CCNA
Routing and Switching
Practice Tests

Jon Buhagiar

A Wiley Brand

Senior Acquisitions Editor: Kenyon Brown
Development Editor: Kim Wimpsett
Technical Editor: Mark Dittmer
Production Editor: Christine O'Connor; Dassi Zeidel
Copy Editor: Judy Flynn
Editorial Manager: Mary Beth Wakefield
Production Manager: Kathleen Wisor
Executive Editor: Jim Minatel
Book Designers: Judy Fung and Bill Gibson
Proofreader: Nancy Carrasco
Indexer: Ted Laux
Project Coordinator, Cover: Brent Savage
Cover Designer: Wiley
Cover Image: ©Getty Images, Inc./Jeremy Woodhouse

Copyright © 2017 by John Wiley & Sons, Inc., Indianapolis, Indiana

Published simultaneously in Canada

ISBN: 978-1-119-36097-1
ISBN: 978-1-119-36099-5 (ebk.)
ISBN: 978-1-1193-6098-8 (ebk.)

Manufactured in the United States of America

I dedicate this book to my wife, Teresa, and my son, Joseph. I love you both.

Acknowledgments

I would like to thank my wife, Teresa. She has had so much patience during the writing of this book. I would also like to thank the many people who made this book possible, including the following: Kenyon Brown at Wiley Publishing for giving me the opportunity to write this book; Kim Wimpsett, for working with me as the developmental editor and making the entire project seamless; Christine O'Conner and Dassi Zeidel, for helping with production editing and guiding me through the process; Mark Dittmer, for serving as technical reviewer to ensure I didn't miss any details; and Judy Flynn, for her many edits that helped make this book a polished product. Thank you to the many other people I've never met who worked behind the scenes to make this book a success.

About the Author

Jon Buhagiar, BS/ITM, MCSE, CCNA   is an information technology professional with two decades of experience in higher education and the private sector.

Jon currently serves as supervisor of network operations at Pittsburgh Technical College. In this role, he manages datacenter and network infrastructure operations and IT operations and is involved in strategic planning of IT projects supporting the quality of education at the College. He also serves as an adjunct instructor in the College's School of Information Technology department, where he teaches courses for Microsoft and Cisco certification. Jon has been an instructor for 18 years with several colleges in the Pittsburgh area, since the introduction of the Windows NT MCSE in 1998.

Jon earned a bachelor of science degree in Information Technology Management from Western Governors University. He also achieved an associate degree in Business Management from Pittsburgh Technical College. He has recently become a Windows Server 2012 R2 Microsoft Certified Solutions Expert (MCSE) and earned the Cisco Certified Network Associate (CCNA) Routing and Switching certification. Other certifications include CompTIA Network+, A+, and Project+.

In addition to his professional and teaching roles, he served as the Technical Editor for the second edition of the *CompTIA Cloud+ Study Guide* by Todd Montgomery (Sybex, 2016). He has spoken at several conferences about spam and email systems. He is an active radio electronics hobbyist and has held a ham radio license for the past 15 years (KB3KGS). He experiments with electronics and has a strong focus on the Internet of Things (IoT).

Contents

Introduction

CCNA Routing and Switching Practice Tests is a companion volume to the *CCNA Routing and Switching Complete Study Guide, Second Edition*. If you're looking to test your knowledge before you take the CCNA exam, this book will help you by providing a combination of 1,500 questions that cover the CCNA objectives.

If you're just starting to prepare for the CCNA exam, I highly recommend that you use the *CCNA Routing and Switching Complete Study Guide, Second Edition* by Todd Lammle (Sybex, 2016) to help you learn about each of the objectives covered in the CCNA exam. Once you're ready to test your knowledge, use this book to help find places where you may need to study more or to practice for the exam itself.

Since it is a companion to the *CCNA Routing and Switching Complete Study Guide, Second Edition*, this book is designed to be similar to taking the CCNA Routing and Switching exam. It contains scenarios and standard multiple-choice questions similar to those you may encounter in the certification exam itself. The book contains nine chapters: seven objective-centric chapters with 140 to 320 questions, weighted by the objectives, and two chapters that contain 50-question practice tests to simulate taking the exam itself. The bulk of the questions are in the routing and switching objectives.

Cisco's Network Certification

It used to be that to secure the holy grail of Cisco certifications—the CCIE—you passed only one written test before being faced with a grueling, formidable hands-on lab. This intensely daunting, all-or-nothing approach made it nearly impossible to succeed and predictably didn't work out too well for most people. Cisco responded to this issue by creating a series of new certifications, which not only made it easier to eventually win the highly coveted CCIE prize, it gave employers a way to accurately rate and measure the skill levels of prospective and current employees. This exciting paradigm shift in Cisco's certification path truly opened doors that few were allowed through before!

Beginning in 1998, obtaining the Cisco Certified Network Associate (CCNA) certification was the first milestone in the Cisco certification climb, as well as the official prerequisite to each of the more advanced levels. But that changed in 2007 when Cisco announced the Cisco Certified Entry Network Technician (CCENT) certification. And then in May 2016, Cisco once again proclaimed updates to the CCENT and CCNA Routing and Switching (R/S) tests. Now the Cisco certification process looks like Figure I.1.

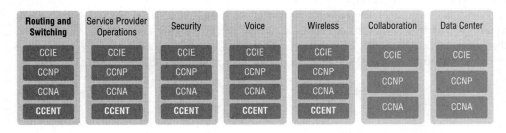

Cisco Certified Entry Network Technician (CCENT)

Don't be fooled by the oh-so-misleading name of this first certification because it absolutely isn't entry level! Okay—maybe entry level for Cisco's certification path, but definitely not for someone without experience trying to break into the highly lucrative yet challenging IT job market! For the uninitiated, the CompTIA A+ and Network+ certifications aren't official prerequisites, but know that Cisco does expect you to have that type and level of experience before embarking on your Cisco certification journey.

All of this gets us to 2017, when the climb to Cisco supremacy got much harder again. The innocuous-sounding siren's call of the CCENT can lure you to some serious trouble if you're not prepared, because it's actually much harder than the old CCNA ever was. This will rapidly become apparent once you start studying, but be encouraged! The fact that the certification process is getting harder really works better for you in the long run, because that which is harder to obtain only becomes that much more valuable when you finally do, right? Yes, indeed!

Another important factor to keep in mind is that the Interconnection Cisco Network Devices Part 1 (ICND1) exam, which is the required exam for the CCENT certification, costs $150 per attempt, and it's anything but easy to pass! However, there is one way to skip the CCENT exam and still meet the prerequisite before moving on to any other certification track, and that path is through the CCNA R/S Composite exam. First, I'll discuss the Interconnecting Cisco Network Devices Part 2 (ICND2) exam, and then I'll tell you about the CCNA Composite exam, which will provide you, when successful, with both the CCENT and the CCNA R/S certification.

Cisco Certified Network Associate Routing and Switching (CCNA R/S)

Once you have achieved your CCENT certification, you can take the ICND2 (200-105) exam in order to achieve your CCNA R/S certification, which is the most popular certification Cisco has by far because it's the most sought-after certification of all employers.

As with the CCENT, the ICND2 exam is also $150 per attempt—although thinking you can just skim a book and pass any of these exams would probably be a really expensive mistake! The CCENT/CCNA exams are extremely hard and cover a lot of material, so you have to really know your stuff. Taking a Cisco class or spending months with hands-on experience is definitely a requirement to succeed when faced with this monster!

And once you have your CCNA, you don't have to stop there—you can choose to continue and achieve an even higher certification, called the Cisco Certified Network Professional (CCNP). There are various ones, as shown in Figure 1.1. The CCNP R/S is still the most popular, with Voice certifications coming in at a close second. And I've got to tell you that the Data Center certification will be catching up fast. Also good to know is that anyone with a CCNP R/S has all the skills and knowledge needed to attempt the notoriously dreaded but coveted CCIE R/S lab. But just becoming a CCNA R/S can land you that job you've dreamed about, and that's what this book is all about: helping you to get and keep a great job!

Still, why take two exams to get your CCNA if you don't have to? Cisco still has the CCNA Routing and Switching Composite (200-125) exam that, if passed, will land you with your CCENT and your CCNA R/S via only one test priced at only $295. Some people like the one-test approach, and some people like the two-test approach. Part of this book covers the ICND2 exam topics.

Why Become a CCENT and CCNA R/S?

Cisco, like Microsoft and other vendors that provide certification, has created the certification process to give administrators a set of skills and to equip prospective employers with a way to measure those skills or match certain criteria. And as you probably know, becoming a CCNA R/S is certainly the initial, key step on a successful journey toward a new, highly rewarding, and sustainable networking career.

The CCNA program was created to provide a solid introduction not only to the Cisco Internetwork Operating System (IOS) and Cisco hardware but also to internetworking in general, making it helpful to you in areas that are not exclusively Cisco's. And regarding today's certification process, it's not unrealistic that network managers—even those without Cisco equipment—require Cisco certifications for their job applicants. Rest assured that if you make it through the CCNA and are still interested in Cisco and internetworking, you're headed down a path to certain success!

What Skills Do You Need to Become a CCNA R/S?

This ICND1 exam (100-105) tests a candidate for the knowledge and skills required to successfully install, operate, and troubleshoot a small branch office network. The exam includes questions on the operation of IP data networks, LAN switching technologies, IPv6, IP routing technologies, IP services, network device security, and basic troubleshooting. The ICND2 exam (200-105) tests a candidate for the knowledge and skills required to successfully install, operate, and troubleshoot a small- to medium-size enterprise branch network. The exam includes questions on LAN switching technologies, IP routing technologies, security, troubleshooting, and WAN technologies.

How Do You Become a CCNA R/S

If you want to go straight for your CCNA R/S and take only one exam, all you have to do is pass the CCNA Composite exam (200-125). Oh, but don't you wish it were that easy? True, it's just one test, but it's a whopper, and to pass it you must possess enough knowledge to understand what the test writers are saying, and you need to know everything I mentioned previously, in the sections on the ICND1 and ICND2 exams! Hey, it's hard, but it can be done!

What does the CCNA Composite exam (200-125) cover? Pretty much the same topics covered in the ICND1 and ICND2 exams. Exam 200-125 tests a candidate's knowledge and skills required to install, operate, and troubleshoot a small to medium-size enterprise branch network.

While you can take the Composite exam to get your CCNA, it's good to know that Cisco offers the two-step process I discussed earlier in this introduction. And this book covers both those exams too! It may be easier than taking that one ginormous exam for you, but don't think the two-test method is easy. It takes work! However, it can be done; you just need to stick with your studies.

The two-test method involves passing the following:

- Exam 100-105: Interconnecting Cisco Networking Devices Part 1 (ICND1)
- Exam 200-105: Interconnecting Cisco Networking Devices Part 2 (ICND2)

Where Do You Take the Exams?

You may take the ICND1, ICND2, or CCNA R/S Composite or any Cisco exam at any of the Pearson VUE authorized testing centers. For information, check www.vue.com or call 877-404-EXAM (3926).

To register for a Cisco exam, follow these steps:

1. Determine the number of the exam you want to take. (The ICND1 exam number is 100-105, ICND2 is 100-205, and CCNA R/S Composite is 200-125.)

2. Register with the nearest Pearson VUE testing center. At this point, you will be asked to pay in advance for the exam. At the time of this writing, the ICND1 and ICND2 exams are $150 each, and the CCNA R/S Composite exam is $295. The exams must be taken within one year of payment. You can schedule exams up to six weeks in advance or as late as the day you want to take it—but if you fail a Cisco exam, you must wait five days before you will be allowed to retake it. If something comes up and you need to cancel or reschedule your exam appointment, contact Pearson VUE at least 24 hours in advance.

3. When you schedule the exam, you'll get instructions regarding all appointment and cancellation procedures, the ID requirements, and information about the testing-center location.

Tips for Taking Your Cisco Exams

The Cisco exams contain about 40–50 questions and must be completed in about 90 minutes or less. This information can change per exam. You must get a score of about 85 percent to pass this exam, but again, each exam can be different.

Many questions on the exam have answer choices that at first glance look identical, especially the syntax questions! So remember to read through the choices carefully because close just doesn't cut it. If you get commands in the wrong order or forget one measly character, you'll get the question wrong. So, to practice, do the hands-on exercises at the end of this book's chapters over and over again until they feel natural to you.

Also, never forget that the right answer is the Cisco answer. In many cases, more than one appropriate answer is presented, but the correct answer is the one that Cisco recommends. On the exam, you will always be told to pick one, two, or three options, never "choose all that apply." The Cisco exam may include the following test formats:

- Multiple-choice single answer
- Multiple-choice multiple answers
- Drag-and-drop
- Router simulations

Cisco proctored exams will not show the steps to follow in completing a router interface configuration, but they do allow partial command responses. For example, show run, sho running, or sh running-config would be acceptable.

Here are some general tips for exam success:

- Arrive early at the exam center so you can relax and review your study materials.

- Read the questions carefully. Don't jump to conclusions. Make sure you're clear about exactly what each question asks. "Read twice, answer once," is what I always tell my students.

- When answering multiple-choice questions that you're not sure about, use the process of elimination to get rid of the obviously incorrect answers first. Doing this greatly improves your odds if you need to make an educated guess.

- You can no longer move forward and backward through the Cisco exams, so double-check your answer before clicking Next since you can't change your mind.

After you complete an exam, you'll get immediate, online notification of your pass or fail status, a printed examination score report that indicates your pass or fail status, and your exam results by section. (The test administrator will give you the printed score report.) Test scores are automatically forwarded to Cisco within five working days after you take the test, so you don't need to send your score to them. If you pass the exam, you'll receive confirmation from Cisco, typically within two to four weeks, sometimes a bit longer.

ICND1 (100-105) Exam Objectives

Exam objectives are subject to change at any time without prior notice and at Cisco's sole discretion. Please visit Cisco's certification website, www.cisco.com/web/learning, for the latest information on the ICND1 exam. Tables 1–5 cover the ICND1 (100-105) exam objectives.

TABLE 1   20% 1.0 Network Fundamentals

Objective	Chapter
1.1 Compare and contrast OSI and TCP/IP models	1
1.2 Compare and contrast TCP and UDP protocols	1
1.3 Describe the impact of infrastructure components in an enterprise network	1
1.3.a Firewalls	1
1.3.b Access points	1
1.3.c Wireless controllers	1
1.4 Compare and contrast collapsed core and three-tier architectures	1
1.5 Compare and contrast network topologies	1
1.5.a Star	1
1.5.b Mesh	1
1.5.c Hybrid	1
1.6 Select the appropriate cabling type based on implementation requirements	1
1.7 Apply troubleshooting methodologies to resolve problems	1
1.7.a Perform fault isolation and document	1
1.7.b Resolve or escalate	1
1.7.c Verify and monitor resolution	1
1.8 Configure, verify, and troubleshoot IPv4 addressing and subnetting	1
1.9 Compare and contrast IPv4 address types	1
1.9.a Unicast	1
1.9.b Broadcast	1
1.9.c Multicast	1
1.10 Describe the need for private IPv4 addressing	1

Objective	Chapter
1.11 Identify the appropriate IPv6 addressing scheme to satisfy addressing requirements in a LAN/WAN environment	1
1.12 Configure, verify, and troubleshoot IPv6 addressing	1
1.13 Configure and verify IPv6 Stateless Address Autoconfiguration	1
1.14 Compare and contrast IPv6 address types	1
1.14.a Global unicast	1
1.14.b Unique local	1
1.14.c Link local	1
1.14.d Multicast	1
1.14.e Modified EUI 64	1
1.14.f Autoconfiguration	1
1.14.g Anycast	1

TABLE 2   26% 2.0 LAN Switching Fundamentals

Objective	Chapter
2.1 Describe and verify switching concepts	2
2.1.a MAC learning and aging	2
2.1.b Frame switching	2
2.1.c Frame flooding	2
2.1.d MAC address table	2
2.2 Interpret Ethernet frame format	2
2.3 Troubleshoot interface and cable issues (collisions, errors, duplex, speed)	2
2.4 Configure, verify, and troubleshoot VLANs (normal range) spanning multiple switches	2

Objective	Chapter
2.4.a Access ports (data and voice)	2
2.4.b Default VLAN	2
2.5 Configure, verify, and troubleshoot interswitch connectivity	2
2.5.a Trunk ports	2
2.5.b 802.1Q	2
2.5.c Native VLAN	2
2.6 Configure and verify Layer 2 protocols	2
2.6.a Cisco Discovery Protocol	2, 7
2.6.b LLDP	2, 7
2.7 Configure, verify, and troubleshoot port security	6
2.7.a Static	6
2.7.b Dynamic	6
2.7.c Sticky	6
2.7.d Max MAC addresses	6
2.7.e Violation actions	6
2.7.f Err-disable recovery	6

TABLE 3 25% 3.0 Routing Fundamentals

Objective	Chapter
3.1 Describe the routing concepts	3
3.1.a Packet handling along the path through a network	3
3.1.b Forwarding decision based on route lookup	3

TABLE 4   15% 4.0 Infrastructure Services

Objective	Chapter
4.1 Describe DNS lookup operation	5
4.2 Troubleshoot client connectivity issues involving DNS	5
4.3 Configure and verify DHCP on a router (excluding static reservations)	5
4.3.a Server	5
4.3.b Relay	5
4.3.c Client	5
4.3.d TFTP, DNS, and gateway options	5
4.4 Troubleshoot client- and router-based DHCP connectivity issues	5
4.5 Configure and verify NTP operating in client/server mode	5
4.6 Configure, verify, and troubleshoot IPv4 standard numbered and named access list for routed interfaces	6
4.7 Configure, verify, and troubleshoot inside source NAT	5
4.7.a Static	5
4.7.b Pool	5
4.7.c PAT	5

TABLE 5   14% 5.0 Infrastructure Maintenance

Objective	Chapter
5.1 Configure and verify device-monitoring using syslog	7
5.2 Configure and verify device management	7
5.2.a Backup and restore device configuration	7

ICND2 (200-105) Exam Objectives

Exam objectives are subject to change at any time without prior notice and at Cisco's sole discretion. Please visit Cisco's certification website (www.cisco.com/web/learning) for the latest information on the ICND2 exam. Tables 6–10 cover the ICND2 (200-105) exam objectives.

TABLE 6   26% 1.0 LAN Switching Technologies

Objective	Chapter
1.1 Configure, verify, and troubleshoot VLANs (normal/extended range) spanning multiple switches	2
1.1.a Access ports (data and voice)	2
1.1.b Default VLAN	2
1.2 Configure, verify, and troubleshoot interswitch connectivity	2
1.2.a Add and remove VLANs on a trunk	2
1.2.b DTP and VTP (v1&v2)	2
1.3 Configure, verify, and troubleshoot STP protocols	2
1.3.a STP mode (PVST+ and RPVST+)	2
1.3.b STP root bridge selection	2
1.4 Configure, verify, and troubleshoot STP-related optional features	2
1.4.a PortFast	2
1.4.b BPDU guard	2
1.5 Configure, verify, and troubleshoot (Layer 2/Layer 3) EtherChannel	2
1.5.a Static	2
1.5.b PAGP	2

Objective	Chapter
1.5.c LACP	2
1.6 Describe the benefits of switch stacking and chassis aggregation	2
1.7 Describe common access layer threat mitigation techniques	6
1.7.a 802.1x	6
1.7.b DHCP snooping	6
1.7.c Nondefault native VLAN	6

TABLE 7   29% 2.0 Routing Technologies

Objective	Chapter
2.1 Configure, verify, and troubleshoot Inter-VLAN routing	3
2.1.a Router on a stick	3
2.1.b SVI	3
2.2 Compare and contrast distance vector and link-state routing protocols	3
2.3 Compare and contrast interior and exterior routing protocols	3
2.4 Configure, verify, and troubleshoot single area and multiarea OSPFv2 for IPv4 (excluding authentication, filtering, manual summarization, redistribution, stub, virtual-link, and LSAs)	3
2.5 Configure, verify, and troubleshoot single area and multiarea OSPFv3 for IPv6 (excluding authentication, filtering, manual summarization, redistribution, stub, virtual-link, and LSAs)	3
2.6 Configure, verify, and troubleshoot EIGRP for IPv4 (excluding authentication, filtering, manual summarization, redistribution, stub)	3
2.7 Configure, verify, and troubleshoot EIGRP for IPv6 (excluding authentication, filtering, manual summarization, redistribution, stub)	3

TABLE 8   16% 3.0 WAN Technologies

Objective	Chapter
3.1 Configure and verify PPP and MLPPP on WAN interfaces using local authentication	4
3.2 Configure, verify, and troubleshoot PPPoE client-side interfaces using local authentication	4
3.3 Configure, verify, and troubleshoot GRE tunnel connectivity	4
3.4 Describe WAN topology options	4
3.4.a Point-to-point	4
3.4.b Hub and spoke	4
3.4.c Full mesh	4
3.4.d Single vs dual-homed	4
3.5 Describe WAN access connectivity options	4
3.5.a MPLS	4
3.5.b MetroEthernet	4
3.5.c Broadband PPPoE	4
3.5.d Internet VPN (DMVPN, site-to-site VPN, client VPN)	4
3.6 Configure and verify single-homed branch connectivity using eBGP IPv4 (limited to peering and route advertisement using Network command only)	4

TABLE 9   14% 4.0 Infrastructure Services

Objective	Chapter
4.1 Configure, verify, and troubleshoot basic HSRP	5
4.1.a Priority	5
4.1.b Preemption	5

TABLE 10   15% 5.0 Infrastructure Maintenance

Objective	Chapter
5.1 Configure and verify device-monitoring protocols	7
5.1.a SNMPv2	7
5.1.b SNMPv3	7
5.2 Troubleshoot network connectivity issues using ICMP echo-based IP SLA	7
5.3 Use local SPAN to troubleshoot and resolve problems	7
5.4 Describe device management using AAA with TACACS+ and RADIUS	6
5.5 Describe network programmability in enterprise network architecture	7
5.5.a Function of a controller	7
5.5.b Separation of control plane and data plane	7
5.5.c Northbound and southbound APIs	7
5.6 Troubleshoot basic Layer 3 end-to-end connectivity issues	3

CCNA Composite (200-125) Exam Objectives

Exam objectives are subject to change at any time without prior notice and at Cisco's sole discretion. Please visit Cisco's certification website (www.cisco.com/web/learning) for the latest information on the CCNA Composite exam. Tables 11–17 cover the ICND2 (200-105) exam objectives.

TABLE 11   15% 1.0 Network Fundamentals

Objective	Chapter
1.1 Compare and contrast OSI and TCP/IP models	1
1.2 Compare and contrast TCP and UDP protocols	1
1.3 Describe the impact of infrastructure components in an enterprise network	1

Objective	Chapter
1.11 Describe the need for private IPv4 addressing	1
1.12 Identify the appropriate IPv6 addressing scheme to satisfy addressing requirements in a LAN/WAN environment	1
1.13 Configure, verify, and troubleshoot IPv6 addressing	1
1.14 Configure and verify IPv6 Stateless Address Autoconfiguration	1
1.15 Compare and contrast IPv6 address types	1
1.15a Global unicast	1
1.15b Unique local	1
1.15c Link local	1
1.15d Multicast	1
1.15e Modified EUI 64	1
1.15f Autoconfiguration	1
1.15g Anycast	1

TABLE 12   21% 2.0 LAN Switching Technologies

Objective	Chapter
2.1 Describe and verify switching concepts	2
2.1a MAC learning and aging	2
2.1b Frame switching	2
2.1c Frame flooding	2
2.1d MAC address table	2
2.2 Interpret Ethernet frame format	2
2.3 Troubleshoot interface and cable issues (collisions, errors, duplex, speed)	2

TABLE 13   23% 3.0 Routing Technologies

Objective	Chapter
3.1 Describe the routing concepts	3
3.1a Packet handling along the path through a network	3
3.1b Forwarding decision based on route lookup	3
3.1c Frame rewrite	3
3.2 Interpret the components of a routing table	3
3.2a Prefix	3
3.2b Network mask	3
3.2c Next hop	3
3.2d Routing protocol code	3
3.2e Administrative distance	3
3.2f Metric	3
3.2g Gateway of last resort	3
3.3 Describe how a routing table is populated by different routing information sources	3
3.3a Admin distance	3
3.4 Configure, verify, and troubleshoot inter-VLAN routing	3
3.4a Router on a stick	3
3.4b SVI	3
3.5 Compare and contrast static routing and dynamic routing	3
3.6 Compare and contrast distance vector and link state routing protocols	3
3.7 Compare and contrast interior and exterior routing protocols	3
3.8 Configure, verify, and troubleshoot IPv4 and IPv6 static routing	3

Objective	Chapter
3.8a Default route	3
3.8b Network route	3
3.8c Host route	3
3.8d Floating static	3
3.9 Configure, verify, and troubleshoot single area and multi-area OSPFv2 for IPv4 (excluding authentication, filtering, manual summarization, redistribution, stub, virtual link, and LSAs)	3
3.10 Configure, verify, and troubleshoot single area and multi-area OSPFv3 for IPv6 (excluding authentication, filtering, manual summarization, redistribution, stub, virtual link, and LSAs)	3
3.11 Configure, verify, and troubleshoot EIGRP for IPv4 (excluding authentication, filtering, manual summarization, redistribution, stub)	3
3.12 Configure, verify, and troubleshoot EIGRP for IPv6 (excluding authentication, filtering, manual summarization, redistribution, stub)	3
3.13 Configure, verify, and troubleshoot RIPv2 for IPv4 (excluding authentication, filtering, manual summarization, redistribution)	3
3.14 Troubleshoot basic Layer 3 end-to-end connectivity issues	3

TABLE 14   10% 4.0 WAN Technologies

Objective	Chapter
4.1 Configure and verify PPP and MLPPP on WAN interfaces using local authentication	4
4.2 Configure, verify, and troubleshoot PPPoE client-side interfaces using local authentication	4
4.3 Configure, verify, and troubleshoot GRE tunnel connectivity	4
4.4 Describe WAN topology options	4
4.4a Point-to-point	4

Objective	Chapter
4.4b Hub and spoke	4
4.4c Full mesh	4
4.4d Single vs dual-homed	4
4.5 Describe WAN access connectivity options	4
4.5a MPLS	4
4.5b Metro Ethernet	4
4.5c Broadband PPPoE	4
4.5d Internet VPN (DMVPN, site-to-site VPN, client VPN)	4
4.6 Configure and verify single-homed branch connectivity using eBGP IPv4 (limited to peering and route advertisement using Network command only)	4
4.7 Describe basic QoS concepts	4
4.7a Marking	4
4.7b Device trust	4
4.7c Prioritization	4
4.7c(i) Voice	4
4.7c(ii) Video	4
4.7c(iii) Data	4
4.7d Shaping	4
4.7e Policing	4
4.7f Congestion management	4

TABLE 15 10% 5.0 Infrastructure Services

Objective	Chapter
5.1 Describe DNS lookup operation	5
5.2 Troubleshoot client connectivity issues involving DNS	5
5.3 Configure and verify DHCP on a router (excluding static reservations)	5

Objective	Chapter
5.3a Server	5
5.3b Relay	5
5.3c Client	5
5.3d TFTP, DNS, and gateway options	5
5.4 Troubleshoot client and router-based DHCP connectivity issues	5
5.5 Configure, verify, and troubleshoot basic HSRP	5
5.5a Priority	5
5.5b Preemption	5
5.5c Version	5
5.6 Configure, verify, and troubleshoot inside source NAT	5
5.6a Static	5
5.6b Pool	5
5.6c PAT	5
5.7 Configure and verify NTP operating in a client/server mode	5

TABLE 16   11% 6.0 Infrastructure Security

Objective	Chapter
6.1 Configure, verify, and troubleshoot port security	6
6.1a Static	6
6.1b Dynamic	6
6.1c Sticky	6
6.1d Max MAC addresses	6
6.1e Violation actions	6

Objective	Chapter
6.1f Err-disable recovery	6
6.2 Describe common access layer threat mitigation techniques	6
6.2a 802.1x	6
6.2b DHCP snooping	6
6.2c Nondefault native VLAN	6
6.3 Configure, verify, and troubleshoot IPv4 and IPv6 access list for traffic filtering	6
6.3a Standard	6
6.3b Extended	6
6.3c Named	6
6.4 Verify ACLs using the APIC-EM Path Trace ACL Analysis tool	6
6.5 Configure, verify, and troubleshoot basic device hardening	6
6.5a Local authentication	6
6.5b Secure password	6
6.5c Access to device	6
6.5c(i) Source address	6
6.5c(ii) Telnet/SSH	6
6.5d Login banner	6
6.6 Describe device security using AAA with TACACS+ and RADIUS	6

TABLE 17   10% 7.0 Infrastructure Management

Objective	Chapter
7.1 Configure and verify device-monitoring protocols	7
7.1a SNMPv2	7
7.1b SNMPv3	7

Using This Book to Practice

This book is composed of nine chapters. Each of the first seven chapters covers a domain, with a variety of questions that can help you test your knowledge of real-world, scenario, and best practices–based networking knowledge. The final two chapters are complete practice exams that can serve as timed practice tests to help determine if you're ready for the CCNA exam.

I recommend taking the first practice exam to help identify where you may need to spend more study time, and then using the domain-specific chapters to test your domain knowledge where it is weak. Once you're ready, take the second practice exam to make sure you've covered all of the material and are ready to attempt the CCNA exam.

The book is separated into nine chapters, seven chapters to reflect the major objectives and two chapters with practice tests:

Chapter 1: Network Fundamentals (Domain 1)

Chapter 2: LAN Switching Technologies (Domain 2)

Chapter 3: Routing Technologies (Domain 3)

Chapter 4: WAN Technologies (Domain 4)

Chapter 5: Infrastructure Services (Domain 5)

Chapter 6: Infrastructure Security (Domain 6)

Chapter 7: Infrastructure Management (Domain 7)

Chapter 8: Practice Test 1

Chapter 9: Practice Test 2

Chapter

1

Network Fundamentals (Domain 1)

THE CCNA EXAM TOPICS COVERED IN THIS PRACTICE TEST INCLUDE THE FOLLOWING:

✓ **1.0 Network Fundamentals (ICND1)**

- 1.1 Compare and contrast OSI and TCP/IP models (ICND1)

- 1.2 Compare and contrast TCP and UDP protocols (ICND1)

- 1.3 Describe the impact of infrastructure components in an enterprise network (ICND1)

- 1.4 Describe the effects of cloud resources on enterprise network architecture (ICND2)

- 1.5 Compare and contrast collapsed core and three-tier architectures (ICND1)

- 1.6 Compare and contrast network topologies (ICND1)

- 1.7 Select the appropriate cabling type based on implementation requirements (ICND1)

- 1.8 Apply troubleshooting methodologies to resolve problems (ICND1)

- 1.9 Configure, verify, and troubleshoot IPv4 addressing and subnetting (ICND1)

- 1.10 Compare and contrast IPv4 address types (ICND1)

- 1.11 Describe the need for private IPv4 addressing (ICND1)

- 1.12 Identify the appropriate IPv6 addressing scheme to satisfy addressing requirements in a LAN/WAN environment (ICND1)

- 1.13 Configure, verify, and troubleshoot IPv6 addressing (ICND1)

- 1.14 Configure and verify IPv6 Stateless Address Autoconfiguration (ICND1)

- 1.15 Compare and contrast IPv6 address types (ICND1)

1. Which statement is a valid reason the OSI reference model was created?
   A. It encourages vendors to create proprietary standards for any component of the OSI.
   B. It allows for changes on one layer to apply to another layer so they can work together.
   C. It prevents industry standardization of network processes.
   D. It divides network communication into smaller components for design and trouble-shooting.

2. When a program uses encryption such as SSL, which layer is responsible?
   A. Presentation layer
   B. Transport layer
   C. Data Link layer
   D. Session layer

3. Which device would primarily function at the Data Link layer?
   A. Routers
   B. Firewalls
   C. Gateways
   D. Switches

4. Which is the proper order of the OSI layers?
   A. Application, Transport, Session, Presentation, Network, Data Link, Physical
   B. Presentation, Application, Session, Transport, Network, Data Link, Physical
   C. Application, Presentation, Session, Transport, Network, Data Link, Physical
   D. Application, Presentation, Transport, Network, Session, Data Link, Physical

5. Which OSI layer is responsible for logical addressing?
   A. Transport layer
   B. Network layer
   C. Application layer
   D. Data Link layer

6. Which OSI layer is responsible for connection-oriented communication?
   A. Transport layer
   B. Presentation layer
   C. Data Link layer
   D. Application layer

7. Which layer is responsible for compression and decompression?
   A. Application layer
   B. Physical layer
   C. Session layer
   D. Presentation layer

8. Which layer of the OSI is responsible for dialog control of applications?

    A. Application layer

    B. Physical layer

    C. Session layer

    D. Network layer

9. At which layer of the OSI can you find DTE and DCE interfaces?

    A. Application layer

    B. Physical layer

    C. Session layer

    D. Transport layer

10. At which DoD model layer does Telnet, TFTP, SNMP, and SMTP function?

    A. Host-to-Host layer

    B. Process/Application layer

    C. Internet layer

    D. Network Access layer

11. An administrator is checking to make sure that SNMP is working properly. Which is the highest layer checked in the OSI if it is working successfully?

    A. Application layer

    B. Presentation layer

    C. Session layer

    D. Network layer

12. The receiving computer checked the checksum of a frame. It had been damaged during transfer, so it is discarded. At which layer of the OSI did this occur?

    A. Physical layer

    B. Data Link layer

    C. Network layer

    D. Session layer

13. Which layer in the DoD model is responsible for routing?

    A. Host-to-Host layer

    B. Process/Application layer

    C. Internet layer

    D. Network Access layer

14. Which devices create collision domains, raising effective bandwidth?

    A. Firewalls

    B. Hubs

    C. Routers

    D. Switches

15. Which device acts like a multiport repeater?

   A. Firewall

   B. Hub

   C. Router

   D. Switch

16. Which layer of the OSI defines the PDU, or protocol data unit, of segments?

   A. Application layer

   B. Session layer

   C. Network layer

   D. Transport layer

17. Which device will create broadcast domains and raise effective bandwidth?

   A. Firewall

   B. Hub

   C. Router

   D. Switch

18. Which is a correct statement about MAC addresses?

   A. Organizationally unique identifiers (OUIs) create a unique MAC address.

   B. The first 24 bits of a MAC address is specified by the vendor.

   C. The IEEE is responsible for MAC address uniqueness.

   D. If the I/G bit is set to 1, then the frame identifies a broadcast or multicast.

19. Which access/contention method is used for Ethernet?

   A. CSMA/CA

   B. CSMA/CD

   C. 802.2

   D. Token passing

20. What is the correct order of encapsulation?

   A. User datagrams, packets, segments, frames, bits

   B. User datagrams, sessions, segments, packets, frames, bits

   C. User datagrams, segments, packets, frames, bits

   D. Bits, frames, sessions, packets, user datagrams

21. Which application provides terminal emulation over a network?

   A. SNMP

   B. Telnet

   C. HTTP

   D. TFTP

22. Which protocol is responsible for identifying upper-layer network protocols at the Data Link layer?

A. LLC

B. MAC

C. 802.3

D. FCS

23. The translation of ASCII to EBCDIC is performed at which layer of the OSI?

A. Application layer

B. Session layer

C. Presentation layer

D. Data Link layer

24. Which is not a common cause for LAN congestion?

A. Broadcasts

B. Multicasts

C. Adding switches for connectivity

D. Using multiple hubs for connectivity

25. Flow control can be found at which layer of the OSI?

A. Transport layer

B. Network layer

C. Data Link layer

D. Session layer

26. Which protocol requires the programmer to deal with lost segments?

A. SSL

B. TCP

C. UDP

D. NMS

27. Which is a correct statement about the Transmission Control Protocol (TCP)?

A. TCP is a connectionless protocol.

B. TCP allows for error detection and correction.

C. TCP is faster than UDP.

D. TCP allows for retransmission of lost segments.

28. Which statement correctly describes what happens when a web browser initiates a request to a web server?

A. The sender allocates a port dynamically above 1024 and associates it with the request.

B. The receiver allocates a port dynamically above 1024 and associates it with the request.

C. The sender allocates a port dynamically below 1024 and associates it with the request.

D. The receiver allocates a port dynamically below 1024 and associates it with the request.

29. Which protocol and port number is associated with SMTP?

    A. UDP/69

    B. UDP/25

    C. TCP/69

    D. TCP/25

30. How does TCP guarantee delivery of segments to the receiver?

    A. Via the destination port

    B. TCP checksums

    C. Window size

    D. Sequence and acknowledgment numbers

31. When a programmer decides to use UDP as a transport protocol, what is a decision factor?

    A. Redundancy of acknowledgment is not needed.

    B. Guaranteed delivery of segments is required.

    C. Windowing flow control is required.

    D. A virtual circuit is required.

32. Which mechanism allows for programs running on a server (daemons) to listen for requests through the process called binding?

    A. Headers

    B. Port numbers

    C. MAC address

    D. Checksums

33. Which is a correct statement about sliding windows used with TCP?

    A. The window size is established during the three-way handshake.

    B. Sliding windows allow for data of different lengths to be padded.

    C. It allows TCP to indicate which upper-layer protocol created the request.

    D. It allows the router to see the segment as urgent data.

34. Why does DNS use UDP?

    A. DNS requires acknowledgment of the request for auditing.

    B. The requests require flow control of UDP.

    C. DNS requests are usually small and do not require connections setup.

    D. DNS requires a temporary virtual circuit.

35. What is required before TCP can begin sending segments?

    A. Three-way handshake

    B. Port agreement

    C. Sequencing of segments

    D. Acknowledgment of segments

36. Which term describes what it is called when more than one wireless access point (WAP) covers the same SSID?

   A. Broadcast domain

   B. Basic service set

   C. Extended server set

   D. Wireless mesh

37. Which protocol allows a Lightweight AP (LWAP) to forward data to the wired LAN?

   A. Spanning Tree Protocol (STP)

   B. Bridge protocol data units (BPDUs)

   C. Orthogonal Frequency Division Multiplexing (OFDM)

   D. Control and Provisioning of Wireless Access Points (CAPWAP)

38. Which component allows wireless clients to roam between access points and maintain authentication?

   A. Basic service set

   B. Extended service set

   C. Wireless LAN controller

   D. Service set ID

39. Which is a valid reason to implement a wireless LAN controller (WLC)?

   A. Centralized authentication

   B. The use of autonomous WAPs

   C. Multiple SSIDs

   D. Multiple VLANs

40. You require a density of 100 wireless clients in a relatively small area. Which design would be optimal?

   A. Autonomous WAPs with a WLC

   B. Lightweight WAPs with a WLC

   C. Autonomous WAPs without a WLC

   D. Lightweight WAPs without a WLC

41. When designing a wireless network, which would be a compelling reason to use 5 GHz?

   A. 5 GHz can go further.

   B. 5 GHz allows for more clients.

   C. There are 24 non-overlapping channels.

   D. There is less interference on 5 GHz.

42. Which allows for seamless wireless roaming between access points?

    A. Single SSID

    B. Single service set

    C. 802.11ac

    D. Wireless LAN controller

43. In the 2.4 GHz spectrum for 802.11, which channels are non-overlapping?

    A. Channels 1, 3, and 11

    B. Channels 1, 3, and 6

    C. Channels 1, 6, and 11

    D. Channels 1 through 6

44. Which is one of the critical functions that a wireless LAN controller performs?

    A. Allows autonomous WAPs

    B. Synchronizes the WAPs with the same IOS

    C. Triangulates users for location lookups

    D. Allows for the use of all frequency channels

45. Which is the contention method 802.11 wireless uses?

    A. CSMA/CA

    B. CSMA/CD

    C. BSSS

    D. OFDM

46. When firewalls are placed in a network, which zone contains Internet-facing services?

    A. Outside zone

    B. Enterprise network zone

    C. Demilitarized zone

    D. Inside zone

47. According to best practices, what is the proper placement of a firewall?

    A. Only between the internal network and the Internet

    B. At key security boundaries

    C. In the DMZ

    D. Only between the DMZ and the Internet

48. Which is a false statement about firewalls?

    A. Firewalls can protect a network from external attacks.

    B. Firewalls can protect a network from internal attacks.

    C. Firewalls can provide stateful packet inspection.

    D. Firewalls can control application traffic.

49. Which of the following options is not a consideration for the management of a firewall?

    A. All physical access to the firewall should be tightly controlled.

    B. All firewall policies should be documented.

    C. Firewall logs should be regularly monitored.

    D. Firewalls should allow traffic by default and deny traffic explicitly.

50. What is the reason firewalls are considered stateful?

    A. Firewalls keep track of the zone states.

    B. Firewalls keep accounting on the state of packets.

    C. Firewalls track the state of a TCP conversation.

    D. Firewalls transition between defense states.

51. You have an Adaptive Security Appliance (ASA) and two separate Internet connections via different providers. How could you apply the same policies to both connections?

    A. Place both connections into the same zone.

    B. Place each connection into an ISP zone.

    C. Apply the same ACL to both of the interfaces.

    D. Each connection must be managed separately.

52. Why should servers be placed in the DMZ?

    A. So that Internet clients can access them

    B. To allow access to the Internet and the internal network

    C. To allow the server to access the Internet

    D. To restrict the server to the Internet

53. Which type of device will detect but not prevent unauthorized access?

    A. Firewall

    B. IPS

    C. IDS

    D. Honey pots

54. When a firewall matches a URI, it is operating at which layer?

    A. Layer 7

    B. Layer 5

    C. Layer 4

    D. Layer 3

55. In which zone should an email server be located?

    A. Inside zone

    B. Outside zone

    C. DNS zone

    D. DMZ

56. Amazon Web Services (AWS) and Microsoft Azure are examples of what?

   A. Public cloud providers

   B. Private cloud providers

   C. Hybrid cloud providers

   D. Dynamic cloud providers

57. You are looking to create a fault tolerant colocation site for your servers at a cloud provider. Which type of cloud provider would you be searching for?

   A. PaaS

   B. IaaS

   C. SaaS

   D. BaaS

58. Which allows for the distribution of compute resources such as CPU and RAM to be distributed over several operating systems?

   A. Physical server

   B. Hypervisor

   C. Virtual machine

   D. Virtual network

59. Which option describes a virtual machine (VM) best?

   A. An operating system that is running directly on hardware

   B. An operating system that is running with dedicated hardware

   C. An operating system that is running on reduced hardware features

   D. An operating system that is decoupled from the hardware

60. What is the physical hardware used in virtualization called?

   A. Host

   B. VM

   C. Hypervisor

   D. Guest

61. Which component connects the virtual machine NIC to the physical network?

   A. vNIC

   B. Trunk

   C. Virtual switch

   D. NX-OS

62. Which component acts as a distribution switch for the physical data center?

   A. Top of Rack switch

   B. End of Row switch

   C. Core switch

   D. Virtual switch

63. Which is not a NIST criteria for cloud computing?

    A. Resource pooling

    B. Rapid elasticity

    C. Automated billing

    D. Measured service

64. Which term describes an internal IT department hosting virtualization for a company?

    A. Public cloud

    B. Elastic cloud

    C. Private cloud

    D. Internal cloud

65. What is the role of a cloud services catalog?

    A. It defines the capabilities for the cloud.

    B. It defines the available VMs for creation in the cloud.

    C. It defines the available VMs running in the cloud.

    D. It defines the drivers for VMs in the cloud.

66. A hosted medical records service is an example of which cloud model?

    A. PaaS

    B. IaaS

    C. SaaS

    D. BaaS

67. A hosted environment that allows you to write and run programs is an example of which cloud model?

    A. PaaS

    B. IaaS

    C. SaaS

    D. BaaS

68. Which cloud connectivity method allows for seamless transition between public clouds?

    A. MPLS VPN

    B. Internet VPN

    C. Intercloud exchange

    D. Private WAN

69. Which statement is not a consideration when converting to an email SaaS application if the majority of users are internal?

    A. Internal bandwidth usage

    B. External bandwidth usage

    C. Location of the users

    D. Branch office connectivity to the Internet

70. Which of the following is a virtual network function (VNF) device?

    A. Virtual switch

    B. Virtual firewall

    C. Database server

    D. File server

71. You purchase a VM on a public cloud and plan to create a VPN tunnel to the cloud provider. Your IP network is 172.16.0.0/12, and the provider has assigned an IP address in the 10.0.0.0/8 network. What VNF will you need from the provider to communicate with the VM?

    A. Virtual switch

    B. Virtual firewall

    C. Virtual router

    D. Another IP scheme at the provider

72. Which protocol would you use to synchronize the VM in the public cloud with an internal time source at your premise?

    A. DNS

    B. rsync

    C. NTP

    D. VPN

73. You need to scale out some web servers to accommodate load. Which method would you use?

    A. Add vCPUs.

    B. Add vRAM.

    C. Add DNS.

    D. Add SLBaaS.

74. You have several VMs in a public cloud. What is a benefit of creating NTP VNF in the public cloud for the VMs?

    A. Better time synchronization

    B. Better response time from the VMs

    C. Lower bandwidth utilization from your premises

    D. Overcoming different time zones

75. When deciding to move DNS into the cloud for an application on the public cloud, what is the primary decision factor?

    A. Bandwidth

    B. Response time

    C. Proper DNS resolution

    D. The cloud provider's requirements

76. Access layer switches in the three-tier design model perform which task?

    A. Connect to other switches for redundancy

    B. Connect to users

    C. Connect campuses

    D. Connect to the Internet

77. Distribution layer switches in the three-tier design model perform which task?

    A. Connect to other switches for redundancy

    B. Connect to users

    C. Connect campuses

    D. Connect to the Internet

78. Core layer switches in the three-tier design model perform which task?

    A. Connect to other switches for redundancy

    B. Connect to users

    C. Connect campuses

    D. Connect to the Internet

79. The two-tier design model contains which layer switches?

    A. Core, distribution, and access

    B. Core and distribution

    C. Distribution and access

    D. Internet, core, distribution, and access

80. You have one campus, which contains 2,000 PCs, and each edge switch will contain 25 to 40 PCs. Based on this layout, which design model should be used?

    A. Collapsed-core model

    B. Three-tier model

    C. DOD model

    D. Access model

81. You have four campuses, each containing 500 PCs, and each edge switch will contain 20 to 30 PCs. Based on this layout, which design model should be used?

    A. Collapsed-core model

    B. Three-tier model

    C. DOD model

    D. Access model

82. Which should only be performed at the core layer?

    A. Routing

    B. Supporting clients

    C. Configuring ACLs

    D. Switching

83. Which layer in the three-tier model is where redistribution of routing protocols should be performed?

  A. Core layer

  B. Distribution layer

  C. Access layer

  D. Routing layer

84. Which layer in the three-tier model is where collision domains should be created?

  A. Core layer

  B. Distribution layer

  C. Access layer

  D. Routing layer

85. Which is an accurate statement about the collapsed-core design concept?

  A. It is best suited for large-scale networks.

  B. It allows for better bandwidth.

  C. It is best suited for small enterprises.

  D. It bottlenecks bandwidth.

86. Which network topology design has a centralized switch connecting all of the devices?

  A. Star topology

  B. Full mesh topology

  C. Partial mesh topology

  D. Hybrid topology

87. Which is a direct benefit of a full mesh topology?

  A. Increased bandwidth

  B. Increased redundancy

  C. Decreased switch count

  D. Increased complexity

88. Where is the hybrid topology most commonly seen in the three-tier design model?

  A. Core layer

  B. Distribution layer

  C. Access layer

  D. Routing layer

89. Where is the full mesh topology commonly seen in the three-tier design model?

  A. Core layer

  B. Distribution layer

  C. Access layer

  D. Routing layer

90. Where is the star topology most commonly seen in the three-tier design model?

   A. Core layer

   B. Distribution layer

   C. Access layer

   D. Routing layer

91. Which topology does the collapsed core layer switch use in a two-tier design model?

   A. Star topology

   B. Full mesh topology

   C. Partial mesh topology

   D. Hybrid topology

92. Define a full mesh topology design.

   A. All links from the central switch connect to the edge switches.

   B. All links between switches are connected to each other redundantly.

   C. Only links between similar switch types are connected to each other redundantly.

   D. All ports are used for connecting only other switches.

93. Define a star topology design.

   A. All links from the central switch connect to the edge switches.

   B. All links between switches are connected to each other redundantly.

   C. Only links between similar switch types are connected to each other redundantly.

   D. All ports are used for connecting other switches.

94. Which topology does an autonomous WAP use?

   A. Star topology

   B. Full mesh topology

   C. Partial mesh topology

   D. Hybrid topology

95. If you had limited cable access for the distribution switches, which topology would you need to plan for?

   A. Star topology

   B. Full mesh topology

   C. Partial mesh topology

   D. Hybrid topology

96. Which cable standard delivers 1 Gb/s using four pairs of CAT5e?

   A. 1000Base-T

   B. 1000Base-SX

   C. 1000Base-LX

   D. 1000Base-X

97. Which fiber optic standard uses a 9 micron core and can span up to 10km?

    A. UTP

    B. Multi-mode

    C. Single-mode

    D. STP

98. Which cable type would you use to connect a router to a switch?

    A. Straight-through cable

    B. Crossover cable

    C. Rolled cable

    D. Shielded cable

99. What is the maximum distance you can run 1000Base-T?

    A. 100 meters

    B. 1,000 meters

    C. 100 feet

    D. 1,000 feet

100. What is the terminal specification to connect to a Cisco router or switch via serial cable?

    A. 9600 baud 8-N-0

    B. 9600 baud 8-N-1

    C. 2400 baud 8-N-1

    D. 115,200 baud 8-N-1

101. Which cable type would you use to connect a switch to a switch?

    A. Straight-through cable

    B. Crossover cable

    C. Rolled cable

    D. Shielded cable

102. Which fiber optic standard utilizes a 50 micron core?

    A. UTP

    B. Multi-mode

    C. Single-mode

    D. STP

103. Which type of cable would be used to connect a computer to a switch for management of the switch?

    A. Straight-through cable

    B. Crossover cable

    C. Rolled cable

    D. Shielded cable

104. Which specification for connectivity is currently used in data centers for cost and simplicity?

    A. 10GBase-T

    B. 40GBase-T

    C. 10GBase-CX

    D. 100GBase-TX

105. If you had an existing installation of Cat5e on your campus, what is the highest speed you could run?

    A. 10 Mb/s

    B. 100 Mb/s

    C. 1 Gb/s

    D. 10 Gb/s

106. You get a call that the Internet is down. When you investigate the Internet router and perform a show interface serial 0/0, you see the following status. What might be the problem?

```
Serial0/0 is administratively down, line protocol is up
  Hardware is MCI Serial
```

    A. The serial line connecting to the ISP is down.

    B. Someone accidentally shut down the serial interface.

    C. Routing to the ISP is not set correctly.

    D. The clocking from the ISP has stopped.

107. When performing troubleshooting for a routing issue, which method should be used first to isolate the problem?

    A. Pinging the destination IP back to the originating IP

    B. Pinging the originating IP to the destination IP

    C. Traceroute from the originating IP to the destination IP

    D. Traceroute from the destination IP to the originating IP

108. Which command would you run to diagnose a possible line speed or duplex issue?

    A. `Switch#show speed`

    B. `Switch#show duplex`

    C. `Switch#show interface status`

    D. `Switch#show diagnostics`

109. Which command would you use, to diagnose a problem with frames that are not getting forwarded to the destination node on a switch?

    A. `Switch#show route`

    B. `Switch#show mac address-table`

    C. `Switch#show mac table`

    D. `Switch#show interface`

110. Which command should you start with when trying to diagnose port security issues?

   A. `Switch#show port-security`

   B. `Switch#show mac address-table`

   C. `Switch#show interface`

   D. `Switch#show security`

111. After solving the root cause of a problem, what should be done?

   A. Isolate the problem.

   B. Perform root cause analysis.

   C. Escalate the problem.

   D. Monitor the solution.

112. What is the first step to troubleshooting a problem?

   A. Isolate the problem.

   B. Perform root cause analysis.

   C. Escalate the problem.

   D. Monitor the solution.

113. Which command should be used to verify that a VLAN is defined on a switch to trouble-shoot a VLAN forwarding issue?

   A. `Switch#show interfaces fast 0/0 switchport`

   B. `Switch#show vlan`

   C. `Switch#show vlans`

   D. `Switch#show vtp`

114. It is reported that users cannot reach an internal server. You only have access to the local switches at your facility. You perform a `show interface fast 0/23` on the user reporting the problem and the status of the switch is up/up. What should you do next?

   A. Isolate the problem.

   B. Perform root cause analysis.

   C. Escalate the problem.

   D. Monitor the solution.

115. You just installed a new switch and you cannot get traffic forwarded to a remote VLAN. You believe there is a problem with trunking. Which command will you start with to verify trunking.

   A. `Switch#show interfaces fast 0/0 switchport`

   B. `Switch#show vlan`

   C. `Switch#show vlans`

   D. `Switch#show trunks`

116. Which class is the IP address 172.23.23.2?

    A. Class A

    B. Class B

    C. Class C

    D. Class D

117. Which is the default subnet mask for a Class A address?

    A. 255.0.0.0

    B. 255.255.0.0

    C. 255.255.255.0

    D. 255.255.255.255

118. Which address is a multicast IP address?

    A. 221.22.20.2

    B. 223.3.40.2

    C. 238.20.80.4

    D. 240.34.22.12

119. Which is true of an IP address of 135.20.255.255?

    A. It is a Class A address.

    B. It is a broadcast address.

    C. It is the default gateway address.

    D. It has a default mask of 255.0.0.0

120. What is the CIDR notation for a subnet mask of 255.255.240.0?

    A. /19

    B. /20

    C. /22

    D. /28

121. You have been given an IP address network of 203.23.23.0. You are asked to subnet it for two hosts per network. What is the subnet mask you will need to use to maximize networks?

    A. 255.255.255.252

    B. 255.255.255.248

    C. 255.255.255.240

    D. 255.255.255.224

122. You have been given an IP address network of 213.43.53.0. You are asked to subnet it for 22 hosts per network. What is the subnet mask you will need to use to maximize networks?

    A. 255.255.255.252

    B. 255.255.255.248

    C. 255.255.255.240

    D. 255.255.255.224

123. Which valid IP is in the same network as 192.168.32.61/26?

    A. 192.168.32.59

    B. 192.168.32.63

    C. 192.168.32.64

    D. 192.168.32.72

124. You are setting up a network in which you need 15 routed networks. You have been given a network address of 153.20.0.0, and you need to maximize the number of hosts in each network. Which subnet mask will you use?

    A. 255.255.224.0

    B. 255.255.240.0

    C. 255.255.248.0

    D. 255.255.252.0

125. An ISP gives you an IP address of 209.183.160.45/30 to configure your end of the serial connection. Which IP address will be on the side at the ISP?

    A. 209.183.160.43/30

    B. 209.183.160.44/30

    C. 209.183.160.46/30

    D. 209.183.160.47/30

126. In the following exhibit, what needs to be changed for Computer A to successfully communicate with Computer B (assume the least amount of effort to fix the problem)?

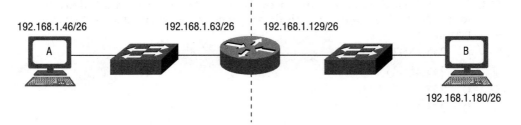

A. Computer A needs to have its IP address changed.

B. Computer B needs to have its IP address changed.

C. The default gateway IP address for Computer A needs to be changed.

D. The default gateway IP address for Computer B needs to be changed.

127. In the following exhibit, what needs to be changed for Computer A to successfully communicate with Computer B (assume the least amount of effort to fix the problem)?

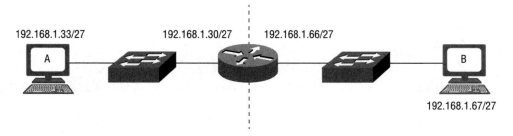

192.168.1.33/27   192.168.1.30/27   192.168.1.66/27

A   B

192.168.1.67/27

A. Computer A needs to have its IP address changed.

B. Computer B needs to have its IP address changed.

C. The default gateway IP address for Computer A needs to be changed.

D. The default gateway IP address for Computer B needs to be changed.

128. Which subnet does host 131.50.39.23/21 belong to?

A. 131.50.39.0/21

B. 131.50.32.0/21

C. 131.50.16.0/21

D. 131.50.8.0/21

129. A computer has an IP address of 145.50.23.1/22. What is the broadcast address for that computer?

A. 145.50.254.255

B. 145.50.255.255

C. 145.50.22.255

D. 145.50.23.255

130. What is the valid IP address range for the network of 132.59.34.0/23?

A. 132.59.34.1 to 132.59.36.254

B. 132.59.34.1 to 132.59.35.254

C. 132.59.34.1 to 132.59.34.254

D. 132.59.34.1 to 132.59.35.255

131. What is the subnet mask for a CIDR notation of /20?

   A. 255.255.224.0

   B. 255.255.240.0

   C. 255.255.248.0

   D. 225.225.252.0

132. What is the number of subnets which you can have for a mask of 255.255.255.248?

   A. 8

   B. 16

   C. 32

   D. 64

133. What is the valid number of hosts for a network with a subnet mask of 255.255.255.224?

   A. 16

   B. 32

   C. 14

   D. 30

134. You have been given the network of 141.23.64.0/19. What is a valid host in this network?

   A. 141.23.120.5/19

   B. 141.23.96.12/19

   C. 141.23.97.45/19

   D. 141.23.90.255/19

135. You have four networks of 141.24.4.0, 141.24.5.0, 141.24.6.0, and 141.24.7.0 that you need to super-net together so you can write one ACL in your firewall. What is the super-netted address you will use?

   A. 141.24.4.0/20

   B. 141.24.4.0/21

   C. 141.24.4.0/22

   D. 141.24.4.0/23

136. You have eight consecutive networks of 132.22.24.0 to 123.22.31.0, which you need to super-net together so you can write one ACL in your firewall. What is the super-netted address you will use?

   A. 132.22.24.0/20

   B. 132.22.24.0/21

   C. 132.22.24.0/22

   D. 132.22.24.0/23

137. You need to use the IP address space of 198.33.20.0/24 and create a VLSM subnet scheme for the network in the following exhibit. What is the network ID for Subnet A?

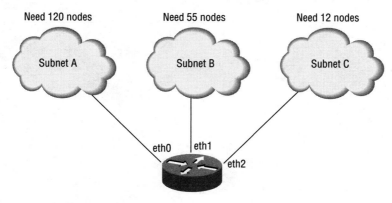

A. 198.33.20.0/25

B. 198.33.20.0/24

C. 198.33.20.0/26

D. 198.33.20.0/28

138. You need to use the IP space of 198.33.20.0/24 and create a VLSM subnet scheme for the network in the following exhibit. What is the network ID for Subnet B?

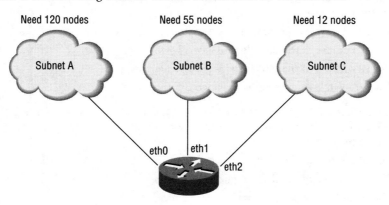

A. 198.33.20.0/25

B. 198.33.20.0/24

C. 198.33.20.0/26

D. 198.33.20.0/28

139. You need to use the IP space of 198.33.20.0/24 and create a VLSM subnet scheme for the network in the following exhibit. What is the network ID for Subnet C?

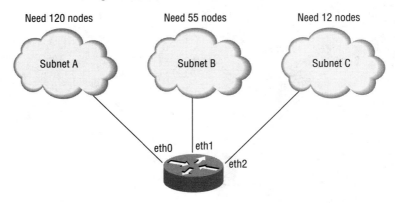

    A.   198.33.20.0/25

    B.   198.33.20.0/24

    C.   198.33.20.0/26

    D.   198.33.20.0/28

140. A computer with an IP address of 172.18.40.5/12 is having trouble getting to an internal server at an IP address of 172.31.2.4. The default gateway of the computer is 172.16.1.1. What is the problem?

    A.   The IP address of the computer is wrong.

    B.   The IP address of the default gateway is wrong.

    C.   The IP address of the internal server is wrong.

    D.   The problem is not the networking configuration.

141. A computer has an IP address of 192.168.1.6/24, and its gateway address is 192.168.1.1. It is trying to reach a server on an IP address of 127.20.34.4. The server is not responding. What is the problem?

    A.   The IP address of the computer is wrong.

    B.   The IP address of the default gateway is wrong.

    C.   The IP address of the internal server is wrong.

    D.   The problem is not the networking configuration.

142. Which is true about a layer 3 broadcast?

    A.   All of the network bits are ones.

    B.   The destination MAC in the frame is always all *F*s.

    C.   The broadcast can be segmented by switches.

    D.   The IP address is always 255.255.255.255.

143. Which method is used to direct communications to a single host?

    A. Unicast

    B. Broadcast

    C. Multicast

    D. Anycast

144. Which method is used to direct communications to the closest IP address to the source?

    A. Unicast

    B. Broadcast

    C. Multicast

    D. Anycast

145. Which method is used to direct communications to a group of computers that subscribe to the transmission?

    A. Unicast

    B. Broadcast

    C. Multicast

    D. Anycast

146. What is the multicast address range?

    A. 224.0.0.0/7

    B. 224.0.0.0/6

    C. 224.0.0.0/5

    D. 224.0.0.0/4

147. Which protocol allows multicast switches to join computers to the multicast group?

    A. ICMP

    B. IGMP

    C. IPMI

    D. IPGRP

148. Which protocol uses broadcasting at layer 3?

    A. ARP

    B. DHCP

    C. IGMP

    D. SNMP

149. Which method is used to direct communications to all computers in a subnet?

    A. Unicast

    B. Broadcast

    C. Multicast

    D. Anycast

150. Which of the following is an example of a multicast address?

   A. 192.168.1.224

   B. 240.23.4.224

   C. 239.45.32.1

   D. 244.23.43.11

151. Which RFC defines private IP addresses?

   A. RFC 1819

   B. RFC 1911

   C. RFC 1918

   D. RFC 3030

152. What is a major reason to use private IP addressing?

   A. It allows for the conservation of public IP addresses.

   B. Since they are non-routable on the Internet, they are secure.

   C. It keeps communications private.

   D. They allow easier setup than public IP addresses.

153. What is required when using private IP addresses to communicate with Internet hosts?

   A. Internet router

   B. IPv4 tunnel

   C. VPN tunnel

   D. Network Address Translation

154. Which is the Class A private IP address range?

   A. 10.0.0.0/8

   B. 10.0.0.0/12

   C. 172.16.0.0/12

   D. 10.0.0.0/10

155. Which is the Class B private IP address range?

   A. 10.0.0.0/8

   B. 10.0.0.0/12

   C. 172.16.0.0/12

   D. 10.0.0.0/10

156. Which is the Class C private IP address range?

   A. 192.168.1.0/24

   B. 192.168.0.0/24

   C. 192.168.0.0/16

   D. 192.168.0.0/12

157. You plug a laptop into a network jack. When you examine the IP address, you see 169.254.23.43. What can you conclude?

    A. The network jack is not working.

    B. Your laptop has a static IP address configured.

    C. The network is configured properly.

    D. The DHCP server is down.

158. You plug a laptop into a network jack. When you examine the IP address, you see 10.23.2.3. What can you conclude?

    A. The network jack is not working.

    B. Your laptop has a static IP address configured.

    C. The network is configured properly.

    D. The DHCP server is down.

159. You want to put a web server online for public use. Which IP address would you use?

    A. 192.168.34.34

    B. 172.31.54.3

    C. 10.55.33.32

    D. 198.168.55.45

160. Who is the governing body that distributes public IP address?

    A. IANA

    B. RFC

    C. IAB

    D. IETF

161. Why is IPv6 needed in the world today?

    A. It does not require NAT to operate.

    B. The IPv4 address space is exhausted.

    C. IPv4 is considered legacy, and IPv6 is the replacement.

    D. IPv6 does not require subnetting.

162. How many bits is an IPv6 address?

    A. 32 bits

    B. 64 bits

    C. 128 bits

    D. 256 bits

163. You have two facilities and both use IPv6 addressing internally. However, both facilities are connected to the Internet via IPv4. What is one recommended method you can use to communicate between the facilities over the Internet?

    A. Dedicated leased line

    B. Frame Relay

    C. Dual stack

    D. 6to4 tunnel

164. Which command is required on a router to support IPv6 static addressing?

    A. `Router(config)#ipv6 address`

    B. `Router(config)#ipv6 routing`

    C. `Router(config)#ipv6 enable`

    D. `Router(config)#ipv6 unicast-routing`

165. Which command would you use on an interface to set the IPv6 address?

    A. `Router(config-if)#ip address 2001:0db8:85aa:0000:0000:8a2e:1343:1337`

    B. `Router(config-if)#ipv6 address 2001:0db8:85aa:0000:0000:8a2e:1343:1337`

    C. `Router(config-if)#ip address 2001:0db8:85aa:0000:0000:8a2e:1343:1337/64`

    D. `Router(config-if)#ipv6 address 2001:0db8:85aa:0000:0000:8a2e:1343:1337/64`

166. Which field of the IPv6 header allows for a dual-stack host to decide which stack to process the packet in?

    A. Version field

    B. Flow label

    C. Source address

    D. Destination address

167. Which command would set the IPv6 default route for a router to interface s0/0?

    A. `Router(config)#ip route 0.0.0.0/0 s0/0`

    B. `Router(config)#ipv6 route 0.0.0.0/0 s0/0`

    C. `Router(config)#ipv6 unicast-route ::/0 s0/0`

    D. `Router(config)#ipv6 route ::/0 s0/0`

168. You want to see all of the interfaces on a router configured with IPv6. Which command would you use?

    A. `Router#show ipv6 interfaces brief`

    B. `Router#show ip interfaces brief`

    C. `Router#show interfaces status`

    D. `Router#show ip addresses`

169. Which dynamic routing protocol(s) can be used with IPv6?

A. RIPng

B. OSPFv3

C. EIGRPv6

D. All of the above

170. You need to see all routes in the routing table for only IPv6. Which command will achieve this?

A. Router#show route

B. Router#show ip route

C. Router#show ipv6 route

D. Router#show route ipv6

171. Which is a valid shortened IPv6 address for 2001:0db8:0000:0000:0000:8a2e:0000:1337?

A. 2001:db8:0000::8a2e::1337

B. 2001:db8:::8a2e:0000:1337

C. 2001:db8::8a2e::1337

D. 2001:db8::8a2e:0:1337

172. Which is the correct expanded IPv6 address of 2001::456:0:ada4?

A. 2001:0000:0000:0456:0000:ada4

B. 2001:0000:0000:0000:456:0000:ada4

C. 2001:0000:0000:0000:0000:0456:0000:ada4

D. 2001:0000:0000:0000:0456:0000:0000:ada4

173. In the IPv6 address of 2001.0db8:1234:0016:0023:8080:2345:88ab/64, what is the subnet quartet?

A. 1234

B. 0016

C. 0023

D. 8080

174. What is the network prefix for the IPv6 address of 2001.db8::8080:2345:88ab/64?

A. 2001:db8::/64

B. 2001:0db8:8080:2345/64

C. 2001:0db8:0000:8080/64

D. 2001:0db8:0000:2345/64

175. You need to verify connectivity to an IPv6 address of fc00:0000:0000:0000:0000:0000:
0000:0004. Which command would you use?

   A. Router#ping fc00::4

   B. Router#ping fc::4

   C. Router#ping6 fc00::4

   D. Router#ping6 fc::4

176. Which address is a valid IPv6 host address?

   A. fe8::1

   B. 2001:db8::2435

   C. ff02::1

   D. ::1

177. Which statement is true of an IPv6 address?

   A. The first 48 bits is the subnet ID.

   B. All IPv6 addresses have a built-in loopback.

   C. A single interface can be assigned multiple IPv6 addresses.

   D. The IPv6 address plan allows for doubling the amount of IPv4 addresses.

178. You have been given an IPv6 prefix of 2001:0db8:aabb:5/52. How many subnets can you have from this address?

   A. 8,192

   B. 4,096

   C. 1,024

   D. 512

179. You work for an ISP. The American Registry for Internet Numbers (ARIN) has given you the 2001:0db8:8/34 IP address block. You need to figure out how many /48 blocks you can assign to your customers.

   A. 32,768

   B. 16,384

   C. 8,192

   D. 4,096

180. How many bits are contained in each field of an IPv6 address between the colons?

   A. 8 bits

   B. 32 bits

   C. 4 bits

   D. 16 bits

181. Which command would be used inside of an interface to configure SLAAC?

   A. Router(config-if)#enable slaac

   B. Router(config-if)#ipv6 address slaac

   C. Router(config-if)#ipv6 address dhcp

   D. Router(config-if)#ipv6 address autoconfig

182. Which address is used for RS (Router Solicitation) messages?

   A. ff00::2

   B. ff02::2

   C. ff00::1

   D. ff02::1

183. Which address is used for RA (Router Advertisement) messages?

   A. ff00:2

   B. ff02:2

   C. ff00:1

   D. ff02:1

184. What protocol/process in IPv6 replaces the IPv4 ARP process?

   A. NDP (NS/NA)

   B. DAD (NS/NA)

   C. SLAAC (RS/RA)

   D. ARPv6(NS/NA)

185. Which layer 3 protocol allows for NDP to process SLAAC?

   A. IGMP

   B. ICMP

   C. ICMPv6

   D. IGMPv6

186. What are stateless DHCPv6 servers used for?

   A. Configuring the default gateway

   B. Configuring the IPv6 address

   C. Configuring the IPv6 prefix length

   D. Configuring the DNS server address

187. Which command will configure an IPv6 DHCP relay agent for an interface?

   A. Router(config-if)#ipv6 helper 2001:db8:1234::1

   B. Router(config-if)#ipv6 dhcp helper 2001:db8:1234::1

   C. Router(config-if)#ipv6 dhcp 2001:db8:1234::1

   D. Router(config-if)#ipv6 dhcp relay destination 2001:db8:1234::1

188. Which mechanism in IPv6 allows for SLAAC to avoid duplicating an IPv6 address?

    A.   NDP (NS/NA)

    B.   DAD (NS/NA)

    C.   SLAAC (RS/RA)

    D.   ARPv6(NS/NA)

189. What is the process of stateful DHCPv6 for IPv6?

    A.   Discover, Offer, Request, Acknowledge

    B.   Solicit, Advertise, Request, Reply

    C.   Neighbor Solicitation, Neighbor Advertisement

    D.   Router Solicitation, Router Advertisement

190. When SLAAC is performed on an IPv6 host, which process happens first?

    A.   A Router Solicitation message is sent from the client.

    B.   A Router Advertisement message is sent from the router.

    C.   A link-local address is auto-configured on the client.

    D.   DAD is performed on the IPv6 address.

191. Which address is a global unicast address?

    A.   fe80:db80:db01:ada0:1112::1

    B.   2005:acd:234:1132::43

    C.   fd00:ac34:34b:8064:234a::7

    D.   ff00:101:4ab0:3b3e::10

192. Which address is a link-local address?

    A.   fe80:db80:db01:ada0:1112::1

    B.   2005:acd:234:1132::43

    C.   fd00:ac34:34b:8064:234a::7

    D.   ff00:101:4ab0:3b3e::10

193. For global unicast addresses, which part of the address is allotted by the RIR, or Regional Internet Registry?

    A.   First 23 bits

    B.   First 32 bits

    C.   First 48 bits

    D.   First 64 bits

194. Which address is a unique-local address?

    A.   fe80:db80:db01:ada0:1112::1

    B.   2005:acd:234:1132::43

    C.   fd00:ac34:34b:8064:234a::7

    D.   ff00::10

195. Which address is a multicast address?

    A. fe80:db80:db01:ada0:1112::1

    B. 2005:acd:234:1132::43

    C. fd00:ac34:34b:8064:234a::7

    D. ff00::10

196. Which IPv6 address type is similar to IPv4 RFC 1918 addresses?

    A. Link-local addresses

    B. Global unicast addresses

    C. EUI-64 addresses

    D. Anycast addresses

197. Which command would configure a single anycast address on a router's interface?

    A. Router(config-if)#ip address 2001:db8:1:1:1::12/64

    B. Router(config-if)#ipv6 address 2001:db8:1:1:1::12/64 anycast

    C. Router(config-if)#ipv6 anycast address 2001:db8:1:1:1::12/128

    D. Router(config-if)#ipv6 address 2001:db8:1:1:1::12/128 anycast

198. You are using the EUI-64 method of allocating the host portion of the IPv6 addresses. The MAC address of the host is f423:5634:5623. Which is the correct IP address that will be calculated for a network ID of fd00:1:1::?

    A. fd00:0001:0001:0000:f623:56ff:fe34:5623/64

    B. fd00:0001:0001:0000:f423:56ff:fe34:5623/64

    C. fd00:0001:0001:0000:fffe:f623:5634:5623/64

    D. fd00:0001:0001:0000:f623:56ff:ff34:5623/64

199. Which address is a EUI-64 generated address?

    A. 2001:db8:33::f629:58fe:ff35:5893/64

    B. fd00:4:33::f680:45ca:ac3b:5a73/64

    C. 2001:db8:aa::f654:56ff:fe34:a633/64

    D. 2001:db8:17:fffe:f623::ff34:5623/64

200. Which command would use the MAC address for the host portion of the IPv6 address on a router interface?

    A. Router(config-if)#ip address eui-64 2001:db8:1234::/64

    B. Router(config-if)#ip address 2001:db8:1234::/64 mac-address

    C. Router(config-if)#ipv6 address 2001:db8:1234::/64 eui-64

    D. Router(config-if)#ipv6 address 2001:db8:1234::/64 mac

201. You are using the EUI-64 method of allocating the host portion of the IPv6 addresses. The MAC address of the host is e5ee:f556:2434. What is the correct IP address that will be calculated for a network ID of fd00:2:2::?

    A. fd00:2:2::e9ee:f5ff:fe56:2434/64

    B. fd00:2:2::fffe:e5ee:f556:2434/64

    C. fd00:2:2::e7ee:f5ff:fe56:2434/64

    D. fd00:2:2::e2ee:f5ff:fe56:2434/64

202. Which command would you use to find the joined multicast groups for an IPv6 interface?

    A. Router#show ipv6 multicast

    B. Router#show ipv6 interface gi 0/1

    C. Router#show ipv6 routes

    D. Router#show mutlicast

203. Which type of IPv6 addressing allows for a one-to-many address for IP services?

    A. Multicast address

    B. Anycast address

    C. Unicast address

    D. Localcast address

204. What type of address is ::1/128?

    A. Multicast address

    B. Anycast address

    C. Unicast address

    D. Loopback address

205. Which type of IPv6 addressing allows for a one-to-closest address for IP services?

    A. Multicast address

    B. Anycast address

    C. Unicast address

    D. Loopback address

206. Which type of automatic address assignment will not allow for EUI-64 addressing?

    A. Static addressing

    B. SLAAC addressing

    C. Stateful DHCPv6 addressing

    D. Stateless DHCPv6 addressing

207. Which type of address always uses the EUI-64 addressing mechanism?

   A. Link-local addresses

   B. Global unicast addresses

   C. SLAAC addresses

   D. Anycast addresses

208. You have been given an IPv6 address of 2030:3454:aabb::/64. What can you conclude?

   A. The IP address is a unique-local address.

   B. The IP has been given to you by the Regional Internet Registry.

   C. The IP has been given to you by the Internet service provider.

   D. The IP has been given to you by IANA.

209. You are using the EUI-64 method of allocating the host portion of the IPv6 addresses. The MAC address of the host is 401e:32e4:ff03. What is the correct IP address that will be calculated for a network ID of fd00:3:3::?

   A. fd00:3:3::fffe:421e:32e4:ff03/64

   B. fd00:3:3::421e:32ff:fee4:ff03/64

   C. fd00:3:3::401e:32ff:fee4:ff03/64

   D. fd00:3:3::421e:32ff:ffe4:ff03/64

210. Which is a valid unique-local address?

   A. fec0:1111:2e3c:eab3::5/64

   B. fe80:d2e1:e24:63::25/64

   C. fd00:1edc:bae:eea4::2478/64

   D. fc00:4fec:ecf2:343::e44/64

Chapter 2

LAN Switching Technologies (Domain 2)

THE CCNA EXAM TOPICS COVERED IN THIS PRACTICE TEST INCLUDE THE FOLLOWING:

✓ **2.0 LAN Switching Technologies (ICND1) (ICND2)**

- 2.1 Describe and verify switching concepts (ICND1)

  - 2.1a MAC learning and aging (ICND1)

  - 2.1b Frame switching (ICND1)

  - 2.1c Frame flooding (ICND1)

  - 2.1d MAC address table (ICND1)

- 2.2 Interpret Ethernet frame format (ICND1)

- 2.3 Troubleshoot interface and cable issues (collisions, errors, duplex, speed) (ICND1)

- 2.4 Configure, verify, and troubleshoot VLANs (normal/extended range) spanning multiple switches (ICND1) (ICND2)

  - 2.4a Access ports (data and voice) (ICND1) (ICND2)

  - 2.4b Default VLAN (ICND1) (ICND2)

- 2.5 Configure, verify, and troubleshoot interswitch connectivity (ICND1) (ICND2)

  - 2.5a Trunk ports (ICND1)

  - 2.5b Add and remove VLANs on a trunk (ICND2)

  - 2.5c DTP, VTP (v1&v2), and 802.1Q (ICND1) (ICND2)

  - 2.5d Native VLAN (ICND1)

- 2.6 Configure, verify, and troubleshoot STP protocols (ICND2)

    - 2.6a STP mode (PVST+ and RPVST+) (ICND2)

    - 2.6b STP root bridge selection (ICND2)

- 2.7 Configure, verify, and troubleshoot STP related optional features (ICND2)

    - 2.7a PortFast (ICND2)

    - 2.7b BPDU guard (ICND2)

- 2.8 Configure and verify Layer 2 protocols (ICND1)

    - 2.8a Cisco Discovery Protocol (ICND1)

    - 2.8b LLDP (ICND1)

- 2.9 Configure, verify, and troubleshoot (Layer 2/Layer 3) EtherChannel (ICND2)

    - 2.9a Static (ICND2)

    - 2.9b PAGP (ICND2)

    - 2.9c LACP (ICND2)

- 2.10 Describe the benefits of switch stacking and chassis aggregation (ICND2)

1. Which benefit to a LAN does a switch provide?
   A. Breaks up broadcast domains
   B. Breaks up collision domains
   C. Forces full-duplex on all ports
   D. Allows for a fast uplink port

2. Where are MAC address tables stored?
   A. Flash
   B. CPU registers
   C. RAM
   D. NVRAM

3. Which advantage(s) are gained using switches?
   A. Low latency
   B. Software switching
   C. High cost
   D. All of the above

4. How do switches forward frames only to the destination computer?
   A. Forward filter decisions based on the MAC address table
   B. Forward filter decisions based on the routing table
   C. Flooding ports for the destination MAC address
   D. Broadcasting for the MAC address

5. Which mechanism does a switch employ to stop switching loops?
   A. Port channels
   B. Spanning Tree Protocol
   C. Ether channels
   D. Trunks

6. How are MAC addresses learned and associated with the port?
   A. Destination MAC address learning
   B. Source MAC address learning
   C. Port listen/learning
   D. Frame type learning

7. How many broadcast domains are present in the network in the following exhibit?

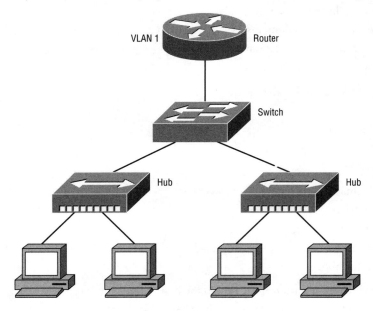

A. One broadcast domain

B. Two broadcast domains

C. Three broadcast domains

D. Seven broadcast domains

8. How many potential collision domains are present in the network in the following exhibit?

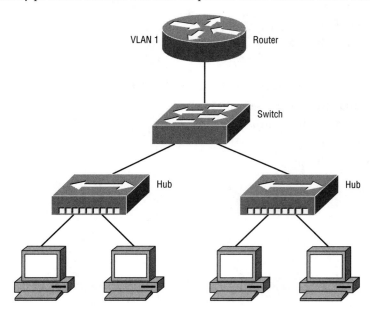

A. One collision domain

B. Two collision domains

C. Three collision domains

D. Seven collision domains

9. In the following exhibit, what will happen first at the switch when Computer A wants to sends Computer B a message?

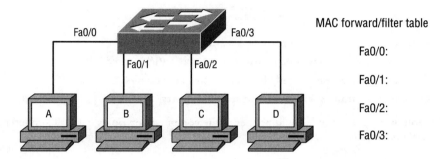

A. The switch will forward the frame to all ports on the switch.

B. The switch will direct communication to port Fa0/1.

C. The switch will record Computer A's MAC address on port Fa0/0.

D. The switch will record Computer B's MAC address on port Fa0/1.

10. In the following exhibit, what will happen first when Computer A wants to sends Computer B a message?

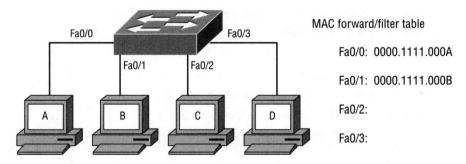

A. The switch will forward the frame to all ports on the switch.

B. The switch will direct communication to port Fa0/1.

C. The switch will record computer A's MAC address on port Fa0/0.

D. The switch will record computer B's MAC address on port Fa0/1.

11. Which command will allow you to see the MAC address table?

A. `Switch#show mac`

B. `Switch#show mac address-table`

C. `Switch#show cam table`

D. `Switch#show mac table`

12. In the following exhibit, what will happen if the computers on ports Fa0/1 (Computer A) and Fa0/4 (Computer B) are swapped?

```
        Mac Address Table
.....................................

Vlan  Mac Address        Type      Ports
.....  ....................  .......   ..........
1      0001.6c58.486e     STATIC    Fa0/1
1      0001.6c58.5606     DYNAMIC   Fa0/2
1      0001.6c58.486e     DYNAMIC   Fa0/3
1      0001.6c58.5406     DYNAMIC   Fa0/4
```

- **A.** Computer A's frames will only be forwarded to port Fa0/1.
- **B.** Computer A's frames will be forwarded to ports Fa0/1 and Fa0/4.
- **C.** Computer A's frames will only be forwarded to port Fa0/4.
- **D.** Computer B's frames will be forwarded to all ports.

13. In the following exhibit, what will happen if the computers on ports Fa0/2 (Computer A) and Fa0/3 (Computer B) are swapped?

```
        Mac Address Table
.....................................

Vlan  Mac Address        Type      Ports
.....  ....................  .......   ..........
1      0001.6c58.486e     STATIC    Fa0/1
1      0001.6c58.5606     DYNAMIC   Fa0/2
1      0001.6c58.486e     DYNAMIC   Fa0/3
1      0001.6c58.5406     DYNAMIC   Fa0/4
```

- **A.** Computer A's frames will only be forwarded to port Fa0/2.
- **B.** Computer A's frames will be forwarded to port Fa0/2 and Fa0/3.
- **C.** Computer A's frames will only be forwarded to port Fa0/3.
- **D.** Computer B's frames will be forwarded to all ports.

14. Which statement is true of an ARP request entering into a switch?
- **A.** The source MAC address of the frame will be all *F*s.
- **B.** The destination MAC address of the frame will be all *F*s.
- **C.** The switch will only forward the ARP request to the port for the destination computer.
- **D.** The switch will respond directly back with an ARP reply.

15. Which command will display all connected ports on a switch and include descriptions?
- **A.** `Switch#show ports`
- **B.** `Switch#show counters interfaces`
- **C.** `Switch#show interfaces counters`
- **D.** `Switch#show interfaces status`

16. Which is a consequence of not using loop avoidance with layer 2 switching?

    A. Duplicate unicast frames

    B. Broadcast storms

    C. MAC address thrashing

    D. All of the above

17. What is the default MAC address aging time for dynamic entries on most switches?

    A. 30 seconds

    B. 60 seconds

    C. 300 seconds

    D. 500 seconds

18. Which is a correct statement when hubs are replaced with switches?

    A. The replacement increases collision domains.

    B. The replacement decreases collision domains.

    C. The replacement increases broadcast domains.

    D. The replacement decreases broadcast domains.

19. In the following exhibit, which statement is true about the computer with a MAC address of 0001.6c58.24ae?

```
          Mac Address Table
          ...............................

     Vlan  Mac Address     Type      Ports
     ....  ..............  ........  ..........
     1     0001.6c58.486e  STATIC    Fa0/1
     1     0001.6c58.5606  DYNAMIC   Fa0/2
     1     0001.6c58.486e  DYNAMIC   Fa0/3
     1     0001.6c58.5406  DYNAMIC   Fa0/4
     1     0001.6c58.2323  DYNAMIC   Gi0/1
     1     0001.6c58.2325  DYNAMIC   Gi0/1
     1     0001.6c58.24ae  DYNAMIC   Gi0/1
```

    A. The computer is directly connected to Gi0/1.

    B. The computer is directly connected to Fa0/1.

    C. The computer is connected to another switch on Gi0/1.

    D. The MAC address table is thrashed, due to a loop.

20. Which command will show the number of entries in a MAC address table?

    A. `Switch#show mac address-table`

    B. `Switch#show mac address-table count`

    C. `Switch#show mac count`

    D. `Switch#show cam count`

21. When a switch receives a frame, what does it use to make a forwarding decision?

   A. Destination MAC address in the frame

   B. Source MAC address in the frame

   C. Source IP address in the frame

   D. Destination IP address in the frame

22. Which switching method checks the CRC as the frame is received by the switch?

   A. Cut-through mode

   B. Frag-free mode

   C. Store-and-forward mode

   D. Fast switching

23. Which statement is true about collision domains?

   A. All computers in the collision domain have the potential to have a frame collision.

   B. All computers in the collision domain have the potential to receive layer 2 broadcast messages.

   C. All computers in the collision domain have the potential to receive layer 3 broadcast messages.

   D. All computers in the collision domain are set to 10 Mb/s full-duplex.

24. In the following exhibit, what will happen when a frame destined for 0001.6c58.486f enters the switch?

```
        Mac Address Table
        ...............................

    Vlan Mac Address      Type      Ports
    ........ ...................... ........ ..........
    1    0001.6c58.486f  DYNAMIC   Fa0/1
    1    0001.6c58.5606  DYNAMIC   Fa0/2
    1    0001.6c58.486e  DYNAMIC   Fa0/3
```

   A. The frame will be forwarded to the uplink port.

   B. The frame will be forwarded to all active ports.

   C. The frame will be dropped.

   D. The frame will be forwarded to a MAC address of ffff.ffff.ffff.

25. Which switch mode operation reads only the first 64 bytes before making a switching decision?

   A. Cut-through mode

   B. Fragment-free mode

   C. Store-and-forward mode

   D. Fast switching

26. Which protocol on the host machine allows for a mapping of IP to MAC address?

    A. MAC Address Resolution Protocol

    B. Address Resolution Protocol

    C. Reverse Address Resolution Protocol

    D. Internet Control Message Protocol

27. A user is complaining of extremely long logon times. Using the following exhibit, what can you conclude?

```
Switch#sh interfaces fastEthernet 0/1
FastEthernet0/1 is up, line protocol is up (connected)
  Hardware is Lance, address is 000a.f36c.1501 (bia 000a.f36c.1501)
[output cut]
    956 packets input, 193351 bytes, 0 no buffer
    Received 956 broadcasts, 0 runts, 0 giants, 0 throttles
    0 input errors, 0 CRC, 235 frame, 0 overrun, 0 ignored, 0 abort
    0 watchdog, 0 multicast, 0 pause input
    0 input packets with dribble condition detected
    2357 packets output, 263570 bytes, 0 underruns
    0 output errors, 212 collisions, 10 interface resets
    0 babbles, 0 late collision, 0 deferred
    0 lost carrier, 0 no carrier
    0 output buffer failures, 0 output buffers swapped out
```

    A. The connection to the computer needs to be upgraded to 100 Mb/s.

    B. The connection to the computer has wiring issues.

    C. The NIC card in the attached computer is going bad and needs replacement.

    D. The interface or computer is running at half-duplex.

28. In the following exhibit, which would be true if the hub was replaced with a switch?

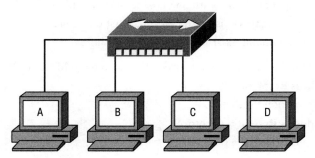

    A. The number of collision domains would increase.

    B. The number of collision domains would decrease.

    C. The number of broadcast domains would increase.

    D. The number of broadcast domains would decrease.

29. Considering the following exhibit, which of the following is a correct statement?

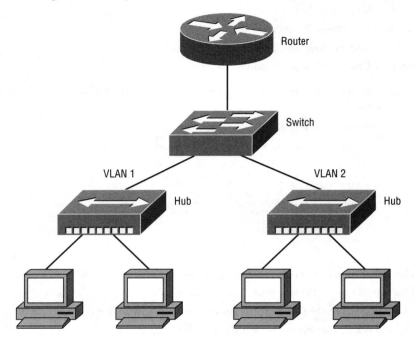

A. One collision domain exists with one broadcast domain.

B. Two collision domains exist with one broadcast domain.

C. Three collision domains exist with two broadcast domains.

D. Seven collision domains exist with two broadcast domains.

30. Which protocol on the host machine allows for a mapping of MAC to IP address?

A. MAC Address Resolution Protocol

B. Address Resolution Protocol

C. Reverse Address Resolution Protocol

D. Internet Control Message Protocol

31. Which command would you use to reset the MAC address table for learned MAC addresses in a switch?

A. `Switch#reset mac address-table`

B. `Switch#clear mac-address-table dynamic`

C. `Switch#clear mac-address-table`

D. `Switch#clear mac table`

32. In the following exhibit, which would cause this issue?

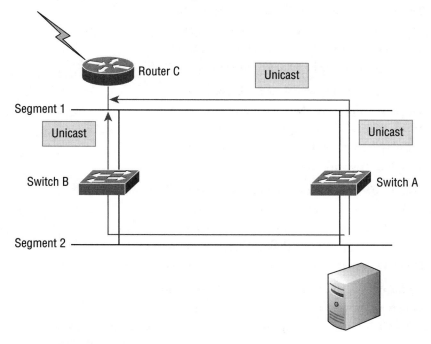

A. STP is not configured.

B. Broadcast control is not configured.

C. VTP is not configured.

D. The MAC address table has duplicate entries.

33. You need to see all of the MAC addresses associated with a single interface. Which command would you use?

A. `Switch>show mac address-table interfaces fast 0/1`

B. `Switch>show address-table interfaces fast 0/1`

C. `Switch#show mac interfaces fast 0/1`

D. `Switch#show address-table fast 0/1`

34. Which switch mode operation reads only the first 6 bytes before making a switching decision?

A. Cut-through mode

B. Frag-free mode

C. Store-and-forward mode

D. Fast switching

35. Which option describes latency in switching?

    A. The delay between routing packets to the destination interface

    B. The delay between switching the frame to the destination interface

    C. The delay in forward lookups to forward packets

    D. The delay in forward lookups to forward frames

36. Which is attributed to lowering switch latency?

    A. The use of higher bandwidth connections

    B. Multiple interfaces aggregated together

    C. Hardware-based bridging (ASICs)

    D. Spanning Tree Protocol

37. What is the difference between a broadcast frame and a flooded frame?

    A. A broadcast frame contains a destination MAC address beginning with ff:ff:ff.

    B. A flooded frame is a frame that is unknown in the MAC address table.

    C. A broadcast frame and a flooded frame are the same.

    D. Flooding of frames only occurs if there are switching loops.

38. What is the most accurate definition of wire speed with switching?

    A. Switching between two ports can happen at wire speed.

    B. The switch can process requests at the incoming speed of the connection.

    C. The switch can process requests at the incoming and outgoing speed of the connection.

    D. The switch can auto-negotiate between several different wire speeds.

39. Which is a function of a layer 2 switch?

    A. Forwarding the date based upon logical addressing

    B. Repeating the electrical signal to all ports

    C. Learning the MAC address by examining the destination MAC addresses

    D. Determining the forwarding interfaces based upon the destination MAC address and tables

40. What is a reason a network administrator would segment a network with a switch?

    A. Create more broadcast domains.

    B. Create isolation of ARP messages.

    C. Create less collision domains.

    D. Isolate traffic between segments.

41. If a switch uses the store and forward method of switching and receives a frame in which its CRC is invalid, what will happen?

    A. The switch will re-create the frame with a new CRC and correct the missing information.

    B. The switch will drop the frame and wait for retransmission of a new frame.

C. The switch will send back a frame for retransmission of the frame.

D. The switch will store the frame until a new frame with a matching CRC is received.

42. What information is added to the MAC address table when a frame is received on an interface?

A. Destination MAC address of the frame and incoming port number

B. Source MAC address of the frame and incoming port number

C. Destination MAC address of the frame and outgoing port number

D. Source MAC address of the frame and outgoing port number

43. Given the information in the following exhibit, which statement is true when Computer A needs to communicate with Computer C?

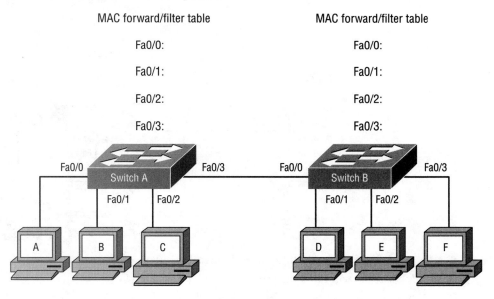

A. Switch A and Switch B will flood the frame across all ports.

B. Only Switch A will flood the frame across all ports.

C. Only Switch B will flood the frame across all ports.

D. Switch A will forward traffic only to Computer C's port.

44. What is the maximum wire speed of a single port on a 48-port Gigabit Ethernet switch?

A. 1,000 Mb/s

B. 2 Gb/s

C. 48 Gb/s

D. 96 Gb/s

45. You need to change the default MAC address aging time on a switch to 400 seconds. Which command would you use?

A. `Switch#set mac aging 400`

B. `Switch#mac aging-time 400 seconds`

C. `Switch#mac-address-table aging-time 400`

D. `Switch#mac address-aging 400`

46. Given the information in the following exhibit, which statement is true when Computer A needs to communicate with Computer F?

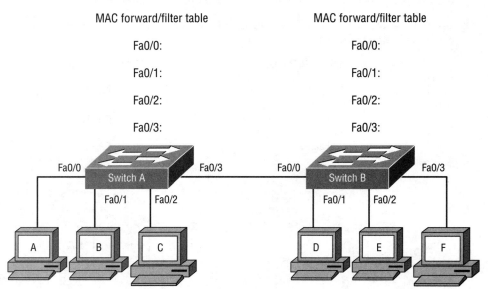

A. Switch A and Switch B will flood the frame across all ports.

B. Only Switch A will flood the frame across all ports.

C. Only Switch B will flood the frame across all ports.

D. Switch A will flood the frame across all ports. Switch B will forward traffic only to Computer F's port.

47. Which statement describes the micro-segmentation that a switch provides?

A. All of the ports on the switch create a single collision domain.

B. Each port on the switch segments broadcasts.

C. Each port on the switch creates its own collision domain.

D. Each port on the switch creates an isolation for layer 2 broadcasts.

48. Given the information in the following exhibit, which statement is true when Computer A needs to communicate with Computer F?

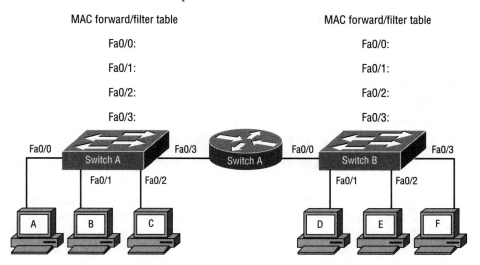

MAC forward/filter table   MAC forward/filter table

Fa0/0:   Fa0/0:

Fa0/1:   Fa0/1:

Fa0/2:   Fa0/2:

Fa0/3:   Fa0/3:

- **A.** Switch A and Switch B will flood the frame across all ports.
- **B.** Only Switch A will flood the frame across all ports.
- **C.** Only Switch B will flood the frame across all ports.
- **D.** Switch A will flood the frame across all ports, Switch B will forward traffic only to Computer F's port.

49. Under which circumstance will a switch drop a frame?

- **A.** If the destination MAC address of the frame is unknown in the MAC address table
- **B.** If the source MAC address of the frame is unknown in the MAC address table
- **C.** If the frame is deemed to be corrupt via the CRC
- **D.** If the destination MAC address exists in another switch's MAC address table

50. What is the issue with the network in the following exhibit?

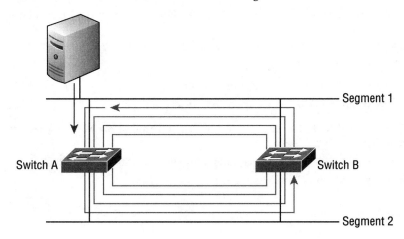

    A. STP is not configured and a broadcast storm is occurring.

    B. MAC table thrashing has occurred.

    C. STP is not configured and duplication of unicast frames is occurring.

    D. An STP loop has occurred.

51. In a layer 2 frame, where is the destination MAC address?

    A. The destination MAC address is in the first 6 bytes after the preamble.

    B. The destination MAC address is in the second 6 bytes after the preamble.

    C. The destination MAC address is the payload data.

    D. The destination MAC address is found in the preamble.

52. What is the significance of the preamble?

    A. The preamble allows the switch to allocate a buffer.

    B. The preamble allows the switch to sense collisions before data is transmitted.

    C. The preamble allows the switch to sync timing for the receipt of information to follow.

    D. The preamble allows the switch to read the sequence and acknowledge receipt of the frame.

53. How many bits is the OUI assigned by the IEEE?

    A. 6 bits

    B. 22 bits

    C. 24 bits

    D. 48 bits

54. What function does the Frame Check Sequence (FCS) perform?

    A. The FCS will error-correct data in a frame.

    B. The FCS will detect errors in a frame's data.

    C. The FCS is used for acknowledgment of receipt of the frame.

    D. Both A and B

55. If the Individual/Group (I/G) bit is set to 1 in the OUI portion of the MAC address, which statement is true?

    A. The MAC address is unique and governed by the IEEE.

    B. The MAC address is locally governed.

    C. The MAC address is a broadcast or multicast.

    D. The MAC address should always be broadcast.

56. If the Group/Local (G/L) bit is set to 1 in the OUI portion of the MAC address, which statement is true?

    A. The MAC address is a unique computer and governed by the IEEE.

    B. The MAC address is locally governed.

    C. The MAC address is a broadcast or multicast.

    D. The MAC address should always be broadcast.

57. Which is a reason that the Ethernet protocol uses physical addresses?

    A. It creates a differentiation between layer 2 and layer 3 communications.

    B. It defines a logical address scheme for devices.

    C. It uniquely identifies devices at layer 2.

    D. It allows the node to decide if the device is remote or local.

58. What is the nominal MTU for LAN communications?

    A. 1,500 bytes

    B. 1,500 bits

    C. 9,000 bytes

    D. 9,000 bits

59. What is the 2-byte type field used for in an Ethernet frame?

    A. It defines the data type contained within the frame.

    B. It identifies the upper-layer protocol for the data contained within the frame.

    C. It is a calculation with the FCS to provide error detection.

    D. It describes the length of data contained within the frame.

60. What is the purpose of the State Frame Delimiter byte in a frame?

    A. It provides physical timing for the frame following.

    B. It divides the data and the physical timing portion of the frame.

    C. It provides a means for the receiving node to know when data begins.

    D. It delimits the destination and source MAC address.

61. In the following exhibit, what can you conclude about the interface or node?

```
Switch#sh int fastEthernet 0/2
FastEthernet0/2 is down, line protocol is down (disabled)
  Hardware is Lance, address is 000a.f36c.1502 (bia 000a.f36c.1502)
[output cut]
   956 packets input, 193351 bytes, 0 no buffer
   Received 956 broadcasts, 0 runts, 0 giants, 0 throttles
   0 input errors, 0 CRC, 0 frame, 0 overrun, 0 ignored, 0 abort
   0 watchdog, 0 multicast, 0 pause input
   0 input packets with dribble condition detected
   2357 packets output, 263570 bytes, 0 underruns
   0 output errors, 0 collisions, 10 interface resets
   0 babbles, 457 late collision, 0 deferred
   0 lost carrier, 0 no carrier
   0 output buffer failures, 0 output buffers swapped out
```

    A. The interface is shut down.

    B. The interface is negotiated at half-duplex.

    C. There is a duplex mismatch on the interface.

    D. The cabling is shorted on the interface.

62. In the following exhibit, what can you conclude about the interface or node?

```
Switch#sh interfaces fastEthernet 0/2
FastEthernet0/2 is administratively down, line protocol is down (disabled)
  Hardware is Lance, address is 000a.f36c.1502 (bia 000a.f36c.1502)
[output cut]
    956 packets input, 193351 bytes, 0 no buffer
    Received 956 broadcasts, 0 runts, 0 giants, 0 throttles
    0 input errors, 0 CRC, 0 frame, 0 overrun, 0 ignored, 0 abort
    0 watchdog, 0 multicast, 0 pause input
    0 input packets with dribble condition detected
    2357 packets output, 263570 bytes, 0 underruns
    0 output errors, 0 collisions, 10 interface resets
    0 babbles, 0 late collision, 0 deferred
    0 lost carrier, 0 no carrier
    0 output buffer failures, 0 output buffers swapped out
```

   A. The interface is shut down.

   B. The interface is negotiated at half-duplex.

   C. There is a duplex mismatch on the interface.

   D. The cabling is shorted on the interface.

63. You have just resolved a problem and now need to monitor the problem on the interface. How would you reset the error counts for a single interface?

   A. `Switch#reset counters interface fast 0/1`

   B. `Switch#clear interface fast 0/1`

   C. `Switch#clear counters interface fast 0/1`

   D. `Switch#clear statistics interface fast 0/1`

64. In the following exhibit, what can you conclude about the interface or node?

```
Switch#sh interfaces fastEthernet 0/1
FastEthernet0/1 is down, line protocol is down (disabled)
  Hardware is Lance, address is 000a.f36c.1501 (bia 000a.f36c.1501)
[output cut]
    956 packets input, 193351 bytes, 0 no buffer
    Received 956 broadcasts, 0 runts, 0 giants, 0 throttles
    0 input errors, 0 CRC, 0 frame, 0 overrun, 0 ignored, 0 abort
    0 watchdog, 0 multicast, 0 pause input
    0 input packets with dribble condition detected
    2357 packets output, 263570 bytes, 0 underruns
    0 output errors, 0 collisions, 10 interface resets
    0 babbles, 0 late collision, 0 deferred
    0 lost carrier, 0 no carrier
    0 output buffer failures, 0 output buffers swapped out
```

   A. The interface is shut down.

   B. The interface is negotiated at half-duplex.

   C. The interface is operating nominally.

   D. The cable is disconnected for the node.

65. A router is connected to the switch via a Fast Ethernet interface. Intermittently you experience an outage. What should be done first to remedy the problem? Refer to the following exhibit.

```
!
interface FastEthernet0/2
  switchport mode access
  switchport access vlan 5
  switchport nonegotiate
[output cut]
```

A. The speed and duplex should be set statically.

B. Change the VLAN to a less crowded VLAN.

C. Change the switchport mode to a trunk.

D. Set the switchport to auto-negotiate.

66. In the following exhibit, what can you conclude about the interface or node?

```
Switch#sh int fastEthernet 0/2
FastEthernet0/2 is up, line protocol is up (connected)
  Hardware is Lance, address is 000a.f36c.1502 (bia 000a.f36c.1502)
BW 10000 Kbit, DLY 1000 usec,
    reliability 255/255, txload 220/255, rxload 80/255
  Encapsulation ARPA, loopback not set
  Keepalive set (10 sec)
  Full-duplex, 10Mb/s
[output cut]
    956 packets input, 193351 bytes, 0 no buffer
    Received 956 broadcasts, 0 runts, 0 giants, 0 throttles
    0 input errors, 0 CRC, 0 frame, 0 overrun, 0 ignored, 0 abort
    0 watchdog, 0 multicast, 0 pause input
    0 input packets with dribble condition detected
    2357 packets output, 263570 bytes, 0 underruns
    0 output errors, 0 collisions, 10 interface resets
    0 babbles, 0 late collision, 0 deferred
    0 lost carrier, 0 no carrier
    0 output buffer failures, 0 output buffers swapped out
```

A. There are no problems with the interface.

B. The interface is auto-negotiating speed and duplex.

C. There are a large number of broadcasts.

D. The node needs a faster network interface.

67. You have statically set an interface to 100 Mb/s full-duplex. However, the device you are plugging in will not work. Which command would you use to set speed and duplex back to auto-negotiate?

A. `Switch(config-if)#speed auto`
   `Switch(config-if)#duplex auto`

B. `Switch(config-if)#speed autonegotiate`
   `Switch(config-if)#duplex autonegotiate`

C. `Switch(config-if)#switchport autonegotiate`

D. `Switch(config-if)#interface autonegotiate`

68. You have auto-negotiation turned off on the node, but it is turned on at the switch's interface connecting the node. The interface is a 10/100/1000 Mb/s interface and the node is 100 Mb/s full-duplex. What will the outcome be when you plug in the node?

A. The switch interface will be set to the 100 Mb/s full-duplex.

B. The switch interface will be set to the 100 Mb/s half-duplex.

C. The switch interface will be set to the 10 Mb/s full-duplex.

D. The switch interface will be set to the 10 Mb/s half-duplex.

69. You plug a 100 Mb/s hub into a switch. What is the expected outcome?

    A. The switch interface will be set to the 100 Mb/s full-duplex.

    B. The switch interface will be set to the 100 Mb/s half-duplex.

    C. The switch interface will be set to the 10 Mb/s full-duplex.

    D. The switch interface will be set to the 10 Mb/s half-duplex.

70. You want to see a status of all speed and duplex negotiations for all interfaces. Which command would you use?

    A. `Switch#show run`

    B. `Switch#show interfaces counters`

    C. `Switch#shower interfaces status`

    D. `Switch#show counters interfaces`

71. You are trying to reprovision a switch in a different part of your network. However, you still see the old VLANs configured from the old network. How can you rectify the problem?

    A. Upgrade the IOS.

    B. Type `erase startup-config`, confirm it, and reload.

    C. Type `clear vlan`, confirm it, and reload.

    D. Delete the `vlan.dat`, confirm it, and reload.

72. Which VLAN is the default VLAN used to configure all switches from the factory?

    A. VLAN 999

    B. VLAN 1002

    C. VLAN 1005

    D. VLAN 1

73. What is the normal range for VLANs before you must use extended VLAN IDs?

    A. VLAN 1 through 1001

    B. VLAN 1 through 1002

    C. VLAN 1 through 1005

    D. VLAN 2 through 1002

74. Which is a benefit to converting a network from a flat layer 2 network to a routed layer 3 VLAN-enabled network?

    A. Increased collision domains for increased bandwidth

    B. Reduced complexity of design and operations

    C. Flexibility of user management and design

    D. Decreased number of broadcast domains for increased bandwidth

75. You have created a VLAN for the Research department. Now you need to configure an interface on the switch for the newly created VLAN. Which command will configure the interface for the respective VLAN?

   A. `Switch(config-if)#switchport vlan research`

   B. `Switch(config-if)#switchport access vlan research`

   C. `Switch(config-if)#switchport access vlan 9`

   D. `Switch(config-if)#switchport vlan 9`

76. You are installing a VoIP phone on the same interface as an existing computer. Which command will allow the VoIP phone to switch traffic onto its respective VLAN?

   A. `Switch(config-if)#switchport voice vlan 4`

   B. `Switch(config-if)#switchport vlan voice 4`

   C. `Switch(config-if)#switchport voip vlan 4`

   D. `Switch(config-if)#switchport access vlan 4 voice`

77. You have configured a new VLAN 9 and applied it to the interface. However, you find that the computer still remains in VLAN 1. What is the problem? Refer to the following exhibit.

```
Switch#sh run
Building configuration...
[output cut]
!
interface FastEthernet0/2
  switchport access vlan 9
  switchport mode trunk
  switchport nonegotiate
  spanning-tree portfast
!
```

   A. The switchport is configured with `switchport nonegotiate`.

   B. The switchport is configured as a trunk and dot1q trunking is intervening.

   C. The switchport is configured as a trunk and the native VLAN is VLAN 1.

   D. Spanning-tree PortFast is configured and defaulting to VLAN 1.

78. Which type of port removes the VLAN ID from the frame before it egresses the interface?

   A. Access port

   B. Trunk port

   C. Voice port

   D. Native port

79. You want to delete VLAN 1 for security reasons. However, the switch will not let you. What is the reason you cannot delete VLAN 1?

   A. The VLAN is still configured on a port.

   B. The VLAN serves as the switch's main management IP.

   C. The VLAN is protected from deletion.

   D. The VLAN is still configured as a native VLAN on a trunk.

80. Which is a true statement about extended VLANs?

    A. You cannot configure extended VLANs until the normal VLANs are all used.

    B. VTP versions 1 and 2 require the switch to be in transparent mode.

    C. Extended VLANs are saved in the VLAN database.

    D. Extended VLANs can only be used for FDDI.

81. What is the extended VLAN range?

    A. VLAN 1002 to 4096

    B. VLAN 1006 to 4096

    C. VLAN 1006 to 4094

    D. VLAN 1006 to 4092

82. You have configured a new VLAN 12 and applied it to the interface. However, you find that the computer still remains in VLAN 1. Which command will fix the issue? Refer to the following exhibit.

```
Switch#sh run
Building configuration...
[output cut]
!
interface FastEthernet0/4
 switchport access vlan 12
 switchport mode trunk
 switchport nonegotiate
 spanning-tree portfast
!
```

    A. `Switch(config-if)#switchport native vlan 12`

    B. `Switch(config-if)#no switchport nonegotiate`

    C. `Switch(config-if)#switchport mode access`

    D. `Switch(config-if)#no spanning-tree portfast`

83. Why is it recommended that you do not use VLAN 1?

    A. It is not a production VLAN.

    B. It cannot be routed via an SVI.

    C. It cannot participate in VTP transfers.

    D. It shouldn't be used for security reasons.

84. You need to create a VLAN to support jumbo frames. Which commands would configure jumbo frame support on a VLAN?

    A. `Switch#vlan 10`
       `Switch(config-vlan)#mtu 9128`

    B. `Switch(config)#vlan 10`
       `Switch(config-vlan)#mtu 9128`

    C. `Switch(config)#vlan 10`
       `Switch(config-vlan)#jumbo frames`

    D. `Switch(config)#vlan 10`
       `Switch(config-vlan)#mtu 1548`

85. What is the command to verify a VLAN and the port(s) it is associated with?

    A. `Switch#show vlans`

    B. `Switch#show vlan`

    C. `Switch#show access vlan`

    D. `Switch#show vlan database`

86. Which command(s) will delete a VLAN?

    A. `Switch(config)#vlan database`
        `Switch(config-vlan)#no vlan 9`

    B. `Switch(config)#vlan database`
        `Switch(config-vlan)#delete vlan 9`

    C. `Switch(config)#no vlan 9`

    D. `Switch(config)#vlan 9 delete`

87. Which is a correct statement about frame and VLANs?

    A. Broadcast frames are sent to ports that are configured in different VLANs.

    B. Unicast frames that are not in the MAC address table are flooded to all ports in all VLANs.

    C. The ports that link switches together must be access links.

    D. Frames with a destination MAC that are not in the MAC address table are flooded to only ports in the respective VLAN.

88. A VLAN is not configured yet, but you mistakenly configure it on an interface via the command `switch access vlan 12`. What will happen?

    A. The command will error.

    B. The command will complete and update the VLAN database.

    C. The command will complete, but before forwarding can happen, the VLAN must be manually created.

    D. The command will need to be negated and performed after the VLAN is manually created.

89. What is the normal range of VLANs that can be modified on a Cisco switch with default configuration?

    A. VLAN 1 to 1002

    B. VLAN 1 to 1001

    C. VLAN 2 to 1002

    D. VLAN 2 to 1001

90. Static VLANs are being used on a switch's interface. Which of the following statements is correct?

   A. Nodes use a VLAN policy server.

   B. Nodes are assigned VLANs based on their MAC address.

   C. Nodes are unaware of the VLAN in which they are configured.

   D. All nodes are in the same VLAN.

91. A switch is configured with a single VLAN of 12 for all interfaces. All nodes auto-negotiate at 100 Mb/s full-duplex. What is true if you add an additional VLAN to the switch.

   A. The switch will decrease its bandwidth due to overhead.

   B. The switch will increase its count of collision domains.

   C. The switch will now require a router.

   D. The switch will increase its bandwidth due to broadcast domains.

92. What is a direct benefit of adding VLANs?

   A. An increase of broadcast domains while decreasing collision domains

   B. An increase of broadcast domains while increasing collision domains

   C. A decrease of broadcast domains while decreasing collision domains

   D. A decrease of broadcast domains while increasing collisions domains

93. Which statement describes dynamic VLANs?

   A. The access port is switched into the respective VLAN based upon user credentials.

   B. The access port is switched into the respective VLAN based upon the computer's IP address.

   C. The access port is switched into the respective VLAN based upon the computer's MAC address.

   D. The access port is switched into the respective VLAN based upon security ACLs.

94. You have changed the name of VLAN 3, and you now want to check your change. Which command will you enter to verify the name change?

   A. `Switch#show vlans`

   B. `Switch#show interface vlan 3`

   C. `Switch#show run`

   D. `Switch#show vlan id 3`

95. You have been asked to segment the network for an R&D workgroup. The requirement is to allow the R&D group access to the existing servers, but no other VLANs should be able to access R&D. How can this be achieved with maximum flexibility?

   A. Create a new VLAN, configure a routed SVI interface, and apply ACLs to the VLAN.

   B. Create a new VLAN, configure a routed SVI interface, and apply ACLs to the R&D ports.

C. Create a new VLAN, and install a new R&D server in the new VLAN.

D. Create a new VLAN, and trunk the existing file server for both the production and R&D network.

96. You have just installed a Cisco VoIP phone and it will not provision. Referring to the following exhibit, what needs to be changed?

```
Switch#sh run
Building configuration...
[output cut]
!
interface FastEthernet0/4
  switchport access vlan 12
  switchport voice vlan 4
  switchport mode access
  no cdp enable
  switchport nonegotiate
  spanning-tree portfast
!
```

A. CDP needs to be enabled.

B. Spanning-tree PortFast needs to be removed.

C. The interface is configured with switchport nonegotiate.

D. The interface needs to be configured as a trunk.

97. You need to verify that an interface is in the proper VLAN. Which command will display the status of the interface, the VLAN configured, and the operational mode?

A. `Switch#show vlan`

B. `Switch#show running-config`

C. `Switch#show interfaces`

D. `Switch#show interfaces switchport`

98. You configured VLAN on an interface, but it is not working. After looking at the VLAN database, you find it has been disabled. Which command will enable the VLAN?

A. `Switch#enable vlan 3`

B. `Switch(config)#enable vlan 3`

C. `Switch#no shutdown vlan 3`

D. `Switch(config)#vlan 3`
`Switch(config-vlan)#no shutdown`

99. Which command will show the operational mode of only Fa0/3?

A. `Switch#show interfaces`

B. `Switch#show interfaces switchport`

C. `Switch#show interfaces FastEthernet 0/3 switchport`

D. `Switch#show interfaces status | i 0/3`

100. The guest VLAN is not allowing traffic to be forwarded. What is the cause of the problem which is not allowing traffic to be forwarded? Refer to the following exhibit.

```
Switch#sh vlan

VLAN Name                             Status    Ports
---- -------------------------------- --------- -------------------------------
1    default                          active    Fa0/1, Fa0/2, Fa0/3, Fa0/4
                                                Fa0/5, Fa0/6, Fa0/7, Fa0/8
                                                Fa0/9, Fa0/10, Fa0/11, Fa0/12
                                                Fa0/13, Fa0/14, Fa0/15, Fa0/16
                                                Fa0/17, Fa0/18, Fa0/19, Fa0/20
                                                Fa0/21, Fa0/22, Fa0/23, Gig0/2
2    office                           active
3    production                       active
4    voip                             active
5    guests                           act/lshut Fa0/24
1002 fddi-default                     active
1003 token-ring-default               active
[output cut]
```

A. The VLAN interface is shut down.

B. The VLAN is disabled.

C. The guest ports are not in the proper VLAN.

D. There is a problem elsewhere.

101. Which of the following is a true statement about static access ports?

A. An access port can carry VLANs via tagging.

B. A client computer can request the VLAN to be placed in.

C. A client computer cannot see any VLAN tagging information.

D. A client computer can see the VLAN tagging information.

102. Which of the following is a true statement, if you have changed the MTU on a VLAN to support jumbo frames?

A. If a normal MTU of 1528 is used, the switch will not forward the traffic.

B. Once jumbo frames are configured, nothing more needs to be done. Clients will auto-detect the new MTU and use jumbo frames.

C. Changing the MTU is an easy and effective method for raising speed.

D. For jumbo frames to be effective, all devices on the VLAN, including switches, must support them.

103. You have configured an access port for a remote office computer. The office has no IT persons on site. You want to stop workers from plugging in a WAP and exposing your company's internal network. Which feature should you configure?

A. Dynamic VLANs

B. Port security

C. ACLs

D. VLAN pruning

104. Which is a benefit of implementing routed VLANs?

A. VLANs can span multiple switches.

B. Implementing routed VLANs will decrease the broadcast domains.

    C. ACLs can be employed to secure VLANs.

    D. All of the above

105. You are running a wireless LAN controller (WLC) for a WLAN. You want to allow for guests to be segmented to the guest VLAN. What will you need to implement on the WLC?

    A. Access control lists for one SSID

    B. Two SSIDs, one configured to the production VLAN and another configured to the guest VLAN

    C. Dynamic VLANs for the SSID

    D. Access control lists for two SSIDs

106. What is the difference between a default VLAN and a native VLAN?

    A. A default VLAN is configured on all access ports of the switch from the factory.

    B. A native VLAN is configured on all access ports of the switch from the factory.

    C. A default VLAN is configured on all trunks for tagged frames.

    D. A native VLAN is configured on all trunks for tagged frames.

107. Where is the extended VLAN configuration stored?

    A. In the `vlan.dat` file

    B. In the running-config

    C. In the VLAN database

    D. In the startup-config

108. You need to create a new VLAN 5 called office and apply it to interface Fa0/4. Which commands will you need to enter?

    A.
```
Switch(config)#vlan 5
Switch(config-vlan)#name office
Switch(config-vlan)#exit
Switch(config)#interface fast 0/4
Switch(config-if)#switchport access vlan 5
```

    B.
```
Switch(config)#vlan 5
Switch(config-vlan)#name office
Switch(config-vlan)#exit
Switch(config)#interface fast 0/4
Switch(config-if)#switchport access vlan office
```

    C.
```
Switch(config)#vlan 5 office
Switch(config)#interface fast 0/4
Switch(config-if)#switchport access vlan 5
```

    D.
```
Switch(config)#vlan 5 name office
Switch(config)#interface fast 0/4
Switch(config-if)#switchport access vlan 5
```

109. In the following exhibit, what is wrong with VLAN 4?

```
Switch#sh vlan

VLAN Name                             Status   Ports
---- -------------------------------- -------- ------------------------------
1    default                          active   Fa0/1, Fa0/2, Fa0/3, Fa0/4
                                               Fa0/5, Fa0/6, Fa0/7, Fa0/8
                                               Fa0/9, Fa0/10, Fa0/11, Fa0/12
                                               Fa0/13, Fa0/14, Fa0/15, Fa0/16
                                               Fa0/17, Fa0/18, Fa0/19, Fa0/20
                                               Fa0/21, Fa0/22, Fa0/23, Gig0/2
2    office                           active
3    production                       active
4    VLAN0004                         active
5    guests                           act/lshut Fa0/24
1002 fddi-default                     active
1003 token-ring-default               active
[output cut]
```

A. The VLAN is shut down.

B. The VLAN is unnamed.

C. The VLAN was created on a non-Cisco switch.

D. The VLAN is suspended.

110. A VLAN was created on another non-Cisco switch. You look at the current VLAN database, but the VLAN is not in the VLAN database. What must be done to correct the issue?

A. Set the correct trunking protocol between the switches.

B. Create the VLAN manually.

C. Configure VTP on both switches.

D. Assign the VLAN to an interface on the other switch.

111. You are trying to implement VLANs. Your proposed drawing is in the following exhibit. What needs to be changed for proper communications?

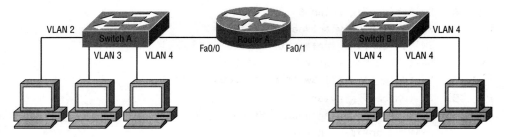

A. A duplicate VLAN database must be created on Switch A and Switch B.

B. A VLAN trunking protocol must be set up on Router A.

C. Switch A and Switch B must be trunked together.

D. Switch A and Switch B must be trunked together and the link to Router A on Fa0/1 removed.

112. You have just configured the network in the following exhibit. The commands you have entered configured the VLAN database and assigned the VLAN IDs to the interfaces. You cannot communicate between VLAN 2 and VLAN 4, but communication within VLAN 4 works. What is wrong?

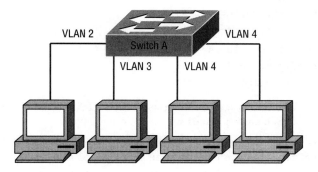

 A. The VLANs must be enabled via the command `no shutdown`.

 B. The network requires routing between the VLANs.

 C. The VLANs require VTP to be configured.

 D. The interfaces are administratively shut down by default and need to be enabled via `no shutdown`.

113. You have configured the network in the following exhibit. Switch A is performing routing functionality via an SVI. You can ping between Computer A and Computer C but cannot ping Computer F. However, Computer F can ping Computers D and E. What is wrong?

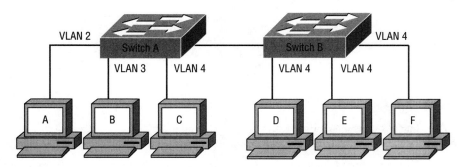

 A. The VLANs require VTP to be configured.

 B. The interfaces are administratively shut down by default and need to be enabled via a `no shutdown`.

 C. Switch B needs to provide routing as well via the SVI.

 D. The link between Switch A and Switch B needs to be a trunk.

114. Which command(s) will rename an existing VLAN 4 from production to office without interruption to the network?

A. `Switch(config)#rename vlan 4 office`

B. `Switch(config)#vlan 4`
`Switch(config-vlan)#name office`

C. `Switch(config)#vlan 4 office`

D. `Switch(config)#no vlan 4`
`Switch(config)#vlan 4`
`Switch(config-vlan)#name office`

115. You have been tasked to configure an interface with a VLAN ID of 8 and support a VoIP phone on VLAN 6. Which commands would achieve the goal?

A. `Switch(config-if)#switchport vlan 8`
`Switch(config-if)#switchport vlan 6 voip`

B. `Switch(config-if)#switchport mode access vlan 8`
`Switch(config-if)#switchport voice vlan 6`

C. `Switch(config-if)#switchport access vlan 8`
`Switch(config-if)#switchport voice vlan 6`

D. `Switch(config-if)#switchport access vlan 8 voice 6`

116. In the following exhibit, you have configured a port for a phone on an existing port for a computer. However, after you are done, only the phone works. What might be the problem?

```
Switch#sh run
Building configuration...
[output cut]
!
interface FastEthernet0/5
  switchport access vlan 8
  switchport voice vlan 4
  switchport mode trunk
  switchport nonegotiate
  spanning-tree portfast
!
```

A. The phone is misconfigured.

B. The computer is misconfigured.

C. The `switchport nonegotiate` command is stopping the computer from negotiating connection.

D. The switchport mode needs to be configured as an access port.

117. You attempt to configure a VLAN on a switch of VLAN 2300. When you finish configuring the VLAN and exit the VLAN database, you receive the error "% Failed to create VLANS 2300." What is wrong?

A. The VLAN database is too large and out of space.

B. The VLAN database cannot be configured for VLAN 2300.

    C. The VTP mode must be transparent to configure VLAN 2300.

    D. The VLAN must be configured on an interface first.

118. You attempt to configure a VLAN with a new name. You receive the error "Default VLAN 1 may not have its name changed." What is wrong?

    A. The VLAN is used on interfaces already.

    B. The VLAN is protected from any changes.

    C. The VLAN is being referenced by its name in interface configuration.

    D. You are not in the VLAN database when committing the change.

119. From the following exhibit, what can you conclude about the computer with the MAC address of 0002.160a.4c37?

```
              Mac Address Table
-------------------------------------------

vlan    Mac Address     Type      Ports
----    -------------   -------   -----
   1    0001.63c8.0a19  DYNAMIC   Gig0/1
   1    0002.160a.4c37  DYNAMIC   Gig0/1
   1    0010.1193.acbb  DYNAMIC   Fa0/1
   2    0001.63c8.0a19  DYNAMIC   Gig0/1
   3    0001.63c8.0a19  DYNAMIC   Gig0/1
   4    0001.63c8.0a19  DYNAMIC   Gig0/1
   5    0001.63c8.0a19  DYNAMIC   Gig0/1
  12    0001.63c8.0a19  DYNAMIC   Gig0/1
```

    A. The computer is the only device on port Gi0/1.

    B. The computer is on a hub connected to port Gi0/1.

    C. The computer is connected to another switch.

    D. The computer's MAC address has not aged out of the table yet.

120. You have configured a VLAN for an MTU of 9128. However, you have noticed a severe performance decrease from the change. What is the problem?

    A. One of the connected switches is still configured for a nominal MTU.

    B. The VLAN configuration must still propagate to the other switches.

    C. The VTP protocol is not configured correctly.

    D. The device does not support jumbo frames.

121. You have connected a Dell switch to the Cisco switch you are configuring and you cannot get a trunk between the two. What must be changed?

    A. The Dell switch must be configured to use ISL.

    B. The Cisco switch must be configured to use 802.1Q.

    C. Both switches need to have duplicated VLAN configurations.

    D. VTP needs to be configured on each of the switches.

122. You need to configure a trunk interface to support the protocol of 802.1Q. Which command will achieve this?

    A. `Switch(config-if)#switchport mode trunk 802.1q`

    B. `Switch(config-if)#switchport trunk encapsulation 802.1q`

   C. `Switch(config-if)#switchport 802.1q`

   D. `Switch(config-if)#switchport encapsulation trunk 802.1q`

123. You are trying to configure a trunk port on an interface for 802.1Q encapsulation. However, after entering the proper command, you receive the error `% Invalid input detected at '^' marker`. What is wrong?

   A. 802.1Q is not supported on the switch you are configuring this on.

   B. The interface will not allow configuration of 802.1Q.

   C. The switch only supports the ISL trunking protocol.

   D. The switch only supports the 802.1Q trunking protocol.

124. You need to view all of the trunks on a switch and verify that they have the proper trunking protocols configured. Which command will display the information?

   A. `Switch#show interfaces brief`

   B. `Switch#show interfaces trunk`

   C. `Switch#show switchport trunk`

   D. `Switch#show switchport brief`

125. When a frame is not tagged with 802.1Q VLAN identifying information, what happens when it traverses a trunk port?

   A. The frame is dropped to the bit bucket.

   B. The frame is forwarded to the default VLAN.

   C. The frame is forwarded to the native VLAN.

   D. The frame is sent to the first VLAN ID configured on the trunk.

126. What is the default VTP mode all switches are configured as by default?

   A. Server

   B. Client

   C. Transparent

   D. Master

127. You need to verify the VTP mode on a switch. Which command will display the information?

   A. `Switch#show vtp`

   B. `Switch#show vtp status`

   C. `Switch#show vtp counters`

   D. `Switch#show running-config`

128. Which commands would you enter on a new switch joining your existing network to configure VTP?

   A. `Switch(config)#vtp mode transparent`
       `Switch(config)#vtp domain corpname`

    B. `Switch(config)#vtp mode client`
        `Switch(config)#vtp domain corpname`

    C. `Switch(config)#vtp domain corpname`

    D. `Switch(config)#vtp client`
        `Switch(config)#vtp corpname`

129. Which protocol is an open standard trunking protocol?

    A. ISL

    B. VTP

    C. 802.1Q

    D. 802.1X

130. Which command will show you the native VLAN for only Fa0/15?

    A. `Switch#show running-config`

    B. `Switch#show interface fastethernet 0/15`

    C. `Switch#show interface fastethernet 0/15 Switchport`

    D. `Switch#show switchport fastethernet 0/15`

131. You need to change the native VLAN for interface Fa0/23 from VLAN 1 to VLAN 999. Which command would you use?

    A. `Switch(config-if)#switchport trunk native vlan 999`

    B. `Switch(config-if)#native vlan 999`

    C. `Switch(config-if)#switchport native vlan 999`

    D. `Switch(config-if)#no switchport native vlan 1`
        `Switch(config-if)#switchport native vlan 999`

132. When you change the native VLAN of a trunk from VLAN 1 to VLAN 999 and you receive the error "%CDP-4-NATIVE_VLAN_MISMATCH: Native VLAN mismatch discovered...," what is the possible problem?

    A. CDP is not running on the other interface, causing a mismatch.

    B. The interface is the first to be changed.

    C. The interface is running ISL.

    D. The version of CDP is wrong on the other switch.

133. You configure a new VLAN of 22 on Switch A. You have configured a few access links with the new VLAN and they work as normal. They do not forward traffic to ports configured in the same VLAN on Switch B. All other VLANs function fine between the switches. What is the problem? Refer to the following exhibit.

```
Current configuration : 202 bytes
!
interface FastEthernet0/32
 description Switch A to Switch B
 switchport trunk encapsulation dot1q
 switchport trunk native vlan 2
 switchport trunk allowed vlan 4,6,12,15
 switchport mode trunk
end
```

- **A.** The native VLAN must be changed.
- **B.** The VLAN is not allowed over the trunk.
- **C.** The trunk encapsulation is wrong.
- **D.** VTP is not set up on the remote switch.

134. Which command will turn off Dynamic Trunking Protocol (DTP) on an interface?

- **A.** `Switch(config-if)#no dtp`
- **B.** `Switch(config-if)#no switchport dtp enable`
- **C.** `Switch(config-if)#switchport dtp disable`
- **D.** `Switch(config-if)#switchport nonegotiate`

135. You need to remove VLANs 2 through 4 from the allowed list on a trunk interface. Which command will remove only these VLANs without interruption to the network?

- **A.** `Switch(config-if)#switchport trunk remove vlan 2-4`
- **B.** `Switch(config-if)#switchport remove vlan 2-4`
- **C.** `Switch(config-if)#switchport trunk allowed vlan remove 2-4`
- **D.** `Switch(config-if)#switchport trunk allowed remove vlan 2-4`

136. You have a list of allowed VLANs over an existing trunk. You need to set the allowed list back to default. Which command will perform this without interruption? Refer to the following exhibit.

```
Current configuration : 202 bytes
!
interface FastEthernet0/32
 description Switch A to Switch B
 switchport trunk encapsulation dot1q
 switchport trunk native vlan 2
 switchport trunk allowed vlan 4,6,12,15
 switchport mode trunk
end
```

- **A.** `Switch(config-if)#no switchport trunk allowed`
- **B.** `Switch(config-if)#no switchport trunk allowed all`
- **C.** `Switch(config-if)#no switchport trunk allowed 1-4096`
- **D.** `Switch(config-if)#switchport trunk allowed vlan all`

137. You are trunking Switch A and Switch B together. On Switch A you have the default of `switchport mode dynamic auto`. On Switch B, which command will you need to configure to allow trunking?

A. `SwitchB(config-if)#switchport mode trunk`

B. `SwitchB(config-if)#switchport mode dynamic trunk`

C. `SwitchB(config-if)#switchport mode dynamic auto`

D. `SwitchB(config-if)#switchport nonegotiate`

138. You need to add VLAN 4 to the allowed list on a trunk interface. Currently VLANs 5 through 8 are allowed. Which command will add only this VLAN without interruption to the network?

A. `Switch(config-if)#switchport trunk allowed vlan add 4`

B. `Switch(config-if)#add allowed vlan 4`

C. `Switch(config-if)#switchport trunk add vlan 4`

D. `Switch(config-if)#switchport trunk allowed add vlan 4`

139. You try to configure the command `switchport mode trunk` on an interface. However, you see the error message "Command rejected: An interface whose trunk encapsulation is Auto cannot be configured to trunk mode." What command will fix the issue?

A. `Switch(config-if)#switchport mode trunk manual`

B. `Switch(config-if)#no switchport mode dynamic auto`

C. `Switch(config-if)#switchport trunk encapsulation dot1q`

D. `Switch(config-if)#no switchport trunk encapsulation auto`

140. You are having an issue with a trunk between two switches. Examining the following exhibit, what can you conclude?

```
---------------------Switch A---------------------
SwitchA#show interfaces fastEthernet 0/2 trunk

Port        Mode            Encapsulation  Status       Native vlan
Fa0/2       Auto            802.1q         other        1

Port        Vlans allowed on trunk
Fa0/2       1-4,7,11,13-4094

Port        Vlans allowed and active in management domain
Fa0/2       1

Port        Vlans in spanning tree forwarding state and not pruned
Fa0/2       1
SwitchA#

---------------------Switch B---------------------
SwitchB#show interfaces fastEthernet 0/8 trunk

Port        Mode            Encapsulation  Status       Native vlan
Fa0/8       off             ISL            other        1

Port        Vlans allowed on trunk
Fa0/8       1-4,7,11,13-4094

Port        Vlans allowed and active in management domain
Fa0/8       1

Port        Vlans in spanning tree forwarding state and not pruned
Fa0/8       1
SwitchB#
```

A. The interfaces on both switches need to be set to trunk mode.

B. DTP is not running on Switch A.

C. All VLANs need to be allowed first.

D. There is a trunking protocol mismatch.

141. What is the function of the VLAN Trunking Protocol (VTP)?

  A. VTP allows for dynamic trunking between links.

  B. VTP allows for propagation of the VLAN database.

  C. VTP detects trunks encapsulations and negotiates trunks.

  D. VTP allows for propagation of the trunking database.

142. Which protocol is a Cisco proprietary protocol used for trunking switches?

  A. ISL

  B. 802.1Q

  C. VTP

  D. CDP

143. How does IEEE 802.1Q tag frames?

  A. 802.1Q adds a 32-bit header to the frame with the VLAN tagging information.

  B. 802.1Q adds a 32-bit header to the packet with the VLAN tagging information.

  C. 802.1Q inserts a 32-bit field between the source MAC address and the type field.

  D. 802.1Q inserts a 32-bit field between the destination MAC address and the type field.

144. Which VTP mode will not allow the switch to participate in VTP traffic but will forward VTP traffic?

  A. Server mode

  B. Transparent mode

  C. Proxy mode

  D. Client mode

145. You have just configured a trunk between two switches, Switch A and Switch B. The trunk operates as normal. However, there are minor issues with some of the switch traffic. What might be the problem? Refer to the following exhibit.

```
SwitchA# show interface fastethernet 3/1 switchport      Switch B# show interface gi 1/1 switchport
Name: Fa3/1                                               Name: Gi1/1
Switchport: Enabled                                      Switchport: Enabled
Administrative Mode: trunk                                Administrative Mode: trunk
Operational Mode: trunk                                   Operational Mode: trunk
Administrative Trunking Encapsulation: dot1q             Administrative Trunking Encapsulation: dot1q
Operational Trunking Encapsulation: dot1q               Operational Trunking Encapsulation: dot1q
Negotiation of Trunking: On                              Negotiation of Trunking: On
Access Mode VLAN: 1 (default)                            Access Mode VLAN: 1 (default)
Trunking Native Mode VLAN: 1 (default)                  Trunking Native Mode VLAN: 10 (inactive)
Voice VLAN: none                                        Voice VLAN: none
Administrative private-vlan host-association: none      Administrative private-vlan host-association: none
Administrative private-vlan mapping: none               Administrative private-vlan mapping: none
Administrative private-vlan trunk native VLAN: none     Administrative private-vlan trunk native VLAN: none
Administrative private-vlan trunk encapsulation: dot1q  Administrative private-vlan trunk encapsulation: dot1q
Administrative private-vlan trunk normal VLANs: none    Administrative private-vlan trunk normal VLANs: none
Administrative private-vlan trunk private VLANs: none   Administrative private-vlan trunk private VLANs: none
Operational private-vlan: none                          Operational private-vlan: none
Trunking VLANs Enabled: ALL                             Trunking VLANs Enabled: ALL
Pruning VLANs Enabled: 2-1001                           Pruning VLANs Enabled: 6-1001
Capture Mode Disabled                                   Capture Mode Disabled
Capture VLANs Allowed: ALL                              Capture VLANs Allowed: ALL
```

  A. Switch A is pruning all VLANs except for VLAN 1.

  B. The switches are on incompatible links.

    C.   Switch B has an inactive native VLAN.

    D.   Both switches have a native VLAN mismatch.

146. Which commands will allow a trunk with another switch configured as mode desirable auto?

    A.   `SwitchB(config-if)#switchport trunk encapsulation dot1q`
         `SwitchB(config-if)#switchport mode trunk`

    B.   `SwitchB(config-if)#switchport mode dynamic auto`
         `SwitchB(config-if)#switchport mode encapsulation dot1q`

    C.   `SwitchB(config-if)#switchport nonegotiate`

    D.   `SwitchB(config-if)#switchport encapsulation dot1q`
         `SwitchB(config-if)#switchport mode trunk`

147. What significance does VTP VLAN pruning provide?

    A.   VLAN pruning removes VLANs from the databases of other switches that they are not configured on.

    B.   VLAN pruning removes VLAN traffic from other switches that are not configured for the respective VLAN.

    C.   VLAN pruning automatically changes the allowed VLANs on all interfaces.

    D.   All of the above

148. Which command enables VTP pruning?

    A.   `Switch(config)#vtp mode pruning`

    B.   `Switch(config)#vtp pruning`

    C.   `Switch(config)#vtp vlan pruning`

    D.   `Switch(config-vlan)#enable pruning`

149. Switch A and Switch B have a trunk. On Switch A, the native VLAN is set to VLAN 10 on Switch B and the native VLAN is defaulted. What problems will occur?

    A.   CDP will not function.

    B.   VTP will not function.

    C.   All broadcasts will be forwarded to Switch B.

    D.   Any traffic not tagged on Switch B when traversing the trunk will be switched onto VLAN 10.

150. When enabling VTP pruning, where does it need to be configured?

    A.   VTP needs to be configured only on the VTP server.

    B.   VTP needs to be configured only on the VTP client.

    C.   VTP needs to be configured only on the VTP transparent.

    D.   VTP needs to be configured on all VTP clients and the server.

151. Which proprietary protocol allows for conformity of VLANs across all Cisco switches?

    A. CDP

    B. VTP

    C. 802.1X

    D. ISL

152. Which statement is correct about native VLANs?

    A. Any traffic tagged will be placed on the native VLAN.

    B. Any traffic that is not allowed over the trunk will be placed on the native VLAN.

    C. Any traffic not tagged will be placed on the native VLAN.

    D. Any traffic that is tagged with ISL on an 802.1Q trunk will be placed on the native VLAN.

153. You have configured a trunk between two switches, Switch A and Switch B, and have connectivity between the two switches. You have also set up VTP between the switches. However, when you configure a new VLAN on Switch A, the VLAN is not present on Switch B. What is the problem? Refer to the following exhibit.

```
---------------------- Switch A --------------------------

SwitchA#sh vtp status
VTP Version                     : 2
Configuration Revision          : 2
Maximum VLANs supported locally : 1005
Number of existing VLANs        : 6
VTP Operating Mode              : Server
VTP Domain Name                 : Cisco
VTP Pruning Mode                : Disabled
VTP V2 Mode                     : Disabled
VTP Traps Generation            : Disabled
MD5 digest                      : 0x9D 0x21 0x11 0xA8 0x00 0x71 0x79 0x39
Configuration last modified by 192.168.1.1 at 3-1-93 00:30:54
Local updater ID is 192.168.1.1 on interface vl1 (lowest numbered VLAN interface found)

---------------------- Switch B --------------------------

SwitchB#sh vtp status
VTP Version                     : 2
Configuration Revision          : 0
Maximum VLANs supported locally : 255
Number of existing VLANs        : 5
VTP Operating Mode              : Client
VTP Domain Name                 : Cisco
VTP Pruning Mode                : Disabled
VTP V2 Mode                     : Disabled
VTP Traps Generation            : Disabled
MD5 digest                      : 0xAA 0xB9 0x0C 0xCD 0xD7 0xE8 0xA6 0xE0
Configuration last modified by 0.0.0.0 at 0-0-00 00:00:00
```

    A. VTP pruning must be enabled.

    B. The operational mode of Switch B should be transparent.

    C. The MD5 digest is not matching on Switch A.

    D. The VTP domain is not correct on Switch B.

154. You have configured a trunk between two switches, Switch A and Switch B, and have connectivity between the two switches. You receive a call from one of the other admins and the person informs you that they are seeing a number of errors. You inspect the trunks of both switches. What could be the problem? Refer to the following exhibit.

```
----------------------- Switch A --------------------------
SwitchA#sh int trunk
Port         Mode         Encapsulation   Status      Native vlan
Gig0/1       on           802.1q          trunking    2

Port         vlans allowed on trunk
Gig0/1       1-1005

Port         vlans allowed and active in management domain
Gig0/1       1,2

Port         vlans in spanning tree forwarding state and not pruned
Gig0/1       1,2

----------------------- Switch B --------------------------
SwitchB#sh int trunk
Port         Mode         Encapsulation   Status      Native vlan
Gig0/1       on           802.1q          trunking    1

Port         vlans allowed on trunk
Gig0/1       1-1005

Port         vlans allowed and active in management domain
Gig0/1       1,2

Port         vlans in spanning tree forwarding state and not pruned
Gig0/1       none
```

A. The trunk mode is incorrect between the two switches and should be ISL.

B. There is a native VLAN mismatch between the two switches.

C. VTP protocol is pruning VLAN 1 and VLAN 2 on Switch B.

D. Both switches do not have support for extended VLANs.

155. You are setting up a switch. When you perform a sh run, you notice that the VLANs are in the running-config. What could be wrong? Refer to the following exhibit.

```
Switch#sh run
Building configuration...

Current configuration : 1139 bytes
[output cut]
spanning-tree mode pvst
!
vlan 2
 name office
!
vlan 3
 name warehouse
!
vlan 4
 name showroom
!
interface FastEthernet0/1
[output cut]
```

A. Nothing is wrong since the VLANs are stored in the running-config.

B. The switch is set up with a VTP mode of client.

C. The switch is set up with a VTP mode of server.

D. The switch is set up with a VTP mode of transparent.

156. You have configured `switchport nonegotiate` on an interface with a default configuration. What effect will it have on the neighboring interface when the other switch is plugged in with its interface in default configuration?

   A. The switchport will transition to a trunk port.

   B. The switchport will remain an access port.

   C. The interface will remain shut down.

   D. The interface will enter an err-disable state.

157. Switch A has the default configuration on its interface. You plug Switch B into its interface with a crossover cable. Which command will force Switch B to become a member of VLAN 5?

   A. `SwitchA(config-if)#switchport mode access`
   `SwitchA(config-if)#switchport access vlan 5`

   B. `SwitchA(config-if)#switchport mode trunk`
   `SwitchA(config-if)#switchport native vlan 5`

   C. `SwitchB(config-if)#switchport mode access`
   `SwitchB(config-if)#switchport access vlan 5`

   D. `SwitchB(config-if)#switchport mode trunk`
   `SwitchB(config-if)#switchport native vlan 5`

158. Switch A is configured with the command of `switchport mode dynamic desirable` on its interface. Which command would you need to configure on Switch B to create a trunk between them?

   A. `SwitchB(config-if)#switchport mode dynamic auto`

   B. `SwitchB(config-if)#switchport mode dynamic desirable`

   C. `SwitchB(config-if)#switchport mode trunk`

   D. All of the above

159. Which statement is correct about the command `switchport mode dynamic auto`?

   A. The interface will become a trunk if requested on the neighboring port.

   B. The interface will become a trunk if the neighboring port is configured the same.

   C. The interface will remain an access link if the neighboring port is configured as a trunk.

   D. The interface will remain an access link if the native VLAN is changed.

160. Which command is similar to `show interfaces trunk` but will show greater detail?

   A. `Switch#show interfaces trunk detail`

   B. `Switch#show switchport`

   C. `Switch#show interfaces switchport`

   D. `Switch#show running-config`

161. You are connecting a VMware ESXi server to an interface on a 3560 switch. The ESXi server will need several VLANs for the VMs running on it. How would you configure the interface?

A.
```
Switch(config-if)#switchport trunk encapsulation dot1q
Switch(config-if)#switchport mode trunk
Switch(config-if)#switchport nonegotiate
```

B.
```
Switch(config-if)#switchport trunk encapsulation dot1q
Switch(config-if)#switchport mode dynamic desirable
```

C.
```
Switch(config-if)#switchport trunk encapsulation dot1q
Switch(config-if)#switchport mode access
```

D.
```
Switch(config-if)#switchport trunk encapsulation dot1q
Switch(config-if)#switchport trunk
Switch(config-if)#switchport nonegotiate
```

162. When you have a native VLAN mismatch on a configured trunk, which protocol will alert you to the issue?

A. VTP

B. CDP

C. 802.1Q

D. ISL

163. How does a VTP client know that the VTP database has been updated?

A. The CDP protocol checks for VTP updates.

B. The VTP protocol checks the MD5 checksum for changes.

C. The VTP protocol checks the database revision number.

D. The VTP protocol pulls a full copy of the database every 60 seconds.

164. You have configured Cisco 2960 called Switch A with the command `switchport mode trunk`. However, Switch B will not form a trunk with Switch A. What is the problem on Switch B? Refer to the following exhibit.

```
SwitchB#sh interfaces gi 0/1 switchport
Name: Gig0/1
Switchport: Enabled
Administrative Mode: static access
Operational Mode: static access
Administrative Trunking Encapsulation: dot1q
Operational Trunking Encapsulation: native
Negotiation of Trunking: on
Access Mode VLAN: 1 (default)
Trunking Native Mode VLAN: 1 (default)
Voice VLAN: none
Administrative private-vlan host-association: none
Administrative private-vlan mapping: none
Administrative private-vlan trunk native VLAN: none
Administrative private-vlan trunk encapsulation: dot1q
Administrative private-vlan trunk normal VLANs: none
Administrative private-vlan trunk private VLANs: none
Operational private-vlan: none
Trunking VLANS Enabled: ALL
Pruning VLANS Enabled: 2-1001
Capture Mode Disabled
Capture VLANS Allowed: ALL
Protected: false
Appliance trust: none
```

    A. Switch B has DTP turned off.

    B. Switch B is set to an access port.

    C. Switch B has its interface administratively disabled.

    D. Switch B has the wrong trunk encapsulation.

165. What can happen by changing the mode of a VTP client to a VTP server and changing one of the VLANs?

    A. The VLAN database can be overwritten in the rest of the network.

    B. The VLAN database can be erased in the rest of the network.

    C. The switch will need to be reloaded before it can function as a server.

    D. Nothing; the switch functions fine in the rest of the network.

166. You need to check the allowed VLANs on a trunk interface. Which command will show you the allowed VLANs?

    A. `SwitchA#show interfaces gi 0/1 trunk`

    B. `SwitchA#show interfaces gi 0/1`

    C. `SwitchA#show interfaces gi 0/1 switchport`

    D. `SwitchA#show interfaces trunk`

167. You are trunking a Hyper-V server to an interface on Switch B. However, the interface will not form a trunk. What is wrong on Switch B? Refer to the following exhibit.

```
SwitchB#sh interfaces gi 0/1 switchport
Name: Gig0/1
Switchport: Enabled
Administrative Mode: dynamic auto
Operational Mode: static access
Administrative Trunking Encapsulation: dot1q
Operational Trunking Encapsulation: native
Negotiation of Trunking: On
Access Mode VLAN: 1 (default)
Trunking Native Mode VLAN: 1 (default)
Voice VLAN: none
Administrative private-vlan host-association: none
Administrative private-vlan mapping: none
Administrative private-vlan trunk native VLAN: none
Administrative private-vlan trunk encapsulation: dot1q
Administrative private-vlan trunk normal VLANs: none
Administrative private-vlan trunk private VLANs: none
Operational private-vlan: none
Trunking VLANS Enabled: ALL
Pruning VLANS Enabled: 2-1001
Capture Mode Disabled
Capture VLANS Allowed: ALL
Protected: false
Appliance trust: none
```

    A. Switch B has DTP turned off.

    B. Switch B is set to an access port.

    C. Switch B must be set to a static trunk.

    D. Switch B is configured with ISL.

168. You need to verify if VTP pruning is enabled. Which command will you use to view the information?

    A. `SwitchA#show vtp status`

    B. `SwitchA#show vtp pruning`

    C. `SwitchA#show vtp details`

    D. `SwitchA#show vlan pruning`

169. You are trying to change the native VLAN from VLAN 1 to VLAN 1002. You have configured both sides with `switchport native vlan 1002`. However, the native VLAN traffic keeps failing. What is wrong?

    A. The native VLAN must be VLAN 1.

    B. The native VLAN cannot be an extended VLAN.

    C. VLAN 1002 is not allowed for Ethernet traffic.

    D. The problem is not the native VLAN; everything is configured properly.

170. You configured a trunk between Switch A and Switch B. Everything works as expected, except you cannot pass traffic for VLAN 9. Which command will fix the issue without causing network interruption? Refer to the following exhibit.

```
SwitchB#sh run
Building configuration...

Current configuration : 1157 bytes
[output cut]
interface FastEthernet0/23
!
interface FastEthernet0/24
!
interface GigabitEthernet0/1
 switchport trunk allowed vlan 1,6-8,10-22,24-798,801-850,853-855,857-1005
 switchport mode trunk
!
interface GigabitEthernet0/2
[output cut]
```

    A. `SwitchB(config-if)#switchport trunk allowed vlan 1-1001`

    B. `SwitchB(config-if)#switchport trunk allowed vlan all`

    C. `SwitchB(config-if)#switchport trunk allowed vlan remove 9`

    D. `SwitchB(config-if)#switchport trunk allowed vlan add 9`

171. What is the IEEE specification for Spanning Tree Protocol?

    A. 802.1x

    B. 802.1w

    C. 802.1d

    D. 802.1s

172. Which statement is correct about Spanning Tree Protocol?

    A. STP runs on a central switch by creating a topology database.

    B. STP runs as a distributed process on each switch and creates a topology database.

    C. STP uses routing protocols to check for network loops.

    D. STP uses the MAC address table to check for switching loops.

173. How does Spanning Tree Protocol detect and monitor loops in networks?

A. STP detects and monitors BPDUs being received on multiple interfaces.

B. STP detects and monitors normal traffic frames being received on multiple interfaces.

C. STP detects and monitors CDP frames being received on multiple interfaces.

D. STP detects and monitors access ports in the same VLAN.

174. How is the root bridge in STP elected?

A. The root bridge is the switch with the highest IP address and priority.

B. The root bridge is the switch with the lowest IP address and priority.

C. The root bridge is the switch with the lowest MAC address and priority.

D. The root bridge is the switch with the highest MAC address and priority.

175. What is the IEEE specification for Rapid Spanning Tree Protocol?

A. 802.1x

B. 802.1w

C. 802.1d

D. 802.1s

176. Why is a root bridge elected for STP to function properly?

A. The root bridge is the logical center of the STP topology.

B. The root bridge allows all forwarding decisions of frames.

C. The root bridge calculates the port cost for the rest of the network.

D. The root bridge calculates the fastest path for the rest of the network.

177. How does a switch calculate the bridge ID?

A. The bridge ID is a 6-byte number containing a 2-byte bridge priority and 4-byte IP address.

B. The bridge ID is an 8-byte number containing a 4-byte bridge priority and 4-byte IP address.

C. The bridge ID is an 8-byte number containing a 2-byte bridge priority and 6-byte MAC address.

D. The bridge ID is a 10-byte number containing a 4-byte bridge priority and 6-byte MAC address.

178. What is the link cost in respect to STP?

A. Link cost is the latency of a frame traversing across the link.

B. Link cost is the calculation of all the ports in the path to the root bridge.

C. Link cost is the monetary cost to traverse a link.

D. Link cost is a numeric value associated with the speed of a link.

179. What is the path cost in respect to RSTP?

A. Path cost is the latency of a frame traversing across the link.

B. Path cost is the calculation of all the ports in the path to the root bridge.

C. Path cost is the monetary cost to traverse a link.

D. Path cost is a numeric value associated with the speed of a link.

180. What is the default wait time for STP convergence to complete?

A. Convergence takes 60 seconds to complete.

B. Convergence takes 5 seconds to complete.

C. Convergence takes 30 seconds to complete.

D. Convergence takes 50 seconds to complete.

181. When a computer is connected to an interface with STP enabled in default mode, which is the correct order of the port transitions?

A. Listening, learning, blocking, forwarding

B. Forwarding, listening, learning, blocking

C. Blocking, listening, learning, forwarding

D. Blocking, learning, listening, forwarding

182. What is the definition of a designated port?

A. A port that is determined to have the lowest cost and placed in a forwarding state for a network segment

B. A port that is determined to have the highest cost and placed in a forwarding state for a network segment

C. A port that is determined to have a lowest path cost to the root bridge and placed in a forwarding state for a network segment

D. A port that is determined to have the highest path cost to the root bridge and placed in a blocking state for a network segment

183. Which is a correct statement about bridge port roles in STP?

A. Every switch, excluding the root bridge, must have at least one root port.

B. Every switch, including the root bridge, must have at least one designated port.

C. Every switch, excluding the root bridge, must have at least one alternate port.

D. Every switch, including the root bridge, must have at least one backup port.

184. What is the definition of an STP root port?

A. A port that is determined to have the lowest cost to the network segment and placed in a forwarding state

B. A port that is determined to have the highest cost to the network segment and placed in a forwarding state

C. A port that is determined to have the lowest path cost to the root bridge and placed in a forwarding state for a network segment

D. A port that is determined to have the highest path cost to the root bridge and placed in a blocking state for a network segment

185. Which statement describes an STP port that is placed into a blocking state?

   A. When a port is placed into a blocking state, it blocks all frames, including BPDUs.

   B. When a port is placed into a blocking state, it blocks redundant frames, excluding BPDUs.

   C. When a port is placed into a blocking state, it blocks all frames, excluding BPDUs.

   D. When a port is placed into a blocking state, it blocks redundant frames, including BPDUs.

186. Which protocol is a Cisco proprietary enhancement for 802.1d that allows separate spanning-tree instances for each VLAN?

   A. IEEE 802.1w

   B. PVST+

   C. CST

   D. RSTP

187. What is the definition of an STP designated port?

   A. A port that is determined to have the lowest cost to the network segment and placed in a forwarding state

   B. A port that is determined to have the lowest path cost to the root bridge and placed in a forwarding state for a network segment

   C. A port that is determined to have the highest path cost to the root bridge and placed in a blocking state for a network segment

   D. A port that is determined to have the highest cost to the network segment and placed in a forwarding state

188. When a computer is connected to an interface with RSTP enabled in default mode, which is the correct order of the port transitions?

   A. Discarding, learning, blocking, forwarding

   B. Discarding, listening, forwarding

   C. Blocking, listening, learning, forwarding

   D. Discarding, learning, forwarding

189. How is the bridge ID calculated for PVST+?

   A. The bridge ID is a 4-byte bridge priority, a 12-byte sys-id-ext, and 6 byte MAC address.

   B. The bridge ID is a 4-byte bridge priority and sys-id-ext and 6-byte MAC address.

   C. The bridge ID is a 4-bit bridge priority, 12-bit sys-id-ext, and 6-byte MAC address.

   D. The bridge ID is a 4-bit bridge priority, 12-bit sys-id-ext, and an 8-byte IP address.

190. What is the default bridge priority for all STP switches?

   A. Bridge priority of 8,192

   B. Bridge priority of 16,384

    C.   Bridge priority of 32,768

    D.   Bridge priority of 65,526

191. Which protocol is a Cisco proprietary enhancement for 802.1w that allows separate spanning-tree instances for each VLAN?

    A.   Rapid PVST+

    B.   PVST+

    C.   CST

    D.   RSTP+

192. Which statement is correct about the Common Spanning Tree?

    A.   CST elects a root bridge for each VLAN.

    B.   CST elects a single root bridge for the entire physical network.

    C.   CST has an immediate convergence because it elects a single root bridge.

    D.   CST is best implemented for really large networks since it scales efficiently.

193. Which statement is correct about Rapid Spanning Tree Protocol?

    A.   RSTP allows for multiple root bridges.

    B.   RSTP is backward compatible with STP.

    C.   RSTP has a convergence time of around 50 seconds.

    D.   RSTP has five port states to which the interfaces could possibly transition.

194. How do switches participating in an STP network become aware of topology changes?

    A.   The root bridge is responsible for sensing the change and sending Topology Change Notification BPDUs.

    B.   Each switch is responsible for sensing the change and sending Topology Change Notification BPDUs.

    C.   The root bridge polls each switch participating in STP for changes.

    D.   The switches participating in STP poll the root bridge for changes.

195. Which of the following standards is an IEEE standard that is to replace Rapid PVST+?

    A.   802.1x

    B.   802.1w

    C.   802.1d

    D.   802.1s

196. Which is a correct statement about bridge port roles in STP?

    A.   A designated port is always in a blocking state.

    B.   Every switch, including the root bridge, must have at least one designated port.

    C.   Every switch, excluding the root bridge, must have at least one non-designated port.

    D.   All ports on the root bridge are in a designated port state.

197. In Rapid Spanning Tree Protocol, which port mode replaces the blocking and listening port states?

    A. Discarding

    B. Learning

    C. Forwarding

    D. Backup

198. You have a network consisting of four switches, all configured with the same bridge priority. Which switch will be elected the root bridge?

    A. 0081.023a.b433

    B. 0011.03ae.d8aa

    C. 0041.0611.1112

    D. 0021.02fa.bdfc

199. What is the default STP mode all Cisco switches run?

    A. 802.1d

    B. 802.1w

    C. Rapid-PVST+

    D. PVST+

200. Which option is a correct statement about alternate ports in RSTP?

    A. An alternate port receives BDPUs from another port on the same switch and therefore can replace the designated port if it fails.

    B. An alternate port receives BPDUs from another switch and therefore can replace the designated port if it fails.

    C. An alternate port is always placed in a forwarding state.

    D. An alternate port receives BPDUs from another switch and therefore can replace the root port if it fails.

201. Which is a correct statement about backup ports in RSTP?

    A. A backup port receives BDPUs from another port on the same switch and therefore can replace the designated port if it fails.

    B. A backup port receives BPDUs from another switch and therefore can replace the designated port if it fails.

    C. A backup port is always placed in a forwarding state.

    D. A backup port receives BPDUs from another switch and therefore can replace the root port if it fails.

202. You have a network consisting of four switches. Which switch will be elected the root bridge?

  A. Priority 32,768 MAC 0013.abea.b562

  B. Priority 32,768 MAC 00ef.0897.8abc

  C. Priority 32,768 MAC 00e8.1212.278e

  D. Priority 16,384 MAC 00f8.034e.bede

203. Which command would configure the priority of 16,384 for VLAN 5?

  A. SwitchB(config)#spanning-tree vlan 5 priority 16384

  B. SwitchB(config)#spanning-tree priority 16384 vlan 5

  C. SwitchB(config-vlan)#spanning-tree priority 16384

  D. SwitchB(config-vlan)#spanning-tree vlan priority 16384

204. Which command will display the VLANs for which the current switch is the root bridge?

  A. SwitchA#show spanning-tree details

  B. SwitchA#show spanning-tree status

  C. SwitchA#show spanning-tree root

  D. SwitchA#show spanning-tree summary

205. Which command will enable Rapid Per-VLAN Spanning Tree on a switch?

  A. SwitchB(config)#spanning-tree rapid-pvst

  B. SwitchB(config)#spanning-tree 802.1w

  C. SwitchB(config)#spanning-tree mode rapid-pvst

  D. SwitchB(config)#spanning-tree mode 802.1w

206. You want to see the spanning tree for one VLAN. Which command would you use?

  A. SwitchC#show vlan 6 spanning-tree

  B. SwitchC#show spanning-tree vlan 6

  C. SwitchC#show vlan 6

  D. SwitchC#show spanning-tree summary vlan 6

207. Which new port state does RTSP have compared to STP?

  A. Learning

  B. Forwarding

  C. Blocking

  D. Discarding

208. In the following exhibit, which switch interfaces will become root ports?

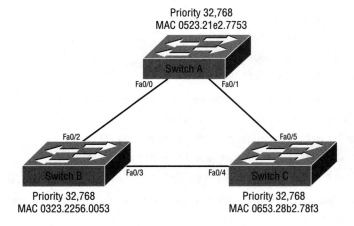

A.   Switch B Fa0/2 and Switch B Fa0/3

B.   Switch A Fa0/0 and Switch C Fa0/4

C.   Switch A Fa0/0 and Switch B Fa0/3

D.   Switch C Fa0/4 and Switch C Fa0/5

209. In the following exhibit, which switch interface will become a non-designated port?

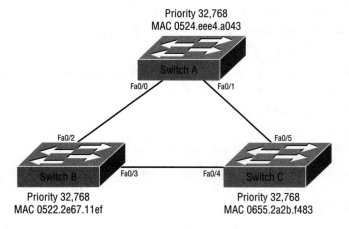

A.   Switch A Fa0/0

B.   Switch A Fa0/1

C.   Switch C Fa0/4

D.   Switch C Fa0/5

210. Using the following exhibit, which option is a correct statement?

```
SwitchA#sh spanning-tree vlan 1
VLAN0001
 Spanning tree enabled protocol ieee
 Root ID Priority 32769
 Address 0021.e455.8848
 Cost 19
 Port 1(FastEthernet0/1)
 Hello Time 2 sec Max Age 20 sec Forward Delay 15 sec
 Bridge ID Priority 32769 (priority 32768 sys-id-ext 1)
 Address 0021.e455.8986
 Hello Time 2 sec Max Age 20 sec Forward Delay 15 sec
 Aging Time 20
Interface Role Sts Cost Prio.Nbr Type
--------------- ---- --- -------- ------- -----------------------------
Fa0/1 Desg FWD 19 128.1 P2p
Fa0/2 Root FWD 19 128.2 P2p
```

A. This switch is the root bridge.

B. This switch is not adjacent to the root bridge.

C. This switch is adjacently connected to the root bridge via Fa0/2.

D. This switch is adjacently connected to the root bridge via Fa0/1.

211. In the following exhibit, which switch interfaces will become the root ports?

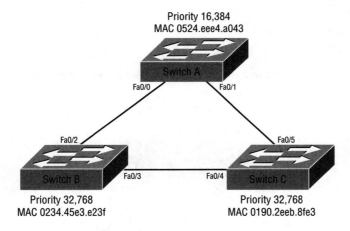

A. Switch A Fa 0/0 and Switch A Fa0/1

B. Switch B Fa 0/2 and Switch B Fa0/3

C. Switch B Fa 0/2 and Switch C Fa0/4

D. Switch B Fa 0/2 and Switch C Fa0/5

212. In the following exhibit, which switch interface will become a non-designated port?

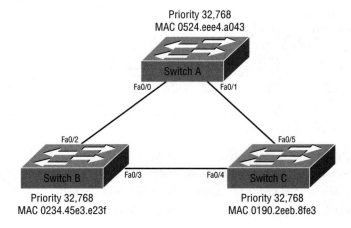

A.   Switch B Fa0/2

B.   Switch A Fa0/0

C.   Switch A Fa0/1

D.   Switch C Fa0/4

213. You have a network configured in the following exhibit. What needs to be changed?

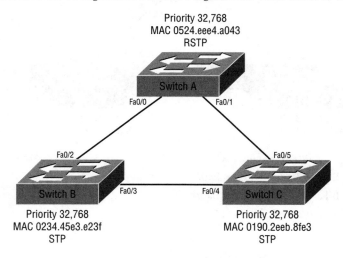

A.   SwitchA(config)#no spanning-tree mode rapid-pvst

B.   SwitchB(config)#spanning-tree mode rapid-pvst
     SwitchC(config)#spanning-tree mode rapid-pvst

C.   SwitchA(config)#spanning-tree priority 16384

D.   Nothing to be further configured

214. In the following exhibit, you are running RSTP. Which switch will become the root bridge?

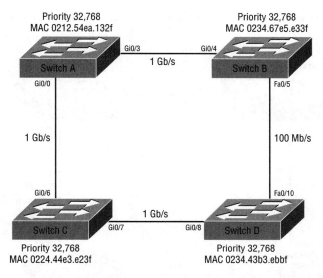

A. Switch A

B. Switch B

C. Switch C

D. Switch D

215. In the following exhibit, you are running RSTP. Which switch interfaces will become root ports?

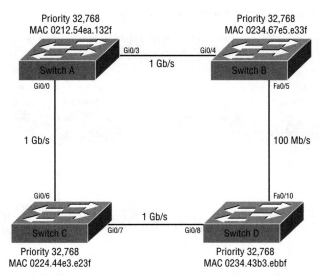

A. Switch A Gi0/0, Switch A Gi0/3

B. Switch B Gi0/4, Switch C Gi0/6

C. Switch B Gi0/4, Switch C Gi0/6, Switch D Gi0/8

D. Switch B Gi0/4, Switch C Gi0/6, Switch D Gi0/10

216. In the following exhibit, you are running RSTP. Which switch interfaces will become root ports?

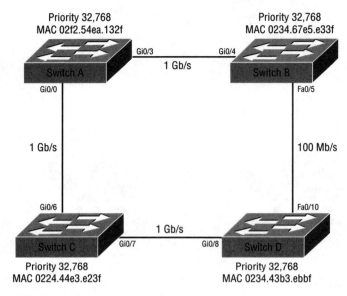

- **A.** Switch C Gi0/6, Switch B Gi0/4, Switch D Fa0/10
- **B.** Switch A Gi0/0, Switch B Gi0/4, Switch D Gi0/8
- **C.** Switch A Gi0/3, Switch C Gi0/6, Switch D Gi0/8
- **D.** Switch C Gi0/7, Switch A Gi0/0, Switch B Fa0/5

217. In the following exhibit, you want to make sure that Switch A always becomes the root bridge. Which command needs to be entered?

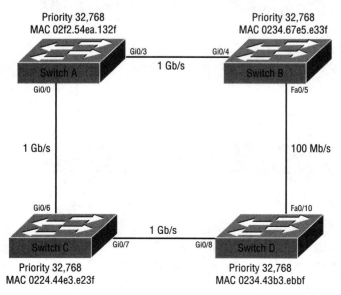

A. `SwitchA(config)#spanning-tree vlan 1 priority 16384`

B. `SwitchA(config)#spanning-tree priority 16384`

C. `SwitchA(config)#spanning-tree priority 1`

D. `SwitchA(config)#spanning-tree vlan 1 priority 1`

218. You have a network configured with three VLANs of users. You want to make sure that the switches connected to the servers for the Sales and Production workgroups become the respective root bridges. Which series of commands would you need to enter? Refer to the following exhibit.

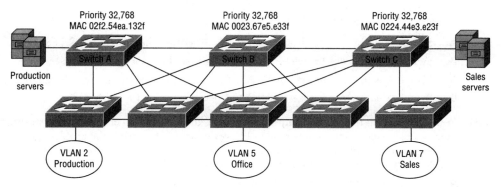

A. `SwitchB(config)#spanning-tree vlan 2 priority 16384`
   `SwitchB(config)#spanning-tree vlan 7 priority 16384`

B. `SwitchA(config)#spanning-tree vlan 2 priority 16384`
   `SwitchC(config)#spanning-tree vlan 7 priority 16384`

C. `SwitchA(config)#spanning-tree vlan 7 priority 16384`
   `SwitchC(config)#spanning-tree vlan 2 priority 16384`

D. `SwitchA(config)#spanning-tree vlan 2 priority 16384`
   `SwitchC(config)#spanning-tree vlan 5 priority 16384`

219. You perform the command `show spanning-tree interface gi 0/1` and see the output in the following exhibit. Why is this interface not a root port for VLAN 5?

```
SwitchB#show spanning-tree interface gi 0/1
Vlan            Role Sts Cost    Prio.Nbr Type
--------------- ---- --- ------- -------- ----------------------------
VLAN0001        Root FWD 4       128.25   P2p
VLAN0005        Altn BLK 19      128.25   P2p
VLAN0007        Root FWD 19      128.25   P2p
```

A. This switch has the lowest MAC address in the network.

B. There is another switch with a lower path cost to the root bridge for VLAN 5.

C. The priority for this switch is the lowest in the network.

D. There is a redundant link on this switch to the same network segment for VLAN 5.

220. Which statement is correct from the information output using the show spanning-tree command? Refer to the following exhibit.

```
SwitchA#sh spanning-tree
VLAN0001
Spanning tree enabled protocol rstp
[output cut]

Bridge ID Priority    32769 (priority 32768 sys-id-ext 1)
             Address     0001.C767.CC31
             Hello Time  2 sec Max Age 20 sec Forward Delay 15 sec
             Aging Time  20

Interface      Role Sts Cost      Prio.Nbr  Type
------------   ------------       --------  ---------------------------
Gi0/1          Desg FWD 4         128.25    P2p
Gi0/2          Desg FWD 4         128.25    P2p
Gi0/3          Desg FWD 4         128.25    P2p
```

A. Switch A is not the root bridge for VLAN 1 because the priority is 32,768.

B. Switch A is the root bridge for VLAN 1 because the priority is 32,768.

C. Switch A is the root bridge for VLAN 1 because all the ports are in a designated state.

D. Switch A is the root bridge for VLAN 1 because the cost is the lowest.

221. You receive a call that when computers boot up, they display an error message stating that they cannot reach a domain controller. However, after a few tries, the problem goes away, and the domain controller can be reached. Which command would you enter into the interface if you suspect spanning-tree convergence problems?

A. SwitchA(config-if)#no switchport spanning-tree

B. SwitchA(config)#switchport spanning-tree portfast

C. SwitchA(config)#spanning-tree portfast default

D. SwitchA(config-if)#spanning-tree portfast

222. On which types of ports should you turn on PortFast mode?

A. Trunk ports

B. Access ports

C. Voice ports

D. Designated ports

223. What will the command of spanning-tree portfast default entered in global configuration mode do?

A. Turn on PortFast mode for all ports.

B. Turn on PortFast mode for all access ports only.

C. Turn off spanning tree on all ports.

D. Turn off spanning tree on all access ports only.

224. What will happen if you plug a hub into two ports on the same switch configured with PortFast on all the interfaces?

A. You will create a temporary switching loop.

B. You will create a switching loop.

C. Both ports will sense the switch and err-disable.

D. One of the links will disable via spanning tree.

225. Which feature will protect a switch immediately if it sees another switch's advertisement?

    A. BPDU Guard

    B. BPDU Detection

    C. Loop Guard

    D. UplinkFast

226. What is the transition of states when PortFast is configured?

    A. Forwarding, listening, learning, blocking

    B. Listening, forwarding, learning, blocking

    C. Listening, learning, forwarding, blocking

    D. Blocking, listening, learning, forwarding

227. Which command would you use to configure BPDU Guard on an interface?

    A. `SwitchA(config-if)#switchport mode bpduguard`

    B. `SwitchA(config-if)#switchport bpduguard enable`

    C. `SwitchA(config-if)#spanning-tree bpduguard enable`

    D. `SwitchA(config-if)#spanning-tree bpduguard`

228. After you configure an access switch on your network, you receive a call that the users have lost connectivity. You examine the trunk interface with the command `show interfaces Gi 0/1`. What might be the problem?

```
SwitchB#sh interfaces gigabitEthernet 0/1
GigabitEthernet0/1 is down, line protocol is down (err-disabled)
  Hardware is Lance, address is 0060.5c22.d319 (bia 0060.5c22.d319)
  BW 1000000 Kbit, DLY 1000 usec,
        reliability 255/255, txload 1/255, rxload 1/255
  Encapsulation ARPA, loopback not set
  Keepalive set (10 sec)
  Full-duplex, 1000Mb/s
  input flow-control is off, output flow-control is off
  ARP type: ARPA, ARP Timeout 04:00:00
  Last input 00:00:08, output 00:00:05, output hang never
  Last clearing of "show interface" counters never
  Input queue: 0/75/0/0 (size/max/drops/flushes); Total output drops: 0
  Queueing strategy: fifo
  output queue :0/40 (size/max)
  [output cut]
```

    A. A spanning-tree loop has been detected.

    B. The switch uplink cable is bad.

    C. BPDU Guard was configured on a trunk.

    D. Flow control is turned off.

229. Which option is a best practice when configuring links on an access switch?

    A. Never configure spanning-tree PortFast mode on an access link.

    B. Always configure BPDU Guard along with PortFast.

    C. Always configure BPDU Guard on trunks.

    D. Always configure BPDU Guard along with UplinkFast.

230. Which command will show you if a port has been configured for PortFast mode?

  A. `Switch#show portfast`

  B. `Switch#show interface fa 0/1`

  C. `Switch#show spanning-tree`

  D. `Switch#show spanning-tree interface fa 0/1`

231. Which command would you use to remove BPDU Guard from an interface?

  A. `Switch(config-if)#switchport bdpugaurd disable`

  B. `Switch(config-if)#spanning-tree bpduguard disable`

  C. `Switch(config-if)#no switchport bpduguard`

  D. `Switch(config-if)#spanning-tree bpduguard disable`

232. You have BPDU Guard configured on an interface. What happens if a BPDU is advertised on the interface?

  A. The interface will become administratively disabled.

  B. The interface will become disabled.

  C. The interface will become err-disabled.

  D. A small switching loop will happen until convergence.

233. Which command will show you if BPDU Guard is enabled by default?

  A. `Switch#show interface gi 0/1`

  B. `Switch#show spanning-tree summary`

  C. `Switch#show spanning-tree vlan 2`

  D. `Switch#show spanning-tree`

234. You are configuring an edge switch and want to make sure that someone does not plug a switch in accidentally. Which feature will you configure?

  A. PortFast

  B. UplinkFast

  C. BackboneFast

  D. BPDU Guard

235. You want to quickly configure an edge switch so all access ports are in PortFast mode. Which command will achieve this?

  A. `SwitchA(config)#spanning-tree portfast default`

  B. `SwitchA(config)#switchport spanning-tree portfast`

  C. `SwitchA(config)#spanning-tree portfast enable`

  D. `SwitchA(config)#spanning-tree portfast`

236. Which protocol is an IEEE standard that collects information from neighboring devices on their identity and capabilities?

    A. CDP

    B. LLDP

    C. 802.1b

    D. 802.1a

237. You want to turn off CDP on a switch. Which command would you enter?

    A. `Switch(config)#cdp disable`

    B. `Switch(config-if)#no cdp enable`

    C. `Switch(config)#no cdp`

    D. `Switch(config-if)#no cdp run`

238. How often are CDP frames sent out of the device by default?

    A. Every 30 seconds

    B. Every 60 seconds

    C. Every 90 seconds

    D. Every 180 seconds

239. Which Cisco proprietary protocol collects information from neighboring devices about their identity and capabilities?

    A. 802.1ab

    B. LLDP

    C. CDP

    D. 802.1a

240. What is the default value of the CDP holddown timer for CDP entries?

    A. 30 seconds

    B. 60 seconds

    C. 90 seconds

    D. 180 seconds

241. You want to turn off CDP on a single interface. Which command would you enter?

    A. `Switch(config)#cdp disable`

    B. `Switch(config-if)#no cdp enable`

    C. `Switch(config)#no cdp`

    D. `Switch(config-if)#no cdp run`

242. Which command gives information that's identical to the output of the show cdp neighbors detail command?

    A. Switch#sh cdp neighbors all

    B. Switch#sh cdp neighbors *

    C. Switch#sh cdp entries all

    D. Switch#sh cdp entry *

243. You have several non-Cisco IP phones and you want to allow automatic power adjustments on the Cisco Power over an Ethernet (PoE) switch. Which command will allow you to achieve this?

    A. Switch#lldp run

    B. Switch(config)#lldp run

    C. Switch(config)#lldp enable

    D. Switch#lldp enable

244. Which command will allow you to see LLDP devices connected to a switch?

    A. Switch#show lldp

    B. Switch#show lldp devices

    C. Switch#show lldp neighbor detail

    D. Switch#show cdp neighbor detail

245. What is the default LLDP advertisement interval?

    A. 30 seconds

    B. 60 seconds

    C. 90 seconds

    D. 120 seconds

246. You want to disable LLDP from sending advertisements on a single interface. Which command will you use?

    A. Switch(config-if)#no lldp

    B. Switch(config-if)#no lldp transmit

    C. Switch(config-if)#no lldp receive

    D. Switch(config-if)#no lldp enable

247. What is the default value of the LLDP holddown timer for entries?

    A. 30 seconds

    B. 60 seconds

    C. 90 seconds

    D. 120 seconds

248. The following image shows the output of the CDP details. Which statement is correct about what is displayed?

```
SwitchB#sh cdp neighbors detail

Device ID: SwitchA
Entry address(es):
  IP address : 192.168.1.1
Platform: Cisco 3560, Capabilities:
Interface: GigabitEthernet0/2, Port ID (outgoing port): GigabitEthernet0/1
Holdtime: 162

Version :
Cisco IOS Software, C3560 Software (C3560-ADVIPSERVICESK9-M),
Version 12.2(37)SE1, RELEASE SOFTWARE (fc1)
Copyright (c) 1986-2007 by Cisco Systems, Inc.
Compiled Thu 05-Jul-07 22:22 by pt_team

advertisement version: 2
Duplex: full
```

- **A.** The advertisement was seen 162 seconds ago.
- **B.** Switch B interface Gi0/1 connects to Switch A.
- **C.** Switch B interface Gi0/2 connects to Switch A.
- **D.** The IP address of Switch B is 192.168.1.1.

249. You have a layer 2 connection to your ISP. You want to make sure that you do not send information on the capabilities of your switch, but you don't want to affect the use of CDP. Which command will you configure?

- **A.** `Switch(config)#cdp disable`
- **B.** `Switch(config-if)#no cdp`
- **C.** `Switch(config-if)#no cdp disable`
- **D.** `Switch(config-if)#no cdp enable`

250. Which command will show the interfaces that CDP is advertising on?

- **A.** `Switch#show cdp`
- **B.** `Switch#show cdp interface`
- **C.** `Switch#show interface`
- **D.** `Switch#show interface cdp`

251. What is the maximum number of interfaces that can be aggregated with EtherChannel and PAgP?

- **A.** 2 interfaces
- **B.** 8 interfaces
- **C.** 16 interfaces
- **D.** 4 interfaces

252. Which is a true statement about EtherChannel?

- **A.** EtherChannel works with 802.1Q to block the redundant lines.
- **B.** EtherChannel can aggregate multiple lines with varying speed.
- **C.** EtherChannel can aggregate interfaces across multiple stand-alone switches.
- **D.** When configured, EtherChannel acts as a single layer 2 connection.

253. You have a switch with 2 Gigabit interface ports and 48 FastEthernet ports and are using PAgP. What is the highest bandwidth you can achieve?

    A. 2 Gb/s

    B. 2.2 Gb/s

    C. 400 Mb/s

    D. 2.6 Gb/s

254. Which negotiation protocol is an IEEE standard?

    A. LACP

    B. 802.1Q

    C. PAgP

    D. 802.1ab

255. You need to form an EtherChannel between a VMware ESXi host and the switch. Which negotiation protocol will you choose?

    A. EtherChannel

    B. LACP

    C. Channel Group

    D. PAgP

256. What is the maximum number of interfaces that can be aggregated with EtherChannel and LACP?

    A. 2 interfaces

    B. 8 interfaces

    C. 16 interfaces

    D. 4 interfaces

257. Which mode forces the aggregation of links without the use of a control protocol?

    A. LACP off mode

    B. PAgP off mode

    C. On mode

    D. 802.3ad mode

258. Which is a correct statement about aggregating ports together?

    A. The term *EtherChannel* is a Cisco proprietary term for port channeling.

    B. PAgP can be used with non-Cisco products.

    C. LACP can only be used with other Cisco switches.

    D. PAgP can bundle several different speeds and duplexes together.

259. Which negotiation protocol is a Cisco proprietary standard?

    A. LACP

    B. 802.1Q

    C. PAgP

    D. 802.1ab

260. How often does PAgP send messages to control the status of the links in the bundle?

    A. Every 30 seconds

    B. Every 60 seconds

    C. Every 90 seconds

    D. Every 120 seconds

261. You want to configure two switches so that LACP is used between the switches. Which mode should you use on both sides to force LACP?

    A. Active mode on both sides

    B. Passive mode on both sides

    C. Auto mode on both sides

    D. Desirable mode on both sides

262. What is the effect of configuring a port channel with one side set to passive mode and the other side set to active mode?

    A. The channel group will use PAgP.

    B. The channel group will not be formed.

    C. The channel group will use LACP.

    D. The channel group will use EtherChannel.

263. Which command is used to verify the negotiation protocol for a port channel?

    A. `Switch#show etherchannel`

    B. `Switch#show port-channel`

    C. `Switch#show interface`

    D. `Switch#show run`

264. What is the effect of configuring a port channel with one side set to passive mode and the other side set to passive mode?

    A. The channel group will use PAgP.

    B. The channel group will not be formed.

    C. The channel group will use LACP.

    D. An unconditional port channel will be formed.

265. What is the effect of configuring a port channel with one side set to on mode and the other side set to on mode?

 A. The channel group will use PAgP.

 B. The channel group will not be formed.

 C. The channel group will use LACP.

 D. An unconditional port-channel will be formed.

266. When a port channel is configured, where do you configure the native VLAN?

 A. On the first port in the channel group

 B. On all of the ports in the channel group

 C. In the port channel created for the channel group

 D. All of the above

267. What is the effect of configuring a port channel with one side set to auto mode and the other side set to desirable mode?

 A. The channel group will use PAgP.

 B. The channel group will not be formed.

 C. The channel group will use LACP.

 D. An unconditional port channel will be formed.

268. Which command will configure one side of an EtherChannel, when the other side is configured with on mode?

 A. ```
SwitchA(config-if)#channel-group 1 mode on
SwitchB(config-if)#channel-group 1 mode on
```

 **B.** ```
SwitchA(config-if)#channel-group 1 mode desirable
SwitchB(config-if)#channel-group 1 mode desirable
```

 C. ```
SwitchA(config-if)#switchport channel-group 1 mode desirable
SwitchB(config-if)#switchport channel-group 1 mode desirable
```

 **D.** ```
SwitchA(config-if)#switchport channel-group 1 mode on
SwitchB(config-if)#switchport channel-group 1 mode on
```

269. What is the default load balancing configuration for EtherChannel?

 A. Destination MAC address

 B. Source IP address

 C. Destination IP address

 D. Source MAC address

270. You want to configure two switches to form a PAgP EtherChannel. Which commands would you enter?

 A. ```
SwitchA(config-if)#channel-group 1 mode pagp
SwitchB(config-if)#channel-group 1 mode pagp
```

 **B.** ```
SwitchA(config-if)#channel-group 1 mode desirable
SwitchB(config-if)#channel-group 1 mode desirable
```

  C. `SwitchA(config-if)#channel-group 1 mode pagp`
     `SwitchB(config-if)#channel-group 1 mode pagp`

  D. `SwitchA(config-if)#channel-group 1 mode desirable`
     `SwitchB(config-if)#channel-group 1 mode desirable`

271. Which command will change the load-balancing criteria of the EtherChannel for the destination IP?

  A. `SwitchA(config-if)#port-channel load-balance dst-ip`

  B. `SwitchA(config)#port-channel load-balance dst-ip`

  C. `SwitchA(config-if)#channel-group load-balance dst-ip`

  D. `SwitchA(config)#channel-group load-balance dst-ip`

272. Which command is used to verify the load-balancing method the switch is using?

  A. `Switch#show etherchannel load-balance`

  B. `Switch#show channel-group load-balance`

  C. `Switch#show port-channel load-balance`

  D. `Switch#show load-balance`

273. You have a router connected to the switch via an EtherChannel. Which type of load-balancing criteria will you use to make sure you have the most optimal load balancing?

  A. Source MAC address

  B. Destination MAC address

  C. Source and destination IP address

  D. Source and destination MAC address

274. What does the non-silent option along with the mode of auto or desirable do?

  A. Configures the interface not to send negotiation notifications

  B. Configures the interface to send negotiation notifications

  C. Configures the interface to send negotiation notifications only if detected

  D. Configures the interface to forward all CDP notifications

275. When a port-channel is configured, where do you configure the access VLAN for connection to a server?

  A. The first port in the channel group

  B. All of the ports in the channel group

  C. In the port-channel created for the channel group

  D. All of the above

276. You check the status of the EtherChannel configured on the switch with the
show etherchannel command. What can be concluded from the output? Refer to the
exhibit below.

```
SwitchA#sh etherchannel
                                   Channel-group listing:
                                   ------------------

Group: 1
---------
Group state = L2
Ports: 2 Maxports = 8
Port-channels: 1 Max Port-channels = 1
Protocol:      -
SwitchA#
```

   A. The EtherChannel is configured with PAgP.

   B. The EtherChannel is configured with LACP.

   C. The EtherChannel is configured with no control protocol.

   D. The EtherChannel is configured as an access port.

277. You are configuring an EtherChannel between two switches. You check your configuration on the first switch and are ready to configure the second switch. What mode do you
need to configure on the other switch? Refer to the following exhibit.

```
SwitchA#sh run
Building configuration...
[output cut]
!
interface Port-channel 1
!
[output cut]
interface GigabitEthernet0/1
 channel-group 1 mode auto
!
interface GigabitEthernet0/2
 channel-group 1 mode auto
[output cut]
```

   A. Switch(config-if)#channel-group 1 mode auto

   B. Switch(config-if)#channel-group 1 mode desirable

   C. Switch(config-if)#channel-group 1 mode active

   D. Switch(config-if)#channel-group 1 mode passive

278. You are configuring an EtherChannel between two switches for trunking. The EtherChannel
will not form. You check your configuration on the first switch. What is the problem on
the other switch? Refer to the following exhibit.

```
SwitchA#sh run
Building configuration...
[output cut]
!
interface Port-channel 1
!
[output cut]
interface GigabitEthernet0/1
 channel-group 1 mode passive
!
interface GigabitEthernet0/2
 channel-group 1 mode passive
[output cut]
```

   A. The other switch is configured as an access link.

   B. The other switch has CDP turned off.

    C.   The other switch is configured for active mode.

    D.   The other switch is configured for passive mode.

279. You have just configured the adjacent side of an EtherChannel from the console and receive the message in the following exhibit. What is the problem?

```
%PM-4-ERR_DISABLE: channel-misconfig error detected on Gig0/1, putting Gig0/1 in err-disable state
%LINK-5-CHANGED: Interface GigabitEthernet0/1, changed state to down
%LINEPROTO-5-UPDOWN: Line protocol on Interface GigabitEthernet0/1, changed state to down
%LINEPROTO-5-UPDOWN: Line protocol on Interface Port-channel 1, changed state to down
%PM-4-ERR_DISABLE: channel-misconfig error detected on Gig0/2, putting Gig0/2 in err-disable state
%LINK-5-CHANGED: Interface GigabitEthernet0/2, changed state to down
%LINEPROTO-5-UPDOWN: Line protocol on Tnterface GigabitEthernet0/2, changed state to down
```

    A.   One of the switches is configured with on mode and the other with desirable mode.

    B.   One of the switches is configured with auto mode and the other with desirable mode.

    C.   One of the switches is configured with active mode and the other with active mode.

    D.   One of the switches is configured with passive mode and the other with passive mode.

280. You have configured the command `channel-group 1 mode active` on a range of interfaces that will participate in an EtherChannel. Which pseudo interface is created for overall management of the EtherChannel?

    A.   ether-channel 1

    B.   port-group 1

    C.   port-channel 1

    D.   channel-group 1

281. You have several 3750 switches located in the same switch closet. You need to add another switch but are out of Gigabit uplink ports. Which technology could you employ with these switches for optimal bandwidth?

    A.   Switch clustering

    B.   Switch stacking

    C.   Daisy chaining the Gigabit ports

    D.   EtherChannel

282. You have several switches configured in a switch stack configuration. You want to make the EtherChannel resilient to failure. Which feature should you use?

    A.   OSPF

    B.   PAgP

    C.   Cross-stack EtherChannel

    D.   EtherChannel load-balancing

283. What is the supported maximum number of 3750 switches that can stacked?

    A.   4 switches

    B.   9 switches

    C.   10 switches

    D.   16 switches

284. You have three switches with LAN Base and two switches with IP Base features sets. You want to stack the switches together. What needs to be done?

A. Upgrade the three switches from LAN Base to IP Base.

B. Downgrade the two switches from IP Base to LAN base.

C. The switch stack will upgrade or downgrade the IOS according to the master switch.

D. All of the above

285. How does traffic flow on the StackWise 3750 platform?

A. Directionally at 32 Gb/s

B. Bidirectionally at 32 Gb/s

C. Counter rotation paths at 16 Gb/s each

D. Counter rotation paths at 32 Gb/s each

286. When you stack Cisco switches together, how do you manage the switch stack?

A. Each switch has its own logical IP address.

B. The entire stack is managed by the master switch IP.

C. All switches in a stack need to have contiguous IP addressing.

D. The entire stack is managed by one IP, and a port number is incremented from 22 for each switch's logical identity.

287. You have a switch in a switch stack that has gone bad. You have received a replacement switch and want to swap it out. How can you swap out the bad switch?

A. You must power the entire stack down to replace the defective switch.

B. You must add the new switch to the last stack member number in the stack and then remove the defective switch.

C. You can remove the defective switch while the stack is on and replace it with the replacement switch.

D. You can swap the defective switch while the stack is on and then the stack requires a reload.

288. Which switch in a stack is responsible for forwarding tables and the central ACL?

A. Slave switch

B. Subordinate switch

C. Topology switch

D. Master switch

289. You have a switch in a stack that needs to be replaced. You are concerned that the configuration will be lost for the switch. What will happen when it is replaced?

A. The replacement switch will automatically download the configuration for the switch member number it's configured for from the master.

B. The replacement switch will need to have the configuration TFTP transferred after replacement manually by the network admin.

   C. The replacement switch will need manual configuration since the interfaces will be renumbered.

   D. The replacement switch will need to have its configuration transferred from the existing switch to be replaced.

290. You want to upgrade the stack's IOS. Assuming you have all the same model of switches in the stack, what needs to be done?

   A. Only the master switch needs to be upgraded.

   B. Each switch needs to be upgraded independently.

   C. Each switch in the stack needs to be configured with a TFTP location to boot from, and then they all must be reloaded.

   D. The IOS image cannot be changed once a stack is configured.

291. Which switch type in a switch stack downloads it configuration, forwarding table, and ACLs?

   A. Provisioned switch

   B. Subordinate switch

   C. Topology switch

   D. Master switch

292. What is the maximum length of a stacking cable for switch stacks?

   A. 1 meter

   B. 3 meters

   C. 5 meters

   D. 10 meters

293. You are connected to a switch stack and want to verify how the stack is cabled. Which command would you use?

   A. `Sw-Stk#show stack`

   B. `Sw-Stk#show stack-ports`

   C. `Sw-Stk#show switch cabling`

   D. `Sw-Stk#show switch stack-ports`

294. You want to verify the master switch in the switch stack, which command will display this information?

   A. `Sw-Stk#show stack`

   B. `Sw-Stk#show switch`

   C. `Sw-Stk#show stack-master`

   D. `Sw-Stk#show stack ids`

295. You want to make sure that the top switch in the stack always becomes the master. How can you guarantee it always wins the election?

    A.   Set the priority to 16.

    B.   Set the priority to 1.

    C.   Set the priority to 0.

    D.   Set the priority to 15.

Chapter 3

Routing Technologies (Domain 3)

THE CCNA EXAM TOPICS COVERED IN THIS PRACTICE TEST INCLUDE THE FOLLOWING:

✓ **3 Routing Technologies (ICND1) (ICND2)**

- 3.1 Describe the routing concepts (ICND1)

  - 3.1a Packet handling along the path through a network (ICND1)

  - 3.1b Forwarding decision based on route lookup (ICND1)

  - 3.1c Frame rewrite (ICND1)

- 3.2 Interpret the components of a routing table (ICND1)

  - 3.2a Prefix (ICND1)

  - 3.2b Network mask (ICND1)

  - 3.2c Next hop (ICND1)

  - 3.2d Routing protocol code (ICND1)

  - 3.2e Administrative distance (ICND1)

  - 3.2f Metric (ICND1)

  - 3.2g Gateway of last resort (ICND1)

- 3.3 Describe how a routing table is populated by different routing information sources (ICND1)

  - 3.3a Admin distance (ICND1)

- 3.4 Configure, verify, and troubleshoot inter-VLAN routing (ICND1) (ICND2)

  - 3.4a Router on a stick (ICND1) (ICND2)

  - 3.4b SVI (ICND2)

- 3.5 Compare and contrast static routing and dynamic routing (ICND1)

- 3.6 Compare and contrast distance vector and link state routing protocols (ICND2)

- 3.7 Compare and contrast interior and exterior routing protocols (ICND2)

- 3.8 Configure, verify, and troubleshoot IPv4 and IPv6 static routing (ICND1)

    - 3.8a Default route (ICND1)

    - 3.8b Network route (ICND1)

    - 3.8c Host route (ICND1)

    - 3.8d Floating static (ICND1)

- 3.9 Configure, verify, and troubleshoot single area and multi-area OSPFv2 for IPv4 (excluding authentication, filtering, manual summarization, redistribution, stub, virtuallink, and LSAs) (ICND2)

- 3.10 Configure, verify, and troubleshoot single area and multi-area OSPFv3 for IPv6 (excluding authentication, filtering, manual summarization, redistribution, stub, virtuallink, and LSAs) (ICND2)

- 3.11 Configure, verify, and troubleshoot EIGRP for IPv4 (excluding authentication, filtering, manual summarization, redistribution, stub) (ICND2)

- 3.12 Configure, verify, and troubleshoot EIGRP for IPv6 (excluding authentication, filtering, manual summarization, redistribution, stub) (ICND2)

- 3.13 Configure, verify, and troubleshoot RIPv2 for IPv4 (excluding authentication, filtering, manual summarization, redistribution) (ICND1)

- 3.14 Troubleshoot basic Layer 3 end-to-end connectivity issues (ICND2)

1. Which criteria are routing decisions based upon?

   A. Source IP

   B. Destination IP address

   C. TTL

   D. Destination MAC address

2. Which type of routing requires network administrator intervention?

   A. Link-state routing

   B. Distance-vector routing

   C. Static routing

   D. Dynamic routing

3. When an IP address is configured on the router's interface, what happens in the routing table?

   A. A route entry is created for the network attached to the IP address on the interface.

   B. A route entry is created for the IP address attached to the interface.

   C. Dynamic routing protocols update all other routers.

   D. All of the above

4. Which is a correct statement about the subnet mask?

   A. The subnet mask is used by the host to determine the destination network.

   B. The subnet mask is used in routing to determine the destination network.

   C. The router uses its subnet mask when routing a packet.

   D. The destination computer checks the subnet mask on the packet to verify that it's intended for that computer.

5. What protocol does the router or host use to find a MAC address for the frame when it determines that the packet is on the local network?

   A. IGMP

   B. RARP

   C. ARP

   D. ICMP

6. When a packet is determined remote from the network of the sending host, what happens?

   A. The destination IP address is changed to the router's IP address.

   B. The destination MAC address is changed to the destination host's MAC address.

   C. The destination MAC address is changed to the router's MAC address.

   D. The source IP address is changed to the router's IP address.

7. Which statement describes correctly what happens when a packet moves through a router?

   A. The destination IP address is changed to the original destination.

   B. The packet's TTL is decremented.

   C. The source MAC address is changed to the original source MAC address.

   D. All of the above

8. What is the entry for the IP address in the routing table called in IOS 15 code when an interface is configured?

   A. IP address route

   B. Local route

   C. Dynamic route

   D. Static route

9. When a packet is determined to be on the local network, what happens?

   A. The destination IP address is changed to the router IP address.

   B. The destination MAC address is changed to the destination host's MAC address.

   C. The destination MAC address is changed to the router's MAC address.

   D. The source IP address is changed to the router's IP address.

10. How does the sending host know if the destination is local or remote in respect to its immediate network?

   A. The host compares the IP address to its internal routing table.

   B. The host performs ANDing on its subnet mask and the destination IP address comparing the result to its own network address.

   C. The host performs ANDing on the destination subnet mask and the destination IP address, comparing the result to its own network address.

   D. The IP address is verified to be local to its network via ICMP.

11. What is the current method Cisco routers use for packet forwarding?

   A. Process switching

   B. Fast switching

   C. Intelligent packet forwarding

   D. Cisco Express Forwarding

12. What is the process called at layer 2 when a packet hops from router to router and eventually to the host?

   A. IP routing

   B. Frame rewrite

   C. Packet hopping

   D. Packet switching

13. When a host sends an ARP request packet out, what is the destination address of the frame?

    A. The router's MAC address

    B. The host's MAC address

    C. The MAC address is in the form of a broadcast.

    D. The MAC address is in the form of a multicast.

14. What does every network device use to limit the amounts of ARP packets?

    A. ARP cache

    B. IP multicasting

    C. Frame casting

    D. IP cache

15. Which statement describes what happens when a packet enters a router?

    A. The router accepts all incoming frames regardless of their destination MAC address.

    B. The router decapsulates the packet and inspects the destination IP address.

    C. Routers do not need to decapsulate packets to inspect the destination IP address.

    D. Routers make routing decisions first by examining the source MAC address.

16. Which command will display the router's ARP cache?

    A. `Router#show arp`

    B. `Router#show arp table`

    C. `Router#show arp cache`

    D. `Router#show ip arp`

17. What is the default time an entry will live in the ARP cache?

    A. 180 seconds

    B. 240 seconds

    C. 300 seconds

    D. 600 seconds

18. What is the relevance of the default gateway address on a host?

    A. The destination IP address is replaced with the default gateway when the destination is remote.

    B. The host sends the default gateway packets that are deemed remote via a broadcast.

    C. The host sends an ARP packet for the default gateway when the destination is remote.

    D. The host creates a dedicated connection with the default gateway for remote traffic.

19. Which command will display the router's routing table?

   A. `Router#show ip route`

   B. `Router#show route`

   C. `Router#show route table`

   D. `Router#show routes`

20. Which type of routing allows for routers to share their routing tables with other routers in the network?

   A. Default routing

   B. Stub routing

   C. Static routing

   D. Dynamic routing

21. Which statement describes what happens during the routing process?

   A. As a packet travels through the routers, the TTL of the packet will increase by one.

   B. When a route to the destination network is found, the router will attach the destination MAC address for the next hop to the packet.

   C. When a packet travels through the router, the transport information will be checked for the destination network.

   D. When a route to the destination network is found, the router will attach the destination IP address for the next hop to the packet.

22. Which protocol allows for testing and connectivity of a route?

   A. IGMP

   B. RARP

   C. ARP

   D. ICMP

23. Which command will clear the ARP cache of the local router?

   A. `Router#clear arp`

   B. `Router#clear arp table`

   C. `Router#clear arp cache`

   D. `Router#clear ip arp`

24. Which routing protocol is a distance-vector routing protocol?

   A. OSPF

   B. RIP

   C. EIGRP

   D. IGRP

25. What uses ICMP to directly check the status of a router?

A. SNMP traps

B. Notifications

C. Ping

D. ARP

26. When an ICMP packet reaches a router for which is has no further route, what happens?

A. The router will discard the packet without notification.

B. The router will change the TTL of the packet to 0.

C. The router will send the packet back to the originating host.

D. The router will send back a destination unreachable message.

27. You have just used the `ping` command for a distant router. You received back five exclamation marks. What do these mean?

A. The distant router is not responding.

B. The distant router has a high response time.

C. The distant router is responding.

D. The distant router has a low response time.

28. Which statement accurately describes a routing loop?

A. Packets are routed out one interface but come back on a different interface.

B. Packets are transmitted within a series of routers and never reach the destination.

C. Packets reach the expiry TTL before reaching the destination network.

D. Packets are routed via an inefficient path.

29. Which routing protocol is a link-state routing protocol?

A. OSPF

B. RIP

C. EIGRP

D. IGRP

30. Where are dynamic routes stored in a router?

A. RAM

B. Flash

C. Startup configuration

D. Running configuration

31. When a static route is made, what is the default administrative distance?

    A. AD of 1

    B. AD of 0

    C. AD of 2

    D. AD of 255

32. You are examining a routing table and see a route marked with S*. Which type of route is this?

    A. Static route

    B. Default route

    C. Dynamic route

    D. OSPF route

33. You are examining a routing table and see the entry in the following exhibit. What does the 4 in the underlined number represent?

    R   172.16.2.0 [120/4] via 1.1.1.13, 00:13:24, FastEthernet0/1

    A. The 4 represents the administrative distance.

    B. The 4 represents the protocol.

    C. The 4 represents the metric.

    D. The 4 represents the position in the routing table.

34. What type of route is the destination of 0.0.0.0/0?

    A. Local route

    B. Dynamic route

    C. Default route

    D. Loopback route

35. In the following exhibit, what does the top line of the output represent?

```
Router#sh ip route
[output cut]

        10.0.0.0/8 is variably subnetted, 3 subnets, 2 masks
C       10.10.0.0/16 is directly connected, Serial0/2/0
L       10.10.1.1/32 is directly connected, Serial0/2/0
S       10.20.0.0/16 [1/0] via 192.168.4.2

[output cut]
```

    A. The 10.0.0.0/8 is a route in the routing table.

    B. The 10.0.0.0/8 is a summarization of the routes in the table.

    C. The 10.0.0.0/8 is the router's network address.

    D. The 10.0.0.0/8 has been populated from another router.

36. You are examining a routing table and see the entry in the following exhibit. What does the underlined number represent?

> R   172.16.2.0 [120/4] via 1.1.1.13, 00:13:24, FastEthernet0/1

- **A.** The number represents the current time.
- **B.** The number represents the delay in micro seconds of the connection.
- **C.** The number represents the time the route has been in the routing table.
- **D.** The number represents the time the interface has been up.

37. You need to create a route for a network of 192.168.4.0/24 through the gateway of serial 0/1 on a 2621 router. Which is the proper command?

- **A.** `Router(config)#ip route 192.168.4.0/24 serial 0/1`
- **B.** `Router(config)#ip route 192.168.4.0 255.255.255.0 serial 0/1`
- **C.** `Router(config)#ip route 192.168.4.0/24 interface serial 0/1`
- **D.** `Router(config)#ip route`
  `Router(config-rtr)#192.168.4.0/24 serial 0/1`

38. You type into the router `ip default-gateway 192.168.11.2`. Why will traffic not route out the default gateway?

- **A.** The `ip default-network` needs to be used in conjunction with `ip default-gateway 192.168.11.2`.
- **B.** The command is only used for the management plane of the router itself.
- **C.** The command is used for dynamic routing only.
- **D.** The specified gateway is wrong.

39. In the following exhibit, which route statement needs to be configured on Router A to allow routing to Network B?

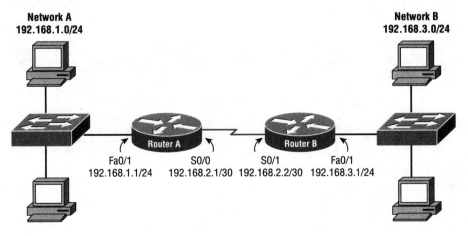

Network A
192.168.1.0/24

Network B
192.168.3.0/24

Router A

Router B

Fa0/1
192.168.1.1/24

S0/0
192.168.2.1/30

S0/1
192.168.2.2/30

Fa0/1
192.168.3.1/24

    A. `RouterA(config)#ip route 192.168.3.0 255.255.255.0 serial 0/1`

    B. `RouterA(config)#ip route 192.168.3.0 255.255.255.0 192.168.2.1`

    C. `RouterA(config)#ip route 192.168.3.0 255.255.255.0 192.168.2.2`

    D. `RouterA(config)#ip route 192.168.3.0 255.255.255.0 192.168.3.1`

40. In the following exhibit, which interface or IP address will a packet be routed to for a destination address of 192.168.4.56?

```
Router#sh ip route
[output cut]
        10.0.0.0/8 is variably subnetted, 3 subnets, 2 masks
C       10.10.0.0/16 is directly connected, Serial0/2/0
L       10.10.1.1/32 is directly connected, Serial0/2/0
S       10.20.0.0/16 [1/0] via 192.168.4.2
        172.16.0.0/16 is variably subnetted, 2 subnets, 2 masks
C       172.16.0.0/16 is directly connected, Serial0/0/0
L       172.16.1.1/32 is directly connected, Serial0/0/0
        192.168.1.0/24 is variably subnetted, 2 subnets, 2 masks
C       192.168.1.0/24 is directly connected, Serial0/0/1
L       192.168.1.1/32 is directly connected, Serial0/0/1
S       192.168.4.0/24 is directly connected, Serial0/0/1
S       192.168.5.0/24 [1/0] via 192.168.4.2
        198.23.24.0/24 is variably subnetted, 2 subnets, 2 masks
C       198.23.24.0/24 is directly connected, Serial0/1/1
L       198.23.24.1/32 is directly connected, Serial0/1/1
S*      0.0.0.0/0 is directly connected, Serial0/2/0
```

    A. Interface Serial 0/0/1

    B. Interface Serial 0/0/0

    C. IP gateway of 192.168.4.1

    D. Interface Serial 0/2/0

41. You configure Router A in the following exhibit with a route statement to get to Network B. However, you cannot ping a host on Network B. What is the problem?

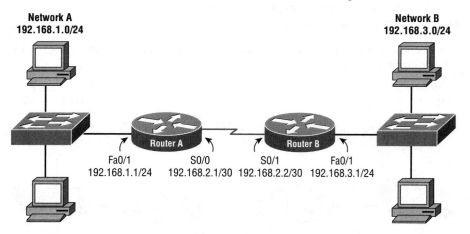

    A. You must issue the `ip routing` command.

    B. The host on Network B is misconfigured.

    C. The host on Network A is misconfigured.

    D. You must enter a network route on Router B for Network A.

42. When you configure an IP address on a router interface, what happens to the routing table?

   A. The router creates a /32 route for the IP address.

   B. The router creates a summary address for the network.

   C. The router creates a routing update if dynamic routing is configured.

   D. All of the above

43. You want to verify the IP addresses configured on the router. Which command will you use?

   A. `Router#show ip`

   B. `Router#show ip interfaces brief`

   C. `Router#show interfaces`

   D. `Router#show ip brief`

44. You configure a brand new IP address on a new router's interface. However, when you look at the routing table, it does not show up. You see a link light on the interface. What is wrong?

   A. The interface is administratively shut down.

   B. The interface speed is incorrect.

   C. The interface bandwidth is not set.

   D. The route will not show up until you save the config.

45. In the following exhibit, which interface or IP address will the packet with a destination of 198.23.34.2 be routed to?

```
Router#sh ip route
[output cut]
         10.0.0.0/8 is variably subnetted, 3 subnets, 2 masks
C        10.10.0.0/16 is directly connected, Serial0/2/0
L        10.10.1.1/32 is directly connected, Serial0/2/0
S        10.20.0.0/16 [1/0] via 192.168.4.2
         172.16.0.0/16 is variably subnetted, 2 subnets, 2 masks
C        172.16.0.0/16 is directly connected, Serial0/0/0
L        172.16.1.1/32 is directly connected, Serial0/0/0
         192.168.1.0/24 is variably subnetted, 2 subnets, 2 masks
C        192.168.1.0/24 is directly connected, Serial0/0/1
L        192.168.1.1/32 is directly connected, Serial0/0/1
S     192.168.4.0/24 is directly connected, Serial0/0/1
S     192.168.5.0/24 [1/0] via 192.168.4.2
         198.23.24.0/24 is variably subnetted, 2 subnets, 2 masks
C        198.23.24.0/24 is directly connected, Serial0/1/1
L        198.23.24.1/32 is directly connected, Serial0/1/1
S*    0.0.0.0/0 is directly connected, Serial0/2/0
```

   A. Interface Serial 0/1/1

   B. Interface Serial 0/0/1

   C. Interface Serial 0/2/0

   D. There is no suitable route.

46. What is a benefit of static routing?

   A. Adding networks is an easy task for network administrators.

   B. It is suited for large networks because changes will not disturb routing.

   C. It reduces bandwidth used by router-to-router communications.

   D. It allows for configuration by any network admin in the network.

47. Where are static routes stored?

    A. RAM

    B. Flash

    C. Startup configuration

    D. Routing database

48. You want to route 192.168.1.0/24, 192.168.2.0/24 to a destination address of 198.43.23.2. How can you accomplish this with one route statement so that other networks are not affected?

    A. `Router(config)#ip route 192.168.0.0 255.255.0.0 198.43.23.2`

    B. `Router(config)#ip route 192.168.0.0 255.255.255.0 198.43.23.2`

    C. `Router(config)#ip route 192.168.0.0 255.255.240.0 198.43.23.2`

    D. `Router(config)#ip route 192.168.0.0 255.255.0.240 198.43.23.2`

49. Why would you create a second route statement to the same network using a different administrative distance and different interface?

    A. If the first one fails to route to the destination, the second route will succeed.

    B. If the first interface goes down, the second route will become active.

    C. If there is a high amount of traffic on the first interface, the second route will become active.

    D. If there is a routing loop on the first interface, the second will overcome the loop.

50. Which route statement is configured when an IP address of 208.43.34.17/29 is configured on an interface?

    A. `S 208.43.34.17/32 is directly connected, Serial 0/0/0`

    B. `S 208.43.34.24/29 is directly connected, Serial 0/0/0`

    C. `S 208.43.34.8/29 is directly connected, Serial 0/0/0`

    D. `S 208.43.34.17/29 is directly connected, Serial 0/0/0`

51. In the following exhibit, which network is routable?

```
Router#sh ip route
[output cut]
        172.16.0.0/16 is variably subnetted, 2 subnets, 2 masks
C       172.16.0.0/16 is directly connected, Serial0/0/0
L       172.16.1.1/32 is directly connected, Serial0/0/0
        192.168.1.0/24 is variably subnetted, 2 subnets, 2 masks
C       192.168.1.0/24 is directly connected, Serial0/0/1
L       192.168.1.1/32 is directly connected, Serial0/0/1
S     192.168.4.0/24 is directly connected, Serial0/0/1
S     192.168.5.0/24 [1/0] via 192.168.4.2
        198.23.24.0/24 is variably subnetted, 2 subnets, 2 masks
C       198.23.24.0/24 is directly connected, Serial0/1/1
L       198.23.24.1/32 is directly connected, Serial0/1/1
```

    A. The 172.30.0/16 network

    B. The 192.168.128.0/24 network

    C. The 192.168.0.0/16 network

    D. The 192.168.4.0/24 network

52. Why can a route have a destination of an interface rather than an IP address?

    A. Serial interfaces are point-to-point connections.

    B. The router on the other side of an interface routes all traffic discovered.

    C. Routing tables cause the destination address to change.

    D. All of the above

53. In the following exhibit is a copy of the running-config. What is the next hop for a destination address of 192.168.4.85?

```
Router#show run
!
[output cut]
ip route 0.0.0.0 0.0.0.0 Serial0/2/0
ip route 192.168.4.0 255.255.255.0 Serial0/0/1
ip route 192.168.5.0 255.255.255.0 192.168.4.2
ip route 10.20.0.0 255.255.0.0 192.168.4.2
ip route 192.168.0.0 255.255.0.0 198.22.34.3
```

    A. Interface Serial 0/2/0

    B. IP address 192.168.4.2

    C. Interface Serial 0/0/1

    D. Interface Serial 198.22.34.3

54. In the following exhibit, what must be configured on Router B to allow routing to Network A?

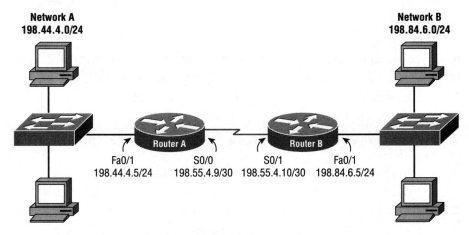

    A. RouterB(config)#ip route 198.44.4.0/24 198.55.4.9

    B. RouterB(config)#ip route 198.44.4.0 255.255.255.0 198.55.4.10

    C. RouterB(config)#ip route 198.44.4.0 255.255.255.0 Serial 0/0

    D. RouterB(config)#ip route 198.44.4.0 255.255.255.0 Serial 0/1

55. Which route statement is configured when an IP address of 203.80.53.22/19 is configured on an interface?

    A. `S 203.80.16.0/19 is directly connected, Serial 0/0/0`

    B. `S 203.80.32.0/19 is directly connected, Serial 0/0/0`

    C. `S 203.80.48.0/19 is directly connected, Serial 0/0/0`

    D. `S 203.80.53.22/19 is directly connected, Serial 0/0/0`

56. Using the following exhibit, if traffic enters Router A for a destination address of 198.44.4.7, what must be configured to allow routing to the host?

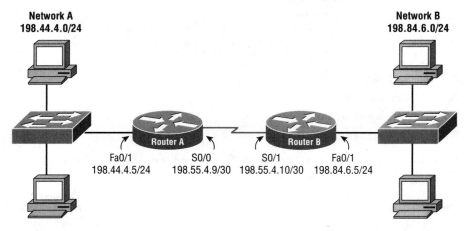

    A. `RouterA(config)#ip route 198.44.4.0 255.255.255.0 198.44.4.5`

    B. `RouterA(config)#ip route 198.44.4.0 255.255.255.0 fast 0/1`

    C. `RouterA(config)#ip route 198.44.4.0/24 fast 0/1`

    D. Nothing needs to be done.

57. Which route statement is configured when an IP address of 194.22.34.54/28 is configured on an interface?

    A. `S 194.22.34.48/28 is directly connected, Serial 0/0/0`

    B. `S 194.22.34.64/28 is directly connected, Serial 0/0/0`

    C. `S 194.22.34.54/28 is directly connected, Serial 0/0/0`

    D. `S 194.22.34.32/28 is directly connected, Serial 0/0/0`

58. You need to create a route for 205.34.54.85/29 and the next hop is 205.34.55.2. Which command would create this route?

    A. `Router(config)#ip route 205.34.54.85/24 205.34.55.2`

    B. `Router(config)#ip route 205.34.54.85 255.255.255.248 205.34.55.2`

    C. `Router(config)# ip route 205.34.54.85 255.255.255.240 205.34.55.2`

    D. `Router(config)#ip route 205.34.55.2 255.255.255.248 205.34.54.85`

59. Which command will create a default route through Serial 0/0 for IPv6?

    A. `Router(config)# ip route 0.0.0.0 0.0.0.0 serial 0/0`

    B. `Router(config)# ipv6 route 0.0.0.0 0.0.0.0 serial 0/0`

    C. `Router(config)# ipv6 route ::/0 serial 0/0`

    D. `Router(config)# ip route ::/0 serial 0/0`

60. Which command would configure the route for an IPv6 network of FC00:0:0:1 with the exit interface of serial 0/0/0?

    A. `Router(config)#ip route fc00:0:0:1 serial 0/0/0`

    B. `Router(config)#ipv6 route fc00:0:0:1/64 serial 0/0/0`

    C. `Router(config)#ip route fc00:0:0:1/64 serial 0/0`

    D. `Router(config)#ipv6 route fc00:0:0:1 serial 0/0/0`

61. In the following exhibit, which interface or IP address will a packet be routed to with a destination address of 192.168.5.6?

```
Router#sh ip route
[output cut]
        172.16.0.0/16 is variably subnetted, 2 subnets, 2 masks
C       172.16.0.0/16 is directly connected, Serial0/0/0
L       172.16.1.1/32 is directly connected, Serial0/0/0
        192.168.1.0/24 is variably subnetted, 2 subnets, 2 masks
C       192.168.1.0/24 is directly connected, Serial0/0/1
L       192.168.1.1/32 is directly connected, Serial0/0/1
S       192.168.4.0/24 is directly connected, Serial0/0/1
S       192.168.5.0/24 [1/0] via 192.168.4.2
S       192.168.5.0/24 [5/0] via 192.168.4.5
        198.23.24.0/24 is variably subnetted, 2 subnets, 2 masks
C       198.23.24.0/24 is directly connected, Serial0/1/1
L       198.23.24.1/32 is directly connected, Serial0/1/1
S*      0.0.0.0/0 is directly connected, Serial0/2/0
```

    A. IP address of 192.168.4.2

    B. IP address of 192.168.4.5

    C. Interface Serial 0/0/1

    D. Interface Serial 0/2/0

62. What is the administrative distance of RIP?

    A. AD of 90

    B. AD of 100

    C. AD of 110

    D. AD of 120

63. Why are administrative distances used with routing tables?

    A. Administrative distances define protocol standards.

    B. Administrative distances define reliability of routing protocols.

    C. Administrative distances allow for the shortest distance between routes.

    D. Administrative distances are programmed by the administrator for path selection.

64. What is the administrative distance of a directly connected network?

    A. The AD is 0.

    B. The AD is 1.

    C. The AD is 5.

    D. Directly connected networks do not have an AD.

65. What is the administrative distance of internal EIGRP?

    A. 90

    B. 100

    C. 110

    D. 120

66. Examining the show ip route statement in the exhibit, which will be the next hop for a destination address of 192.168.1.5?

```
Router#show ip route
[output cut]
192.168.1.0/24 is subnetted, 1 subnets
C 192.168.1.0/24 is directly connected, Serial 0/0
O 192.168.1.0/24 [110/421356] via 172.16.1.200, 00:00:33, Ethernet 0
R 192.168.1.0/24 [90/2] via 172.16.1.100, 00:00:16, Ethernet0
```

    A. The gateway 172.16.1.200

    B. The exit interface Serial 0/0

    C. The gateway 172.16.1.100

    D. The exit interface Ethernet0

67. What is the administrative distance of OSPF?

    A. 90

    B. 100

    C. 110

    D. 120

68. Which statement is true when there are multiple route statements from different routing protocols for the same destination network?

    A. The route is chosen with the highest administrative distance.

    B. The route chosen has the lowest metric.

    C. The route is chosen with the lowest administrative distance.

    D. The route chosen has the highest metric.

69. Which command will configure a static route with an administrative distance higher than RIP?

    A. Router(config)#ip route 192.168.2.0 255.255.255.0 192.168.4.1 110

    B. Router(config)#ip route 192.168.2.0 255.255.255.0 192.168.4.1 130

    C. Router(config)#ip route 110 192.168.2.0 255.255.255.0 192.168.4.1

    D. Router(config)#ip route 130 192.168.2.0 255.255.255.0 192.168.4.1

70. A router has three routes to the same network: one route from a RIP with a metric of 4, another from OSPF with a metric of 3053092, and another from EIGRP with a metric of 4039043. Which of the three routes will be used for the routing decision?

    A. EIGRP

    B. OSPF

    C. RIP

    D. All of the above

71. Which is a correct statement about SVI inter-VLAN routing (IVR)?

    A. Latency is low with SVI inter-VLAN routing because of ASICs.

    B. Latency is high with SVI inter-VLAN routing because of resource use.

    C. SVI inter-VLAN routing is a cheaper alternative to ROAS.

    D. Bandwidth is limited compared to ROAS.

72. Which is a disadvantage of using router on a stick (ROAS)?

    A. The lack of ISL support for VLANs

    B. The number of VLANs you can route is tied to the number of physical ports.

    C. Scalability of ROAS for the number of VLANs

    D. The lack of dynamic routing protocol support

73. What is the purpose of issuing the command `no switchport` on a layer 3 switch?

    A. It configures a Switched Virtual Interface.

    B. It configures an access port.

    C. It configures a trunk port.

    D. It configures a port as a routed interface.

74. Which is a correct statement about inter-VLAN routing (IVR)?

    A. Each VLAN requires a unique IP network.

    B. IVR reduces the number of broadcast domains.

    C. It does not support ACLs.

    D. IVR restricts the use of subnetting.

75. You need to configure a router that has three interfaces to route five VLANs. Which method would you choose to accomplish this?

    A. Purchase another router with additional interfaces.

    B. Configure the router as a ROAS.

    C. Purchase a new router with five interfaces.

    D. Configure a dynamic routing protocol.

76. Which command do you need to enter on a switch to allow routing between VLANs?

   A. `Switch(config)#routing`

   B. `Switch(config)#ip router`

   C. `Switch(config)#ip routing`

   D. `Switch(config)#ip route`

77. What is the method of using a single router interface to route between VLANs called?

   A. Interface routing

   B. ROAS routing

   C. SVI routing

   D. Bridge routing

78. When routing between VLANs with a router's interface, which trunking protocol is always supported?

   A. 802.1x

   B. 802.1Q

   C. ISL

   D. VTP

79. What is a disadvantage of routing between VLANs on a router's interface?

   A. Routers do not handle large amounts of traffic very well.

   B. When using ROAS, bandwidth problems are encountered.

   C. Security cannot be implemented with ROAS.

   D. Broadcast traffic is increased.

80. What is the method of routing between VLANs on a layer 3 switch?

   A. Interface routing

   B. ROAS routing

   C. SVI routing

   D. Bridge routing

81. Which command would configure the interface on the ROAS configuration as the native VLAN?

   A. `Router(config-subif)#switchport native vlan 2`

   B. `Router(config-if)#interface gi 0/1.2 native`

   C. `Router(config-subif)#native vlan 2`

   D. `Router(config-subif)#encapsulation dot1q 2 native`

82. Which commands would you use to configure an IP address on an SVI?

    A.   `Switch(config)#interface vlan 10`
        `Switch(config-if)#ip address 192.168.10.0 255.255.255.0`
        `Switch(config-if)#no shutdown`

    B.   `Switch(config)#interface vlan 10`
        `Switch(config-if)#ip address 192.168.10.0/24`

    C.   `Switch(config)#interface vlan 10`
        `Switch(config-if)#ip address 192.168.10.0/24`
        `Switch(config-if)#no shutdown`

    D.   `Switch(config)#vlan 10`
        `Switch(config-vlan)#ip address 192.168.10.0 255.255.255.0`
        `Switch(config-vlan)#no shutdown`

83. When configuring ROAS, which mode must the switch port on the switch be configured to?

    A. Trunk mode

    B. Access mode

    C. Routed mode

    D. Switched mode

84. When configuring the subinterfaces on a router for ROAS, what is a best practice when naming the subinterface?

    A. Always name the subinterface the same as the VLAN name.

    B. Always name the subinterface the same as the VLAN number.

    C. Always name the subinterface the same as the default gateway address.

    D. Always name the subinterface the same as the switch's interface number.

85. Which command enables the routers to direct the frames for a particular VLAN to the subinterface?

    A.   `Router(config-if)#interface gi 0/1.5`

    B.   `Router(config-subif)#vlan 5`

    C.   `Router(config-subif)#encapsulation dot1q 5`

    D.   `Router(config-subif)#switchport access vlan 5`

86. Which command must be entered on 2960-XR switches to enable IP routing?

    A.   `Switch(config)#ip lanbase`

    B.   `Switch(config)#sdm prefer lanbase-routing`

    C.   `Switch(config)#sdm lanbase-routing`

    D.   `Switch(config)#sdm routing`

87. You want to verify the configured SVI VLAN interfaces. Which command will show you the configured IP addresses on each of the SVI VLAN interfaces?

   A. `Switch#show ip interface brief`

   B. `Switch#show interfaces status`

   C. `Switch#show svi`

   D. `Switch#show switchports ip`

88. You enter the command `ip address 192.168.2.0 255.255.255.0` on interface VLAN 2. When you enter the command, you receive a "Bad mask /24 for address" error. What is the problem?

   A. The subnet mask is incorrect.

   B. The subnet of 192.168.2.0 cannot be used for this interface.

   C. The IP address is invalid.

   D. The VLAN has not been configured yet.

89. You have purchased a layer 3 switch with the LAN Base feature. When you enter `ip routing` in global configuration mode, you receive an "Invalid input detected" error. What is the problem?

   A. There are no IP addresses configured on the switch.

   B. The SDM of LAN Base routing has not been enabled.

   C. There is not enough memory for routing tables.

   D. The IP Base feature is required.

90. You have a 3560 switch that supports layer 3 routing. You need to configure a physical interface to route a subnet. Which command needs to be used?

   A. `Switch(config-if)#switchport routed`

   B. `Switch(config-if)#no ip-routing`

   C. `Switch(config-if)#no switchport`

   D. `Switch(config-if)#ip address 192.168.2.1 255.255.255.0`

91. Which command will allow you to examine a switch's port to see if it is routed or switched?

   A. `Switch#show interface gi 0/2 switchport`

   B. `Switch#show interface gi 0/2 state`

   C. `Switch#show switchport interface gi 0/2`

   D. `Switch#show status interface gi 0/2`

92. You need more bandwidth to your switch from the router. Currently you have one Gigabit Ethernet connection in use and both your router and switch have another available Gigabit Ethernet connection. What can you do to get more bandwidth?

   A. Nothing. Routers cannot aggregate bandwidth from multiple connections.

   B. Use RIP to balance the bandwidth.

    C. Bundle both Gigabit Ethernet connections in an EtherChannel.

    D. Use the switch to perform inter-VLAN routing.

93. You need to configure ROAS on a router's interface to route VLAN 5 with ISL. Which command will specify the encapsulation and achieve this?

    A. `Router(config-if)#encapsulation 5`

    B. `Router(config-if)#encapsulation isl 5`

    C. `Router(config-subif)#switchport encapsulation isl 5`

    D. `Router(config-subif)#encapsulation isl 5`

94. You have just configured a new VLAN and have configured the SVI with an IP address and `no shutdown` command on the interface. However, when you perform a `show ip route`, it does not show a valid directly connected route for the SVI. What is the problem?

    A. The VLAN is in a shutdown state.

    B. No interfaces have been configured with the new VLAN yet.

    C. The `show ip route` command will not display SVI directly connected routes.

    D. No dynamic routing protocols have been configured.

95. Which of the following is a correct statement about Router On A Stick?

    A. Using a ROAS is a highly efficient alternative to routed SVIs.

    B. Using a ROAS is a cheaper alternative to inter-VLAN routing on a switch.

    C. A ROAS can only be used with 802.1Q.

    D. A ROAS is limited to a maximum of 16 routes.

96. Before configuring ROAS, which command should be entered in the interface connecting to the switch?

    A. `Router(config-if)#ip routing`

    B. `Router(config-if)#no ip address`

    C. `Router(config-if)#ip encapsulation dot1q`

    D. `Router(config-if)#sdm routing`

97. You have configured a Router On A Stick and set up the switch to connect to the router. However, you cannot route between VLANs. Which command would you use on the switch to verify operations?

    A. `Switch#show ip route`

    B. `Switch#show interface status`

    C. `Switch#show interface trunk`

    D. `Switch#show switchport`

98. When configuring a router in an ROAS configuration, which command will enable the interface to accept frames tagged for VLAN 10?

   A. `Switch(config-subif)#encapsulation vlan 10 dot1q`

   B. `Switch(config-if)#interface Fa 0/0.10`

   C. `Switch(config-subif)#encapsulation dot1q 10`

   D. `Switch(config-subif)#ip address 192.168.10.1 255.255.255.0`

99. Which statement is correct about ARP in relation to ROAS?

   A. Each physical interface has a unique MAC address, which responds to ARP requests.

   B. Each subinterface has a unique MAC address, which responds to ARP requests.

   C. Each IP address has a unique MAC address, which responds to ARP requests.

   D. All of the above

100. Which statement is correct about implementing ROAS?

   A. Each IP address is configured on the subinterface as the gateway for the VLAN.

   B. The main interface must be configured with the summary IP address for all VLANs.

   C. You must configure at least one native VLAN.

   D. All of the above

101. Which is a reason for using a dynamic routing protocol?

   A. You have a network with only a few routers and network per branch.

   B. You have a network with only a few VLANs and one router.

   C. You have a network with a large amount of VLANs and only one router.

   D. You have a network with a few VLANs and many routers.

102. Which routing technique is a type of static routing?

   A. OSPF routing

   B. EIGRP routing

   C. Default routing

   D. RIP routing

103. Which is an advantage of using static routing?

   A. There is less administrative overhead.

   B. It is extremely secure.

   C. It can create resiliency in a network.

   D. It is extremely scalable without issues.

104. Which routing technique has the lowest bandwidth overhead?

   A. RIP routing

   B. OSPF routing

   C. EIGRP routing

   D. Static routing

105. Which routing technique requires no administrator intervention when a route goes down?

   A. Dynamic routing

   B. Directly connected routes

   C. Default routing

   D. Static routing

106. Which routing technique requires increased time for configuration as networks grow?

   A. RIP routing

   B. OSPF routing

   C. Static routing

   D. Default routing

107. Which routing technique requires the lowest amount of router RAM consumption?

   A. RIP routing

   B. OSPF routing

   C. Static routing

   D. Default routing

108. Which dynamic routing protocol has the lowest overhead?

   A. BGP

   B. OSPF

   C. RIP

   D. EIGRP

109. Which is an advantage of dynamic routing protocols?

   A. Resiliency when routes become unavailable

   B. Lower router RAM usage

   C. Lower router CPU usage

   D. Less bandwidth usage

110. Which type of routing technique allows for route summarization to be computed automatically by routers?

   A. Dynamic routing

   B. Directly connected routes

   C. Default routing

   D. Static routing

111. Which routing technique requires administrator intervention when a route goes down?

   A. Dynamic routing

   B. Directly connected routes

   C. Default routing

   D. Static routing

112. Which routing protocol broadcasts updates for routes?

   A. RIP

   B. OSPF

   C. EIGRP

   D. BGP

113. What is an advantage of dynamic routing protocols?

   A. Centralized routing tables

   B. Optimized route selection

   C. Ease of configuration

   D. Lower bandwidth utilization

114. You have several routes configured on a router. Which command will show only the static routes?

   A. `Router#show static routes`

   B. `Router#show ip static routes`

   C. `Router#show ip routes static`

   D. `Router#show ip routes`

115. Which routing technique is best suited for small networks in which the administrator wants control of routing?

   A. OSPF routing

   B. EIGRP routing

   C. Static routing

   D. RIP routing

116. Which protocol is a distance-vector protocol?

   A. RIP

   B. OSPF

   C. EIGRP

   D. BGP

117. Which protocol is a true link-state protocol?

   A. RIP

   B. OSPF

   C. EIGRP

   D. BGP

118. Which protocol is considered a hybrid protocol?

   A. RIP

   B. OSPF

   C. EIGRP

   D. BGP

119. What is an attribute of distance-vector protocols?

    A. They track the status of routes learned.

    B. They re-advertise routes learned.

    C. Each router keeps its own topology database.

    D. Each router checks the routes it learns.

120. Which type of network are distance-vector protocols best suited for?

    A. Networks containing fewer than 255 routes

    B. Networks containing fewer than 15 routers

    C. Networks containing more than 15 routers

    D. Networks containing more than 255 routers

121. You have a network with varied bandwidths and need to choose a dynamic routing protocol. Which would you choose for optimal performance?

    A. RIPv1

    B. RIPv2

    C. EIGRP

    D. BGP

122. Which problem could arise from use of a distance-vector routing protocol?

    A. Routing loops

    B. Router compatibility

    C. Complexity of configuration

    D. Default route propagation

123. Which dynamic routing protocol uses the Dijkstra routing algorithm?

    A. RIP

    B. EIGRP

    C. OSPF

    D. BGP

124. Why don't link-state protocols suffer from routing loops like distance-vector protocols do?

    A. Link-state protocols require routers to maintain their own topology database of the network.

    B. Link-state protocols share the topology database between all routers.

    C. Link-state protocols allow routers to maintain a link-state database of all routers.

    D. Link-state protocols use multiple routes to the same destination.

125. Which dynamic routing protocol uses the Diffusing Update Algorithm as its routing algorithm?

    A. RIP

    B. EIGRP

    C. OSPF

    D. BGP

126. Which is a disadvantage of distance-vector routing protocols?

    A. Router compatibility for RIP

    B. Slow convergence of routing tables

    C. Resource usage of CPU and RAM

    D. The complexity of RIP design

127. What is an advantage of a link-state dynamic routing protocol?

    A. The only metric needed is hop count.

    B. Link-state dynamic routing protocols support CIDR and VLSM.

    C. OSPF requires only a small amount of resources such as CPU and RAM.

    D. Link-state dynamic routing protocols use triggered updates for recalculation of routing tables.

128. What type of network is best suited for a link-state routing protocol such as OSPF?

    A. Extremely small networks of three routers

    B. Networks with routers that have a limited amount of RAM and CPU

    C. Large hierarchical networks, like global networks

    D. Networks within organizations with limited training of network admins

129. Which dynamic routing protocol uses the Bellman-Ford routing algorithm?

    A. RIP

    B. EIGRP

    C. OSPF

    D. BGP

130. Which is a design concept used to stop routing loops with distance-vector dynamic routing protocols?

    A. Use of a topology database

    B. Use of holddown timers

    C. Use of anti-flapping ACLs

    D. Use of counting-to-infinity conditions

131. Which is an exterior gateway routing protocol?

    A. RIP v1

    B. OSPF

    C. EIGRP

    D. BGP

132. Which protocol is a Cisco proprietary interior gateway protocol?

    A. RIP v1

    B. OSPF

    C. EIGRP

    D. BGP

133. Which statement is correct about interior gateway protocols (IGPs) vs. exterior gateway protocols (EGPs)?

    A. Interior routing protocols are used to exchange information between autonomous systems.

    B. Exterior routing protocols are used to exchange information between routers within an autonomous system.

    C. Interior routing protocols are used to exchange information between routers within an autonomous system.

    D. Exterior routing protocols are used in the core of an internal network.

134. How are routers managed with interior gateway protocols?

    A. Routers are grouped into autonomous systems.

    B. Routing protocols are redistributed between ASs.

    C. All routers use the same interior routing protocol.

    D. All network IDs are advertised with the same autonomous system number.

135. Which statement is correct about interior gateway protocols?

    A. IGPs require a small number of resources, such as CPU and RAM.

    B. IGPs function within an administrative domain.

    C. An EGP is an example of an interior gateway protocol.

    D. IGPs use autonomous system numbers (ASN) that have been assigned by ARIN.

136. Why would you need to use an exterior gateway protocol?

    A. You need to connect your company to the Internet.

    B. You have been delegated a large number of IP addresses.

    C. You want to achieve fast routing to the Internet.

    D. You are dual-homed with two different ISPs.

137. You need to use BGP to advertise routes. Which do you need to obtain before you could use BGP?

    A. An autonomous system number from IANA

    B. An area ID from IANA

    C. The process ID from IANA

    D. A BGP routing path

138. How are BGP routes calculated?

- **A.** The number of hops to the destination network
- **B.** The bandwidth to the destination network
- **C.** The shorted AS path to the destination network
- **D.** The most reliable path to the destination network

139. Which is an example of an interior gateway protocol that is nonproprietary?

- **A.** EGP
- **B.** OSPF
- **C.** EIGRP
- **D.** BGP

140. You have several sites, each with different administrative units in your company. Which routing protocol should you choose?

- **A.** BGP
- **B.** OSPF
- **C.** RIPv2
- **D.** EGP

141. Which command will allow you to verify the IPv6 addresses configured on a router?

- **A.** `Router#show ipv6`
- **B.** `Router#show ip interfaces brief`
- **C.** `Router#show ipv6 interfaces brief`
- **D.** `Router#show ipv6 brief`

142. On interface Serial 0/1, you type `ipv6 address 2000:db8:4400:2300::1234/64`. Which statement is true?

- **A.** The router will calculate a network ID of 2000:0db8::.
- **B.** The IPv6 address of 2000:0db8:4400:2300:1234:0000:0000:0000/128 will be assigned to Serial 0/0.
- **C.** The router will calculate a network ID of 2000:0db8:4400:2300::/64 for Serial 0/0.
- **D.** The router will calculate a network ID of 2000:db8:4400:2300:0000/64 for Serial 0/0.

143. When you check the IPv6 addresses configured on the interfaces, you find two IPv6 addresses: One address is a 2001:db8::/64 address, and the other is an ff80::/64 address. However, you do not see a route statement for the ff80::/64 address in the routing table. Why?

- **A.** Multicast addresses do not get added to the routing tables.
- **B.** Link-local addresses do not get added to the routing tables.

C.   Only one route statement can be in the routing table at a time for an interface.

D.   Broadcast addresses do not get added to the routing tables.

144. Which command will show you the IPv6 routes in the routing table?

A.   Router#show ipv6 route

B.   Router#show ip route

C.   Router#show ipv6 route summary

D.   Router#show ipv6 route brief

145. In the following exhibit, which route statement will need to be added to the routers to allow routing between the networks?

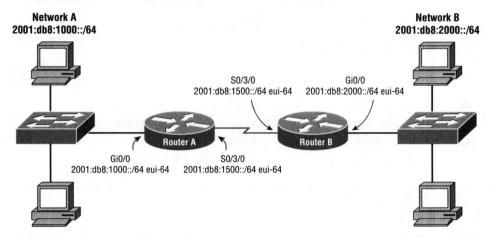

A.   RouterA(config)#ip route 2001:db8:1000/64 serial 0/3/0
     RouterB(config)#ip route 2001:db8:2000/64 serial 0/3/0

B.   RouterA(config)#ip route 2001:db8:2000::/64 serial 0/3/0
     RouterB(config)#ip route 2001:db8:1000::/64 serial 0/3/0

C.   RouterA(config)#ipv6 route 2001:db8:2000::/64 serial 0/3/0
     RouterB(config)#ipv6 route 2001:db8:1000::/64 serial 0/3/0

D.   RouterA(config)#ipv6 route 2001:db8:2000::/64 2001:db8:1500::/64 eui-64
     RouterB(config)#ipv6 route 2001:db8:1000::/64 2001:db8:1500::/64 eui-64

146. Which command will only show you all of the directly connected routes for IPv6?

A.   Router#show ipv6 interface summary

B.   Router#show ipv6 route connected

C.   Router#show ipv6 interface brief

D.   Router#show ipv6 summary

147. In the following exhibit, you need to configure Router B so that hosts on Network B can reach the Internet. Which statement on Router B will allow host to reach the Internet?

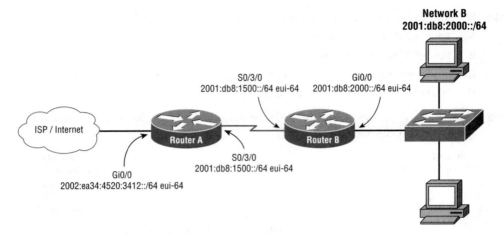

Network B
2001:db8:2000::/64

S0/3/0
2001:db8:1500::/64 eui-64

Gi0/0
2001:db8:2000::/64 eui-64

ISP / Internet

Router A

Router B

S0/3/0
2001:db8:1500::/64 eui-64

Gi0/0
2002:ea34:4520:3412::/64 eui-64

A. RouterB(config)#ipv6 route 0.0.0.0 0.0.0.0 serial 0/3/0

B. RouterB(config)#ipv6 route 2002:ea34:4520:3412::/64 serial 0/3/0

C. RouterB(config)#ipv6 route ::/0 serial 0/3/0

D. RouterB(config)#ipv6 route ::/0 2001:db8:1500::/64 eui

148. In the following exhibit, which route statement will need to be added to the routers to allow routing between the networks?

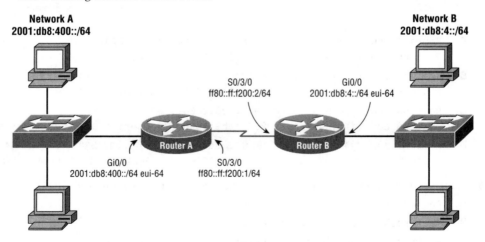

Network A
2001:db8:400::/64

Network B
2001:db8:4::/64

S0/3/0
ff80::ff:f200:2/64

Gi0/0
2001:db8:4::/64 eui-64

Router A

Router B

Gi0/0
2001:db8:400::/64 eui-64

S0/3/0
ff80::ff:f200:1/64

A. RouterA(config)#ip route 2001:db8:4/64 ff80::ff:f200:2
RouterB(config)#ip route 2001:db8:400/64 ff80::ff:f200:1

B. RouterA(config)#ip route 2001:db8:400::/64 serial 0/3/0
RouterB(config)#ip route 2001:db8:4::/64 serial 0/3/0

C. `RouterA(config)#ipv6 route 2001:db8:400::/64 serial 0/3/0`
`RouterB(config)#ipv6 route 2001:db8:4::/64 serial 0/3/0`

D. `RouterA(config)#ipv6 route 2001:db8:4/64 ff80::ff:f200:2`
`RouterB(config)#ipv6 route 2001:db8:400/64 ff80::ff:f200:1`

149. In the following exhibit, RIP is running on all of the routers. On Router A, you want to make sure that if Router B fails then a backup route is used through Router C to Network B. Which statement will achieve this?

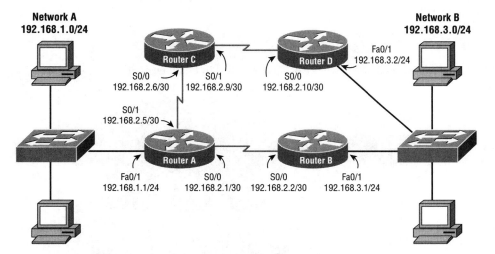

A. `RouterA(config)#ip route 192.168.2.8 255.255.255.252 192.168.2.6`

B. `RouterA(config)#ip route 192.168.3.0 255.255.255.0 192.168.2.6 220`

C. `RouterA(config)#ip route 192.168.3.0 255.255.255.0 192.168.2.6 90`

D. `RouterA(config)#ip route 192.168.3.0 255.255.255.0 192.168.2.10`

150. In the following exhibit, which command on Router B will allow hosts on Network B to reach the Internet?

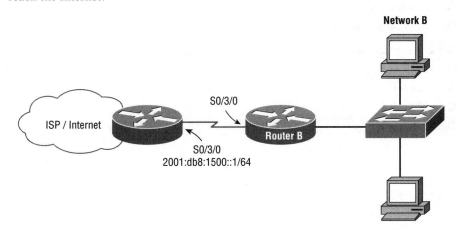

    A. `RouterB(config-if )#ipv6 address default`

    B. `RouterB(config)#ip route ::/0 serial 0/3/0`

    C. `RouterB(config-if)#ipv6 address autoconfig default`

    D. `RouterB(config-if)#ipv6 address slaac`

151. Which area must be present when using the OSPF routing protocol with multiple areas?

    A. Area 0

    B. Area 1

    C. Area 10

    D. Area 4

152. In the following exhibit, what is Router A called in OSPF terminology?

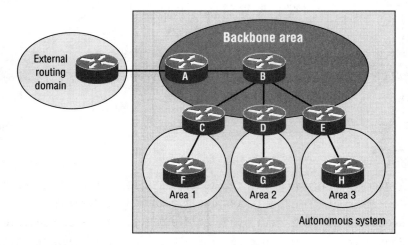

    A. Area border router

    B. Autonomous system router

    C. Autonomous system boundary router

    D. Area backup router

153. Which multicast address is used by OSPF for neighbor discovery?

    A. 224.0.0.4

    B. 224.0.0.5

    C. 224.0.0.6

    D. 224.0.0.7

154. In the following exhibit, what are Routers C, D, and E called in OSPF terminology?

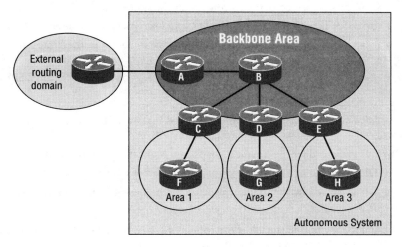

A. Area border routers

B. Autonomous system routers

C. Autonomous system boundary routers

D. Area backup routers

155. Which statement is true about OSPF?

A. OSPF is a distance-vector protocol.

B. OSPF performs default auto-summarization.

C. OSPF broadcasts changes to the routing tables.

D. OSPF updates are event triggered.

156. How do Cisco routers determine their router ID (RID)?

A. The lowest IP address configured on the loopback interfaces

B. The highest IP address configured on the router

C. The lowest IP address configured on the router

D. The highest MAC address configured on the router

157. What is the definition of an OSPF link?

A. Two routers participating in OSPF routing

B. Two routers that share the same area ID

C. A routed interface added to the OSPF process

D. Two routers that share the same AS number

158. Which statement is correct about adjacency with OSPF on a broadcast network (LAN)?

    A. An adjacency is formed between routers on the same link.

    B. An adjacency is formed between the DR and every neighbor router on the same LAN.

    C. An adjacency is formed between the DR and every router in the same autonomous system.

    D. An adjacency is formed between the DR and every router in the same OSPF area.

159. How is a designated router elected for OSPF?

    A. The DR is elected by the highest priority and highest RID in the same autonomous system.

    B. The DR is elected by the lowest priority and highest RID in the same area.

    C. The DR is elected by the lowest priority and lowest RID.

    D. The DR is elected by the highest priority and highest RID in the same broadcast network.

160. In which database can you see all of the routers discovered in the OSPF network in which hello packets were sent and acknowledged?

    A. The routing table database

    B. The neighborship database

    C. The topological database

    D. The link state database

161. Which is a correct statement about OSPF?

    A. OSPF uses autonomous systems for scalability.

    B. OSPF uses process IDs for scalability.

    C. OSPF uses areas for scalability.

    D. OSPF uses RID for scalability.

162. Which is an example of a broadcast (multi-access) network?

    A. An X.25 network

    B. Frame Relay

    C. ATM network

    D. A LAN

163. Which multicast address is used by OSPF for communication between the designated router and adjacencies formed?

    A. 224.0.0.4

    B. 224.0.0.5

    C. 224.0.0.6

    D. 224.0.0.7

164. What is the Cisco metric for OSPF?

    A. 10^8/bandwidth

    B. Delay, bandwidth, reliability, load

    C. K metrics

    D. Bandwidth

165. What does the command `router ospf 20` configure?

    A. An OSPF router process of 20

    B. An OSPF router area of 20

    C. An OSPF router autonomous system of 20

    D. An OSPF cost of 20

166. Which command will verify the bandwidth of an interface participating in OSPF?

    A. `Router#show ospf`

    B. `Router#show interface`

    C. `Router#show running-config`

    D. `Router#show ospf interface`

167. Which command will tune the cost of the OSPF metrics for integration with non-Cisco routers to participate in OSPF?

    A. `Router(config-if)#ip cost 20000`

    B. `Router(config)#ip ospf cost 20000`

    C. `Router(config)#ip cost 20000`

    D. `Router(config-if)#ip ospf cost 20000`

168. Which command will configure a network of 192.168.1.0/24 for OSPF area 0?

    A. `Router(config)#router ospf 0`
        `Router(config-router)#network 192.168.1.0 0.0.0.255`

    B. `Router(config)#router ospf 0`
        `Router(config-router)#network 192.168.1.0 0.0.0.255`

    C. `Router(config)#router ospf 0`
        `Router(config-router)#network 192.168.1.0 255.255.255.0`

    D. `Router(config)#router ospf 1`
        `Router(config-router)#network 192.168.1.0 0.0.0.255 area 0`

169. What is the default number of equal-cost routes for OSPF on Cisco routers?

    A. 4 routes

    B. 8 routes

    C. 16 routes

    D. 32 routes

170. You want to advertise a network of 131.40.32.0/27 with OSPF. Which wildcard mask will you need to use?

  A. 255.255.224.0

  B. 0.0.32.255

  C. 0.0.31.255

  D. 0.0.224.255

171. Which command will allow changing the number of equal-cost routes for OSPF?

  A. `Router(config)#ospf equal-cost 10`

  B. `Router(config-router)#ospf equal-cost 10`

  C. `Router(config)#ospf maximum-paths 10`

  D. `Router(config-router)#maximum-paths 10`

172. What is the maximum number of equal-cost routes that can be configured for OSPF on Cisco routers?

  A. 4 routes

  B. 8 routes

  C. 16 routes

  D. 32 routes

173. Which command will allow you to verify the router's RID for OSPF?

  A. `Router#show ip ospf`

  B. `Router#show ip interface`

  C. `Router#show ip ospf rid`

  D. `Router#show ip ospf neighbor`

174. You want to advertise a network of 192.168.1.16/28 with OSPF. Which wildcard mask will you need to use?

  A. 0.0.0.16

  B. 255.255.255.240

  C. 0.0.0.15

  D. 0.0.0.240

175. Which command will allow you to verify if a remote router has formed an adjacency with the current router?

  A. `Router#show ip ospf neighbor`

  B. `Router#show router adjacency`

  C. `Router#show ip ospf`

  D. `Router#show ip ospf router`

176. What is the default OSPF hello interval in which hello packets are sent out on a broadcast (multi-access) network?

  A. 5 seconds

  B. 10 seconds

    C. 30 seconds

    D. 60 seconds

177. You are running OSPF on a router. One of the interfaces, Gi0/1, connects to your ISP. You want to make sure you do not forward any OSPF packets to your ISP. How can you achieve this?

    A. `Router(config-if)#passive-interface`

    B. `Router(config-router)#passive-interface gigabitethernet 0/1`

    C. `Router(config)#passive-interface gigabitethernet 0/1`

    D. `Router(config-if)#passive-interface default`

178. Which command will help verify which interfaces hello packets are being sent out for OSPF?

    A. `Router#show interfaces`

    B. `Router#show ip routes`

    C. `Router#show ip ospf interface`

    D. `Router#show ip ospf brief`

179. Which command will statically set the RID for OSPF and override all others?

    A. `Router(config)#interface fa 0/1`
       `Router(config-if)#ip address 192.168.1.5 255.255.255.0`

    B. `Router(config)#interface loopback 0`
       `Router(config-if)#ip address 192.168.1.5 255.255.255.0`

    C. `Router(config-router)#rid 192.168.1.5`

    D. `Router(config-router)#router-id 192.168.1.5`

180. Which command(s) will only allow interface Gi0/2 to send hello packets for OSPF?

    A. `Router(config-router)#active-interface gigabitethernet 0/2`

    B. `Router(config-router)#passive-interface default`
       `Router(config-router)#active-interface gigabitethernet 0/2`

    C. `Router(config-router)#passive-interface default`
       `Router(config-router)#no passive-interface gigabitethernet 0/2`

    D. `Router(config-router)#passive-interface gigabitethernet 0/2`

181. After changing the router's RID for OSPF, which command needs to be entered?

    A. `Router#clear ip ospf`

    B. `Router(config-router)#shut`
       `Router(config-router)#no shut`

    C. `Router(config-router)#clear ip ospf`

    D. `Router#clear ospf`

182. Which statement about OSPF area border routers is correct?

    A. ABRs sit between an autonomous system and OSPF.

    B. ABRs exchange Type 1 Link-State Advertisements between areas.

    C. ABRs exchange Type 2 Link-State Advertisements between areas.

    D. ABRs exchange Type 3 Link-State Advertisements between areas.

183. In the following exhibit, you have two areas in which you want OSPF to advertise routes for. Which command(s) will achieve this?

Area 0
128.24.1.0/24
128.24.0.0.24

Area 1
128.24.2.0/24
128.24.3.0/24

A. Router(config-router)#network 128.24.0.0/22 area 0
Router(config-router)#network 128.24.0.0/22 area 1

B. Router(config-router)#network 128.24.0.0 0.0.252.255 area 0
Router(config-router)#network 128.24.0.0 0.0.252.255 area 1

C. Router(config-router)#network 128.24.0.0 0.0.254.255 area 0
Router(config-router)#network 128.24.0.0 255.254.255 area 1

D. Router(config-router)#network 128.24.0.0 0.0.255.255

184. Which command will allow you to see the summary of OSPF Link-State Advertisements?

A. Router#show ip ospf database

B. Router#show ip ospf states

C. Router#show ip ospf neighbors

D. Router#show ip ospf topology

185. You have configured OSPF on Router B. The network command entered was
network 197.234.3.0 0.0.0.63 area 0. You find out that one of the interfaces is not participating in OSPF. Which interface is not participating? Refer to the following exhibit.

```
RouterB#show ip interface brief
Interface              IP-Address      OK? Method Status                Protocol
GigabitEthernet0/0     197.234.3.65    YES manual up                    up
GigabitEthernet0/1     unassigned      YES unset  administratively down down
GigabitEthernet0/2     unassigned      YES unset  administratively down down
Serial0/3/0            unassigned      YES manual up                    up
Serial0/3/0.1          197.234.3.17    YES manual up                    up
Serial0/3/0.2          197.234.3.33    YES manual up                    up
Serial0/3/0.3          197.234.3.49    YES manual up                    up
RouterB#
```

A. Interface Serial 0/3/0

B. Interface Serial 0/3/0.1

C. Interface Serial 0/3/0.2

D. Interface GigabitEthernet 0/0

186. Two routers, called Router A and Router B, are configured in the same area and share a common LAN. However, they cannot form an adjacency. What could the problem be?

A. There is a static route configured between the two routers.

B. Router A is configured with multiple area IDs.

C. Router A is configured with a hello timer of 30.

D. Router B is configured with a hello timer of 10.

187. Which is a direct benefit of a hierarchical OSPF design?

    A. Fast convergence

    B. Reduction of configuration complexity

    C. Increased bandwidth

    D. Better security

188. In the following exhibit, which router is the designated router?

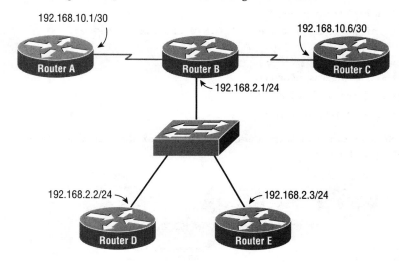

```
RouterB#sh ip ospf neighbor

Neighbor ID      Pri   State          Dead Time    Address        Interface
192.168.10.1     0     FULL/ -        00:00:30     192.168.10.1   Serial0/3/0
192.168.10.6     0     FULL/ -        00:00:36     192.168.10.6   Serial0/3/1
192.168.2.2      1     FULL/DROTHER   00:00:34     192.168.2.2    GigabitEthernet0/0
192.168.2.3      1     FULL/BDR       00:00:30     192.168.2.3    GigabitEthernet0/0
RouterB#
```

    A. Router C

    B. Router B

    C. Router D

    D. Router E

189. In the following exhibit, what is Router B called in this hierarchy?

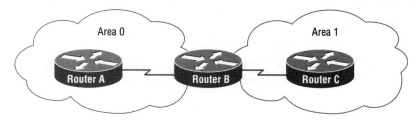

   A. ASBR

   B. ABR

   C. DR

   D. BDR

190. You have configured a router with the following command. However, when you enter `show ip routes` you do not see any routes for OSPF. What is the problem?

```
Router(config)#router ospf 255
Router(config-router)#network 10.0.0.0 255.0.0.0 area 255
```

   A. The process ID is incorrect.

   B. The area number is incorrect.

   C. The wildcard mask is incorrect.

   D. The network ID is incorrect.

191. In the following exhibit, Router A and Router B will not form an adjacency. What is the cause of the problem?

```
RouterA#show ip ospf interface                              RouterB#show ip ospf interface
Serial0/3/0 is up, line protocol is up                      Serial0/3/0 is up, line protocol is up
  Internet address is 192.168.10.1/30, Area 0                 Internet address is 192.168.10.2/30, Area 0
  Process ID 1, Router ID 192.168.10.1, Network Type          Process ID 23, Router ID 192.168.10.5, Network Type
  POINT-TO-POINT, Cost: 64                                    POINT-TO-POINT, Cost: 64
  Transmit Delay is 1 sec, State POINT-TO-POINT, Priority 0   Transmit Delay is 1 sec, State POINT-TO-POINT, Priority 0
  No designated router on this network                        No designated router on this network
  No backup designated router on this network                 No backup designated router on this network
  Timer intervals configured, Hello 30, Dead 40, Wait 40,     Timer intervals configured, Hello 10, Dead 40, Wait 40,
  Retransmit 5                                                Retransmit 5
      Hello due in 00:00:03                                       Hello due in 00:00:08
  Index 2/2, flood queue length 0                             Index 2/2, flood queue length 0
  Next 0x0(0)/0x0(0)                                          Next 0x0(0)/0x0(0)
[output cut]                                                 [output cut]
```

   A. The hello/dead timer does not match.

   B. The link is a point-to-point connection.

   C. The process IDs do not match.

   D. The area IDs do not match.

192. Which state in the neighbor table indicates that the router has successfully downloaded the LSA information from a neighboring router?

   A. FULL state

   B. EXSTART state

C. INIT state

D. EXCHANGE state

193. In the following exhibit, which is a correct statement about the neighbor ID of 192.168.2.2?

```
RouterB#sh ip ospf neighbor

Neighbor ID    Pri  State          Dead Time  Address       Interface
192.168.10.1   0    FULL/ -        00:00:30   192.168.10.1  Serial0/3/0
192.168.10.6   0    FULL/ -        00:00:36   192.168.10.6  Serial0/3/1
192.168.2.2    1    2WAY/          00:00:34   192.168.2.2   GigabitEthernet0/0
192.168.2.3    1    FULL/BDR       00:00:30   192.168.2.3   GigabitEthernet0/0
RouterB#
```

A. The neighbor is having a problem forming an adjacency.

B. The neighbor's OSPF process is recalculating cost.

C. This router's OSPF process is recalculating cost.

D. Both routers have formed an adjacency.

194. You have two links that enter the same OSPF router with the same bandwidth. You want to prefer one route over the other yet allow the second as a backup route. Which command would you use to achieve this?

A. `Router(config-router)#ip ospf priority 25`

B. `Router(config-if)#ip ospf route primary`

C. `Router(config-if)#ip ospf cost 25`

D. `Router(config-router)#passive interface gi 0/0`

195. Referring to the following exhibit, which is a correct statement about router ID 192.168.2.2?

```
RouterB#sh ip ospf neighbor

Neighbor ID    Pri  State          Dead Time  Address       Interface
192.168.10.1   0    FULL/ -        00:00:30   192.168.10.1  Serial0/3/0
192.168.10.6   0    FULL/ -        00:00:36   192.168.10.6  Serial0/3/1
192.168.2.2    1    FULL/DROTHER   00:00:34   192.168.2.2   GigabitEthernet0/0
192.168.2.3    1    FULL/BDR       00:00:30   192.168.2.3   GigabitEthernet0/0
RouterB#
```

A. It is in the process of forming an adjacency.

B. It is the designated router.

C. It is not participating in this OSPF area.

D. It will only form an adjacency with the DR or BDR.

196. Refer to the following exhibit. You want to make Router D the designated router. Which command will assure that it becomes the designated router?

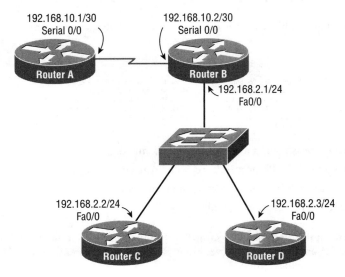

192.168.10.1/30
Serial 0/0

192.168.10.2/30
Serial 0/0

192.168.2.1/24
Fa0/0

192.168.2.2/24
Fa0/0

192.168.2.3/24
Fa0/0

   A. RouterD(config-router)#ospf priority
   B. RouterD(config-if)#ip ospf priority 10
   C. RouterD(config-if)#ip address 192.168.5.2 255.255.255.0
   D. RouterD(config-if)#ip ospf cost 15

197. Which command will display the designated router for a LAN?
   A. Router#show ip ospf neighbor
   B. Router#show ip ospf database
   C. Router#show ip ospf dr
   D. Router#show ip ospf interfaces

198. In the following exhibit, Router A will not form an adjacency with Router B. What is the problem?

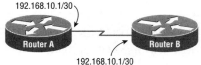

192.168.10.1/30

192.168.10.1/30

```
RouterA#show ip ospf interface
Serial0/3/0 is up, line protocol is up
   Internet address is 192.168.10.1/30, Area 0
   Process ID 1, Router ID 192.168.10.1, Network Type POINT-TO-POINT, Cost: 64
   Transmit Delay is 1 sec, State POINT-TO-POINT, Priority 0
   No designated router on this network
   No backup designated router on this network
   Timer intervals configured, Hello 10, Dead 40, Wait 40, Retransmit 5
      Hello due in 00:00:03
   Index 2/2, flood queue length 0
   Next 0x0(0)/0x0(0)
[output cut]
```

```
RouterB#show ip ospf interface
Serial0/3/0 is up, line protocol is up
   Internet address is 192.168.10.2/30, Area 1
   Process ID 23, Router ID 192.168.10.5, Network Type POINT-TO-POINT, Cost: 64
   Transmit Delay is 1 sec, State POINT-TO-POINT, Priority 0
   No designated router on this network
   No backup designated router on this network
   Timer intervals configured, Hello 10, Dead 40, Wait 40, Retransmit 5
      Hello due in 00:00:08
   Index 2/2, flood queue length 0
   Next 0x0(0)/0x0(0)
[output cut]
```

   A. The hello/dead timer does not match.
   B. There is no designated router on the network.

   C. The process IDs do not match.

   D. The area IDs do not match.

199. In the following exhibit, you have one OSPF area and want to populate the default route to all routers in the OSPF area. Which command would you use?

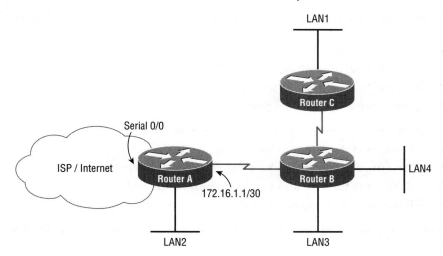

   A. `RouterA(config)#ip route 0.0.0.0 0.0.0.0 serial 0/0`

   B. `RouterA(config-router)#default-route originate`

   C. `RouterA(config-router)#default-information originate`

   D. `RouterA(config-router)#network 0.0.0.0 0.0.0.0 area 0`

200. Which command will set the bandwidth of an interface to 2.048 Mb/s?

   A. `Router(config-if)#bandwidth 2048`

   B. `Router(config-if)#bandwidth 2048000000`

   C. `Router(config-if)#bandwidth 2.048`

   D. `Router(config-if)#bandwidth 2048000`

201. In the following exhibit, Router A will not form an adjacency with Router B. What is the problem?

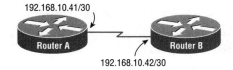

```
RouterA#show ip ospf interface                              RouterB#show ip ospf interface
Serial0/3/0 is up, line protocol is up                      Serial0/3/0 is up, line protocol is up
  Internet address is 192.168.10.41/30, Area 0                Internet address is 192.168.10.42/30, Area 0
  Process ID 1, Router ID 192.168.10.41, Network Type POINT-TO-POINT, Cost: 64    Process ID 23, Router ID 192.168.10.42, Network Type POINT-TO-POINT, Cost: 64
  Transmit Delay is 1 sec, State POINT-TO-POINT, Priority 0   Transmit Delay is 1 sec, State POINT-TO-POINT, Priority 0
  No designated router on this network                        No designated router on this network
  No backup designated router on this network                 No backup designated router on this network
  Timer intervals configured, Hello 10, Dead 40, Wait 40, Retransmit 5    Timer intervals configured, Hello 10, Dead 40, Wait 40, Retransmit 5
  oob-resync timeout 40                                       oob-resync timeout 40
  No Hellos (Passive interface)                               No Hellos (Passive interface)
[output cut]                                                 [output cut]
```

A. The routers are not in the same network.

B. The routers have mismatched process IDs.

C. The routers have passive interfaces.

D. The hello/dead interval is wrong for serial links.

202. Which command will allow you to see the networks the current router is advertising for OSPF?

A. `Router#show ip protocols`

B. `Router#show ip ospf`

C. `Router#show ip ospf database`

D. `Router#show ip ospf neighbors`

203. Which statement is true of routers in the same area?

A. All routers in the same area have the same neighbor table.

B. All routers in the same area have the same hello/dead timers.

C. All routers in the same area have same topology table.

D. All routers in the same area have the same process IDs.

204. Which command would you use to make sure Router A never becomes a designated router?

A. `Router(config)#no ospf designated`

B. `Router(config-router)#no ospf designated`

C. `Router(config-router)#passive interface gi 0/0`

D. `Router(config-if)#ip ospf priority 0`

205. You enter a `show ip route` command and see the following line. What does the `[110/1]` identify?

```
O    192.168.3.0/24 [110/1] via 192.168.10.6, 00:58:55, Serial0/3/1
```

A. Administrative distance of 110 and a 100 Mb/s link

B. Administrative distance of 110 and a 10 Mb/s link

C. Administrative distance of 1 and a 110 Mb/s link

D. Administrative distance of 110 and a 1 Gb/s link

206. Which command will start an OSPFv3 process with an ID of 4?

A. `Router(config)#router ospfv3 4`

B. `Router(config)#ip router ospfv3 4`

C. `Router(config)#ipv6 router ospf 4`

D. `Router(config)#router ospf3 4`

207. Which IPv6 address does OSPFv3 use to communicate with designated routers?

A. ff02::6

B. ff02::5

    C. fe02::5

    D. fe02::6

208. When configuring OSPFv3, how do you configure the router ID?

    A. The router ID is configured as a 128-bit IPv6 address.

    B. The router ID is configured as the 64-bit host section of an IPv6 address.

    C. The router ID is configured as a 32-bit IPv4 address.

    D. The router ID is configured as a 48-bit MAC address.

209. You are configuring an OSPFv3 process of 4 for an interface of Serial 0/0 with an IPv6 address of 2001:db8:1:2::1/64 in area 0. Which command will you use?

    A. `Router(config-router)#network 2001:db8:1:2/64 area 0`

    B. `Router(config-if)#ipv6 ospf 4 area 0`

    C. `Router(config-rtr)#network 2001:db8:1:2/64 area 0`

    D. `Router(config-if)#ipv6 ospf area 0`

210. You have an interface of Serial 0/0, which is connected to your ISP. You want to suppress OSPFv3 LSAs on the IPv6 link to the ISP. Which command will you use?

    A. `Router(config-rtr)#passive-interface serial 0/0`

    B. `Router(config-router)#passive-interface serial 0/0`

    C. `Router(config-if)#passive-interface`

    D. `Router(config-if)#ipv6 passive-interface`

211. You have a number of routers with 10 Gb/s and 1 Gb/s links running OSPFv3. You need to adjust the cost for all links on the router. Which command will allow you to achieve this with the fewest commands?

    A. `Router(config-rtr)#auto-cost 10000`

    B. `Router(config-rtr)#auto-cost reference-bandwidth 10000`

    C. `Router(config)#auto-cost reference-bandwidth 10000`

    D. `Router(config-rtr)#auto-cost reference-bandwidth 10000000`

212. Which IPv6 address does OSPFv3 use to send LSA hello packets?

    A. ff02::6

    B. ff02::5

    C. fe02::5

    D. fe02::6

213. Which command will allow you to verify only OSPFv3 routes?

    A. `Router#show ip route opsf3`

    B. `Router#show ip route opsfv3`

    C. `Router#show ipv6 route opsf3`

    D. `Router#show ipv6 route ospf`

214. Which command would you use to verify that the hello/dead timers match for OSPFv3?

   A. Router#show ip ospf interface

   B. Router#show ipv6 ospf interface

   C. Router#show ipv6 ospfv3 interface

   D. Router#show ipv6 database

215. A common problem with IPv6 and OSPFv3 is MTU. Why is it a common problem with IPv6 and not IPv4?

   A. OSPFv3 ignores MTU settings.

   B. IPv4 fragments packets.

   C. IPv6 addresses are large and require jumbo frames.

   D. IPv4 uses TCP to transmit OSPF packets.

216. You need to configure OSPFv3 for the network 2001:db8:2:3/64 with an area of 0. Which configuration would you use?

   A. Router(config-rtr)#network 2001:db8:2:3/64 area 0

   B. Router(config-router)#network 2001:db8:2:3/64 area 0

   C. Router(config-if)#ip ospf 2 area 0

   D. Router(config-if)#ipv6 ospf 2 area 0.0.0.0

217. You begin to configure OSPFv3 but get the error % IPv6 routing not enabled. Which command needs to be entered?

   A. Router(config)#enable ipv6

   B. Router(config)#enable ipv6 routing

   C. Router(config)#ipv6 unicast-routing

   D. Router(config)#enable ipv6 unicast-routing

218. You have configured OSPFv3 with a process ID of 5. You want to view only the OSPFv3 process ID of 5. Which command will achieve this?

   A. Router#show ip ospf 5

   B. Router#show ipv6 ospf 5

   C. Router#show ospfv3 5

   D. Router#show ipv6 ospfv3 5

219. You have two routers that will not form an OPSFv3 adjacency. You've identified that the hello timer on Router B has been changed. Which command will rectify the problem?

   A. RouterB(config-if)#no ipv6 ospf hello-interval

   B. RouterB(config-if)#no ipv6 ospf hello timer

   C. RouterB(config-rtr)#no ipv6 ospf hello-interval

   D. RouterB(config-rtr)#no ipv6 ospf hello timer

220. After you configure a new router ID for an OSPFv3 process, which command must be
entered for the change to take effect?

A. `Router#clear ipv6 ospf process`

B. `Router(config)#restart ipv6 ospf process`

C. `Router(config-if)#restart ipv6 ospf process`

D. `Router(config-rtr)#clear ipv6 ospf`

221. In the following exhibit, you must configure Router B to support the OSPFv3 structure.
Which commands will configure Router B?

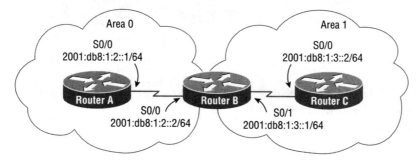

A. `Router(config)#ipv6 router ospf 1`
`Router(config)#interface serial 0/0`
`Router(config-if)#ipv6 ospf 1 area 0`
`Router(config)#interface serial 0/1`
`Router(config-if)#ipv6 ospf 1 area 1`

B. `Router(config)#ipv6 router ospf 1`
`Router(config)#ipv6 router ospf 2`
`Router(config)#interface serial 0/0`
`Router(config-if)#ipv6 ospf 1 area 0`
`Router(config)#interface serial 0/1`
`Router(config-if)#ipv6 ospf 2 area 1`

C. `Router(config)#ipv6 router ospf 1`
`Router(config-rtr)#router-id 2.2.2.2`
`Router(config)#interface serial 0/0`
`Router(config-if)#ipv6 ospf 1 area 0`
`Router(config)#interface serial 0/1`
`Router(config-if)#ipv6 ospf 1 area 1`

D. `Router(config)#ipv6 router ospf 1`
`Router(config-rtr)#router-id 1.1.1.1`
`Router(config)#ipv6 router ospf 2`
`Router(config-rtr)#router-id 2.2.2.2`
`Router(config)#interface serial 0/0`
`Router(config-if)#ipv6 ospf 1 area 0`
`Router(config)#interface serial 0/1`
`Router(config-if)#ipv6 ospf 2 area 1`

222. In the following exhibit, you have configured Router A, Router B, and Router C with router IDs of 1.1.1.1, 2.2.2.2, and 3.3.3.3 respectively. When you perform the command show ipv6 ospf neighbors, you only see router 1.1.1.1 as a neighbor. What could the problem be?

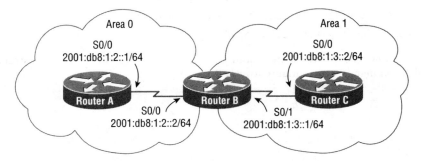

    A.   Router C is the designated router.

    B.   Router C is misconfigured.

    C.   Router C is in a different area than Router A.

    D.   Router C is the backup designated router.

223. When configuring OSPFv3, what is an alternative to specifying a router ID?

    A.   Configuring a loopback interface

    B.   Configuring the highest IP address on the network

    C.   Specifying the command ipv6 ospf 1 area 0 on an IPv4 interface

    D.   Specifying the command router-id autoconfigure

224. Which statement is correct about OSPFv3 vs. OSPFv2?

    A.   OSPFv3 will advertise all networks configured on a link.

    B.   OSFPv3 requires directed broadcast enabled on the router.

    C.   OSPFv3 can run a maximum of four instances per router.

    D.   OSPFv3 can load-balance links of unequal cost.

225. In the following exhibit, Router A and Router B will not form an adjacency. What is the problem?

```
RouterA#show ipv6 ospf interface fa0/0
FastEthernet0/0 is up, line protocol is up
  Link Local Address FE80::1212:2234:AE23:0011, Interface ID 2
  Area 0, Process ID 2, Instance ID 0, Router ID 2.2.2.2
  Network Type BROADCAST, Cost: 1
  Transmit Delay is 1 sec, State DR, Priority 1
  [output cut]
  Neighbor Count is 0, Adjacent neighbor count is 0
  Suppress hello for 0 neighbors

RouterB#show ipv6 ospf interface fa0/0
FastEthernet0/0 is up, line protocol is up
  Link Local Address FE80::1212:2234:AE23:0022, Interface ID 2
  Area 0, Process ID 2, Instance ID 0, Router ID 2.2.2.2
  Network Type BROADCAST, Cost: 1
  Transmit Delay is 1 sec, State DR, Priority 1
  [output cut]
  Neighbor Count is 0, Adjacent neighbor count is 0
  Suppress hello for 0 neighbors
```

   A. Both routers have the same process ID.

   B. Both routers have the same router ID configured.

   C. Both routers are the designated router.

   D. Both routers are using a link-local address.

226. Which dynamic routing protocol is a Cisco proprietary routing protocol?

   A. RIPv2

   B. BGP

   C. OSPFv3

   D. EIGRP

227. By default, which metrics are used by EIGRP to calculate path cost?

   A. Bandwidth and delay

   B. Bandwidth and MTU

   C. Bandwidth and reliability

   D. Bandwidth and hop count

228. Which is a requirement for EIGRP routers to create a neighborship?

   A. Matching bandwidth metrics

   B. Matching delay metrics

   C. Matching K metrics

   D. Matching areas

229. Which IPv4 multicast address is used by EIGRP?

   A. 224.0.0.5

   B. 224.0.0.6

   C. 224.0.0.10

   D. 224.0.0.4

230. What is the default formula for metric calculation for EIGRP?

   A. metric = ((107 / least-bandwidth) + cumulative-delay) * 256

   B. metric = ([K1 * bandwidth + (K2 * bandwidth) / (256 − load) + K3 * delay] * [K5 / (reliability + K4)]) * 256

   C. metric = least-bandwidth + cumulative-delay

   D. metric = least-bandwidth + cumulative-delay / 256

231. Which condition must be met for two routers participating in EIGRP to become neighbors?

   A. Matching area numbers

   B. Matching autonomous system numbers

   C. Matching hello/dead timers

   D. Matching MTUs

232. What is the default hop count of EIGRP?

    A. 15

    B. 100

    C. 255

    D. Infinite

233. What mechanism does EIGRP have for scalability?

    A. Reliable Transport Protocol

    B. Diffusing Update Algorithm

    C. Holddown timers

    D. Autonomous system numbers

234. How often are hello messages sent between EIGRP participating routers by default?

    A. Every 5 seconds

    B. Every 15 seconds

    C. Every 30 seconds

    D. Every 40 seconds

235. When does the EIGRP protocol advertise the entire database?

    A. When a route update is sent

    B. Every 30 seconds

    C. Upon forming an adjacency

    D. Every 5 seconds

236. What is the maximum stable hop count for EIGRP?

    A. 15

    B. 100

    C. 255

    D. Infinite

237. Which table is used to feed information to the topology table with EIGRP?

    A. Neighbor table

    B. Routing table

    C. RTP table

    D. Feasibility table

238. Which mechanism does RTP use if an established neighbor does not respond to a multi-cast hello packet for EIGRP?

    A. Holddown timers

    B. Unicast packets

    C. Hello packet proxy

    D. Broadcasts

239. What happens when a hold interval for EIGRP has expired?

    A. The hello message is retransmitted via unicast packets.

    B. The hello message is retransmitted via broadcast packets.

    C. The neighbor is considered down.

    D. The link is considered down.

240. How many equal-cost links can EIGRP load-balance?

    A. 4 links

    B. 8 links

    C. 16 links

    D. 32 links

241. Which routing algorithm does EIGRP use?

    A. Shortest Path First

    B. Dijkstra

    C. Bellman-Ford

    D. DUAL

242. After a router has been acknowledged, which table is built from the network routes discovered for the EIGRP protocol?

    A. The neighbor table

    B. The topology table

    C. The routing table

    D. The adjacency table

243. A router has learned two routes to the same network. EIGRP has a route to the destination network with a cost of 202342520. OSPF has a route to the destination network with a cost of 64. Which route will be used to the destination network?

    A. The OSPF route with a cost of 64

    B. The EIGRP route with a cost of 202342520

    C. Both routes will be used with load balancing.

    D. The routes will be used in a spill and fill configuration.

244. What is the default hold interval for EIGRP?

    A. 5 seconds

    B. 15 seconds

    C. 30 seconds

    D. 40 seconds

245. Which metric is considered to be infinite for an EIGRP route in which the router will not try to route packets to the destination network?

  A. 15 hops

  B. 255 hops

  C. $2^{24} - 1$

  D. $2^{32} - 1$

246. Which statement is correct about EIGRP and how it works with updates?

  A. EIGRP sends its full routing table during each hello interval.

  B. EIGRP sends its link state during each hello interval.

  C. EIGRP sends its full routing table every 30 seconds.

  D. EIGRP sends changes to routes only when they are detected.

247. Which table is a router added to when it acknowledges a hello packet for EIGRP?

  A. The neighbor table

  B. The topology table

  C. The routing table

  D. The adjacency table

248. Which is a condition that must be met for a router to become a neighbor router for EIGRP?

  A. Both routers have the same hello/hold interval.

  B. Both routers are on the same subnet.

  C. Both routers have the same area ID.

  D. Both routers have the same link types.

249. What is the definition of the reported distance for EIGRP?

  A. The local router's calculated metric for the remote network

  B. The remote router's calculated metric for the remote network

  C. The local router's calculated metric for the local network

  D. The remote router's calculated metric for the local network

250. Which route will be entered into the routing table from EIGRP calculation of metrics?

  A. The feasible successor route

  B. The feasible distance route

  C. The successor route

  D. The reported distance route

251. Which table does EIGRP use to calculate the feasible distance of a remote route?

  A. The neighbor table

  B. The topology table

C. The routing table

D. The adjacency table

252. In the following exhibit, packets with a destination of 192.168.4.0/24 from 192.168.1.0/24 travel from Router A to Router B. However, the best path is Router A to Router C to Router B. Which configuration change for EIGRP will allow the best path to be used?

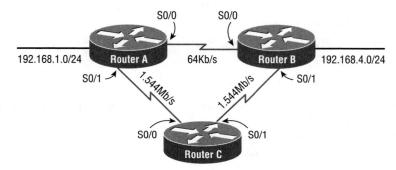

A. ```
RouterA(config)#interface serial 0/0
RouterA(config-if)#bandwidth 64
RouterB(config)#interface serial 0/0
RouterB(config-if)#bandwidth 64
```

B. ```
RouterA(config)#interface serial 0/1
RouterA(config-if)#bandwidth 1544
RouterC(config)#interface serial 0/0
RouterC(config-if)#bandwidth 1544
RouterC(config)#interface serial 0/1
RouterC(config-if)#bandwidth 1544
RouterB(config)#interface serial 0/1
RouterB(config-if)#bandwidth 1544
```

C. ```
RouterA(config)#interface serial 0/0
RouterA(config-if)#bandwidth 64000
RouterB(config)#interface serial 0/0
RouterB(config-if)#bandwidth 64000
```

D. ```
RouterA(config)#ip route 192.168.4.0 255.255.255.0 serial 0/1
```

253. Which command will create a routing process for EIGRP using an autonomous system number (ASN) of 20?

A. `Router(config)#eigrp 20`

B. `Router(config)#ip eigpr 20`

C. `Router(config)#router eigrp 20`

D. `Router(config)#router eigrp asn 20`

254. What is the default variance of EIGRP?

    A. 0

    B. 1

    C. 2

    D. 128

255. Which command will change the router ID of an EIGRP router?

    A. `Router(config-router)#router-id 2.2.2.2`

    B. `Router(config-router)#eigrp router-id 2.2.2.2`

    C. `Router(config)#eigrp router-id 2.2.2.2`

    D. `Router(config)#ip eigrp router-id 2.2.2.2`

256. Which command should be used when configuring networks with discontiguous IP addresses for EIGRP?

    A. `Router(config-router)#network discontiguous`

    B. `Router(config-router)#no auto-summary`

    C. `Router(config)#network discontiguous`

    D. `Router(config)#no auto-summary`

257. Which command will advertise the network 192.168.1.0/24 for an EIGRP ASN of 20?

    A. `Router(config-router)#network 192.168.1.0 0.0.0.255`

    B. `Router(config-router)#network 192.168.1.0 255.255.255.0`

    C. `Router(config-router)#network 192.168.1.0/24`

    D. `Router(config-router)#network 192.168.1.0 0.0.0.255 20`

258. In the following exhibit, Router A will not form an EIGRP adjacency with Router B. What is the problem?

```
RouterA#show ip protocols                                 RouterB#show ip protocols
Routing Protocol is "eigrp 10"                            Routing Protocol is "eigrp 20"
  Outgoing update filter list for all interfaces is not set   Outgoing update filter list for all interfaces is not set
  Incoming update filter list for all interfaces is not set   Incoming update filter list for all interfaces is not set
  Default networks flagged in outgoing updates              Default networks flagged in outgoing updates
  Default networks accepted from incoming updates           Default networks accepted from incoming updates
  Redistributing: eigrp 10                                  Redistributing: eigrp 20
  EIGRP-IPv4 Protocol for AS(10)                            EIGRP-IPv4 Protocol for AS(20)
    Metric weight K1=1, K2=0, K3=1, K4=0, K5=0               Metric weight K1=1, K2=0, K3=1, K4=0, K5=0
    NSF-aware route hold timer is 240                        NSF-aware route hold timer is 240
    Router-ID: 192.168.3.1                                   Router-ID: 192.168.2.1
  [output cut]                                              [output cut]
  Routing for Networks:                                     Routing for Networks:
    172.16.0.0/16                                            192.168.0.0/16
  Routing Information Sources:                               Routing Information Sources:
    Gateway      Distance    Last Update                     Gateway      Distance    Last Update
  Distance: internal 90 external 170                        Distance: internal 90 external 170
```

    A. The router IDs are in the wrong subnets.

    B. The K metrics do not match.

    C. Router A is advertising networks that are not in the same subnet as Router A.

    D. The ASNs do not match.

259. You need to verify the adjacent routers participating in EIGRP. Which command will allow you to see the adjacent routers?

    A.   `Router#show ip eigrp`

    B.   `Router#show ip eigrp adajcent`

    C.   `Router#show ip eigrp database`

    D.   `Router#show ip eigrp neighbors`

260. Which command will allow you to inspect the K metrics for EIGRP?

    A.   `Router#show ip protocols`

    B.   `Router#show ip eigrp interfaces`

    C.   `Router#show ip eigrp detail`

    D.   `Router#show ip eigrp neighbors`

261. You need to suppress EIGRP hello advertisements on the interface connecting you to your ISP. Which command will suppress EIGRP hello packets?

    A.   `Router(config-if)#eigrp 20 passive-interface`

    B.   `Router(config-if)#eigrp passive-interface`

    C.   `Router(config-router)#passive-interface serial 0/0`

    D.   `Router(config-if)#ip eigrp 20 suppress-hello`

262. You want to confirm a Feasible-Successor route for EIGRP. Which command will allow you to verify this?

    A.   `Router#show ip route eigrp`

    B.   `Router#show ip eigrp topology`

    C.   `Router#show running-configuration`

    D.   `Router#show ip eigrp route`

263. You have two paths you want to load-balance that have slightly different delays. Which command will allow you to tune the unequal paths so they will load-balance with EIGRP?

    A.   `Router(config-if)#variance 2`

    B.   `Router(config-router)#variance 2`

    C.   `Router(config-if)#variance 2 asn 20`

    D.   `Router(config-if)#variance 20 2`

264. When is the command `no passive-interface serial 0/0` used with EIGRP?

    A.   When you want to suppress hello packets exiting on interface serial 0/0

    B.   When you want to suppress hello packets from entering interface serial 0/0

    C.   When you want to allow hello packets exiting on interface serial 0/0

    D.   When you want to allow hello packets to enter interface serial 0/0

265. In the following exhibit, Router A will not form an EIGRP adjacency with Router B. What is the problem?

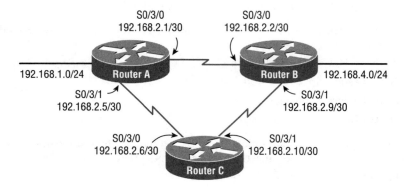

```
RouterA#show ip protocols
Routing Protocol is "eigrp 10"
  Outgoing update filter list for all interfaces is not set
  Incoming update filter list for all interfaces is not set
  Default networks flagged in outgoing updates
  Default networks accepted from incoming updates
  Redistributing: eigrp 10
  EIGRP-IPv4 Protocol for AS(10)
    Metric weight K1=1, K2=0, K3=1, K4=0, K5=0
    NSF-aware route hold timer is 240
    Router-ID: 192.168.3.1
  [output cut]
  Routing for Networks:
    172.16.0.0/16
  Routing Information Sources:
    Gateway    Distance    Last Update
  Distance: internal 90 external 170
```

```
RouterB#show ip protocols
Routing Protocol is "eigrp 10"
  Outgoing update filter list for all interfaces is not set
  Incoming update filter list for all interfaces is not set
  Default networks flagged in outgoing updates
  Default networks accepted from incoming updates
  Redistributing: eigrp 10
  EIGRP-IPv4 Protocol for AS(10)
    Metric weight K1=1, K2=1, K3=1, K4=0, K5=0
    NSF-aware route hold timer is 240
    Router-ID: 192.168.2.1
  [output cut]
  Routing for Networks:
    192.168.0.0/16
  Routing Information Sources:
    Gateway    Distance    Last Update
  Distance: internal 90 external 170
```

A. The router IDs are in the wrong subnets.

B. The K metrics do not match.

C. Router A is advertising networks that are not in the same subnet as Router A.

D. The ASNs do not match.

266. In the following exhibit, which route will the packet from 192.168.1.5 to 192.168.4.9 take?

S0/3/0
192.168.2.1/30

S0/3/0
192.168.2.2/30

192.168.1.0/24   **Router A**   **Router B**   192.168.4.0/24

S0/3/1
192.168.2.5/30

S0/3/1
192.168.2.9/30

S0/3/0
192.168.2.6/30

S0/3/1
192.168.2.10/30

Router C

```
RouterA#sh ip route
[output cut]
      192.168.1.0/24 is variably subnetted, 2 subnets, 2 masks
C       192.168.1.0/24 is directly connected, GigabitEthernet0/0
L       192.168.1.1/32 is directly connected, GigabitEthernet0/0
      192.168.2.0/24 is variably subnetted, 5 subnets, 2 masks
C       192.168.2.0/30 is directly connected, Serial0/3/0
L       192.168.2.1/32 is directly connected, Serial0/3/0
C       192.168.2.4/30 is directly connected, Serial0/3/1
L       192.168.2.5/32 is directly connected, Serial0/3/1
D       192.168.2.8/30 [90/2681856] via 192.168.2.6, 00:32:41, Serial0/3/1
D       192.168.4.0/24 [90/2682112] via 192.168.2.6, 00:06:12, Serial0/3/1
Router A#
```

   A.   Router A to Router B

   B.   Router A to Router C to Router B

   C.   Both Router A to Router B and Router A to Router C

   D.   Router B to Router A

267. In the following exhibit, EIGRP is used to advertise routes on both Router A and Router B. Why will packets not route from 172.16.2.0/24 to 172.16.4.0/24?

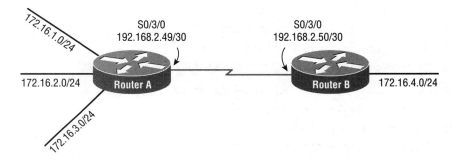

   A.   Router A and Router B serial interfaces are not on the same subnet.

   B.   EIGRP only advertises classful addresses.

   C.   The serial line is not supported for EIGRP.

   D.   Auto-summarization is prohibiting proper routing.

268. Which mechanism in EIGRP allows for EIGRP to support multiple protocols?

   A.   Reliable Transport Protocol

   B.   Protocol-dependent module

   C.   Diffusing Update Algorithm

   D.   Auto-summarization

269. Two routers, Router A and Router B, will not form an adjacency with EIGRP. You discover that someone configured a custom K metric. Which command will configure the router's K metrics back to their default setting?

   A.   `Router(config-router)#metric 0 0 0 0 0`

   B.   `Router(config-router)#no k-metric`

   C.   `Router(config-router)#no metric weights`

   D.   `Router(config-router)#metric weights 1 1 1 1 1`

270. Which command will allow you to verify the routes advertised by EIGRP?

   A.   `Router#show ip protocols`

   B.   `Router#show ip eigrp database`

   C.   `Router#show ip eigrp neighbors`

   D.   `Router#show ip eigrp topology`

271. What is the IPv6 address for EIGRPv6 neighbor discovery?

    A. ff02::6

    B. ff03::5

    C. ff02::a

    D. ff03::c

272. Which command must be entered before EIGRPv6 can be configured?

    A. `Router(config)#enable ipv6`

    B. `Router(config)#enable ipv6 routing`

    C. `Router(config)#ipv6 unicast-routing`

    D. `Router(config)#enable ipv6 unicast-routing`

273. Which command must be entered to start the EIGRPv6 router instance?

    A. `Router(config-rtr)#no shutdown`

    B. `Router(config-rtr)#run`

    C. `Router(config-rtr)#start eigrp`

    D. `Router(config)#ipv6 eigrp 10`

274. You have configured EIGRPv6 with an ASN of 10. Which command will add networks to be advertised?

    A. `Router(config-rtr)#interface serial 0/0`

    B. `Router(config-rtr)#network 2001:db8:2:3::1/64`

    C. `Router(config-if)#ipv6 eigrp 10`

    D. `Router(config-if)#ipv6 eigrp asn 10`

275. When configuring a router with EIGRPv6 and only IPv6 is configured on the router, which command is necessary for EIGRPv6 operations?

    A. `Router(config-rtr)#router id 1.1.1.1`

    B. `Router(config)#router-id 1.1.1.1`

    C. `Router(config-rtr)#router-id 1.1.1.1`

    D. `Router(config-if)#eigrp router-id 1.1.1.1`

276. You have configured EIGRPv6 on a router that also faces your Internet service provider. Which command should you use to restrict hello packets from being directed to the ISP?

    A. `Router(config-if)#ipv6 eigrp 10 passive-interface`

    B. `Router(config-rtr)#passive-interface serial 0/0`

    C. `Router(config-if)#ipv6 eigrp passive-interface`

    D. `Router(config-rtr)#ipv6 passive-interface serial 0/0`

277. You want to verify the K metrics that EIGRPv6 is using. Which command will display the K metrics?

    A. Router#show running-configuration

    B. Router#show ip protocols

    C. Router#show ipv6 eigrp interfaces

    D. Router#show ipv6 protocols

278. Which command will help you verify that a router has created an adjacency with EIGRPv6?

    A. Router#show ipv6 eigrp

    B. Router#show ipv6 eigrp adjacency

    C. Router#show ipv6 eigrp database

    D. Router#show ipv6 eigrp neighbors

279. Which command will show only the EIGRPv6 routes?

    A. Router#show ipv6 route

    B. Router#show ipv6 route eigrp

    C. Router#show ipv6 eigrp

    D. Router#show ipv6 eigrp route

280. You need to verify the interfaces that are participating in EIGRPv6. Which command will show this?

    A. Router#show ipv6 interface

    B. Router#show ipv6 eigrp neighbors

    C. Router#show ipv6 eigrp topology

    D. Router#show ipv6 protocols

281. Which command will change the hello timer for EIGRPv6 ASN from 10 to 5 seconds?

    A. Router(config)#ip hello-timer eigrp 10 5

    B. Router(config)#ipv6 hello- interval eigrp 10 5

    C. Router(config-rtr)#ipv6 hello-interval eigrp 5

    D. Router(config-if)#ipv6 hello-interval eigrp 10 5

282. Which statement is true for EIGRP but not for EIGRPv6?

    A. Interfaces must be on the same subnet for an adjacency to form.

    B. K metrics must match for an adjacency to form.

    C. Hello and holddown timers must match for an adjacency to form.

    D. Router IDs must match.

283. You need to calculate a variance for EIGRPv6. Which table will allow you to calculate the variance for unequal-cost load balancing?

   A. `Router#show ipv6 eigrp adjacency`

   B. `Router#show ipv6 eigrp topology`

   C. `Router#show ipv6 eigrp interfaces`

   D. `Router#show ipv6 eigrp neighbors`

284. In the following exhibit, a host on the 2001:db8:0500::/64 network sends a packet to a host on the 2001:db8:3000::/64 network. Which path will the packet take?

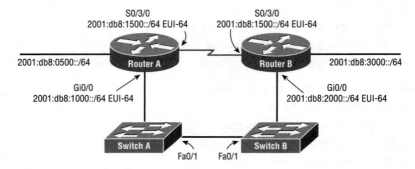

```
RouterA#show ipv6 eigrp topology
[Output Cut]
P 2001:DB8:1000::/64, 1 successors, FD is 2816
    via Connected, GigabitEthernet0/0
P 2001:DB8:1500::/64, 1 successors, FD is 2169856
    via Connected, Serial0/3/0
P 2001:DB8:2000::/64, 1 successors, FD is 3072
    via FE80::201:96FF:FE6B:B301 (3072/2816), GigabitEthernet0/0
    via FE80::201:96FF:FE6B:B301 (2170112/2816), Serial0/3/0
P 2001:DB8:2500::/64, 1 successors, FD is 2170112
    via FE80::201:96FF:FE6B:B301 (2170112/2169856), GigabitEthernet0/0
    via FE80::201:96FF:FE6B:B301 (2681856/2169856), Serial0/3/0
P 2001:DB8:3000::/64, 1 successors, FD is 2170368
    via FE80::201:96FF:FE6B:B301 (2170368/2170112), GigabitEthernet0/0
    via FE80::201:96FF:FE6B:B301 (2682112/2170112), Serial0/3/0
RouterA#
```

   A. Router A to Switch A to Switch B to Router B

   B. Router A to Router B

   C. Load-balanced Router A to Router B and Router A to Switch A to Switch B to Router B

   D. Router B to Router A

285. In the following exhibit, how can you force packets from hosts on the 2001:db8:0500::/64 network destined to the 2001:db8:3000::/64 network through Serial 0/3/0 statically?

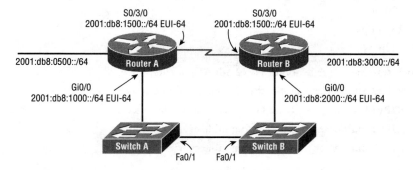

```
RouterA#show ipv6 eigrp topology
[Output Cut]
P 2001:DB8:1000::/64, 1 successors, FD is 2816
      via Connected, GigabitEthernet0/0
P 2001:DB8:1500::/64, 1 successors, FD is 2169856
      via Connected, Serial0/3/0
P 2001:DB8:2000::/64, 1 successors, FD is 3072
      via FE80::201:96FF:FE6B:B301 (3072/2816), GigabitEthernet0/0
      via FE80::201:96FF:FE6B:B301 (2170112/2816), Serial0/3/0
P 2001:DB8:2500::/64, 1 successors, FD is 2170112
      via FE80::201:96FF:FE6B:B301 (2170112/2169856), GigabitEthernet0/0
      via FE80::201:96FF:FE6B:B301 (2681856/2169856), Serial0/3/0
P 2001:DB8:3000::/64, 1 successors, FD is 2170368
      via FE80::201:96FF:FE6B:B301 (2170368/2170112), GigabitEthernet0/0
      via FE80::201:96FF:FE6B:B301 (2682112/2170112), Serial0/3/0
RouterA#
```

A. RouterA(config)#int gi 0/0
   RouterA(config-if)#passive-interface
   RouterB(config)#int gi 0/0
   RouterB(config-if)#passive-interface

B. RouterA(config-rtr)#passive-interface gi 0/0
   RouterB(config-rtr)#passive-interface gi 0/0

C. RouterA(config)#int gi 0/0
   RouterA(config-if)#no bandwidth
   RouterB(config)#int gi 0/0
   RouterB(config-if)#no bandwidth

D. RouterA(config)#int serial 0/3/0
   RouterA(config-if)#no bandwidth
   RouterB(config)#int serial 0/3/0
   RouterB(config-if)#no bandwidth

286. What is the maximum hop count for RIP?

    A. 15 hops

    B. 100 hops

    C. 255 hops

    D. 16 hops

287. Which statement is true about RIPv2 advertisements?

    A. RIPv2 allows for neighborship through hello packets.

    B. RIPv2 broadcasts only updates on all active interfaces.

    C. RIPv2 multicasts the full routing table every 30 seconds.

    D. RIPv2 multicasts the full routing table every 60 seconds.

288. Which metric does RIPv2 use to calculate routes?

    A. Delay

    B. Bandwidth

    C. Hop count

    D. Bandwidth and delay

289. Which multicast address does RIPv2 use for advertising routes?

    A. 224.0.0.5

    B. 224.0.0.9

    C. 224.0.0.6

    D. 224.0.0.2

290. When RIP is configured on a router, what must be configured to allow for classless routing?

    A. `Router(config)#ip classless`

    B. `Router(config)#router rip v2`

    C. `Router(config-router)#ip classless`

    D. `Router(config-router)#version 2`

291. You need to configure the advertisement of the network 192.168.1.0/24 for RIPv2. Which command will achieve this?

    A. `Router(config-router)#network 192.168.1.0`

    B. `Router(config-router)#network 192.168.1.0 0.0.0.255`

    C. `Router(config-router)#network 192.168.1.0/24`

    D. `Router(config-router)#network 192.168.1.0 255.255.255.0`

292. Which command will allow you to see the next advertisement interval for RIPv2?

    A. `Router#show ip protocols`

    B. `Router#show ip rip database`

    C.   `Router#show ip rip`

    D.   `Router#show ip interface`

293. Which command will allow you to inspect RIPv2 calculations for routes discovered?

    A.   `Router#show ip protocols rip`

    B.   `Router#show ip rip database`

    C.   `Router#show ip interface`

    D.   `Router#show ip rip topology`

294. You have RIPv2 configured on an Internet-facing router. Which command will propagate the default route to all other RIPv2 routers?

    A.   `Router(config-router)#network 0.0.0.0`

    B.   `Router(config-router)#default-route advertise`

    C.   `Router(config-router)#network 0.0.0.0 default`

    D.   `Router(config-router)#default-information originate`

295. Which command will allow you to inspect RIPv2 advertisements?

    A.   `Router#show ip protocols`

    B.   `Router#debug rip`

    C.   `Router#show ip rip`

    D.   `Router#debug ip rip`

296. You need to advertise the routes of 192.168.1.0/24, 192.168.2.0/24, and 192.168.3.0/24. Which configuration will achieve this?

    A.   `Router(config-router)#network 192.168.0.0`

    B.   `Router(config-router)#network 192.168.1.0`
         `Router(config-router)#network 192.168.2.0`
         `Router(config-router)#network 192.168.3.0`

    C.   `Router(config-router)#network 192.168.0.0/16`

    D.   `Router(config-router)#network 192.168.0.0 0.0.255.255`

297. You have RIPv2 configured on an Internet-facing router. Which command will suppress RIPv2 advertisements on the interface link?

    A.   `Router(config-if)#ip rip passive-interface`

    B.   `Router(config-if)#rip passive-interface`

    C.   `Router(config-router)#passive-interface serial 0/0`

    D.   `Router(config-if)#ip rip suppress-advertisement`

298. What is the default invalid timer for RIPv2?

    A.   60 seconds

    B.   90 seconds

    C.   180 seconds

    D.   240 seconds

299. Which is a problem with using RIPv2 in a network?

    A. Complex configuration

    B. Slow convergence

    C. The use of broadcasts

    D. Routing support for classless networks

300. Which technique is used to stop routing loops with RIPv2?

    A. Split horizons

    B. Advertisement intervals

    C. Zoning

    D. Invalid timers

301. Which algorithm does RIPv2 use to calculate routes?

    A. Shortest Path First

    B. Dijkstra

    C. Bellman-Ford

    D. DUAL

302. Which command will need to be configured for support of discontinuous networks?

    A. `Router(config-router)#network discontiguous`

    B. `Router(config)#network discontiguous`

    C. `Router(config)#no auto-summary`

    D. `Router(config-router)#no auto-summary`

303. Which command configures RIPv2 on a router and advertises a network of 192.168.20.0/24?

    A.
```
Router(config)#ip router ripv2
Router(config-router)#network 192.168.20.0
```

    B.
```
Router(config)#router rip
Router(config-router)#version 2
Router(config-router)#network 192.168.20.0
```

    C.
```
Router(config)#router rip
Router(config-router)#version 2
Router(config-router)#network 192.168.20.0 0.0.0.255
```

    D.
```
Router(config)#ip router rip
Router(config-router)#version 2
Router(config-router)#network 192.168.20.0 0.0.0.255
```

304. What is the purpose of the RIPv2 holddown timer?

    A. Holddown timers allow for time between when a route becomes invalid and it is flushed from the routing table.

    B. Holddown timers allow for time between when a route has become unreachable and when it can be updated again.

    C. Holddown timers define the time when a route becomes invalid.

    D. Holddown timers define the time when a valid route is present in the routing table.

305. In the following exhibit, a packet from network 192.168.1.0/24 is destined for 192.168.4.0/24. The route the packet will take will be Router A to Router B, determined by RIPv2. However, the bandwidth is only 64 Kb/s. How can you force packets to travel over the 1.544 Mb/s links?

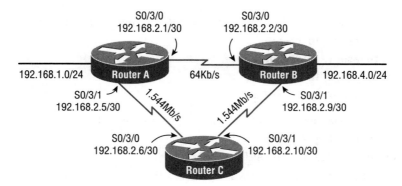

```
RouterA#sh ip route
[output cut]
     192.168.1.0/24 is variably subnetted, 2 subnets, 2 masks
C       192.168.1.0/24 is directly connected, GigabitEthernet0/0
L       192.168.1.1/32 is directly connected, GigabitEthernet0/0
     192.168.2.0/24 is variably subnetted, 5 subnets, 2 masks
C       192.168.2.0/30 is directly connected, Serial0/3/0
L       192.168.2.1/32 is directly connected, Serial0/3/0
C       192.168.2.4/30 is directly connected, Serial0/3/1
L       192.168.2.5/32 is directly connected, Serial0/3/1
R       192.168.2.8/30 [120/1] via 192.168.2.6, 00:00:25, Serial0/3/1
R       192.168.4.0/24 [120/1] via 192.168.2.2, 00:00:22, Serial0/3/0
RouterA#
```

    A. `RouterA(config-router)#passive interface serial 0/3/0`
        `RouterB(config-router)#passive interface serial 0/3/0`

    B. `RouterA(config)#ip route 192.168.4.0 255.255.255.0 serial 0/3/1`
        `RouterB(config)#ip route 192.168.1.0 255.255.255.0 serial 0/3/1`

    C. `RouterA(config-router)#cost 2 serial 0/3/0`
        `RouterB(config-router)#cost 2 serial 0/3/0`

    D. `RouterA(config-if)#metric 2 serial 0/3/0`
        `RouterB(config-if)#metric 2 serial 0/3/0`

306. What is the default number of equal-cost routes RIPv2 will load balance?

A. 2 routes

B. 4 routes

C. 8 routes

D. 16 routes

307. Which protocol will support IPv6 for RIP?

A. RIPv1

B. RIPv2

C. RIPv6

D. RIPng

308. Which command will display which routes the RIPv2 router is advertising?

A. Router#show ip route

B. Router#show ip rip database

C. Router#show ip rip

D. Router#show ip interface

309. How would you configure a router to use split horizons for RIPv2?

A. Router(config)#ip rip split-horizon

B. Router(config-if)#ip split-horizon

C. Router(config-router)#ip split-horizon

D. Router(config-router)#rip split-horizon

310. In the following exhibit, when will a route be removed from the routing table for RIPv2?

```
RouterA#show ip protocols
Routing Protocol is "rip"
Sending updates every 30 seconds, next due in 12 seconds
Invalid after 180 seconds, hold down 180, flushed after 240
Outgoing update filter list for all interfaces is not set
Incoming update filter list for all interfaces is not set
Redistributing: rip
[Output Cut]
  Routing Information Sources:
    Gateway         Distance      Last Update
    192.168.2.6          120      00:00:25
    192.168.2.2          120      00:00:18
Distance: (default is 120)
```

A. 30 seconds

B. 180 seconds

C. 360 seconds

D. 240 seconds

311. Which command will allow you to check basic connectivity at layer 3?

A. Router#show ip route

B. Router#ping 192.168.4.1

C. Router#pathping 192.168.4.1

D. Router#ip ping 192.168.4.1

312. Which command will allow you to see the path on which a packet gets routed to its destination?

   A.   `Router#show ip route`

   B.   `Router#tracert 192.168.7.56`

   C.   `Router#pathping 192.168.7.56`

   D.   `Router#traceroute 192.168.7.56`

313. You perform a ping to a host on the network. However, the first packet is dropped. Why did the first packet drop?

   A.   The local router dropped the first packet.

   B.   The routing table was updating.

   C.   The ARP request timed out the ping packet.

   D.   The remote router dropped the first packet.

314. Which command on Windows will allow you to verify your IP address, subnet mask, default gateway, and MAC address?

   A.   `C:\>ipconfig`

   B.   `C:\>ipstatus`

   C.   `C:\>ipconfig /all`

   D.   `C:\>hostname`

315. Which command on Windows will allow you to verify the path a packet gets routed through on the network?

   A.   `C:\>tracert 198.78.34.2`

   B.   `C:\>ping 198.78.34.2`

   C.   `C:\>traceroute 198.78.34.2`

   D.   `C:\>route print`

316. You ping from a router to another router and receive back ! ! ! ! !. What does this mean?

   A.   All packets have been dropped.

   B.   All packets are successfully acknowledged.

   C.   There is congestion in the path.

   D.   The packets were received, but after the ICMP timeout.

317. You want to ping a router on your network from interface Serial 0/0 and not the path in the routing table. How can you achieve this?

   A.   This cannot be done; packets cannot disregard the routing table.

   B.   Enter the interface in configuration mode, and ping the remote router.

   C.   Enter extended ping, and specify the exit interface.

   D.   Configure a temporary route for the router exiting the interface.

318. You perform a traceroute to a destination network and receive back several lines of output. On the end of each line are three parameters such as
`1 192.168.1.1 20 msec 34 msec 67 msec`. What do they mean?

   A. They are the three response times of each ICMP request.

   B. They are the minimum, maximum, and average of the ICMP query.

   C. They are the minimum, average, and maximum of the ICMP query.

   D. They are the maximum, average, and minimum of the ICMP query.

319. You need to make a Telnet connection to a remote router from a router you are configuring. Which command will allow you to do this?

   A. `Router#198.56.33.3`

   B. `Router#connect 198.56.33.3`

   C. `Router#remote 198.56.33.3`

   D. `Router#vty 198.56.33.3`

320. An administrator calls you and states that they believe an interface is down on a router you maintain. Which command will show only the interface, the IP address configured, and the status of the interface?

   A. `Router#show ip interface`

   B. `Router#show interface`

   C. `Router#show ip interface brief`

   D. `Router#show interface brief`

321. You need to ping an IPv6 address of 2001:db8:3:4::2. Which command will achieve this?

   A. `Router#ping 2001:db8:3:4::2`

   B. `Router#ipv6 ping 2001:db8:3:4::2`

   C. `Router#pingv6 2001:db8:3:4::2`

   D. `Router#ping6 2001:db8:3:4::2`

322. Which IPv6 command will verify that you have received a Router Advertisement message from a local router?

   A. `Router#show ipv6 neighbors`

   B. `Router#show ipv6 cache`

   C. `Router#show ipv6 ra`

   D. `Router#show neighbors`

Chapter 4

WAN Technologies (Domain 4)

THE CCNA EXAM TOPICS COVERED IN THIS PRACTICE TEST INCLUDE THE FOLLOWING:

✓ **4.0 WAN Technologies (ICND2)**

- 4.1 Configure and verify PPP and MLPPP on WAN interfaces using local authentication (ICND2)

- 4.2 Configure, verify, and troubleshoot PPPoE client-side interfaces using local authentication (ICND2)

- 4.3 Configure, verify, and troubleshoot GRE tunnel connectivity (ICND2)

- 4.4 Describe WAN topology options (ICND2)

  - 4.4a Point-to-point (ICND2)

  - 4.4b Hub and spoke (ICND2)

  - 4.4c Full mesh (ICND2)

  - 4.4d Single vs. dual-homed (ICND2)

- 4.5 Describe WAN access connectivity options (ICND2)

  - 4.5a MPLS (ICND2)

  - 4.5b Metro Ethernet (ICND2)

  - 4.5c Broadband PPPoE (ICND2)

  - 4.5d Internet VPN (DMVPN, site-to-site VPN, client VPN) (ICND2)

- 4.6 Configure and verify single-homed branch connectivity using eBGP IPv4 (limited to peering and route advertisement using Network command only) (ICND2)

- 4.7 Describe basic QoS concepts (ICND2)

  - 4.7a Marking (ICND2)

  - 4.7b Device trust (ICND2)

  - 4.7c Prioritization (ICND2)

  - 4.7c(i) Voice (ICND2)

  - 4.7c(ii) Video (ICND2)

  - 4.7c(iii) Data (ICND2)

  - 4.7d Shaping (ICND2)

  - 4.7e Policing (ICND2)

  - 4.7f Congestion management (ICND2)

1. Which is the default encapsulation on a serial connection for Cisco?

   A. MPLS

   B. HDLC

   C. PPP

   D. PPPoE

2. You are connecting a Cisco router to a leased line serial connection. The other side of the connection has non-Cisco equipment. Which protocol should you choose for compatibility?

   A. HDLC

   B. PPP

   C. PPPoE

   D. X.25

3. Which sub-protocol inside of the PPP suite is responsible for tagging layer 3 protocols so that multiple protocols can be used over a PPP connection?

   A. MPLS

   B. NCP

   C. LCP

   D. PCP

4. Which command will configure PPP on a serial interface?

   A. `Router(config-if)#encapsulation ppp`

   B. `Router(config-if)#protocol ppp`

   C. `Router(config-if)#ppp enable`

   D. `Router(config-if)#ppp protocol`

5. Which sub-protocol inside of the PPP suite is responsible for authentication?

   A. MPLS

   B. NCP

   C. LCP

   D. ACP

6. Which encapsulation protocol is used with PPP to transmit data over serial links?

   A. PPPoE

   B. HDLC

   C. MPLS

   D. X.25

7. Which authentication method used with PPP uses a nonce (random number) to hash the password and prevent replay attacks?

   A. PAP

   B. PSAP

   C. CHAP

   D. NTLM

8. Which sub-protocol inside of the PPP suite facilitates multilink connections?

   A. MPLS

   B. NCP

   C. LCP

   D. ACP

9. Which is a benefit of using MLPPP?

   A. Simplified layer 3 configuration

   B. Does not require routing protocols

   C. Does not require authentication protocols

   D. Provides end-to-end encryption

10. Which configuration will create the multilink interface for an MLPPP connection to an adjoining router?

   A.
```
RouterA(config)#interface multilink 1
RouterA(config-if)#encapsulation ppp
RouterA(config-if)#ppp multilink
RouterA(config-if)#ip address 192.168.1.1 255.255.255.0
RouterA(config-if)#ppp multilink group 1
```

   B.
```
RouterA(config)#interface multilink 1
RouterA(config-if)#ppp multilink
RouterA(config-if)#ip address 192.168.1.1 255.255.255.0
```

   C.
```
RouterA(config)#interface multilink 1
RouterA(config-if)#encapsulation ppp multilink
```

   D.
```
RouterA(config)#interface multilink 1
RouterA(config-if)#ip address 192.168.1.1 255.255.255.0
RouterA(config-if)#ppp multilink group 1
```

11. Which command will allow verification of the active links in a multilink connection?

   A. `Router#show multilink`

   B. `Router#show ppp multilink`

   C. `Router#show ppp`

   D. `Router#show run`

12. You need to set up PPP authentication for RouterA. The adjoining router is named RouterB, and both routers will have a matching password of *cisco*. Which commands will achieve this?

- **A.** RouterA(config)#username RouterA password cisco
  RouterA(config)#interface serial 0/1/0
  RouterA(config-if)#ppp authentication chap pap

- **B.** RouterA(config)#username RouterB password cisco
  RouterA(config)#interface serial 0/1/0
  RouterA(config-if)#ppp authentication chap pap

- **C.** RouterA(config)#username RouterA cisco
  RouterA(config)#interface serial 0/1/0
  RouterA(config-if)#ppp authentication chap pap

- **D.** RouterA(config)#username RouterA password cisco
  RouterA(config)#interface serial 0/1/0
  RouterA(config-if)#authentication chap pap

13. Which command will allow you to diagnose PPP authentication failures?

- **A.** Router#debug ppp authentication
- **B.** Router#debug ppp
- **C.** Router#show interface
- **D.** Router#debug ppp events

14. Which command will allow you to see the authentication protocol that PPP has authenticated with on the adjoining router?

- **A.** RouterA#show interface
- **B.** RouterA#show ppp all
- **C.** RouterA#debug ppp
- **D.** RouterA#show running-configuration

15. In the following exhibit, what does the line LCP closed mean?

```
RouterA#show interface s0/3/0
Serial0/0 is up, line protocol is down
  Hardware is PowerQUICC Serial
  Internet address is 10.0.1.1/24
  MTU 1500 bytes, BW 1544 Kbit, DLY 20000 usec,
  reliability 233/255, txload 1/255, rxload 1/255
  Encapsulation PPP, loopback not set
  Keepalive set (10 sec)
  LCP Closed
  Closed: IPCP, CDPCP
```

- **A.** The LCP process has completed.
- **B.** The router does not have an IP address configured.
- **C.** The serial line is disconnected.
- **D.** The LCP process has not completed.

16. Which command will configure PPP to support CHAP first and PAP if CHAP is not supported?

A. Router(config-if)#authentication pap chap

B. Router(config-if)#ppp authentication chap pap

C. Router(config-if)#authentication chap pap

D. Router(config-if)#ppp authentication chap

17. In the following exhibit, Router A is configured for PPP multilink to Router B. However, the multilink is not functioning properly. What is the problem?

```
RouterA#show run
[output cut]
interface Multilink1
 encapsulation ppp
 ppp multilink
 ip address 192.168.1.1 255.255.255.0
 ppp multilink group 1
!
interface Serial0/3/0
no ip address
encapsulation ppp
ppp multilink
multilink-group 1
!
interface Serial0/3/1
no ip address
encapsulation ppp
ppp multilink
multilink-group 2
[output cut]
```

A. The serial interfaces are not configured with an IP address.

B. The serial interfaces should not be configured with the encapsulation.

C. All links in the multicast bundle must have the same multilink group.

D. The multilink group should not be configured on the multilink interface.

18. In the following exhibit, Router A will not form a PPP connection with Router B. What is the problem?

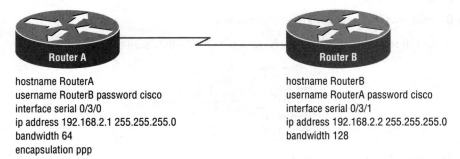

hostname RouterA
username RouterB password cisco
interface serial 0/3/0
ip address 192.168.2.1 255.255.255.0
bandwidth 64
encapsulation ppp

hostname RouterB
username RouterA password cisco
interface serial 0/3/1
ip address 192.168.2.2 255.255.255.0
bandwidth 128

A. The username on Router A should match Router A's hostname and the username on Router B should match Router B's hostname.

B. The bandwidth should be configured the same on both routers.

    C. The interfaces on Router A and Router B should be matching for authentication purposes.

    D. The encapsulation on both routers should be configured as PPP.

19. You have set up a PPP multilink connection between two routers. You want to add authentication. Where should you configure the authentication?

    A. On the multilink interface

    B. On the first serial interface in the bundle

    C. On both serial interfaces in the bundle

    D. On the multilink group that joins the bundle

20. In the following exhibit, Router A will not form a PPP connection with Router B. What is the problem?

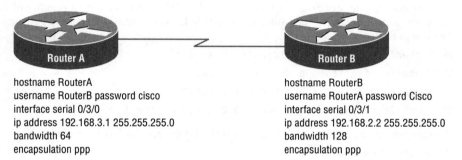

```
hostname RouterA
username RouterB password cisco
interface serial 0/3/0
ip address 192.168.3.1 255.255.255.0
bandwidth 64
encapsulation ppp
```

```
hostname RouterB
username RouterA password Cisco
interface serial 0/3/1
ip address 192.168.2.2 255.255.255.0
bandwidth 128
encapsulation ppp
```

    A. The IP addresses on Router A and Router B are not in the same subnet.

    B. The bandwidth should be configured the same on both routers.

    C. The username on Router A should match Router A's hostname and the username on Router B should match Router B's hostname.

    D. The passwords on both routers do not match.

21. What encapsulation is used with DSL connections?

    A. PPPoE

    B. HDLC

    C. MPLS

    D. PPP

22. What is the maximum transmission unit that should be set for PPPoE?

    A. 1,400

    B. 1,492

    C. 1,500

    D. 1,548

23. In the following exhibit, which router interface gets configured with an IP address?

Customer router   ISP router

A. Router A Interface G0/1

B. Router A Interface G0/2

C. Router B Interface G0/2

D. Router A Interface G0/2 and Router B Interface G0/2

24. You are configuring PPPoE and have configured a dialer interface with a number of 1. Interface Gi0/1 connected the router to the ISP. Which command will set the gateway of last resort to the ISP?

A. `Router(config)#ip default-gateway gi 0/1`

B. `Router(config-if)#ppp default-gateway`

C. `Router(config)#ip route 0.0.0.0 0.0.0.0 gi 0/1`

D. `Router(config)#ip route 0.0.0.0 0.0.0.0 dialer 1`

25. Which command can be used to diagnose if the PPPoE session has been established?

A. `Router#show ppp`

B. `Router#show pppoe users`

C. `Router#show pppoe session`

D. `Router#show running-configuration`

26. Which protocol is responsible in configuring the dialer interface for PPPoE with an IP address?

A. LCP

B. PPP

C. IPCP

D. CHAP

27. In the following exhibit, which interface is configured with the PPP authentication protocol for PPPoE?

Customer router   ISP router

A. Interface Dialer1 (customer router)

B. Interface G0/2 (customer router)

C. Interface G0/2 (ISP router)

D. Interface G0/2 (both customer and ISP router)

28. In the following exhibit, Router A cannot establish a PPPoE session with Router B. What is the problem?

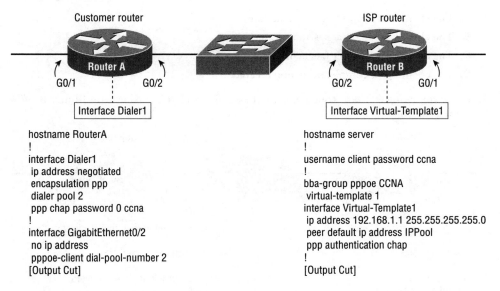

Customer router

Router A

G0/1   G0/2

Interface Dialer1

ISP router

Router B

G0/2   G0/1

Interface Virtual-Template1

```
hostname RouterA
!
interface Dialer1
 ip address negotiated
 encapsulation ppp
 dialer pool 2
 ppp chap password 0 ccna
!
interface GigabitEthernet0/2
 no ip address
 pppoe-client dial-pool-number 2
[Output Cut]
```

```
hostname server
!
username client password ccna
!
bba-group pppoe CCNA
 virtual-template 1
interface Virtual-Template1
 ip address 192.168.1.1 255.255.255.0
 peer default ip address IPPool
 ppp authentication chap
!
[Output Cut]
```

A. Router A does not have the correct hostname configured.

B. Router B does not have the correct hostname configured.

C. The interface Dialer1 must match the dialer pool number.

D. The passwords do not match on Router A and Router B.

29. Which command will allow you to see how many PPPoE sessions are terminated on the aggregation router (ISP router)?

A. `Router#show pppoe states`

B. `Router#show pppoe users`

C. `Router#show pppoe summary`

D. `Router#show running-configuration`

30. In the following exhibit, you have entered the command show pppoe sessions on the aggregation router. What does a state of PTA mean?

```
RouterA#show pppoe session
[Output Cut]
Uniq ID        PPPoE    RemMAC          Port    VT    VA          State
               SID      LocMAC                        VA-st       Type
    1           1       0012.2345.ee23  Fa0/1   1     Vi1.1       PTA
                        0013.3454.e2e2                UP
    2           2       0012.2567.e2e3  Fa0/1   1     Vi1.2       PTA
                        0014.3634.4e46                UP
RouterA#
```

A. The client is attempting to authenticate.

B. The client has a partial session created.

C. The aggregation router has denied the session.

D. The client has a completed session created.

31. In the following exhibit, Router A cannot establish a PPPoE session with Router B. What is the problem?

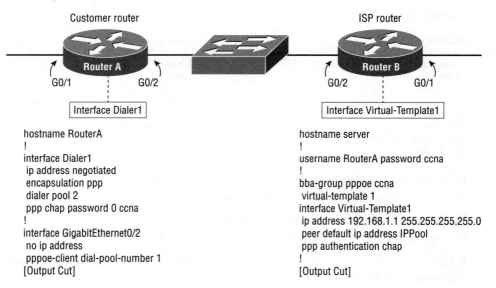

Customer router   ISP router

Router A   Router B

G0/1   G0/2   G0/2   G0/1

Interface Dialer1   Interface Virtual-Template1

hostname RouterA   hostname server
!   !
interface Dialer1   username RouterA password ccna
 ip address negotiated   !
 encapsulation ppp   bba-group pppoe ccna
 dialer pool 2   virtual-template 1
 ppp chap password 0 ccna   interface Virtual-Template1
!   ip address 192.168.1.1 255.255.255.255.0
interface GigabitEthernet0/2   peer default ip address IPPool
 no ip address   ppp authentication chap
 pppoe-client dial-pool-number 1   !
[Output Cut]   [Output Cut]

A. Router B does not have the correct hostname configured.

B. The interface Dialer1 must match the dialer pool number.

C. The dialer pool must match the dialer pool number.

D. The passwords do not match on Router A and Router B.

32. Which command creates an IP pool for PPPoE on the aggregation router?

    A. `Router(config)#ip pool poolname 192.168.1.0 255.255.255.0`

    B. `Router(config)#ip local pool poolname 192.168.1.2 192.168.1.254`

    C. `Router(config)#ip pool poolname 192.168.1.2 192.168.1.254`

    D. `Router(config)#ip local pool poolname 192.168.1.0`

33. In the following exhibit, Router A cannot establish a PPPoE session with Router B. What is the problem?

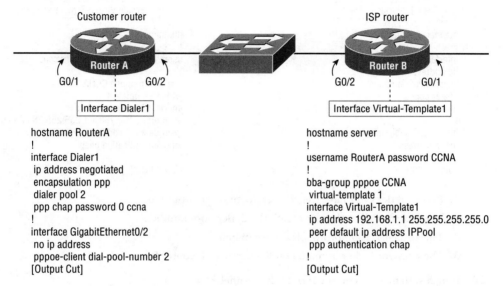

    A. Router B does not have the correct hostname configured.

    B. The interface dialer1 must match the dialer pool number.

    C. The authentication protocols do not match.

    D. The passwords do not match on Router A and Router B.

34. Which is a disadvantage of PPPoE?

    A. Higher level of security

    B. Smaller MTU per packet

    C. Single point of aggregation for bandwidth

    D. Lower speeds than leased lines

35. In the following exhibit, Router A cannot establish a PPPoE session with Router B. What is the problem?

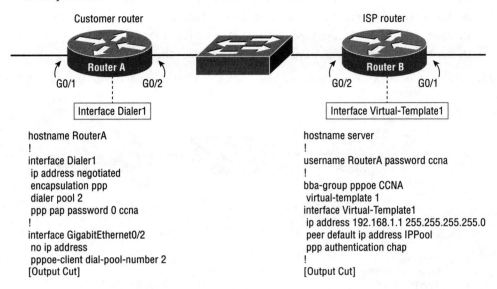

A. Router B does not have the correct hostname configured.

B. The interface dialer1 must match the dialer pool number.

C. The authentication protocols do not match.

D. The passwords do not match on Router A and Router B.

36. Which statement is correct about GRE tunnels?

A. GRE uses IPSec security.

B. GRE uses a protocol of 57.

C. GRE provides per-packet authentication.

D. GRE provides packet-in-packet encapsulation.

37. Which tunnel protocol is a Cisco proprietary protocol?

A. GRE

B. PPP

C. IPSec

D. SSL

38. Which layer 3 protocol does GRE use?

A. Protocol 4

B. Protocol 43

C. Protocol 47

D. Protocol 57

39. In the following exhibit, you are configuring a GRE tunnel. What is wrong with this configuration?

```
Router A#show run                               Router B#show run
interface serial0/0/1                           interface serial0/0/1
 ip address 198.34.54.2 255.255.255.0            ip address 198.44.34.5 255.255.255.0
!                                               !
interface tunnel0                               interface tunnel0
 ip address 192.168.2.1 255.255.255.0            ip address 192.168.2.2 255.255.255.0
 tunnel mode gre ip                              tunnel mode gre ip
 tunnel source serial0/0/1                       tunnel source serial0/0/1
 tunnel destination 198.44.34.5                  tunnel destination 198.34.54.2
 interface GigbitEthernet 0/1                    interface GigbitEthernet 0/1
 ip address 192.168.2.1                          ip address 192.168.2.1
!                                               !
[Output Cut]                                    [Output Cut]
```

A. Nothing is wrong with the configuration.

B. The destination on Router A of the tunnel is incorrect.

C. The network is un-routable.

D. The serial interfaces are on different networks.

40. In the following exhibit, you are configuring a GRE tunnel and need to configure a route statement on Router A. Which is the correct route statement?

```
Router A#show run                               Router B#show run
interface serial0/0/1                           interface serial0/0/1
 ip address 198.34.54.2 255.255.255.0            ip address 198.44.34.5 255.255.255.0
!                                               !
interface tunnel0                               interface tunnel0
 ip address 192.168.2.1 255.255.255.0            ip address 192.168.2.2 255.255.255.0
 tunnel mode gre ip                              tunnel mode gre ip
 tunnel source serial0/0/1                       tunnel source serial0/0/1
 tunnel destination 198.44.34.5                  tunnel destination 198.34.54.2
 interface GigbitEthernet 0/1                    interface GigbitEthernet 0/1
 ip address 192.168.2.1                          ip address 192.168.2.1
!                                               !
[Output Cut]                                    [Output Cut]
```

A. `Router(config)#ip route 192.168.3.0 255.255.255.0 tunnel 0`

B. `Router(config)#ip route 192.168.2.0 255.255.255.0 tunnel 0`

C. `Router(config)#ip route 192.168.3.0 255.255.255.0 serial 0/0/1`

D. `Router(config)#ip route 192.168.3.0 255.255.255.0 192.168.2.2`

41. What is the MTU of a Generic Router Encapsulation (GRE) tunnel?

A. MTU 1476

B. MTU 1492

C. MTU 1500

D. MTU 1528

42. Which command will help you verify the source and destination of a GRE tunnel?

A. `Router#show ip tunnel 0`

B. `Router#show interface tunnel 0`

C. `Router#show ip gre`

D. `Router#show ip route`

43. In the following exhibit, If you do a traceroute on Router A to a destination of 192.168.3.50, how many hops will show?

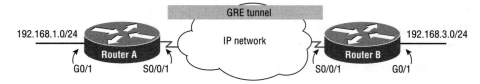

```
Router A#show run                              Router B#show run
interface serial0/0/1                          interface serial0/0/1
  ip address 198.34.54.2 255.255.255.0           ip address 198.44.34.5 255.255.255.0
!                                              !
interface tunnel0                              interface tunnel0
  ip address 192.168.2.1 255.255.255.252         ip address 192.168.2.2 255.255.255.252
  tunnel mode gre ip                             tunnel mode gre ip
  tunnel source serial0/0/1                      tunnel source serial0/0/1
  tunnel destination 198.44.34.5                 tunnel destination 198.34.54.2
interface GigbitEthernet 0/1                   interface GigbitEthernet 0/1
  ip address 192.168.2.1                         ip address 192.168.2.1
!                                              !
ip route 192.168.3.0 255.255.255.0 192.168.2.2 ip route 192.168.1.0 255.255.255.0 192.168.2.1
[Output Cut]                                   [Output Cut]
```

A. One hop

B. Two hops

C. Four hops

D. Zero hops

44. Refer to the following exhibit. You are configuring a GRE tunnel. However, you cannot ping from Router A to 192.168.3.1. What is the problem?

```
Router A#show run                                    Router B#show run
interface serial0/0/1                                interface serial0/0/2
 ip address 198.34.54.45 255.255.255.0                ip address 198.44.34.5 255.255.255.0
!                                                    !
interface tunnel1                                    interface tunnel0
 ip address 192.168.2.45 255.255.255.252              ip address 192.168.2.46 255.255.255.252
 tunnel mode gre ip                                   tunnel mode gre ip
 tunnel source serial0/0/1                            tunnel source serial0/0/2
 tunnel destination 198.44.34.5                       tunnel destination 198.34.54.2
 interface GigbitEthernet 0/1                         interface GigbitEthernet 0/1
 ip address 192.168.2.1                               ip address 192.168.2.1
!                                                    !
ip route 192.168.3.0 255.255.255.0 198.44.34.5       ip route 192.168.1.0 255.255.255.0 198.34.54.45
[Output Cut]                                         [Output Cut]
```

A. The tunnel numbers do not match.

B. The destination on Router A of the tunnel is incorrect.

C. The routes are wrong.

D. The serial interfaces do not match.

45. Which protocol helps resolve and direct traffic for DMVPN connections?

A. HSRP

B. NHRP

C. ARP

D. GRE

46. What is the default keepalive for serial interfaces?

A. 1 second

B. 5 seconds

C. 10 seconds

D. 60 seconds

47. Which technology is a point-to-point dedicated line between two private facilities?

A. DMVPN

B. T1 leased line

C. Wireless WAN

D. VPN

48. Refer to the following exhibit. You have configured a point-to-point dedicated line between two locations. However, you cannot ping between the two routers. What is the problem?

Network A
192.168.0.0/24

Network B
192.168.2.0/24

Router A

Router B

FaO/1
192.168.0.1/24

S0/0
192.168.1.21/30

S0/1
192.168.1.22/30

FaO/1
192.168.2.1/24

RouterA#show interfaces serial 0/0
Serial0/0 is up, line protocol is down (disabled)
  Hardware is HD64570
  Internet address is 192.168.1.21/30
  MTU 1500 bytes, BW 1544 Kbit, DLY 20000 usec,
    reliability 255/255, txload 1/255, rxload 1/255
  Encapsulation HDLC, loopback not set, keepalive set (10 sec)
[Output Cut]
RouterA#

RouterB#show interfaces serial 0/1
Serial0/1 is up, line protocol is down (disabled)
  Hardware is HD64570
  Internet address is 192.168.1.22/30
  MTU 1500 bytes, BW 1544 Kbit, DLY 20000 usec,
    reliability 255/255, txload 1/255, rxload 1/255
  Encapsulation PPP, loopback not set, keepalive set (10 sec)
[Output Cut]
RouterB#

A. The interface is administratively shut down.

B. There is a wiring problem.

C. There is a protocol mismatch.

D. There is an IP mismatch.

49. Which topology will allow for fault tolerance to a single ISP?

A. Single-homed

B. Dual-homed

C. Single multi-homed

D. Dual multi-homed

50. Which topology provides no fault tolerance?

A. Single-homed

B. Dual-homed

C. Single multi-homed

D. Dual multi-homed

51. What is the function of a keepalive on a dedicated line?

A. It keeps the connection alive by transmitting small amounts of data.

B. It sends the clocking information.

C. It helps routers know when a connection no longer functions.

D. It helps identify congestion.

52. Refer to the following exhibit. You have configured a point-to-point dedicated line between two locations. However, you cannot ping between the two routers. What is the problem?

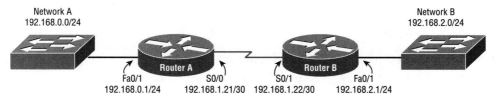

Network A
192.168.0.0/24

Network B
192.168.2.0/24

Router A   Router B

FaO/1   S0/0   S0/1   FaO/1
192.168.0.1/24   192.168.1.21/30   192.168.1.22/30   192.168.2.1/24

```
RouterA#show interfaces serial 0/0
Serial0/0 is up, line protocol is up (connected)
  Hardware is HD64570
  Internet address is 192.168.1.21/30
  MTU 1500 bytes, BW 1544 Kbit, DLY 20000 usec,
    reliability 255/255, txload 1/255, rxload 1/255
  Encapsulation HDLC, loopback not set, keepalive set (10 sec)
[Output Cut]
RouterA#
```

```
RouterB#show interfaces serial 0/1
Serial0/1 is up, line protocol is up (connected)
  Hardware is HD64570
  Internet address is 192.168.1.25/30
  MTU 1500 bytes, BW 1544 Kbit, DLY 20000 usec,
    reliability 255/255, txload 1/255, rxload 1/255
  Encapsulation HDLC, loopback not set, keepalive set (10 sec)
[Output Cut]
RouterB#
```

- **A.** The interface is administratively shut down.
- **B.** There is a wiring problem.
- **C.** There is a protocol mismatch.
- **D.** There is an IP mismatch.

53. Which technology is primarily used as a point-to-point connection?
- **A.** DMVPN
- **B.** MLPPP
- **C.** E-LAN services
- **D.** E-Tree services

54. Which technology provides for a hub-and-spoke design?
- **A.** E-Tree services
- **B.** Wireless WAN
- **C.** E-Line services
- **D.** E-LAN services

55. Which technology provides for a dedicated point-to-point design?
- **A.** E-Tree services
- **B.** Wireless WAN
- **C.** E-Line services
- **D.** E-LAN services

56. Which technology provides for a mesh design?

    A. E-Tree services

    B. Wireless WAN

    C. E-Line services

    D. E-LAN services

57. Which is a typical use case for hub-and-spoke WAN design?

    A. Connections for an enterprise spread over a metropolitan area

    B. Connections for an Internet service provider to its customers

    C. Connections between two or more corporate locations

    D. Connection internally inside of a service provider's network

58. In the following exhibit, you have configured a serial connection. What is the most likely problem?

```
RouterA#show interfaces serial 0/3/0
Serial0/3/0 is down, line protocol is down (disabled)
  Hardware is HD64570
  Internet address is 192.168.1.21/30
  MTU 1500 bytes, BW 1544 Kbit, DLY 20000 usec,
      reliability 0/255, txload 1/255, rxload 1/255
  Encapsulation HDLC, loopback not set, keepalive set (10 sec)
[Output Cut]
RouterA#
```

    A. The interface is administratively shut down.

    B. There is a wiring problem.

    C. There is a protocol mismatch.

    D. There is an IP mismatch.

59. You are configuring a serial interface for a point-to-point connection. You want to verify that clocking has been detected. Which command will help you verify clocking?

    A. `Router#show controllers serial 0/0`

    B. `Router#show clocking serial 0/0`

    C. `Router#show interface serial 0/0`

    D. `Router#show ip protocols`

60. In a DS1 serial connection, how many DS0 channels exist?

    A. 12 DS0 channels

    B. 23 DS0 channels

    C. 24 DS0 channels

    D. 32 DS0 channels

61. PPPoE is an example of which topology?

    A. Point-to-point

    B. Hub-and-spoke

    C. Full-mesh

    D. Dual-homed

62. You are configuring a serial point-to-point connection between two routers and need to provide clocking. Which command will configure the router as a DCE device?

    A. `Router(config-if)#mode dce`

    B. `Router(config-if)#dce clocking`

    C. `Router(config-if)#clock-rate 64000`

    D. `Router(config-if)#clock 64000`

63. In a leased line point-to-point configuration, what is responsible for sending the clocking for data alignment?

    A. Both of the customer's routers

    B. A single side of the customer's routers

    C. The CSU/DSU

    D. The Telco provider network

64. MLPPP is an example of which topology?

    A. Single-homed

    B. Dual-homed

    C. Single multi-homed

    D. Dual multi-homed

65. DMVPN is an example of which topology?

    A. Point-to-point

    B. Hub-and-spoke

    C. Full-mesh

    D. Dual-homed

66. Why would you use Multiprotocol Label Switching (MPLS) as a connectivity option?

    A. You need support for multicast packets.

    B. You need support for both IPv4 and IPv6 packets.

    C. You need a high amount of bandwidth.

    D. You require encryption.

67. What does the term *customer edge* describe with respect to MPLS?

    A. The provider's router closest to the customer

    B. The router in the provider's network that switches customer packets

    C. The customer's router that sits at the edge of the customer's network

    D. The path that the packet travels in an MPLS network

68. What is the field in the layer 3 header that helps MPLS support quality of service?

A. QoS

B. DSCP

C. 802.1p

D. VOIP

69. What does the term *provider edge* describe with respect to MPLS?

A. The provider's router closest to the customer edge router

B. The router in the provider's network that switches customer packets

C. The customer's router that sits at the edge of the customer's network

D. The path that the packet travels in an MPLS network

70. Which WAN option provides a layer 2 connection between sites?

A. Wireless WAN

B. GRE tunnels

C. MPLS

D. Metro Ethernet

71. What is MPLS referred to as?

A. Layer 2 protocol

B. Layer 2.5 protocol

C. Layer 3 protocol

D. Layer 1 protocol

72. Which benefit of using a secure VPN allows verification that a packet was not tampered with in transit?

A. Authentication

B. Data integrity

C. Anti-replay

D. Confidentiality

73. Which Cisco technology is often used to create VPN tunnels between sites?

A. Catalyst switches

B. Cisco routers

C. Adaptive Security Appliance

D. Policy-based routing

74. You have several remote workers who enter patient information and require a high level of security. Which technology would best suit the connectivity for these workers?

A. GRE tunnels

B. Wireless WAN

C. Client SSL/VPN

D. Site-to-site VPN

75. You have obtained an ADSL circuit at a remote office for central office connectivity. What will you need to configure on the remote office router?

A. Metro Ethernet

B. PPPoE

C. PPP

D. MPLS

76. What is the term used to describe the telephone company's switching office?

A. Demarcation point

B. Network edge

C. Central office

D. Main data frame

77. Which is a correct statement about private WANs?

A. Private WANs have built-in encryption.

B. Private WANs secure by isolation.

C. Private WANs use GRE tunnels.

D. Private WANs use PPPoE for authentication.

78. What is the definition of an Ethernet virtual circuit (EVC)?

A. An EVC defines two endpoints for Metro Ethernet customers.

B. An EVC defines two endpoints for MPLS customers.

C. An EVC defines the path that a PPPoE packet will travel.

D. An EVC defines the path that an MPLS packet will travel.

79. What is the term that defines the access point for the service provider's services?

A. Demarcation point

B. Point of presence

C. Customer edge

D. Network edge

80. When implementing routing protocols such as OSPF with E-LAN Metro Ethernet, which statement is true?

A. All routers in an E-LAN service will become neighbors.

B. All routers in an E-LAN service require a unique network ID.

C. All of the E-LAN service sites require a unique area ID.

D. Only the leaf routers and the root will become neighbors.

81. Which routing protocol do MPLS providers typically use internally in the provider's network?

    A. MP-BGP

    B. EIGRP

    C. OSPF

    D. IS-IS

82. What device connects the remote office DSL modem to the telco's PSTN and the Internet?

    A. DSL access multiplier

    B. DSL concentrator

    C. 5ESS switch

    D. Digital cross-connect System

83. Which protocol does IPSec use to encrypt data packets?

    A. AH

    B. ESP

    C. IKE

    D. ISAKMP

84. What is a benefit of site-to-site IPSec VPNs?

    A. Lower bandwidth requirements

    B. Lower latency

    C. Scalability

    D. Support for multicast

85. You have been asked to recommend a private WAN technology. All of the remote offices have varied physical connectivity paths. Which private WAN technology should you recommend?

    A. MPLS

    B. Metro Ethernet

    C. PPPoE

    D. GRE tunnels

86. Which statement is true about implementing routing protocols such as OSPF with E-Tree Metro Ethernet?

    A. All routers in an E-Tree service will become neighbors.

    B. All routers in an E-Tree service require a unique network ID.

    C. All of the E-Tree service sites require a unique area ID.

    D. Only the leaf routers and the root will become neighbors.

87. Which statement about using MPLS and dynamic routing protocols is true?

   A. CE routers form neighbor relations with other CE routers.

   B. CE routers form neighbor relations with PE routers.

   C. CE routers receive their routing updates with route redistribution from PE routers.

   D. CE routers receive their routing updates with route redistribution from other CE routers.

88. When using MPLS and OSPF, the PE routers function as what?

   A. Autonomous system boundary routers

   B. Super backbone routers

   C. Area border routers

   D. Point-to-multipoint routers

89. Which mechanism does a service provider use for controlling overages on Metro Ethernet services?

   A. ACLs on the SP network

   B. Policing of traffic

   C. Ethernet virtual circuits

   D. Shaping of traffic

90. When working with the MPLS provider on providing QOS, which is a consideration for the customer?

   A. MPLS support of DSCP markings

   B. MPLS support of multiple access link technologies

   C. Redistribution of routing protocols

   D. Internal speed of the customer network

91. Which protocol does IPSec use to check integrity of data packets?

   A. AH

   B. ESP

   C. IKE

   D. ISAKMP

92. When creating GRE tunnels, what is a consideration that can restrict tunnel creation?

   A. The tunnel interface number

   B. ACLs on the firewall

   C. Speed of the tunnel

   D. Number of hops between the source and destination

93. When purchasing a Metro Ethernet connection, which option is generally tied to the monthly reoccurring cost of the connection?

A. IP addresses used to support the service

B. Routing protocols used to support the service

C. The committed information rate on the EVC

D. The use of QOS

94. Which mechanism can a Metro Ethernet customer employ to ensure proper QoS?

A. ACLs on the SP network

B. Policing of traffic

C. Ethernet virtual circuits

D. Shaping of traffic

95. When a customer purchases MPLS and supports EIGRP, which statement is correct?

A. The customer can opt to have the PE provide EIGRP.

B. The customer can configure all of the EIGRP routers to use the same Autonomous System Number (ASN).

C. The customer must configure all of the EIGRP routers to use different Autonomous System Numbers (ASNs).

D. All of the routers must share the super backbone.

96. Which Exterior Gateway Protocol (EGP) is used to route Internet traffic?

A. IS-IS

B. OSPF

C. eBGP

D. iBGP

97. Which statement correctly identifies the differences between iBGP and eBGP?

A. eBGP routers peer with other eBGP routers in the same AS.

B. iBGP routers peer with other iBGP routers in the same AS.

C. An iBGP router advertises prefixes with other iBGP routers in which the router has learned.

D. iBGP connects enterprise networks with ISPs.

98. How are BGP neighbors formed?

A. Via BGP discovery

B. Via BGP hello packets

C. Via static BGP neighbor assignment

D. BGP multicasting

99. Which statement is correct about Exterior Border Gateway Protocol (eBGP)?

   A. eBGP is a very scalable routing protocol.

   B. Any AS number can be used for connecting to the Internet.

   C. eBGP has extremely fast convergence.

   D. eBGP is a link-state protocol.

100. What does eBGP use to determine best path?

   A. Speed

   B. Path attributes

   C. Delay

   D. Reliability

101. Which algorithm is used with eBGP for path selection?

   A. Best path algorithm

   B. Dijkstra algorithm

   C. Bellman-Ford algorithm

   D. Edge disjoint shortest pair algorithm

102. Where is it common to find single-homed eBGP connections?

   A. The link connecting ISPs to larger ISPs

   B. The link between internal ISP structures

   C. The link connecting an enterprise with the ISP

   D. The link providing redundancy for an ISP

103. How are eBGP messages exchanged by peers?

   A. Via multicasts

   B. Via broadcasts

   C. Via TCP/179

   D. Via UDP/179

104. Which statement is correct about prefix advertisements with eBGP?

   A. Private and public address blocks should be advertised with eBGP.

   B. All network addresses, including subnets, should be advertised with eBGP.

   C. Only subnets of address blocks should be advertised with eBGP as they are used in a network.

   D. Only public network address blocks should be advertised with eBGP.

105. What can an ISP employ with eBGP to reduce load on the enterprise router?

   A. Condensed prefix advertisement

   B. Default route advertisement

   C. AS reduction advertisement

   D. Redistribution of eBGP to IGP protocols

106. Which command will start a BGP router process for an AS of 2001?

    A. Router(config)#router bgp 2001

    B. Router(config)#bgp 2001

    C. Router(config)#ip bgp 2001

    D. Router(config)#ip router bgp 2001

107. What is the administrative distance of eBGP?

    A. 20

    B. 40

    C. 90

    D. 200

108. Which command will configure and advertise a network of 120.187.230.0/24 for BGP?

    A. Router(config-router)#network 120.187.230.0/24

    B. Router(config-router)#network 120.187.230.0 255.255.255.0

    C. Router(config-router)#network 120.187.0.0

    D. Router(config-router)#network 120.187.230.0 mask 255.255.255.0

109. Which command will allow you to verify the BGP neighbors the router is peered with?

    A. Router#show ip bgp

    B. Router#show ip bgp summary

    C. Router#show ip bgp neighbors

    D. Router#show ip route

110. Which command will perform a soft reset of BGP for a neighbor?

    A. Router#bgp reset 198.23.45.2

    B. Router#clear ip bgp 198.23.45.2 soft in

    C. Router#clear bgp 198.23.45.2

    D. Router#clear ip bgp 198.23.45.2

111. In the following exhibit, you are configuring Router A to peer with the ISP router. Which command will you configure on Router A to accomplish this task?

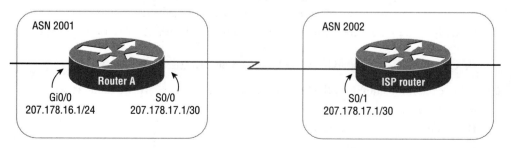

    A. `Router(config-router)#network 207.178.16.0 mask 255.255.255.0`

    B. `Router(config-router)#bgp neighbor 207.178.17.1 remote-as 2001`

    C. `Router(config-router)#bgp neighbor 207.178.17.1 remote-as 2002`

    D. `Router(config-router)#neighbor 207.178.17.1 remote-as 2002`

112. Which command will allow you to verify that you are connected to a BGP peer and can receive data?

    A. `Router#show ip bgp`

    B. `Router#show bgp`

    C. `Router#show tcp brief`

    D. `Router#show ip tcp brief`

113. Which command will allow you to temporarily disable a BGP peer?

    A. `Router(config)#no router bgp 200`

    B. `Router(config-router)#disable neighbor 198.45.32.2`

    C. `Router(config-router)#neighbor 198.45.32.2 shutdown`

    D. `Router(config)#clear ip bgp neighbor 198.45.32.2`

114. You have several /29 blocks of public IPs configured on Router A. You need to advertise the entire /24 block to your ISP with BGP. Which command will allow you to achieve this?

    A. `Router(config-router)#network 194.56.32.0 mask 255.255.255.0`

    B. `Router(config)#ip route 194.56.32.0 255.255.255.0 null0`

    C. `Router(config-router)#network 194.56.32.0`

    D. `Router(config)#ip route 194.56.32.0 255.255.255.0 lo0`

115. Which command will allow you to verify routes line-by-line in a subset of the general route statement?

    A. `Router#show ip route 160.45.23.0 255.255.255.0 longer-prefixes`

    B. `Router#show ip route 160.45.23.0 255.255.255.0`

    C. `Router#show ip route bgp`

    D. `Router#show ip route`

116. Which measurement describes the speed of a link?

    A. Bandwidth

    B. Delay

    C. Jitter

    D. Loss

117. Where should QoS marking be performed?

    A. Closest to the source of the traffic

    B. Closest to the Internet router

    C. On every device in the network

    D. On the core router in the network

118. Which measurement describes the time a packet takes from source to destination?

A. Bandwidth

B. Delay

C. Jitter

D. Loss

119. How do routers classify traffic for QoS?

A. Access control lists

B. Layer 2 ASICs

C. Route tables

D. Frame filters

120. Which measurement describes the variation of consecutive packet time from source to destination?

A. Bandwidth

B. Delay

C. Jitter

D. Loss

121. Which is a true statement about the Class of Service field?

A. The Class of Service field is a layer 3 field.

B. The Class of Service field is only present in 802.1Q frames.

C. The Class of Service field is present from end to end of a transmission.

D. The Class of Service field is 6 bits.

122. What is the measurement of packets discarded due to congestion of queues?

A. Bandwidth

B. Delay

C. Jitter

D. Loss

123. Which technology is used to identify and mark applications such as Bittorrent and Netflix for QoS?

A. ACLs

B. Routing tables

C. NBAR2

D. Tail drop

124. Which layer 3 protocol is used for marking packets with QoS?

A. DSCP

B. 802.1Q

    C. CoS

    D. QoE

125. Which is a correct statement about device trust boundary for QoS?

    A. The trust boundary should always be an asset IT controls.

    B. The switch should always be set as the trust boundary.

    C. Only routers can create trust boundaries.

    D. Only IP phones can become trust boundaries.

126. Which DSCP marking has the highest priority?

    A. DSCP AF 43

    B. DSCP EF 46

    C. DSCP AF 11

    D. DSCP AF 00

127. What is the recommended maximum delay VoIP traffic should not exceed?

    A. 10 ms

    B. 90 ms

    C. 150 ms

    D. 300 ms

128. Which QoS queue has priority over all other queues in the scheduler?

    A. CBWFQ

    B. LLQ

    C. FIFO

    D. CIR

129. Which method helps combat queue starvation for QoS queuing?

    A. LLQ

    B. Policing

    C. CBWFQ

    D. FIFO

130. Which statement is correct about shaping of traffic for QoS?

    A. Shaping holds packets in the queue over the configured bit rate to cause delay.

    B. Shaping drops packets over the configured bit rate to cause loss.

    C. Shaping holds packets in the queue over the configured bit rate to cause jitter.

    D. Shaping slows packets in the queue over the configured bit rate to adhere to the speed.

131. Which QoS method uses a round-robin scheduler for packet queuing?

    A. LLQ

    B. FIFO

    C. CBWFQ

    D. PQ

132. Which statement is correct about policing of traffic for QoS?

    A. Policing holds packets in the queue over the configured bit rate to cause delay.

    B. Policing drops packets over the configured bit rate to cause loss.

    C. Policing holds packets in the queue over the configured bit rate to cause jitter.

    D. Policing slows packets in the queue over the configured bit rate to adhere to the bit rate.

133. When should QoS policing be implemented?

    A. To help police LAN applications

    B. To maintain a contracted CIR

    C. To help police WAN applications

    D. To maintain a contracted burst rate

134. Which statement is correct about tail drop with QoS queues?

    A. Tail drop is a method of QoS.

    B. Tail drop happens when the queues round-robin.

    C. Tail drop happens when the queues are full.

    D. Tail drop helps slow down protocols that are monopolizing bandwidth.

135. When should QoS shaping be implemented?

    A. When maintaining a contracted burst rate

    B. When LAN applications require a minimum bit rate

    C. When WAN applications require a minimum bit rate

    D. When the service provider is policing traffic

136. Which command will allow the CoS value to be trusted for a VoIP phone?

    A. `Switch(config-if)#auto qos trust cos`

    B. `Switch(config-if)#qos trust cos`

    C. `Switch(config-if)#cos trust qos`

    D. `Switch(config-if)#auto qos`

137. When configuring QoS for packet shaping, which is an important guideline to follow?

    A. Always make the bit rate small.

    B. Always make the time interval small.

    C. Always make the time interval large.

    D. Always use the maximum bit rate.

138. How do congestion avoidance tools help to prevent tail drop?

    A. When the queue depth is full, a percentage of TCP packets are dropped.

    B. When the queue depth is empty, a percentage of TCP packets are dropped.

    C. When the queue depth is below the minimum threshold, a percentage of TCP packets are dropped.

    D. When the queue depth is above the minimum threshold, a percentage of TCP packets are dropped.

139. Which command on a Cisco switch will show the default CoS value?

    A. `Switch#show qos interface`

    B. `Switch#show mls qos interface`

    C. `Switch#show interface`

    D. `Switch#show qos`

140. If a traffic is marked with AF31 and another traffic pattern is marked with AF41, which statement explains the traffic markings?

    A. AF31 marked traffic has a better queue than AF41 marked traffic.

    B. AF41 marked traffic has a better queue than AF31 marked traffic.

    C. Both AF31 and AF41 marked traffic has an equal queue.

    D. During high congestion, AF41 queues will be dropped and AF31 queues won't.

Chapter

5

Infrastructure Services (Domain 5)

THE CCNA EXAM TOPICS COVERED IN THIS PRACTICE TEST INCLUDE THE FOLLOWING:

✓ **5.0 Infrastructure Services (ICND1) (ICND2)**

- 5.1 Describe DNS lookup operation (ICND1)

- 5.2 Troubleshoot client connectivity issues involving DNS (ICND1)

- 5.3 Configure and verify DHCP on a router (excluding static reservations) (ICND1)

  - 5.3a Server (ICND1)

  - 5.3b Relay (ICND1)

  - 5.3c Client (ICND1)

  - 5.3d TFTP, DNS, and gateway options (ICND1)

- 5.4 Troubleshoot client-and router-based DHCP connectivity issues (ICND1)

- 5.5 Configure, verify, and troubleshoot basic HSRP (ICND2)

  - 5.5a Priority (ICND2)

  - 5.5b Preemption (ICND2)

  - 5.5c Version (ICND2)

- 5.6 Configure, verify, and troubleshoot inside source NAT (ICND1)

  - 5.6a Static (ICND1)

  - 5.6b Pool (ICND1)

  - 5.6c PAT (ICND1)

- 5.7 Configure and verify NTP operating in a client/server mode (ICND1)

1. Which method provides a distributed database that is used to resolve FQDNs to an IP address?

    A. Hostnames

    B. Hosts files

    C. DNS

    D. ARP

2. What statement is correct about forward lookups?

    A. Forward lookups resolve IP addresses from the queried DNS server, without the help of other DNS servers.

    B. Forward lookups resolve FQDNs to IP addresses.

    C. Forward lookups resolve IP addresses to FQDNs.

    D. A forward lookup forwards a request to another DNS server.

3. Which protocol and port number does DNS use for direct queries?

    A. UDP/53

    B. TCP/53

    C. UDP/55

    D. UDP/68

4. Which statement describes FQDNs?

    A. A DNS server always processes the entire FQDN.

    B. FQDNs are always registered with a registrar.

    C. FQDNs are significant from left to right, starting with a period for the root.

    D. FQDNs are significant from right to left, starting with a period for the root.

5. Which statement is correct about reverse lookups?

    A. A reverse lookup is when the request needs to be reversed to another DNS server.

    B. A reverse lookup is the resolution of an IP address to FQDN.

    C. A reverse lookup is when the DNS queried can answer the request without asking another DNS server.

    D. A reverse lookup is the resolution of an FQDN to an IP address.

6. Which record type is used for an IPv4 address to FQDN for DNS queries?

    A. The A record

    B. The CName record

    C. The PTR record

    D. The AAAA record

7. What gets appended to hostname queries for DNS resolution?

   A. The DNS domain name

   B. The DNS zone

   C. The host header

   D. The hostname PTR record

8. Which is the most secure method of name resolution for routers and switches?

   A. DNS

   B. PTR records

   C. Static hostname entries

   D. LLMNR

9. Which type of DNS record holds the IPv4 IP address for a hostname?

   A. The A record

   B. The CName record

   C. The PTR record

   D. The AAAA record

10. What limits the amount of time that a DNS entry is available in DNS cache?

   A. A record

   B. TTL

   C. SOA

   D. Default of 5 minutes

11. Which is an alternative to DNS lookup on routers?

   A. Static ARP

   B. LLMNR

   C. Hosts table file

   D. Static hostname entries

12. Which record type is used for IPv6 hostname lookup for DNS queries?

   A. The A record

   B. The CName record

   C. The PTR record

   D. The AAAA record

13. Which protocol and port number is used for DNS domain zone transfers?

   A. UDP/53

   B. TCP/53

   C. UDP/55

   D. UDP/68

14. What is a reason to configure DNS on a router or switch?

    A. ACLs can dynamically reverse hostnames to IPs.

    B. Configuration allows access to the router or switch by the FQDN.

    C. Configuration allows ease of administration from the router or switch when connecting to other devices by FQDN.

    D. Configuration allows secure communications via HTTPS.

15. You are were trying to type the `ping` command into the router and mistype it and receive the output of `Translating "png"... domain server (255.255.255.255)`, which halts you from continuing. Which command will stop this behavior?

    A. `RouterA#no domain-lookup`

    B. `RouterA#no ip dns`

    C. `RouterA(config)#no ip dns-lookup`

    D. `RouterA(config)#no ip domain-lookup`

16. Which command will set the resolution of a host so that DNS does not need to be used for resolution?

    A. `RouterA(config)#hostname routerb 10.1.2.3`

    B. `RouterA(config)#hostname 10.1.2.3 routerb`

    C. `RouterA(config)#ip hostname routerb 10.1.2.3`

    D. `RouterA(config)#ip host routerb 10.1.2.3`

17. Which command will configure the router or switch to use a specific DNS server for hostname lookups?

    A. `RouterA(config)#ip domain server 172.16.1.5`

    B. `RouterA(config)#ip dns-server 172.16.1.5`

    C. `RouterA(config)#ip name-server 172.16.1.5`

    D. `RouterA(config)#ip domain-server 172.16.1.5`

18. Which command will configure the domain name to append to a DNS query?

    A. `RouterA(config)#ip domain sybex.com`

    B. `RouterA(config)#dns-domain sybex.com`

    C. `RouterA(config)#ip dns-domain sybex.com`

    D. `RouterA(config)#ip domain-name sybex.com`

19. What is at the end of all FQDN addresses?

    A. A period, which signifies root

    B. Top-level domain names

    C. Generic top-level domain names

    D. The domain name

20. When configuring the name server(s) for domain lookup, what is a best practice?

    A. Always use public DNS servers.

    B. Always use TLD servers.

    C. Always use private DNS servers.

    D. Always use a mixture of public and private DNS servers for fault tolerance.

21. Which command will help verify the hostnames that are statically configured?

    A. `RouterA#show hostname`

    B. `RouterA#show hosts`

    C. `RouterA#show ip hosts`

    D. `RouterA#show ip host-names`

22. Your DNS administrator has changed the DNS entry for RouterB. You clear the DNS cache and ping `routerb.sybex.com` again but still ping the original address. All other DNS addresses work fine. What is the problem?

    A. The router is configured to the wrong DNS server.

    B. RouterB has a host entry configured.

    C. The DNS administrator made an error.

    D. The domain name of the router is incorrect.

23. You have configured a router to point to the DNS server with the IP address 10.2.2.2 and configured the domain name of `sybex.com`. However, you cannot resolve the host `routerb.sybex.com`. Which Windows command will help you verify DNS name resolution?

    A. `C:\>ping routerb.sybex.com`

    B. `C:\>tracert routerb.sybex.com`

    C. `C:\>nslookup routerb.sybex.com`

    D. `C:\>dig routerb.sybex.com`

24. Which command will allow you to verify the DNS server you are using for name resolution?

    A. `RouterA#show hosts`

    B. `RouterA#show running-configuration`

    C. `RouterA#show ip domain`

    D. `RouterA#show dns`

25. You have configured the domain name of `sybex.com` and the DNS server 10.2.3.4 on a router. However, after you type `ping routerb`, the console promptly returns "% Unrecognized host or address or protocol not running." What is wrong?

    A. The DNS server is wrong.

    B. The domain server is wrong.

    C. The hostname is wrong.

    D. All of the above

26. Your DNS administrator has changed the DNS entry for RouterB. You ping `routerb.sybex`
`.com` again, but still ping the original address. All other DNS addresses work fine. What is
the problem?

   A. The DNS administrator made an error.

   B. The router is configured to the wrong DNS server.

   C. The router's DNS cache needs to be cleared.

   D. The domain name of the router is incorrect.

27. Which statement is true about the following exhibit?

```
RouterA#show hosts
Default Domain is sybex.com
Name/address lookup uses domain service
Name servers are 10.0.0.3
[Output Cut]

Host                Port  Flags       Age Type  Address(es)
routerb.sybex.com   None  (temp, OK)  9   IP    10.1.0.2
routerc.sybex.com   None  (temp, OK)  6   IP    10.1.0.3
routerd.sybex.com   None  (perm, OK)  0   IP    10.1.0.4
routere.sybex.com   None  (temp, OK)  4   IP    10.1.0.5
RouterA#
```

   A. RouterB has not accessed the cache in 9 hours.

   B. RouterD is expired in the cache.

   C. RouterE has 4 hours left in the cache.

   D. RouterC has 6 minutes left in the cache.

28. Which command will remove the entry `routerb.sybex.com` out of the DNS cache or a
switch without affecting the rest of the cache?

   A. `Router#clear host`

   B. `Router#clear host *`

   C. `Router(config)#clear host routerb.sybex.com`

   D. `Router#clear host routerb.sybex.com`

29. Given the output in the following exhibit, what error message will you see when you try to
ping `routerb.sybex.com`?

```
Router#show run
[Output Cut]
!
ip ssh version 1
ip domain-name sybex.local
ip name-server 8.8.8.8
!
interface FastEthernet0/0
 ip address 10.0.0.1 255.255.255.0
 duplex auto
 speed auto
[Output Cut]
```

   A. The DNS server is unreachable.

   B. The IP address is private.

   C. The DNS server is a public server.

   D. The DNS domain name is wrong.

30. In the following exhibit, you have configured Router B for DNS lookups. From Host B, you can resolve DNS for `routerb.sybex.com`, and from Host A you can ping the DNS server. However, Router A will not resolve the DNS hostname of `routerb.sybex.com`. What is the problem?

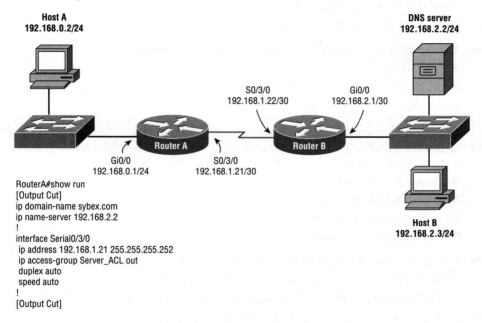

```
RouterA#show run
[Output Cut]
ip domain-name sybex.com
ip name-server 192.168.2.2
!
interface Serial0/3/0
  ip address 192.168.1.21 255.255.255.252
  ip access-group Server_ACL out
  duplex auto
  speed auto
!
[Output Cut]
```

A. The DNS server on Router A is wrong.

B. UDP/53 is being blocked on Router B.

C. UDP/53 is blocked outbound on Router A.

D. There is a routing issue.

31. Which statement is true about the Discover packet of DHCP?

A. The layer 3 destination is a unicast to the DHCP server.

B. The layer 2 destination is the MAC address of the DHCP server.

C. The layer 2 source is the MAC address of the client.

D. The layer 3 source is a link-local address of the client.

32. Which command will configure a router to use DHCP for IP address assignment?

A. `RouterA(config)#ip address dhcp`

B. `RouterA(config-if)#ip address auto`

C. `RouterA(config-if)#ip address dhcp`

D. `RouterA(config)#ip address auto`

33. Which command will allow you to verify the IP address assigned to a router's interface?

    A. `Router#show ip dhcp bindings`

    B. `Router#show ip interface`

    C. `Router#show ip lease`

    D. `Router#show ip dhcp lease`

34. Which port and protocol does the client use for DHCP messages?

    A. UDP/68

    B. TCP/68

    C. UDP/67

    D. TCP/67

35. Which command will allow you to verify the active DHCP server that has assigned an IP address to the router?

    A. `Router#show dhcp lease`

    B. `Router#show ip dhcp lease`

    C. `Router#show ip lease`

    D. `Router#show ip interface`

36. Which statement is true about the Offer packet of DHCP?

    A. The layer 3 destination is a unicast to the DHCP client.

    B. The layer 2 destination is the MAC address of the DHCP client.

    C. The layer 2 source is the MAC address of the server.

    D. The layer 3 source is a link-local address of the client.

37. Which command will configure a DHCP relay agent on an interface to the DHCP server of 10.10.1.101?

    A. `Router(config)#ip dhcp server 10.10.1.101`

    B. `Router(config-if)#ip dhcp server 10.10.1.101`

    C. `Router(config-if)#ip relay-agent 10.10.1.101`

    D. `Router(config-if)#ip helper-address 10.10.1.101`

38. Which DHCP field helps a DHCP server decide which scope to serve to the DHCP relay agent?

    A. CIADDR

    B. GIADDR

    C. SIADDR

    D. CHADDR

39. Which port and protocol does the server use to await connections for DHCP?

   A. TCP/68

   B. UDP/68

   C. TCP/67

   D. UDP/67

40. In the following exhibit, what is required on the network to allow Host A to receive an IP address from the DHCP server?

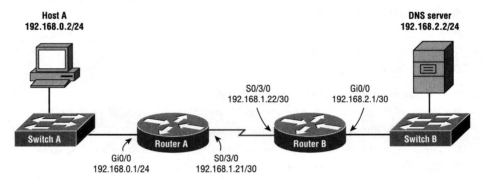

   A. A second DHCP server on the Host A network

   B. A DHCP relay agent on Router B interface Gi0/0

   C. A DHCP relay agent on Switch A

   D. A DHCP relay agent on Router A interface Gi0/0

41. Which Windows command will allow you to see the DHCP server that has configured the client computer with an IP address?

   A. `C:\>ipconfig`

   B. `C:\>ipconfig /all`

   C. `C:\>ipconfig /showclassid`

   D. `C:\>ipstatus`

42. Which message is sent from the DHCP client to the DHCP server to confirm the offer of an IP address?

   A. Acknowledgment

   B. Discover

   C. Offer

   D. Request

43. What form of communications does a DHCP client use to initially acquire an IP address?

    A. Layer 3 broadcast

    B. Layer 3 multicast

    C. Layer 3 802.1Q

    D. Layer 3 unicast

44. At what point of the lease time will the client ask for a renewal of the IP address from the DHCP server?

    A. One-quarter of the lease

    B. One-half of the lease

    C. Seven-eighths of the lease

    D. End of the lease

45. Which statement is correct about the DHCP process?

    A. The DHCP server is responsible for maintaining the life cycle of an IP address.

    B. DHCP uses multicasting between the client and server.

    C. The DHCP client is responsible for maintaining the life cycle of an IP address.

    D. The DHCP lease is negotiated between client and server.

46. Which transport protocol does DHCP use?

    A. UDP

    B. ICMP

    C. TCP

    D. RARP

47. Which command will allow you to diagnose DHCP relay agent messages on a router or switch?

    A. `Router#debug dhcp`

    B. `Router#show ip dhcp detail`

    C. `Router#debug ip dhcp server packet`

    D. `Router#debug ip dhcp`

48. What is DHCPv6 used for when a network is configured for Stateless Address Autoconfiguration (SLAAC)?

    A. Stateful configuration of clients for IPv6 addressing

    B. Configuration of clients with the IPv6 network IDs

    C. Configuration of clients with IPv6 options

    D. Stateless configuration of clients for IPv6 addressing

49. The DHCP server in the network went down. What happens to clients that have obtained IP addresses from the DHCP server?

    A. They lose their IP address immediately.

    B. They lose their IP address after one-half of their lease has expired.

C. They lose their IP address after seven-eighths of their lease has expired.

D. They lose their IP address after their entire lease has expired.

50. Which command will configure a router as a DHCPv6 relay agent for a stateful DHCPv6 server?

A. Router(config)#ip dhcp server 2001:db8:1:2::2

B. Router(config-if)#ipv6 dhcp relay destination 2001:db8:1:2::2

C. Router(config-if)#ip dhcp server 2001:db8:1:2::2

D. Router(config-if)#ipv6 helper-address 2001:db8:1:2::2

51. You need to configure a lease duration of 4 hours for a DHCP pool. Which command will achieve this?

A. Router(dhcp-config)#lease 0 4 0

B. Router(dhcp-config)#lease-duration 0 4 0

C. Router(dhcp-config)#lease 4 0 0

D. Router(dhcp-config)#dhcp lease 0 4 0

52. Which command will create an exclusion of 192.168.1.16 to 192.168.1.31 in the DHCP pool?

A. Router(dhcp-config)#exclusion 192.168.1.16 192.168.1.31

B. Router(dhcp-config)#dhcp exclusion 192.168.1.16 192.168.1.31

C. Router(dhcp-config)#ip dhcp exclusion-address 192.168.1.16 192.168.1.31

D. Router(config)#ip dhcp exclusion-address 192.168.1.16 192.168.1.31

53. When configuring a DHCP pool, which option(s) will configure the client to boot from a PXE server?

A. Router(dhcp-config)#option pxe 10.1.1.5

B. Router(dhcp-config)#option 66 10.1.1.5

C. Router(dhcp-config)#option 60 ascii PXEClient
   Router(dhcp-config)#option 66 ip 10.1.1.5

D. Router(dhcp-config)#option 66 ip 10.1.1.5
   Router(dhcp-config)#bootfile boot\x86\wdsnbp.com

54. Which command will configure the default gateway option for a DHCP pool?

A. Router(dhcp-config)#option gateway 10.1.1.1

B. Router(dhcp-config)#default-router 10.1.1.1

C. Router(dhcp-config)#default-gateway 10.1.1.1

D. Router(dhcp-config)#gateway 10.1.1.1

55. Which option will configure the DNS servers for the DHCP clients?

A. Router(dhcp-config)#dns-server 10.1.1.5

B. Router(dhcp-config)#dns 10.1.1.5

C. Router(dhcp-config)#option 53 10.1.1.5

D. Router(dhcp-config)#option 55 ip 10.1.1.5

56. Which command will configure a DHCP pool to serve the IP addresses for
192.168.1.0/24?

   A. `Router(dhcp-config)#dhcp-range 192.168.1.0`

   B. `Router(dhcp-config)#network 192.168.1.0`

   C. `Router(dhcp-config)#network 192.168.1.0 255.255.255.0`

   D. `Router(dhcp-config)#dhcp-network 192.168.1.0 255.255.255.0`

57. Which statement is correct about stateful DHCPv6?

   A. Stateful DHCPv6 supplies the network ID and host ID.

   B. Stateful DHCPv6 supplies the network ID, host ID, and default router.

   C. Stateful DHCPv6 communicates via broadcasts.

   D. Stateful DHCPv6 works in conjunction with SLAAC.

58. Which command will configure a router interface to obtain its IP address via a stateful
DHCPv6?

   A. `RouterA(config)#ipv6 address dhcp gi 0/0`

   B. `RouterA(config-if)#ipv6 address dhcpv6`

   C. `RouterA(config-if)#ipv6 address dhcp`

   D. `RouterA(config)#ipv6 address stateless`

59. Which command will allow you to verify the IPv6 configuration for stateful DHCPv6?

   A. `RouterA#show ipv6 dhcp bindings`

   B. `RouterA#show ipv6 dhcp interface`

   C. `RouterA#show ipv6 address`

   D. `RouterA#show ipv6 interface`

60. What happens if you delete a current lease on the DHCP server?

   A. The server will contact the client to immediately relinquish the IP address.

   B. The client will immediately renew its lease for the current IP address.

   C. The server will offer the IP address to another node, which will cause a duplicate
   address.

   D. The server will offer the IP address to another node, at which time the original client
   will relinquish the IP address.

61. What happens at the client when the lease for an IP address reaches seven-eighths of the
lease cycle?

   A. The DHCP client will perform a DHCP rebinding.

   B. Nothing. The DHCP client will retain the lease.

   C. The DHCP client will renew its lease.

   D. The DHCP client will relinquish the use of the IP address.

62. Which command is used on a router to request a renewal lease on a DHCP interface?

   A. Router#renew dhcp gi 0/0

   B. Router(config)#renew dhcp gi 0/0

   C. Router#clear interface gi 0/0

   D. Router#clear dhcp gi 0/0

63. How are nodes and leased IPs tracked in the DHCP bindings table on a switch or router?

   A. GUID address

   B. UUID address

   C. MAC address

   D. DHCP ID

64. During the DHCP rebinding, which message is sent from the client?

   A. DHCP Discover

   B. DHCP Request

   C. DHCP Ack

   D. DHCP Offer

65. You have just finished configuring a new router name Router A. With the configuration in the following exhibit, what will the first host receive as an IP address?

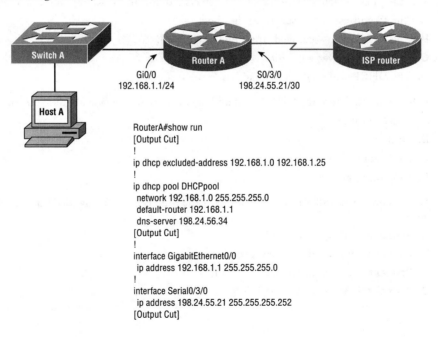

```
RouterA#show run
[Output Cut]
!
ip dhcp excluded-address 192.168.1.0 192.168.1.25
!
ip dhcp pool DHCPpool
  network 192.168.1.0 255.255.255.0
  default-router 192.168.1.1
  dns-server 198.24.56.34
[Output Cut]
!
interface GigabitEthernet0/0
  ip address 192.168.1.1 255.255.255.0
!
interface Serial0/3/0
  ip address 198.24.55.21 255.255.255.252
[Output Cut]
```

    A. 192.168.1.2

    B. 192.168.1.254

    C. 192.168.1.26

    D. 192.168.1.252

66. You have configured a DHCP server on a router interface. You test a Windows client and receive the address 169.254.24.56. What can you conclude?

    A. You have successfully configured the scope of 169.254.24.0/24.

    B. The client had a static IP address of 169.254.24.0/24 configured.

    C. The DHCP server is not configured properly and the client has configured itself with a link-local address.

    D. The DHCP server is configured for APIPA.

67. What mechanism is used by DHCP clients to avoid IP address conflicts with other DHCP clients?

    A. ARP

    B. RARP

    C. GARP

    D. Ping

68. What happens when a router or switch detects a duplicate IP address for a DHCP process?

    A. The IP address is still served to the client.

    B. The IP address is removed from the DHCP pool.

    C. The DHCP server will halt.

    D. The DHCP will serve the IP address in the future.

69. Before you configure the DHCP pool and network, which option should you configure?

    A. Lease duration

    B. Options

    C. Exclusions

    D. Domain name

70. Which command will allow you to check if the router or switch handed out a duplicate IP address?

    A. `Router#show ip conflict`

    B. `Router#show ip dhcp conflict`

    C. `Router#show ip dhcp duplication`

    D. `Router#show ip duplication`

71. Refer to the following exhibit. You have configured DHCP on Router A. However, you cannot serve any DHCP clients. What is wrong?

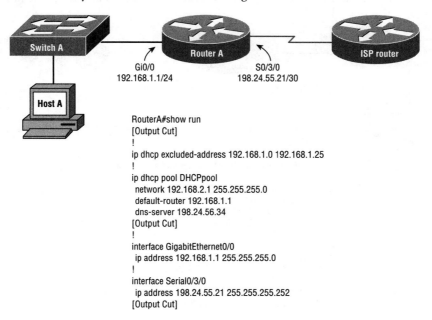

```
RouterA#show run
[Output Cut]
!
ip dhcp excluded-address 192.168.1.0 192.168.1.25
!
ip dhcp pool DHCPpool
 network 192.168.2.1 255.255.255.0
 default-router 192.168.1.1
 dns-server 198.24.56.34
[Output Cut]
!
interface GigabitEthernet0/0
 ip address 192.168.1.1 255.255.255.0
!
interface Serial0/3/0
 ip address 198.24.55.21 255.255.255.252
[Output Cut]
```

    A. The DNS server is incorrect.

    B. The DHCP exclusions are incorrect.

    C. The DHCP pool is administratively shut down.

    D. The DHCP pool network is incorrect.

72. Which command will allow you to see the current utilization of the DHCP pools configured?

    A. `Router#show dhcp`

    B. `Router#show ip dhcp`

    C. `Router#show dhcp status`

    D. `Router#show ip dhcp pool`

73. How can an address be removed from the DHCP conflict table?

    A. `Router#clear ip conflict 192.168.1.6`

    B. `Router#clear ip dhcp conflict 192.168.1.6`

    C. `Router#remove ip conflict 192.168.1.6`

    D. `Router(config)#clear ip dhcp conflict 192.168.1.6`

74. Refer to the following exhibit. You have just finished configuring a DHCP scope on Router A. However, it will not serve an IP address to Host A. What is the problem?

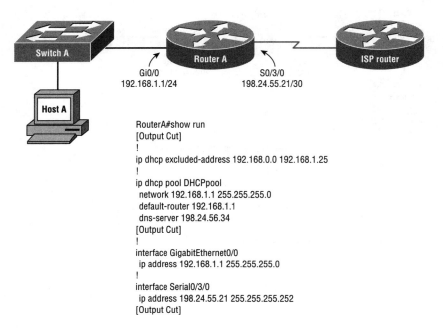

```
RouterA#show run
[Output Cut]
!
ip dhcp excluded-address 192.168.0.0 192.168.1.25
!
ip dhcp pool DHCPpool
  network 192.168.1.1 255.255.255.0
  default-router 192.168.1.1
  dns-server 198.24.56.34
[Output Cut]
!
interface GigabitEthernet0/0
 ip address 192.168.1.1 255.255.255.0
!
interface Serial0/3/0
 ip address 198.24.55.21 255.255.255.252
[Output Cut]
```

A. The DNS server is incorrect.

B. The DHCP exclusions are incorrect.

C. The DHCP pool is administratively shut down.

D. The DHCP pool network is incorrect.

75. Which command will allow you to verify the current DHCP leases on a router or a switch?

A. `Router#show ip dhcp bindings`

B. `Router#show ip interface`

C. `Router#show ip lease`

D. `Router#show ip dhcp lease`

76. Which protocol is an IEEE standard that is supported openly as a first hop redundancy protocol (FHRP)?

A. Proxy ARP

B. VRRP

C. GLBP

D. HSRP

77. In the MAC address 0000.0c07.ac0a, what is the well-known Hot standby Router Protocol (HSRP) ID?

A. 0000.0c

B. c007

C. 0a

D. 07.ac

78. Which protocol is a Cisco Proprietary protocol for load-balancing routers?

A. Proxy ARP

B. VRRP

C. GLBP

D. HSRP

79. In the MAC address 0000.0c07.ac01, what is the HSRPv1 group number?

A. 0000.0c

B. c007

C. 01

D. 07.ac

80. What is the default priority of HSRP?

A. 100

B. 110

C. 200

D. 10

81. What is the maximum number of HSRPv1 groups that can be created?

A. 8

B. 16

C. 255

D. 256

82. Which port and protocol are used by HSRP for communications?

A. UDP/1935

B. UDP/1985

C. UDP/1895

D. UCP/3222

83. Which statement is correct about HSRP?

A. All routers in an HSRP group are active.

B. Only one router in an HSRP group can be active.

C. The virtual router sends hello packets to the HSRP group.

D. HSRP allows for per-packet load balancing.

84. What type of communication is used between HSRP members?

    A. Unicast

    B. Broadcast

    C. Multicast

    D. Layer 2 flooding

85. When a host sends an outgoing packet to an HSRP group, which router provides the destination address for the default gateway?

    A. Virtual router

    B. Active router

    C. Standby router

    D. Monitor router

86. Which timer must expire for a standby router in an HSRP group to become the active router?

    A. Hello timer

    B. Standby timer

    C. Hold timer

    D. Virtual timer

87. Which port and protocol are used by Gateway Load Balancing Protocol (GLBP) for communications?

    A. UDP/1935

    B. UDP/1985

    C. UDP/1895

    D. UDP/3222

88. Which is a difference between HSRPv1 and HSRPv2?

    A. HSRPv2 does not use hello packets.

    B. HSRPv1 uses broadcasts, and HSRPv2 uses multicasts.

    C. HSRPv1 supports IPv6.

    D. HSRPv2 uses milliseconds.

89. Which statement is correct about Gateway Load Balancing Protocol (GLBP)?

    A. The active router is responsible for responding to clients with the virtual router's MAC address.

    B. The active virtual gateway will respond with a MAC address of the active router.

    C. The active virtual gateway will respond with a MAC address of an active virtual forwarder.

    D. The virtual router is responsible for responding to tracking requests.

90. Which router is elected to become the GLBP active virtual gateway?

A. The router with the lowest priority

B. The router with the highest priority

C. The router with the lowest priority and lowest IP address

D. The router with the highest priority and highest IP address

91. How many active virtual forwarders are supported per the Gateway Load Balancing Protocol (GLBP) group?

A. 2

B. 4

C. 16

D. 1,024

92. Which command will allow Router B to always become the active router for HSRP?

A. `Router(config-if)#standby 1 priority 150`

B. `Router(config-if)#standby 1 priority 70`

C. `Router(config-if)#hsrp 1 priority 150`

D. `Router(config-if)#hsrp 1 priority 90`

93. What is the maximum number of Hot Standby Router Protocol version 2 groups that can be created?

A. 255

B. 256

C. 1,024

D. 4,096

94. Your company is running a first hop redundancy protocol (FHRP). You notice that the MAC address of the default gateway is 0000.0c9f.f123. Which FHRP is being employed?

A. HSRPv1

B. GLBP

C. HSRPv2

D. VRRP

95. What is the definition of preemption for Hot Standby Router Protocol (HSRP)?

A. It allows the protocol to effectively load-balance per packet.

B. It watches an upstream interface and fails over when the interface goes down.

C. It ignores the priorities of the routers and elects an active router by highest IP address.

D. When a standby router comes online, it allows for a re-election of the active router.

96. Which is a method of configuring Hot Standby Router Protocol (HSRP) so that traffic is not directed to one router?

A. Configure version 2 for all HSRP groups.

B. Configure an HSRP group per VLAN and alternate the priority above 100.

C. Configure PPPoE on the router interfaces.

D. Configure all routers in the HSRP as active routers.

97. Which command will allow you to verify the state of the current router for HSRP?

A. RouterA#show hsrp

B. RouterA#show ip standby

C. RouterA#show standby

D. RouterA#show ip hsrp

98. You have just changed the priority on Router A to 150. All other routers have the default priority. What is wrong?

A. The default priority is 150.

B. The hold timer is set too high and needs to timeout.

C. The HSRP group is not set for preemption.

D. Router A has too low of an IP address.

99. Which command will allow you to enable preemption for HSRP?

A. Router(config)#standby 1 preemption

B. Router(config-if)#standby 1 preemption

C. Router(config-if)#hsrp 1 preempt

D. Router(config-if)#standby 1 preempt

100. Which command will configure VRRP on an interface with an IP address of 10.1.2.3?

A. Router(config)#vrrp 1 10.1.2.3 gi 0/0

B. Router(config-if)#vrrp 1 ip 10.1.2.3

C. Router(config-if)#vrrp 1 10.1.2.3

D. Router(config-if)#standby 1 10.1.2.3
   Router(config-if)#standby 1 vrrp

101. Refer to the following exhibit. You are running HSRP on Router A and Router B. You intermittently have ISP outages. What command should you configure to alert HSRP to the outage?

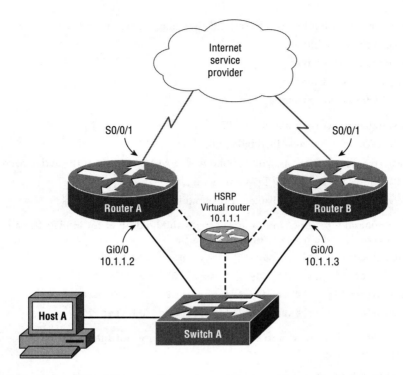

A. RouterA(config-if)#standby 1 interface tracking serial 0/0/1
RouterB(config-if)#standby 1 interface tracking serial 0/0/1

B. RouterA(config-if)#standby 1 tracking serial 0/0/1
RouterB(config-if)#standby 1 tracking serial 0/0/1

C. RouterA(config-if)#standby 1 track serial 0/0/1
RouterB(config-if)#standby 1 track serial 0/0/1

D. RouterA(config-if)#interface serial 0/0/1
RouterA(config-if)#standby 1 interface tracking
RouterA(config-if)#interface serial 0/0/1
RouterB(config-if)#standby 1 interface tracking

102. Which command from the host will allow you to see the router your packets have been routed with?

A. C:\ping 10.1.2.33

B. C:\tracert 10.1.2.33

C. C:\arp -g

D. C:\ipconfig /all

103. Which command will allow you to see real-time diagnostics of HSRP?

   A. Router#show ip hsrp

   B. Router#debug ip hsrp

   C. Router#debug standby

   D. Router#debug ip standby

104. Which statement is correct about GLBP?

   A. GLBP allows for per-host load balancing.

   B. The active virtual gateway will respond with a MAC address of the active router.

   C. GLBP allows for per-subnet load balancing.

   D. The virtual router is responsible for responding to tracking requests.

105. Which command will allow you to set the hello and hold timer for HSRPv2 to a hello of 200 milliseconds and a hold of 700 milliseconds?

   A. RouterA(config-if)#standby 1 timers msec 200 msec 700

   B. RouterA(config-if)#standby 1 timers 200 msec 700 msec

   C. RouterA(config-if)#standby 1 timers 700 msec 200 msec

   D. RouterA(config-if)#standby 1 timers msec 700 msec 200

106. Which method will allow you to use RFC 1918 addresses for Internet requests?

   A. CIDR

   B. Classful addressing

   C. NAT

   D. VPN

107. Which is a disadvantage of using NAT?

   A. Creates switching path delays

   B. Introduces security weaknesses

   C. Requires address renumbering

   D. Increases bandwidth utilization

108. Which type of Network Address Translation is used for one-to-one mapping between local and global addresses?

   A. Dynamic NAT

   B. Static NAT

   C. NAT Overloading

   D. Symmetric NAT

109. In the following exhibit, what is the inside local IP address?

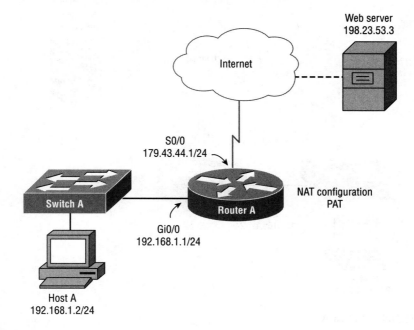

A. 192.168.1.2 Host A

B. 192.168.1.1 Router A Gi0/0

C. 179.43.44.1 Router A S0/0

D. 198.23.53.3 web server

110. Which type of Network Address Translation is used for one-to-one mapping (sometimes called many-to-many) on the fly between local and global addresses that are allocated from a pool of addresses?

A. Dynamic NAT

B. Static NAT

C. NAT Overloading

D. Full cone NAT

111. Which type of Network Address Translation is used for a many-to-one translation in which the source and destination ports are tracked?

A. Dynamic NAT

B. Static NAT

C. NAT Overloading

D. Full cone NAT

112. In the following exhibit, what is the inside global IP address?

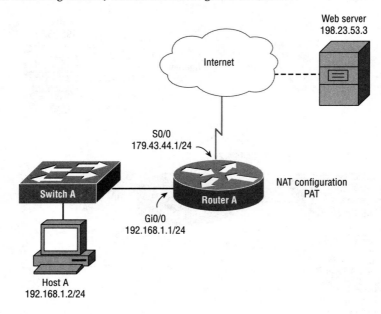

A. 192.168.1.2 Host A

B. 192.168.1.1 Router A Gi0/0

C. 179.43.44.1 Router A S0/0

D. 198.23.53.3 web server

113. In the following exhibit, what is the outside global IP address?

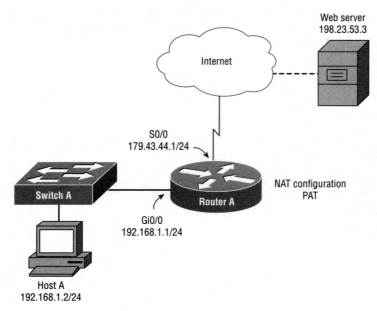

    A. 192.168.1.2 Host A

    B. 192.168.1.1 Router A Gi0/0

    C. 179.43.44.1 Router A S0/0

    D. 198.23.53.3 web server

114. Which statement is correct about static NAT?

    A. The translation is always present in the NAT table.

    B. The translation is never present in the NAT table.

    C. Static NAT is less secure than dynamic NAT.

    D. Static NAT has less latency than dynamic NAT.

115. Network Address Translation overloading is also called what?

    A. Static NAT

    B. PAT

    C. CEF NAT

    D. I-NAT

116. What is an advantage of Network Address Translation?

    A. Decreased memory utilization

    B. Decreased utilization of public IP addresses

    C. Decreased latency of packets

    D. Increased network application compatibility

117. Which is a practical application of static Network Address Translation?

    A. Address overlap for an enterprise

    B. Internet access for an enterprise from private IP addressing

    C. Publishing a web server on the Internet from a private IP address

    D. All of the above

118. Which term describes the IP address of the internal host before NAT?

    A. Inside local

    B. Outside local

    C. Inside global

    D. Outside global

119. Which of the following is an advantage to using Port Address Translation?

    A. Lower levels of jitter

    B. Lower levels of packet loss

    C. Flexibility of Internet connections

    D. Lower memory usage than other NAT types

120. Which command would you configure on the private network interface for NAT?

    A. `Router(config-if)#ip nat outside`

    B. `Router(config)#ip nat inside gi0/0`

    C. `Router(config-if)#ip nat private`

    D. `Router(config-if)#ip nat inside`

121. Which command will allow you to view the NAT translations active on the router?

    A. `Router#show ip nat translations`

    B. `Router#show nat translations`

    C. `Router#debug ip nat translations`

    D. `Router#show translations nat`

122. Which command will allow you to view the current number of active NAT translations on the router?

    A. `Router#show ip nat translations`

    B. `Router#show ip nat summary`

    C. `Router#show ip nat status`

    D. `Router#show ip nat statistics`

123. In the following exhibit, which command will configure static NAT for the internal web server?

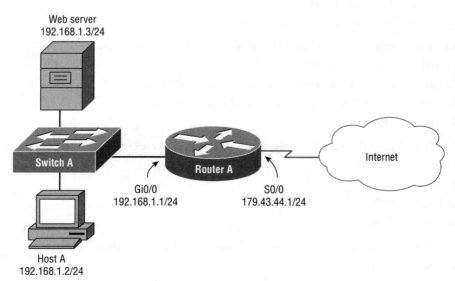

    A. `RouterA(config)#ip nat inside source static 192.168.1.3 179.43.44.1`

    B. `RouterA(config)#nat source static 192.168.1.3 179.43.44.1`

    C. `RouterA(config)#ip nat static 192.168.1.3 179.43.44.1`

    D. `RouterA(config)#ip nat source static 192.168.1.3 179.43.44.1`

124. In the following exhibit, the enterprise owns the address block of 179.43.44.0/28. Which command will create a NAT pool for Dynamic NAT?

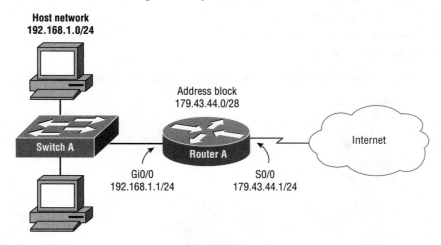

A. RouterA(config)#ip nat pool EntPool 179.43.44.0/28

B. RouterA(config)#ip pool EntPool 179.43.44.2 179.43.44.15
netmask 255.255.255.0

C. RouterA(config)#ip nat pool EntPool 179.43.44.1 179.43.44.15
netmask 255.255.255.240

D. RouterA(config)#ip nat pool EntPool 179.43.44.2 179.43.44.15
netmask 255.255.255.0

125. When configuring dynamic NAT, why must you configure an access list?

A. The access list allows incoming access from outside global addresses.

B. The access list allows outgoing access from inside local addresses.

C. The access list allows outgoing access from outside local addresses.

D. The access list allows outgoing access from inside global addresses.

126. Which command will wipe out all current NAT translations in the NAT table?

A. Router#no ip nat translation

B. Router#clear ip nat translation

C. Router#clear ip nat translation *

D. Router#clear ip nat

127. What happens to host communications when the NAT table is manually cleared?

A. No disturbance in communications will be observed.

B. Established UDP sessions will need to reestablish and will disturb communications.

C. Established TCP sessions will need to reestablish and will disturb communications.

D. Established TCP sessions will need to reestablish and will not disturb communications.

128. Which command will allow you to see real time Network Address Translations?

    A. Router#show ip translations

    B. Router#debug ip nat

    C. Router#debug ip translations

    D. Router#show ip nat

129. In the following exhibit, which command will configure Port Address Translation?

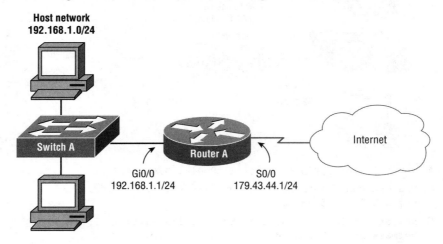

    A. RouterA(config)#access-list 1 permit 192.168.1.0 0.0.0.255
       RouterA(config)#ip nat pool EntPool 179.43.44.1 179.43.44.1
       RouterA(config)#ip nat inside source list 1 pool EntPool

    B. RouterA(config)#ip nat pool EntPool 179.43.44.1 179.43.44.1
       netmask 255.255.255.0
       RouterA(config)#ip nat source pool EntPool

    C. RouterA(config)#access-list 1 permit 192.168.1.0 0.0.0.255
       RouterA(config)#ip nat pool EntPool 179.43.44.1 179.43.44.1
       netmask 255.255.255.0
       RouterA(config)#ip nat inside source list 1 pool EntPool overload

    D. RouterA(config)#access-list 1 permit 192.168.1.0 0.0.0.255
       RouterA(config)#ip nat pool EntPool 179.43.44.1 179.43.44.1
       netmask 255.255.255.0
       RouterA(config)#ip nat inside source list 1 pool EntPool

130. In the following exhibit, how would you configure Port Address Translation on a DHCP-enabled interface?

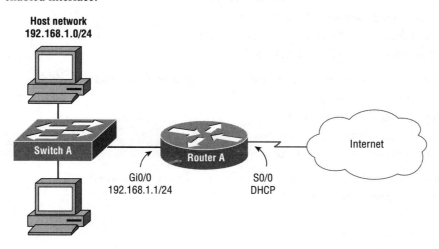

Host network
192.168.1.0/24

Switch A

Router A

Internet

Gi0/0
192.168.1.1/24

S0/0
DHCP

A. RouterA(config)#access-list 1 permit 192.168.1.0 0.0.0.255
   RouterA(config)#ip nat pool EntPool serial 0/0
   RouterA(config)#ip nat inside source list 1 pool EntPool overload

B. RouterA(config)#access-list 1 permit 192.168.1.0 0.0.0.255
   RouterA(config)#ip nat pool EntPool dhcp
   RouterA(config)#ip nat inside source list 1 pool EntPool overload

C. RouterA(config)#access-list 1 permit 192.168.1.0 0.0.0.255
   RouterA(config)#ip nat inside source list 1 serial 0/0

D. RouterA(config)#access-list 1 permit 192.168.1.0 0.0.0.255
   RouterA(config)#ip nat inside source list 1 interface serial
   0/0 overload

131. Which protocol helps synchronize time for routers and switches?

   A. SNMP

   B. NTP

   C. Syslog

   D. ICMP

132. Why is time synchronization important for routers and switches?

   A. It is important for serialized communication frame alignment.

   B. It is important for quality of service queuing.

   C. It is important for logging accuracy.

   D. It helps delivery of packets via timed queues.

133. Which command will allow your router to synchronize with a time source of 129.6.15.28?

    A. `Router(config)#ntp server 129.6.15.28`

    B. `Router#ntp server 129.6.15.28`

    C. `Router(config)#ntp client 129.6.15.28`

    D. `Router#ntp client 129.6.15.28`

134. Which command configures the router or switch to trust its internal time clock?

    A. `Router(config)#ntp server`

    B. `Router(config)#ntp master`

    C. `Router(config)#ntp clock source`

    D. `Router(config)#ntp trusted`

135. Which command will allow you to see if the router or switch is using NTP?

    A. `Router#show clock detail`

    B. `Router#show ntp`

    C. `Router#show time`

    D. `Router#show time source`

136. Which command will allow you to view the time details from a configured server?

    A. `Router#show clock detail`

    B. `Router#show ntp detail`

    C. `Router#show ntp associations detail`

    D. `Router#show ntp skew`

137. Which protocol and port does NTP use for time synchronization?

    A. TCP/161

    B. TCP/123

    C. UDP/69

    D. UDP/123

138. Which command will help you diagnose if the router or switch is getting an answer back from an NTP server?

    A. `Router#show ntp`

    B. `Router#show ip ntp`

    C. `Router#debug ntp packets`

    D. `Router#debug ntp messages`

139. Which is a best practice for setting up NTP?

   A. Always configure the time source to a DNS address.

   B. Configure all devices to a public NTP server.

   C. Configure all devices to different NTP servers for redundancy.

   D. Configure all devices as master servers.

140. Which command will allow you to view the time drift observed by NTP?

   A. Router#show ntp

   B. Router#show ip ntp status

   C. Router#show ntp status

   D. Router#debug ntp drift

Chapter

6

Infrastructure Security (Domain 6)

THE CCNA EXAM TOPICS COVERED IN THIS PRACTICE TEST INCLUDE THE FOLLOWING:

✓ **6.0 Infrastructure Security (ICND2)**

- 6.1 Configure, verify, and troubleshoot port security (ICND1)
  - 6.1a Static (ICND1)
  - 6.1b Dynamic (ICND1)
  - 6.1c Sticky (ICND1)
  - 6.1d Max MAC addresses (ICND1)
  - 6.1e Violation actions (ICND1)
  - 6.1f Err-disable recovery (ICND1)
- 6.2 Describe common access layer threat mitigation techniques (ICND2)
  - 6.2a 802.1x (ICND2)
  - 6.2b DHCP snooping (ICND2)
  - 6.2c Nondefault native VLAN (ICND2)
- 6.3 Configure, verify, and troubleshoot IPv4 and IPv6 access list for traffic filtering (ICND1) (ICND2)
  - 6.3a Standard (ICND2)
  - 6.3b Extended (ICND2)
  - 6.3c Named (ICND2)
- 6.4 Verify ACLs using the APIC-EM Path Trace ACL Analysis tool (ICND2)

- 6.5 Configure, verify, and troubleshoot basic device hardening (ICND1)

  - 6.5a Local authentication (ICND1)

  - 6.5b Secure password (ICND1)

  - 6.5c Access to device (ICND1)

  - 6.5c(i) Source address (ICND1)

  - 6.5c(ii) Telnet/SSH (ICND1)

  - 6.5d Login banner (ICND1)

- 6.6 Describe device security using AAA with TACACS+ and RADIUS (ICND2)

1. Which method can restrict a user from plugging a wireless access point into a corporate network?

   A. Access control lists

   B. Port security

   C. Wired Equivalent Privacy

   D. Static MAC addresses

2. What does port security use to block unauthorized access?

   A. Source MAC addresses

   B. Destination MAC addresses

   C. Source IP addresses

   D. Destination IP addresses

3. Which command will enable port security?

   A. `Switch(config)#switchport port-security`

   B. `Switch(config)#port-security enable`

   C. `Switch(config-if)#switchport port-security`

   D. `Switch(config-if)#port-security enable`

4. If port security is enabled on an interface, what is the maximum number of MAC addresses allowed by default?

   A. 1 MAC address

   B. 2 MAC addresses

   C. 0 MAC addresses

   D. 10 MAC addresses

5. Which layer of the OSI model does port security use for securing a port?

   A. Layer 0

   B. Layer 1

   C. Layer 2

   D. Layer 3

6. Why would a network admin choose to configure port security on an interface?

   A. To allow or disallow VLANs

   B. To allow or disallow IP addresses

   C. To prevent unauthorized access by MAC address

   D. To prevent unauthorized access by user

7. Which statement is correct about port security?

A. Port security works best in mobile environments.

B. Port security requires a higher amount of memory.

C. Port security works best in static environments.

D. Port security always results in admin intervention to reset the port.

8. When configuring port security on a port that contains a VoIP phone with a voice VLAN and a computer connected to the phone, how many MAC addresses must you allow?

A. 1 MAC address

B. 2 MAC addresses

C. 0 MAC addresses

D. 10 MAC addresses

9. What is the default action of port security on the interface when the maximum number of MAC addresses is exceeded?

A. Administrative shutdown

B. Err-disabled shutdown

C. Restricted access without logging

D. Restricted access with logging

10. You are configuring a port for port security and receive the error "Command rejected: FastEthernet0/1 is a dynamic port." Which commands will help you configure the port?

A. `SwitchA(config-if)#no switchport dynamic`
`SwitchA(config-if)#switchport port-security`

B. `SwitchA(config-if)#switchport mode access`
`SwitchA(config-if)#switchport port-security`

C. `SwitchA(config-if)#switchport mode access`
`SwitchA(config-if)#switchport nonnegotiate`
`SwitchA(config-if)#switchport port-security`

D. `SwitchA(config-if)#switchport mode access`
`SwitchA(config-if)#no dynamic`
`SwitchA(config-if)#switchport port-security`

11. Which command will allow you to configure two MAC addresses for port security?

A. `SwitchA(config-if)#switchport maximum 2`

B. `SwitchA(config-if)#switchport port-security maximum 2`

C. `SwitchA(config-if)#port-security maximum 2`

D. `SwitchA(config-if)#switchport port-security limit 2`

12. Which command will limit devices via port security without disabling the port and logging the restricted device?

A. Switch(config-if)#switchport port-security violation shutdown

B. Switch(config-if)#switchport port-security restrict

C. Switch(config-if)#switchport port-security violation protect

D. Switch(config-if)#switchport port-security violation restrict

13. Which command will allow you to inspect the status of a port that has been configured for port security?

A. Switch#show running-configuration

B. Switch#show port-security interface gi 2/13

C. Switch#show port-security details interface gi 2/13

D. Switch#show port-security gi 2/13

14. Which command will limit devices via port security and send an SNMP trap notification?

A. Switch(config-if)#switchport port-security violation shutdown

B. Switch(config-if)#switchport port-security restrict

C. Switch(config-if)#switchport port-security violation protect

D. Switch(config-if)#switchport port-security violation restrict

15. Which command will limit devices via port security without disabling the port and not provide logging for a security violation counter?

A. Switch(config-if)#switchport port-security violation shutdown

B. Switch(config-if)#switchport port-security restrict

C. Switch(config-if)#switchport port-security violation protect

D. Switch(config-if)#switchport port-security violation restrict

16. Which command will allow you to see logged security violations for port security?

A. Switch#show violations

B. Switch#show port-security violations

C. Switch#show port-security

D. Switch#show psec violations

17. You have been tasked to secure ports with port security. You need to make sure that only the computers installed can access the network. The computers are installed already. Which type of configuration for port security would require the least amount of administration?

A. Static port security

B. Dynamic port security

C. Sticky port security

D. Time limit port security

18. Refer to the following exhibit. You received a call that a port is no longer active. The port has post security configured on it. What is the problem?

```
SwitchA#show interfaces fastEthernet 0/1
FastEthernet0/1 is down, line protocol is down (err-disabled)
    Hardware is Lance, address is 0002.17ac.a601 (bia 0002.17ac.a601)
    MTU 1500 bytes, BW 100000 Kbit, DLY 1000 usec,
          reliability 255/255, txload 1/255, rxload 1/255
    Encapsulation ARPA, loopback not set
    Keepalive set (10 sec)
    Half-duplex, 100Mb/s
    input flow-control is off, output flow-control is off
    ARP type: ARPA, ARP Timeout 04:00:00
[Output Cut]
```

A. The port has been administratively shut down.

B. The port has an access violation on it.

C. The port has bad wiring.

D. The port on the switch is configured as a trunk.

19. Which command will allow the first MAC address learned on the port to be allowed to only pass traffic on the port via port security?

A. `SwitchA(config-if)#switchport port-security mac-address sticky`

B. `SwitchA(config-if)#switchport port-security mac-address dynamic`

C. `SwitchA(config-if)#switchport port-security mac-address static`

D. `SwitchA(config-if)#switchport port-security mac-address learn`

20. Refer to the following exhibit. You receive a call that a port on the switch is not working. You determine that a port-security violation has been experienced. Once the violation has been remediated, how will you reset the port so that it functions again?

```
SwitchA#show interfaces fastEthernet 0/1
FastEthernet0/1 is down, line protocol is down (err-disabled)
    Hardware is Lance, address is 0002.17ac.a601 (bia 0002.17ac.a601)
    MTU 1500 bytes, BW 100000 Kbit, DLY 1000 usec,
        reliability 255/255, txload 1/255, rxload 1/255
    Encapsulation ARPA, loopback not set
    Keepalive set (10 sec)
    Half-duplex, 100Mb/s
    input flow-control is off, output flow-control is off
    ARP type: ARPA, ARP Timeout 04:00:00
[Output Cut]
```

A. `SwitchA(config-if)#no port-security`

B. `SwitchA(config-if)#no shutdown`

C. `SwitchA(config-if)#no switchport port-security`

D. `SwitchA(config-if)#shutdown`
   `SwitchA(config-if)#no shutdown`

21. Which command will configure the port with only the MAC address you want to allow via port security?

A. `SwitchA(config-if)#switchport port-security mac-address sticky`

B. `SwitchA(config-if)#switchport port-security mac-address 0334.56f3.e4e4`

C. `SwitchA(config-if)#switchport port-security mac-address static`
   `0334.56f3.e4e4`

D. `SwitchA(config-if)#switchport port-security static 0334.56f3.e4e4`

22. Which command is used to see the output in the following exhibit?

```
Secure Port  MaxSecureAddr  CurrentAddr  SecurityViolation  Security Action
                            (Count)        (Count)           (Count)
--------------------------------------------------------------------------------
      Gi2/1        1           1              0               Restrict
      Gi2/2        1           1              0               Restrict
      Gi2/3        1           1              0               Restrict
      Gi2/4        1           1              0               Restrict
      Gi2/5        1           1              0               Restrict
      Gi2/6        1           1              0               Restrict
      Gi2/7        1           1              0               Restrict
      Gi2/8        1           1              0               Restrict
      Gi2/9        1           1              0               Restrict
     Gi2/10        1           1              0               Restrict
     Gi2/11        1           1              0               Restrict
     Gi2/12        1           1              0               Restrict
     Gi2/13        1           1              0               Restrict
     Gi2/14        1           1              0               Restrict
```

   A. Switch#show port-security details

   B. Switch#show mac address-table secure

   C. Switch#show port-security address

   D. Switch#show port-security

23. Which command will allow you to globally reset all ports with an err-disable state with minimal disruption?

   A. Switch#clear err-disable

   B. Switch#clear switchport port-security

   C. Switch#clear port-security violation

   D. Switch(config)#errdisable recovery cause psecure_violation

24. You need to verify the sticky MAC addresses learned on a port on the switch. Which command will allow you to verify the addresses learned?

   A. SwitchA#show running-configuration

   B. SwitchA#show port-security

   C. SwitchA#show port-security details

   D. SwitchA#show port-security status

25. Which is a correct statement about sticky MAC addresses learned on a switchport?

   A. Sticky MAC addresses are removed by performing a shutdown on the port.

   B. Sticky MAC addresses become part of the running-configuration.

   C. Sticky MAC addresses can be explicitly configured manually.

   D. Sticky MAC addresses automatically become part of the startup-configuration.

26. You need to change a device on a port with which a sticky MAC address is associated. Which command will allow you to change the device and allow for a new sticky MAC address to be learned?

   A. Switch#clear switchport port-security f 0/0

   B. Switch(config-if)#no switchport port-security

   C. Switch#clear port-security f 0/0

   D. Switch(config-if)#no switchport port-security mac-address sticky
      0045.2342.e4c3

27. Referring to the following exhibit, which statement is correct about the status of port security?

```
SwitchA#sh port-security interface g 2/43
Port Security            : Enabled
Port Status              : Secure-up
Violation Mode           : Restrict
Aging Time               : 0 mins
Aging Type               : Absolute
SecureStatic Address Aging : Disabled
Maximum MAC Addresses    : 2
Total MAC Addresses      : 2
Configured MAC Addresses : 0
Sticky MAC Addresses     : 2
Last Source Address:Vlan : 000b.8278.ce5b:4
Security Violation Count : 0
[Output Cut]|
```

A. Only one MAC address is learned on the interface.

B. The port is currently in an access violation status.

C. The port is currently up and normal.

D. The MAC addresses have been seen 0 minutes ago.

28. Which command will allow you to see all the dynamically learned MAC addresses for port security?

A. SwitchA#show running-configuration

B. SwitchA#show mac address-table

C. SwitchA#show port-security details

D. SwitchA#show port-security address

29. Referring to the following exhibit, which statement is correct about the status of port security?

```
SwitchA#sh port-security interface g 2/43
Port Security            : Enabled
Port Status              : Secure-shutdown
Violation Mode           : Shutdown
Aging Time               : 0 mins
Aging Type               : Absolute
SecureStatic Address Aging : Disabled
Maximum MAC Addresses    : 1
Total MAC Addresses      : 2
Configured MAC Addresses : 0
Sticky MAC Addresses     : 1
Last Source Address:Vlan : 00aa.8278.c55b:4
Security Violation Count : 326
[Output Cut]|
```

A. Two MAC address are allowed on the interface.

B. The port is currently in an access violation status.

C. The port is currently up and normal.

D. The MAC addresses have been seen 0 minutes ago.

30. Which command is used to see the output in the following exhibit?

Vlan	Mac Address	Type	Ports	Remaining Age (mins)
21	e42b.cbce.6630	SecureSticky	Gi2/1	-
21	e42b.cba0.6d77	SecureSticky	Gi2/2	-
21	e42b.cbce.5812	SecureSticky	Gi2/3	-
21	e42b.cbce.609d	SecureSticky	Gi2/4	-
21	e42b.cbce.5b50	SecureSticky	Gi2/5	-
21	e42b.cba0.1307	SecureSticky	Gi2/6	-
21	e42b.cbce.5b6c	SecureSticky	Gi2/7	-
21	e42b.cbce.6356	SecureSticky	Gi2/8	-
21	e42b.cba0.0ab4	SecureSticky	Gi2/9	-

A. Switch#show port-security details

B. Switch#show mac address-table secure

C. Switch#show port-security address

D. Switch#show port-security

31. In which interface mode should you configure port security for end devices?

A. Dynamic

B. Access

C. Trunk

D. Voice

32. Which statement is correct about the configuration in the following exhibit?

```
interface GigabitEthernet2/23
 description Point of Sale system
 switchport access vlan 23
 switchport mode access
 switchport port-security violation  restrict
 switchport port-security mac-address sticky
 switchport port-security mac-address sticky 782b.cb9f.6431
 switchport port-security
 spanning-tree portfast
end
```

A. The port will restrict the MAC address of 782b.cb9f.6431.

B. The port will be in an err-disable state when the maximum threshold is exceeded.

C. The maximum number of MAC addresses is one.

D. The port should be set to shutdown to stop unauthorized access.

33. Which command is used to see the output in the following exhibit?

```
Port Security : Enabled
Port Status : Secure-up
Violation Mode : Shutdown
Aging Time : 0 mins
Aging Type : Absolute
SecureStatic Address Aging : Disabled
Maximum MAC Addresses : 1
Total MAC Addresses : 1
Configured MAC Addresses : 0
Sticky MAC Addresses : 0
Last Source Address : 0004.00d5.285d
Security Violation Count : 0
```

    A. `Switch#show port-security details`

    B. `Switch#show mac address-table gi 2/3`

    C. `Switch#show port-security gi 2/3`

    D. `Switch#show port-security interface gi 2/3`

34. You have default configuration on a port, which is also configured for port security. One of your junior admins is switching out equipment on the port. Which command will need to be entered so the port does not go into the violation mode?

    A. `Switch#clear port-security dynamic interface gi 2/3`

    B. `Switch(config-if)#no port-security mac-address`

    C. `Switch(config-if)#switchport port-security maximum 2`

    D. `Switch#clear port-security interface gi 2/3`

35. Which command would configure a port to forget the dynamically learned MAC address after 24 hours?

    A. `Switch(config-if)#switchport port-security aging 1440`

    B. `Switch(config-if)#switchport port-security aging time 1440`

    C. `Switch(config-if)#switchport port-security time 1440`

    D. `Switch(config-if)#switchport port-security maximum time 1440`

36. Which term describes the area outside of the corporate firewall?

    A. DMZ area

    B. Perimeter area

    C. Internal area

    D. Trusted area

37. How does DHCP snooping track DHCP messages and mitigate attacks?

    A. DHCP filtering

    B. DHCP binding table

    C. Untrusted ports

    D. IOS ACLs

38. Which term describes the area accessible to the Internet yet protected by the corporate firewall?

    A. DMZ

    B. Perimeter

    C. Internal

    D. Trusted

39. Which type of device can prevent an intrusion on your network?

   A. Honey pots

   B. IDS

   C. IPS

   D. HIDS

40. When dealing with firewalls, the term *trusted network* is used to describe what?

   A. Internal network

   B. The Internet

   C. The DMZ

   D. A network with SSL

41. Which is a common attack method used to overwhelm services from traffic from multiple Internet sources?

   A. Denial of service

   B. Distributed denial of service

   C. IP address spoofing

   D. Session hijacking

42. Which type of device can detect an intrusion on your network?

   A. Honey pots

   B. IDS

   C. IPS

   D. HIDS

43. When you configure DHCP snooping on a network, which mode are clients configured in?

   A. Untrusted mode

   B. Trusted mode

   C. Client mode

   D. Access mode

44. What method does DHCP snooping employ to thwart DHCP starvation attacks?

   A. DHCP guard

   B. DHCP filtering

   C. Rate limiting

   D. IOS ACLs

45. Which method will allow you to mitigate from a spurious DHCP attack?

   A. DHCP snooping

   B. DHCP filtering

   C. Rate limiting

   D. IOS ACLs

46. Which method can be used to stop ping sweep scans?

    A. Deploying host intrusion detection systems

    B. Deploying network intrusion detection systems

    C. Blocking RFC 1918 addresses at the perimeter

    D. Blocking ICMP echo-requests and echo-replies at the perimeter

47. Which appliance can be used to mitigate denial of service attacks?

    A. Honey pots

    B. IDS

    C. IPS

    D. HIDS

48. Which is a common attack method used to attempt to gain access to a system using a false identity?

    A. Denial of service

    B. Distributed denial of service

    C. IP address spoofing

    D. Session hijacking

49. Which method would prevent tampering of data in transit?

    A. Access control lists

    B. Spoofing mitigation

    C. Secure Sockets Layer

    D. Encryption of the data

50. A rouge wireless access point is created with the same SSID as the corporate SSID. The attacker has employees connect to the SSID and watches the information as it's relayed to the original SSID. What type of attack is described here?

    A. Smurf attack

    B. Compromised key attack

    C. Sniffer attack

    D. Man in the middle attack

51. What can you use to protect against spoofing of internal IP addresses on the perimeter of your network?

    A. Access control lists

    B. Intrusion detection systems

    C. Secure Sockets Layer

    D. Host intrusion detection systems

52. Which is a requirement for the use of DHCP snooping to protect a device?

   A. The device is on a layer 2 switched port on the same VLAN.

   B. The DHCP server is running on the layer 2 switch.

   C. The device is on a layer 3 routed port on the same VLAN.

   D. Configuration of a dedicated IP for monitoring DHCP transactions.

53. What attack vector can be used for a man in the middle attack?

   A. DHCP

   B. DNS

   C. Wireless

   D. All of the above

54. What is the default mode port configured on a switch for DHCP snooping?

   A. Trusted

   B. Internal

   C. External

   D. Untrusted

55. Which VLAN is the default native VLAN for Cisco switches?

   A. VLAN 1

   B. VLAN 2

   C. VLAN 255

   D. VLAN 1024

56. You have just configured DHCP snooping. Which ports should be trusted?

   A. Ports connecting to clients

   B. Ports connecting to web servers

   C. Ports connecting to other switches

   D. Ports connecting to the DNS server

57. Which is a correct statement about how DHCP snooping works?

   A. Untrusted ports allow Discover and Offer messages to be switched.

   B. Untrusted ports drop Discover and Offer messages.

   C. Untrusted ports drop Offer and Acknowledgment messages.

   D. Untrusted ports allow Offer and Acknowledgment messages to be switched.

58. Which attack can be used on a native VLAN?

   A. Double tagging

   B. VLAN traversal

   C. Trunk popping

   D. Denial of service

59. Which command is used to view the DHCP snooping database?

A. `Switch#show dhcp binding`

B. `Switch#show ip dhcp binding`

C. `Switch#show ip dhcp snooping database`

D. `Switch#show ip dhcp snooping binding`

60. Which command is used to configure the port of a switch as trusted for DHCP snooping?

A. `Switch(config-if)#ip dhcp snooping trust`

B. `Switch(config-if)#dhcp snooping trust`

C. `Switch(config)#ip dhcp snooping trust interface gi 2/3`

D. `Switch(config-if)#ip dhcp trust`

61. Why should you always change the native VLAN?

A. The native VLAN contains frames from all VLANs.

B. The native VLAN is configured on all switches for logging.

C. The native VLAN is the default on all switchports.

D. The native VLAN provides no encryption.

62. Which technology will give selective access to the network based upon authentication?

A. 802.1Q

B. ACLs

C. 802.1x

D. Firewall

63. What is the end device that sends credentials for 802.1x called?

A. Authenticator

B. Supplicant

C. AAA server

D. RADIUS server

64. What is the switch called in an 802.1x configuration?

A. Authenticator

B. Supplicant

C. AAA server

D. RADIUS server

65. What protocol does the supplicant communicate to the authenticator for 802.1x?

A. 802.1x layer 2 protocol

B. UDP

C. TCP

D. IP

66. What is the attack in which DTP is exploited by a malicious user?

    A. Native VLAN

    B. VLAN hopping

    C. VLAN traversal

    D. Trunk popping

67. Which protocol is used by 802.1x for end-to-end authentication from the supplicant to the authentication server?

    A. 802.1x authentication headers

    B. IPSec

    C. EAP

    D. RADIUS

68. Which device is the supplicant during the 802.1x authentication process?

    A. The device requesting access

    B. The server that is providing authentication

    C. The device that is controlling access via 802.1x

    D. The device connecting the layer 3 network

69. Which mechanism is used to authenticate EAP-TLS during the 802.1x authentication process?

    A. MD5

    B. Certificates

    C. SSH

    D. Passwords

70. Which port must be open to the RADIUS or AAA server for authentication from the authenticator?

    A. UDP/49

    B. UDP/1821

    C. UDP/1812

    D. UDP/1813

71. What is the range of a standard access list?

    A. 1 to 99

    B. 1 to 100

    C. 100 to 199

    D. 100 to 200

72. Which statement is correct about a standard access control list?

    A. Conditions can be based upon only the destination address.

    B. Conditions can be based upon only the source address and source port.

    C. Conditions can be based upon only the source address.

    D. Conditions can be based upon the source or destination address and source or destination port.

73. What is the range of an extended access list?

    A. 1 to 99

    B. 1 to 100

    C. 100 to 199

    D. 100 to 200

74. What is at the end of every access control list?

    A. Permit any any

    B. Deny any any

    C. Log all

    D. End of ACL marker

75. Which statement is correct about an access control list?

    A. Packets are compared sequentially against each line in an access list, and the last matching condition is the action taken.

    B. Packets are compared sequentially against each line in an access list until a match is made.

    C. Packets are compared, and if no matching rule exists, they are allowed.

    D. At the end of the access control list, there is an implicit allow.

76. What is an advantage of using a standard access control list?

    A. More secure

    B. Less processing overhead

    C. More specific rules

    D. Blocking of applications

77. What is the expanded range of a standard access list?

    A. 1000 to 1999

    B. 1100 to 1299

    C. 1300 to 1999

    D. 2000 to 2699

78. You need to filter traffic for the 172.16.0.0/12 network. Which wildcard mask would you use?

    A. 255.240.0.0

    B. 0.0.240.255

    C. 0.15.255.255

    D. 255.3.0.0

79. Which command would configure an ACL to block traffic coming from 192.168.1.0/24?

    A. `Router(config)#ip access-list 20 192.168.1.0 0.0.0.255`

    B. `Router(config)#ip access-list 100 192.168.1.0 0.0.0.255`

    C. `Router(config)#ip access-list 1 192.168.1.0/24`

    D. `Router(config)#ip access-list 2 192.168.1.0 255.255.255.0`

80. If you configure a rule with the address of 0.0.0.0 and wildcard mask of 255.255.255.255, what are you doing?

    A. Defining the broadcast address

    B. Defining no addresses

    C. Defining the network address

    D. Defining all addresses

81. Which statement is correct about applying ACLs to an interface?

    A. An access control list can be applied in only one direction.

    B. An access control list can be applied only to a single protocol.

    C. An access control list can be applied only to a single port.

    D. All of the above

82. You need to filter an application. Which type of access list will you use to complete the task?

    A. Standard

    B. Extended

    C. Dynamic

    D. Expanded

83. What is the expanded range of an extended access list?

    A. 1000 to 1999

    B. 1100 to 1299

    C. 1300 to 1999

    D. 2000 to 2699

84. You need to filter traffic for the 192.168.1.0/25 network. Which wildcard mask would you use?

   A. 255.255.255.128

   B. 0.0.0.128

   C. 0.0.0.127

   D. 0.0.0.63

85. Which type of access control list allows for removing a single entry without removing the entire ACL?

   A. Standard

   B. Dynamic

   C. Extended

   D. Named

86. Which type of access control list allows you to open a port only after someone has successfully logged into the router?

   A. Standard

   B. Dynamic

   C. Extended

   D. Named

87. Which statement configures a standard access list?

   A. `Router(config)#access-list 20 deny 172.16.0.0 0.255.255.255`

   B. `Router(config)#access-list 180 permit udp any 172.16.0.0 0.255.255.255 eq 161`

   C. `Router(config)#access-list 130 permit permit ip any any`

   D. `Router(config)#access-list 150 deny any 172.16.0.0 0.255.255.255`

88. Which statement can be used in lieu of `access-list 5 permit 192.168.1.5 0.0.0.0`?

   A. `Router(config)#access-list 5 permit 192.168.1.5`

   B. `Router(config)#access-list 5 permit 192.168.1.5/24`

   C. `Router(config)#access-list 5 permit host 192.168.1.5`

   D. `Router(config)#access-list 5 permit 192.168.1.0 0.0.0.255`

89. Referring to the following exhibit, you need to block traffic from the host 192.168.2.6 to the HR web application server but allow it to get to all other servers and the Internet. Which command(s) will achieve this?

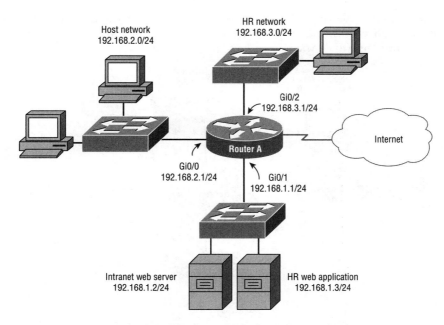

- **A.** Router(config)#access-list 101 deny tcp host 192.168.2.6 host 192.168.1.3 eq 80 Router(config)#access-list 101 permit any any
- **B.** Router(config)#access-list 101 deny tcp host 192.168.2.6 host 192.168.1.3 eq 80 Router(config)#access-list 101 permit ip any any
- **C.** Router(config)#access-list 101 deny host 192.168.2.6 host 192.168.1.3 eq 80 Router(config)#access-list 101 permit any any
- **D.** Router(config)#access-list 101 deny tcp host 192.168.2.6 host 192.168.1.3 eq 80 Router(config)#access-list 101 permit ip any any eq 80

90. Which type of access list limits you to describing traffic by source address?
- **A.** Extended
- **B.** Named
- **C.** Dynamic
- **D.** Standard

91. Which statement will block traffic for a server of 192.168.1.5 for SSH?
- **A.** Router(config)#access-list 90 deny ip host 192.168.1.5 eq 22
- **B.** Router(config)#access-list 90 deny tcp any host 192.168.1.5 eq 22
- **C.** Router(config)#access-list 199 deny tcp host 192.168.1.5 any eq 23
- **D.** Router(config)#access-list 199 deny tcp any host 192.168.1.5 eq 22

92. Referring to the following exhibit, you need to block traffic from the host network to the HR web application and allow all traffic to get to the intranet web server. Which type of access control list would you use?

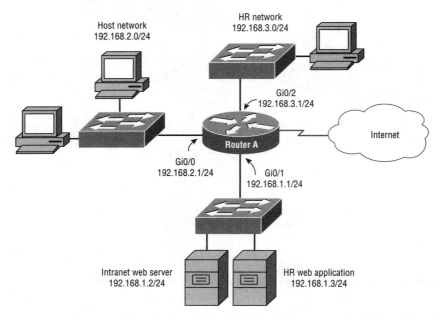

A. Standard

B. Dynamic

C. Extended

D. Expanded

93. Which statement configures a valid access list?

A. Router(config)#access-list 99 deny tcp host 192.168.2.7 eq 443

B. Router(config)#access-list 189 deny any host 192.168.1.5 eq 22

C. Router(config)#access-list 143 permit tcp host 192.168.8.3 eq 80 any

D. Router(config)#access-list 153 permit any host 192.168.4.5 eq 22

94. You want to apply an access list of 198 to an interface to filter traffic into the interface. Which command will achieve this?

A. Router(config)#ip access-list 198 in fast 0/1

B. Router(config-if)#ip access-list 198 in

C. Router(config-if)#ip access-class 198 in

D. Router(config-if)#ip access-group 198 in

95. Referring to the following exhibit, you want to block the host network from accessing the HR network. Which commands will place the access list on the proper interface to make it effective?

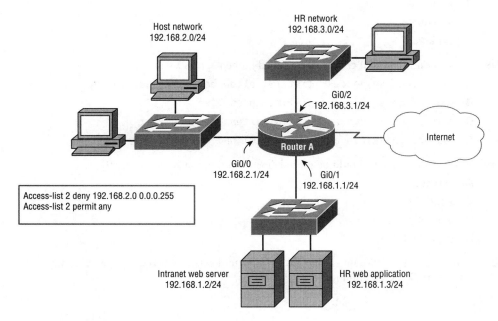

A. Router(config)#interface gi 0/0
   Router(config-if)#ip access-group 2 in

B. Router(config)#interface gi 0/0
   Router(config-if)#ip access-group 2 out

C. Router(config)#interface gi 0/2
   Router(config-if)#ip access-group 2 in

D. Router(config)#interface gi 0/2
   Router(config-if)#ip access-group 2 out

96. Which command will allow you to see the output in the following exhibit with the line numbers?

```
[Output Cut]
Extended IP access list named_list
    10 permit ip any any
    20 permit tcp host 192.168.1.6 host 192.168.2.3 eq 22
    30 permit udp any host 192.168.2.3 eq 123

Switch#
```

A. Switch#show access-list named_list

B. Switch#show ip access-list named_list

C. Switch#show running-configuration

D. Switch#show ip access-list

97. Which type of ACL should be placed closest to the source of traffic?

A. Extended

B. Standard

C. Dynamic

D. Expanded

98. Which command will create an extended named access list?

A. `Router(config)#access-list 101 allow host 192.168.1.5 any`

B. `Router(config)#ip access-list named_list`

C. `Router(config)#ip access-list extended named_list`

D. `Router(config)#ip access-list 101 named_list`

99. Which type of ACL should be placed closest to the destination of traffic?

A. Extended

B. Standard

C. Dynamic

D. Expanded

100. Referring to the following exhibit, you want to delete the `allow ip permit any any` statement. Which command will achieve this?

```
[Output Cut]
Extended IP access list named_list
    10 permit ip any any
    20 permit tcp any 192.168.2.3 eq 22
    30 permit udp any host 192.168.2.3 eq 123
Switch#
```

A. `Switch(config)#no ip access-list named_list`

B. `Switch(config-nacl)#remove 10`

C. `Switch(config-nacl)#no 10`

D. `Switch(config)#no ip access-list named_list 10`

101. After several edits to a named access control list, the numbers are no longer 10, 20, and 30, and you have no room to perform future edits. Which command will fix the problem with no disruption?

A. `Switch(config)#ip access-list named_list renumber`

B. `Switch#clear ip access-list named_list line-numbers`

C. `Switch(config)#ip access-list re-number named_list`

D. `Switch(config)#ip access-list resequence named_list 10 10`

102. Which command will apply the named access control list called named_list to the interface in an inbound direction?

   A. Router(config)#ip access-list named_list in fast 0/1

   B. Router(config-if)#ip access-list named_list in

   C. Router(config-if)#ip access-class named_list in

   D. Router(config-if)#ip access-group named_list in

103. In the following exhibit, you will need to block the servers from communicating to the Internet while allowing internal communications. Which commands will achieve this?

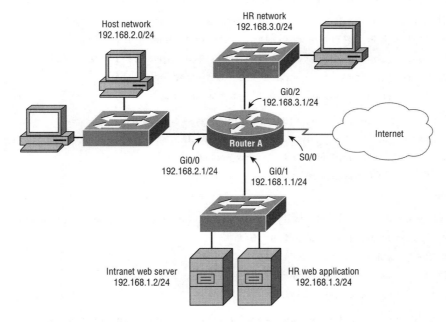

   A. Router(config)#ip access-list 6 deny 192.168.1.2
   Router(config)#ip access-list 6 deny 192.168.1.3
   Router(config)#ip access-list 6 permit any
   Router(config)#interface serial 0/0
   Router(config-if)#ip access-list 6 out

   B. Router(config)#ip access-list 6 deny 192.168.1.0 0.0.0.255
   Router(config)#ip access-list 6 permit any
   Router(config)#interface serial 0/0
   Router(config-if)#ip access-group 6 out

    C. `Router(config)#ip access-list 6 deny 192.168.1.0 0.0.0.255`
       `Router(config)#ip access-list 6 permit any`
       `Router(config)#interface serial 0/0`
       `Router(config-if)#ip access-list 6 out`

    D. `Router(config)#ip access-list 6 deny 192.168.1.0 0.0.0.255`
       `Router(config)#ip access-list 6 permit any`
       `Router(config)#interface serial 0/0`
       `Router(config-if)#ip access-group 6 in`

104. Which command will create an IPv6 access list?

    A. `Router(config)#ip access-list extended named_list ipv6`

    B. `Router(config)#ip access-list deny 2100 ipv6 2001:db8::1/64`

    C. `Router(config)#ipv6 access-list extended named_list`

    D. `Router(config)#ipv6 access-list named_list`

105. What is a difference between IPv6 and IPv4 access control lists?

    A. Implicit allow of any any at the end of the ACL

    B. Implicit allow of Neighbor Discovery packets

    C. The use of wildcard masks

    D. All of the above

106. Which command will help verify that an access control list is applied to an interface?

    A. `Router#show interface fast 0/1`

    B. `Router#show ip access-list`

    C. `Router#show ip interface fast 0/1`

    D. `Router#show access-list`

107. Which command will allow notes to be added to an access control list?

    A. `Router(config-nacl)#remark This is a note about the ACL`

    B. `Router(config-nacl)#note This is a note about the ACL`

    C. `Router(config-nacl)#banner ^This is a note about the ACL^`

    D. `Router(config-nacl)#info This is a note about the ACL`

108. Which command will allow you to see matching statistics for an access control list?

    A. `Router#debug ip access-list 2`

    B. `Router#show ip access-list 2`

    C. `Router#show ip interface fast 0/1`

    D. `Router#show access-list`

109. You want to see if a particular rule is matching packets in real time. Which command will allow you to do this?

   A. `Switch(config)#ip access-list 101 permit tcp host 192.168.1.6 any eq 80 debug`

   B. `Switch(config)#ip access-list 101 permit tcp host 192.168.1.6 any eq 80 log`

   C. `Switch(config)#ip access-list 101 log tcp host 192.168.1.6 any eq 80 debug`

   D. `Switch(config)#ip access-list 101 debug tcp host 192.168.1.6 any eq 80 debug`

110. If the Neighbor Discovery Protocol for IPv6 is blocked via an ACL, what is the negative effect?

   A. The gateway of the router will never be used.

   B. A duplicate IPv6 address is possible.

   C. Autoconfiguration of the network will be disabled.

   D. All of the above

111. What is the earliest version of the APIC-EM (Application Policy Infrastructure Controller Enterprise Module) required to use the Path Trace ACL Analysis tool?

   A. Version 0.9

   B. Version 1.0

   C. Version 1.1

   D. Version 1.2

112. What will you need to do before performing a path trace ACL analysis?

   A. Perform an ACL detection.

   B. Perform an environment discovery.

   C. Copy all ACLs into the APIC-EM.

   D. Manually enter all routers and switches into the APIC-EM.

113. What type of application is the Path Trace ACL Analysis tool?

   A. Base controller

   B. Basic application

   C. Solutions application

   D. DevNet application

114. Where do you download the APIC-EM?

   A. The Cisco software download site

   B. A Cisco partner download site

   C. The Cisco DevNet site

   D. The Cisco Network Academy site

115. In the following exhibit, what does the output from the trace path ACL analysis mean?

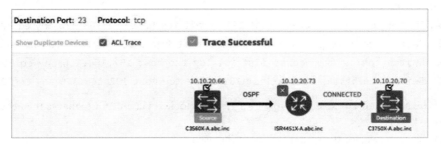

- **A.** The ISR4451X-A router is down.
- **B.** The ISR4451X-A router is not participating in OSPF.
- **C.** The ISR4451X-A has an ACL blocking the destination traffic.
- **D.** The link to ISR4451X-A is down.

116. What does the APIC-EM Path Trace ACL Analysis tool perform?
- **A.** It performs end-to-end analysis of ACLs for a given path.
- **B.** It performs analysis of ACLs to make sure they are correct.
- **C.** It helps create ACLs for data paths.
- **D.** All of the above

117. Which statement is correct about the Path Trace ACL Analysis tool?
- **A.** When performing an analysis, you must start by selecting the Path Trace option.
- **B.** When performing an analysis, you must start by selecting the ACL Analysis option.
- **C.** The Path Trace ACL Analysis tool helps you create ACLs.
- **D.** The Path Trace ACL Analysis tool helps with what-if scenarios.

118. What must be selected when performing a path trace ACL analysis?
- **A.** The type of ACL to be examined
- **B.** The path of the analysis
- **C.** The egress and ingress ports
- **D.** The data payload for the test

119. In the following exhibit, what does the output from the trace path ACL analysis mean?

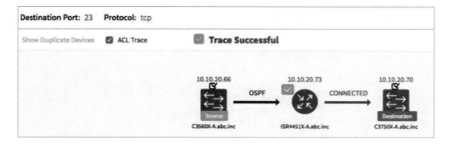

    A. The ISR4451X-A router has an ACL that is permitting the destination traffic.

    B. The ISR4451X-A router is participating in OSPF.

    C. The ISR4451X-A router is up.

    D. The link to ISR4451X-A is up.

120. If a device is blocking traffic for a path trace ACL analysis, what information does the interface give you to diagnose the problem?

    A. The tool will give you the correction to the ACL.

    B. The tool will allow you to perform a what-if scenario.

    C. The tool will show you the access control entry blocking traffic.

    D. The tool will allow you to create a new ACL.

121. Which command will configure the enable password for a router or switch?

    A. `Router(config)#password enable Password20!`

    B. `Router(config)#enable Password20!`

    C. `Router(config)#enable secret Password20!`

    D. `Router(config)#secret enable Password20!`

122. You need to set the login password for Telnet. Which command will you type first?

    A. `Switch(config)#interface vlan 1`

    B. `Switch(config)#line console 1`

    C. `Switch(config)#line aux 1`

    D. `Switch(config)#line vty 0 5`

123. You have set the enable password using `enable password Password20!`. However, when you try to get to a privileged exec prompt the router states that you are using an incorrect password. What is the problem?

    A. You originally entered the wrong password.

    B. The `enable secret` password is set to something else.

    C. The password *Password20!* contains a special character.

    D. The password is too long and has been truncated.

124. Which command(s) will set a password and require login for a line?

    A. `Router(config-line)#set password Password20!`
       `Router(config-line)#request login`

    B. `Router(config-line)#password Password20!`
       `Router(config-line)#login password`

    C. `Router(config-line)#password Password20!`
       `Router(config-line)#login`

    D. `Router(config-line)#login password Password20!`

125. You telnet to a switch and receive the error `Password required, but none set .[Connection to 192.168.1.1 closed by foreign host]`. What is the problem?

    A. The enable secret is not set.

    B. The enable password is not set.

    C. The line login password is not set.

    D. The line is administratively shut down.

126. What is required before generating the encryption keys for SSH on a router or switch?

    A. Setting the time and date

    B. Setting the hostname and domain name

    C. Setting the key strength

    D. Setting the key repository

127. Which command will enable SSH version 2 for logins?

    A. `Router(config)#ip ssh version 2`

    B. `Router(config-line)#version 2`

    C. `Router(config-ssh)#version 2`

    D. `Router(config)#ssh version 2`

128. Which command will configure the router or switch to allow SSH as a protocol for management with a fallback of Telnet?

    A. `Switch(config)#login ssh telnet`

    B. `Switch(config-line)#login ssh telnet`

    C. `Switch(config-line)#transport ssh telnet`

    D. `Switch(config)#transport ssh telnet`

129. Why should Telnet be replaced with SSH?

    A. Telnet has weak encryption.

    B. SSH allows for file copy.

    C. SSH makes it easier to create ACLs for access.

    D. SSH is encrypted.

130. Which command will create and apply an access list to secure router or switch management?

    A. `Switch(config)#access-list 1 permit host 192.168.1.5`

        `Switch(config)#interface vlan 1`

        `Switch(config-if)#ip access-group 1 in`

    B. `Switch(config)#access-list 1 permit host 192.168.1.5`

        `Switch(config)#line vty 0 5`

        `Switch(config-line)#ip access-group 1 in`

C. `Switch(config)#access-list 1 permit host 192.168.1.5`

   `Switch(config)#line vty 0 5`

   `Switch(config-line)#ip access-class 1 in`

D. `Switch(config)#access-list 1 permit host 192.168.1.5`

   `Switch(config)#ip access-group 1 in`

131. You have created the SSH encryption keys, but you cannot enable SSH version 2. What is the problem?

A. The time and date need to be corrected.

B. The key strength needs to be 768 bits or higher.

C. The DNS server is not configured.

D. There is no host record for the switch or router.

132. Which command will configure a local user for SSH access?

A. `Router(config)#username user1 password Password20!`

B. `Router(config)#account user1`

   `Router(config-acct)#password Password20!`

C. `Router(config)#user user1 Password20!`

D. `Router(config)#user-account user1 password Password20!`

133. You configured the password for Telnet access, but when you perform a `show running-configuration`, the password shows in clear text. Which command should be run?

A. `Router(config)#password encryption`

B. `Router(config)#service password-encryption`

C. `Router(config)#service encryption`

D. `Router(config)#password-encryption service`

134. Which command will generate the encryption keys for SSH?

A. `Router(config)#generate crypto key rsa`

B. `Router(config)#crypto key generate rsa`

C. `Router(config)#crypto generate key rsa`

D. `Router#crypto key generate rsa`

135. Which command will disable auto-disconnect for idle privileged exec sessions?

A. `Switch(config-line)#exec-timeout 0 0`

B. `Switch(config)#exec-timeout 0`

C. `Switch(config-line)#timeout 0 0`

D. `Switch(config-line)#no exec-timeout`

136. In the following exhibit, you have listed all management sessions on the switch. On which line are you connected?

```
Switch#show users
      Line      User    Host(s)       Idle      Location
    0 con 0     admin                 00:00:20
  * 1 vty 0     admin   10.30.2.3     00:00:00  10.30.2.3
    2 vty 1     admin   10.30.2.4     00:00:00  10.30.2.4
    3 vty 2     admin   10.30.2.5     00:00:00  10.30.2.5
```

A. Console 0

B. VTY 0

C. VTY 1

D. VTY 2

137. You want to turn on local authentication so that a user must supply a username and password when managing the switch. You have created the username and password combinations on the switch. Which command will direct SSH and Telnet to use this authentication model?

A. `Switch(config)#new aaa model`

B. `Switch(config)#local authentication`

C. `Switch(config-line)#local authentication`

D. `Switch(config-line)#login local`

138. During a recent external security audit, it was determined that your enable password should be secured with SHA-256 scrypt. Which command will change the password strength on the switches and routers?

A. `Switch(config)#enable secret 9`

B. `Switch(config)#service password-encryption scrypt`

C. `Switch(config)#enable secret algorithm-type scrypt`

D. `Switch(config)#enable algorithm-type scrypt secret Password20!`

139. What is the default encryption method for passwords, when you configure a line password?

A. MD5

B. SHA-128

C. SHA-256

D. Clear text

140. You need to change the default idle time before disconnection of privileged exec mode for network administrators. Which command will change it to 30 minutes?

A. `Switch(config)#exec-timeout 30 0`

B. `Switch(config-line)#exec-timeout 30 0`

C. `Switch(config-line)#exec-timeout 0 30`

D. `Switch(config-line)#timeout 30 0`

141. You need to disconnect a network admin from the switch or router. Which command would you use?

A. `Switch(config)#no enable secret`

B. `Switch#no line vty 2`

C. `Switch#disconnect line vty 2`

D. `Switch#clear line vty 2`

142. Which banner can deliver a message only to authenticated users regardless of connection type?

A. MOTD banner

B. Login banner

C. Exec banner

D. Incoming banner

143. Which banner will be displayed first when a user connects to a Cisco device via SSH?

A. MOTD banner

B. Login banner

C. Exec banner

D. Incoming banner

144. Which command will configure the login banner to read "CCNA Routing and Switching"?

A. `Router(config)#login banner CCNA Routing and Switching`

B. `Router(config)#banner login CCNA Routing and Switching`

C. `Router(config)#banner login ^CCNA Routing and Switching^`

D. `Router(config-line)#banner login ^CCNA Routing and Switching^`

145. You have configured a message of the day (MOTD) banner, but it only shows up after you have logged into the router. What is the problem?

A. You are connecting via SSH.

B. You are connecting via Telnet.

C. You are connecting via the console.

D. You do not have an enable password set.

146. Which server will centralize authentication for all Cisco routers and switches?

A. Active Directory server

B. AAA server

C. 802.1x server

D. Terminal server

147. Which protocol and port does RADIUS authentication use?

   A. UDP/1845

   B. UDP/1645

   C. TCP/1645

   D. UDP/1911

148. Which is an authentication protocol for AAA servers to secure Telnet authentication?

   A. 802.1x

   B. TACACS+

   C. AD

   D. EAP

149. Which port and protocol does TACACS+ use?

   A. UDP/69

   B. TCP/74

   C. UDP/47

   D. TCP/49

150. Which is a benefit of using TACACS+ for authentication of users?

   A. It is an open standard.

   B. It encrypts the password of users.

   C. It supports authenticating a user to a subset of commands.

   D. It supports authenticating a user to a length of time.

151. Which command will configure the router to use a TACACS+ server and a backup of local for authentication of logins?

   A. `Router(config)#aaa authentication login default group tacacs+ local`

   B. `Router(config)#authentication login group tacacs+ local`

   C. `Router(config)#aaa-authentication login default tacacs+ local`

   D. `Router(config)#aaa authentication login tacacs+ local`

152. You configured the AAA authentication for login to default local but forgot to create a local AAA user. What will happen when you log out?

   A. The enable secret will work.

   B. The console will still be available.

   C. The router will lock you out.

   D. Nothing, since a username and password have not been set.

153. Why should you always provide a second method of local when setting up AAA remote authentication with a router or switch?

   A. To allow for a backdoor

   B. To provide a backup if the TACACS+ server is down or unreachable

   C. The local second method is required

   D. All of the above

154. Which command will configure the RADIUS server 192.168.1.5 with a secret of aaaauth?

   A. `Router(config)#radius host 192.168.1.5 key aaaauth`

   B. `Router(config)#radius-server host 192.168.1.5 key aaaauth`

   C. `Router(config)#radius-server 192.168.1.5 key aaaauth`

   D. `Router(config)#radius-server host 192.168.1.5 secret aaaauth`

155. Which protocol will encrypt the entire packet from the switch or router to the AAA server?

   A. 802.1x

   B. IPSEC

   C. RADIUS

   D. TACACS+

Chapter

7

Infrastructure Management (Domain 7)

THE CCNA EXAM TOPICS COVERED IN THIS PRACTICE TEST INCLUDE THE FOLLOWING:

✓ **7.0 Infrastructure Management (ICND1) (ICND2)**

- 7.1 Configure and verify device-monitoring protocols (ICND1) (ICND2)

  - 7.1a SNMPv2 (ICND2)

  - 7.1b SNMPv3 (ICND2)

  - 7.1c Syslog (ICND1)

- 7.2 Troubleshoot network connectivity issues using ICMP echo-based IP SLA (ICND2)

- 7.3 Configure and verify device management (ICND1)

  - 7.3a Backup and restore device configuration (ICND1)

  - 7.3b Using Cisco Discovery Protocol or LLDP for device discovery (ICND1)

  - 7.3c Licensing (ICND1)

  - 7.3d Logging (ICND1)

  - 7.3e Timezone (ICND1)

  - 7.3f Loopback (ICND1)

- 7.4 Configure and verify initial device configuration (ICND1)

- 7.5 Perform device maintenance (ICND1)

  - 7.5a Cisco IOS upgrades and recovery (SCP, FTP, TFTP, and MD5 verify) (ICND1)

  - 7.5b Password recovery and configuration register (ICND1)

  - 7.5c File system management (ICND1)

- 7.6 Use Cisco IOS tools to troubleshoot and resolve problems (ICND1)

  - 7.6a Ping and traceroute with extended option (ICND1)

  - 7.6b Terminal monitor (ICND1)

  - 7.6c Log events (ICND1)

  - 7.6d Local SPAN (ICND2)

- 7.7 Describe network programmability in enterprise network architecture (ICND2)

  - 7.7a Function of a controller (ICND2)

  - 7.7b Separation of control plane and data plane (ICND2)

  - 7.7c Northbound and southbound APIs (ICND2)

1. Which version of Simple Network Management Protocol (SNMP) supports the Inform SNMP message?

   A. SNMP version 1

   B. SNMP version v2

   C. SNMP version 2c

   D. SNMP version 3

2. Which protocol and port number does SNMP use for polling from the NMS?

   A. UDP/161

   B. TCP/162

   C. UDP/162

   D. UDP/514

3. Which version of SNMP offers authentication and encryption?

   A. SNMP version 1

   B. SNMP version 2e

   C. SNMP version 2c

   D. SNMP version 3

4. What is the database of variables that SNMP uses to allow for collection of data called?

   A. Object identifiers

   B. Management information base

   C. SNMP agent

   D. SNMP community

5. What is the component that an SNMP agent sends information to?

   A. Syslog

   B. Network management station

   C. Object identifier

   D. Management Information Base

6. What type of SNMP message is sent to a network management station when an interface goes down?

   A. Get-request message

   B. Get-response message

   C. Set-request message

   D. Trap message

7. Which of the following is a hierarchical set of variables that make up the management information base?

   A. Object IDs

   B. The SNMP community

   C. The SNMP agent

   D. SNMP messages

8. What is the difference between trap messages and inform messages for SNMP?

   A. Trap messages are always encrypted.

   B. Inform messages do not use acknowledgment.

   C. Trap messages always use acknowledgment.

   D. Inform messages always use acknowledgment.

9. Which security method does SNMP version 2c employ?

   A. Encryption

   B. User authentication

   C. Community strings

   D. Message integrity

10. Which command will configure the SNMP agent with a read-only community of "snmpreadonly"?

   A. `Switch(config)#snmp-agent community snmpreadonly ro`

   B. `Switch(config)#snmp-server snmpreadonly ro`

   C. `Switch(config)#ip snmp-server community snmpreadonly ro`

   D. `Switch(config)#snmp-server community snmpreadonly read-only`

11. Which of the following can be used in conjunction with an SNMP agent configuration for added security?

   A. Encrypted communities

   B. Access control lists

   C. SNMP callback security

   D. SHA-256

12. Which command will allow you to configure contact information for SNMP for Sybex Publishing?

   A. `Switch(config)#snmp-agent location main-idf4-ru23`

   B. `Switch(config)#snmp-server contact Sybex Publishing`

   C. `Switch(config)#snmp-server contact-info Sybex Publishing`

   D. `Switch(config)#snmp contact Sybex Publishing`

13. Which command(s) will configure SNMPv2c to trap messages to a network management station in the event of component failure?

    A. `Switch(config)#snmp-server 192.168.1.5 version 2c C0mmun1ty`
       `Switch(config)#snmp-server enable traps`

    B. `Switch(config)#snmp-server host 192.168.1.5 version 2c`
       `Switch(config)#snmp-server enable traps`

    C. `Switch(config)#snmp-server host 192.168.1.5 version 2c C0mmun1ty`
       `Switch(config)#snmp-server enable traps`

    D. `Switch(config)#snmp contact trap 192.168.1.5 version 2c`

14. Which command will allow you to verify the configured ACL applied to the SNMP agent?

    A. `Switch#show snmp`

    B. `Switch#show snmp community`

    C. `Switch#show snmp acl`

    D. `Switch#show ip interface`

15. Which protocol and port number does SNMP use for trap and inform messages to the NMS?

    A. UDP/161

    B. TCP/162

    C. UDP/162

    D. UDP/514

16. Which command will allow you to verify the network management station that is configured to receive trap notifications?

    A. `Switch#show snmp`

    B. `Switch#show snmp community`

    C. `Switch#show snmp host`

    D. `Switch#show snmp notifications`

17. When you configure SNMPv3 for a restricted OID, what is the first step?

    A. Configuring a group

    B. Configuring a view

    C. Configuring a user

    D. Configuring a community

18. When you configure an SNMPv3 group, which parameter will configure authentication and encryption of data?

    A. `auth`

    B. `noauth`

    C. `priv`

    D. `enc`

19. Which command will configure an SNMP view named INT-VIEW, which will include the ifIndex OID?

   A. `Switch(config)#snmp-server view INT-VIEW ifIndex include`

   B. `Switch(config)#snmp-server v3 view INT-VIEW ifIndex include`

   C. `Switch(config)#snmp-server view INT-VIEW ifIndex`

   D. `Switch(config)#snmp-server INT-VIEW ifIndex`

20. Which command will allow you to verify a user's authentication and encryption settings for SNMPv3?

   A. `Switch#show user auth`

   B. `Switch#show user priv`

   C. `Switch#show snmp user`

   D. `Switch#show snmp user auth`

21. Which command will allow you to verify the view associated with a group?

   A. `Switch#show group view`

   B. `Switch#show snmp group`

   C. `Switch#show snmp group view`

   D. `Switch#show snmp group-view`

22. Which protocol and port number does syslog use?

   A. UDP/161

   B. TCP/162

   C. UDP/162

   D. UDP/514

23. Which command will configure all event logs to be sent to a syslog server?

   A. `Router(config)#logging server 192.168.1.6`

   B. `Router(config)#logging 192.168.1.6`

   C. `Router(config)#logging host 192.168.1.6`

   D. `Router(config)#syslog server 192.168.1.6`

24. Which command will allow you to verify the syslog server set for logging and the logging level set?

   A. `Router#show logging`

   B. `Router#show syslog`

   C. `Router#show log-server`

   D. `Router#show ip logging`

25. Which command will configure the severity level of syslog events that will be sent to the syslog server for debugging?

   A. `Router(config)#syslog debugging`

   B. `Router(config)#logging debugging`

   C. `Router(config)#logging trap debugging`

   D. `Router(config)#log-level debugging`

26. What is a service-level agreement (SLA) for network connectivity?

   A. It is an agreement of bandwidth between the ISP and the customer.

   B. It is a quality of service agreement between the ISP and the customer.

   C. It is an agreement of uptime between the ISP and the customer.

   D. All of the above

27. Which feature in Cisco routers can a network administrator use to check the provider's SLA?

   A. IP SLA

   B. Syslog

   C. ACLs and policy-based routing

   D. SNMP

28. On which device(s) can you configure the Cisco IP SLA feature to allow for statistics' collection?

   A. Routers and switches

   B. Switches only

   C. Routers only

   D. Router, switches, and all other Cisco devices

29. Which type of IP SLA check does not require an SLA responder?

   A. UDP jitter probe

   B. VoIP jitter probe

   C. ICMP echo probe

   D. MPLS probe

30. What is the term used for the IP SLA router that sends packets and collects and compiles statistics on the packets?

   A. IP SLA responder

   B. IP SLA sender

   C. IP SLA collector

   D. IP SLA source

31. Which command(s) will configure an IP SLA for ICMP echo probe?

   A. `Router(config)#ip sla icmp-echo 192.168.1.2`

   B. `Router(config)#ip sla 1`
      `Router(config-ip-sla)#icmp-echo 192.168.1.2`

   C. `Router(config)#ip sla 1`
      `Router(config-ip-sla)#icmp 192.168.1.2`

   D. `Router(config)#ip sla 1 icmp-echo 192.168.1.2`

32. What is the default timer (frequency) for an IP SLA ICMP echo probe?

   A. 60 seconds

   B. 120 seconds

   C. 60 minutes

   D. 5 minutes

33. Which command will configure an IP SLA schedule for a probe?

   A. `Router(config-ip-sla)#ip sla schedule life forever start-time now`

   B. `Router(config)#ip sla 1 schedule life forever start-time now`

   C. `Router(config)#ip sla 1 schedule forever start-time now`

   D. `Router(config)#ip sla 1 schedule life start-now`

34. Which command will allow you to view the statistics of an IP SLA ICMP echo probe for all configured buckets?

   A. `Router#show ip sla`

   B. `Router#show ip sla statistics 1`

   C. `Router#show ip sla history 1`

   D. `Router#show sla summary`

35. You have running on your router an IP SLA ICMP echo probe that checks the ISP connection. When you view the historical statistics, you notice that several of the tests in the probe have a result of 4 in the Sense column. What happened during those tests?

   A. The test for the probe ran successfully.

   B. The test for the probe did not receive a response.

   C. The test for the probe exceeded a set threshold.

   D. The test for the probe was out of sequence.

36. Which command will allow you to verify the size of storage for flash as well as how much free space is available?

   A. `Switch#show storage`

   B. `Switch#show file storage`

   C. `Switch#show file systems`

   D. `Switch#show file free`

37. Where is the startup-config stored?

   A. Flash

   B. NVRAM

   C. System

   D. RAM

38. If power is lost, which command will retain the configuration for bootup?

   A. `Router#copy running-config startup-config`

   B. `Router#save running-config`

   C. `Router#cp running-config startup-config`

   D. `Router#write running-config startup-config`

39. You need to decommission a router. You want to clear only the configuration off the router. Which command will achieve this?

   A. `Router#clear startup-config`

   B. `Router#format flash:`

   C. `Router#format startup-config`

   D. `Router#erase startup-config`

40. Which command will allow you to verify the IOS images you have on the flash file system?

   A. `Router#show flash: filesystem`

   B. `Router#show boot`

   C. `Router#dir flash:`

   D. `Router#dir /flash`

41. Which command will back up the startup-config for a device to a server?

   A. `Switch#archive startup-config tftp:`

   B. `Switch#backup startup-config tftp://192.168.1.2`

   C. `Switch#copy startup-config tftp:`

   D. `Switch#copy startup-config server:`

42. Which command will restore configuration to the running-config for a device from a server?

   A. `Switch#archive tftp: running-config`

   B. `Switch#restore tftp://192.168.1.2 running-config`

   C. `Switch#copy tftp: running-config`

   D. `Switch#copy server: running-config`

43. You have been given the task of mapping a network. You have several routers and switches that are interconnected. Which Cisco tool will help you map the network?

A. CDP

B. Running-config

C. OSPF neighbor table

D. EIGRP neighbor table

44. You are contracted to fix a networking issue. The technical staff has given you the network logins for all the routers and switches. You discover that the problem is not on the router you are connected to but on a neighboring router. How can you obtain the management IP address of the neighboring router?

A. `RouterA#show ip route`

B. `RouterA#show ip interface`

C. `RouterA#show ip protocols`

D. `RouterA#show cdp neighbors detail`

45. You have neighboring equipment on the switch that is running LLDP. Which command(s) will allow you to see the neighboring equipment's management IP addresses?

A. `Switch(config)#enable lldp`
`Switch(config)#exit`
`Switch#show lldp neighbors detail`

B. `Switch(config)#lldp run`
`Switch(config)#exit`
`Switch#show lldp neighbors detail`

C. `Switch#show lldp neighbors detail`

D. `Switch(config)#enable lldp`
`Switch(config)#exit`
`Switch#show lldp neighbors *`

46. What is the term used to describe Cisco's current IOS image naming convention, which contains all the feature sets and is licensed upon feature use?

A. Universal image

B. Unified image

C. Fusion image

D. Central image

47. What allows you to download the current IOS from Cisco for your router or switch?

A. Cisco provides upgrades for free; nothing is required.

B. You need a current SMARTnet contract for the device.

C. One free upgrade is permitted per the life of the device.

D. An activation key is required, which is purchased from a retailer.

48. You have a new router and you have purchased the IP Base license along with it. You want to use the voice feature set on the router. What is required?

  A. A current SMARTnet contract for the device is required.

  B. Cisco provides one free feature set upgrade.

  C. An activation key is required, which is purchased from a retailer.

  D. A new Cisco IOS with the feature set included is required.

49. Which tool allows you to manage all of your Cisco device licensing needs through a single user interface?

  A. Cisco SMARTnet

  B. Cisco License Manager

  C. Cisco Network Assistant

  D. Cisco Prime Infrastructure

50. Which command would you use to obtain a device's product ID (PID) and unique device identifier (UDI) for the activation process?

  A. `Switch#show version`

  B. `Switch#show license`

  C. `Switch#show license udi`

  D. `Switch#show licensing`

51. Which command will show which features are activated, available, and in evaluation mode on a router or switch?

  A. `Switch#show license feature`

  B. `Switch#show version`

  C. `Switch#show features`

  D. `Switch#show licensing`

52. Which license will allow a Cisco router to enable a feature set for evaluation?

  A. UDI license

  B. Right-to-use license

  C. Evaluation license

  D. Enforcement license

53. You are connected to the console of a switch. As you are configuring the switch, console logging is disrupting your commands and making it hard to configure the switch properly. Which command will allow the console message to still appear but not disrupt what you are typing?

  A. `Switch#no logging inline`

  B. `Switch(config)#logging synchronous`

  C. `Switch(config-line)#logging synchronous`

  D. `Switch#logging synchronous`

54. Which command sets the time zone of a router for Pacific Standard Time?

A. `Router(config)#clock timezone pacific`

B. `Router(config)#clock timezone pst -8`

C. `Router(config)#timezone pacific`

D. `Router(config)#timezone pst -8`

55. Which command will send all warnings to the syslog server?

A. `Switch(config)#logging server 4`

B. `Switch(config)#logging trap 4`

C. `Switch(config)#logging trap 5`

D. `Switch(config)#logging server 5`

56. Which command will send logging with time stamps rather than sequence numbers?

A. `Switch(config)#logging timestamps log datetime`

B. `Switch(config)#logging timestamps datetime`

C. `Switch(config)#service datetime timestamps`

D. `Switch(config)#service timestamps log datetime`

57. Which command will configure Eastern Daylight Time?

A. `Switch(config)#clock timezone EST -5 daylight`

B. `Switch(config)#clock daylight-savings`

C. `Switch(config)#clock summer-time EDT recurring`

D. `Switch(config)#clock tz EDT -5`

58. Which command will limit console logging to the severity level of alerts?

A. `Router(config)#logging console 0`

B. `Router(config-line)#logging level 0`

C. `Router(config)#logging console 7`

D. `Router(config-line)#logging level 7`

59. You are configuring NTP on your switch. You want to configure the switch so if any interface fails, NTP will still be available. Which type of interface should you use?

A. Tunnel interface

B. NTP interface

C. Loopback interface

D. Switched Virtual Interface (SVI)

60. Which command will configure NTP to use the internal loopback interface?

A. `Switch(config)#ntp source loopback 0`

B. `Switch(config)#ntp loopback 0`

C. `Switch(config)#ntp master loopback 0`

D. `Switch(config)#ntp clock loopback 0`

61. Which command will configure a loopback interface with an address of 192.168.1.2/24?

    A. `Router(config)#interface loopback 0`
       `Router(config-if)#ip address 192.168.1.2/24`

    B. `Router(config)#interface loopback 0`
       `Router(config-if)#ip address 192.168.1.2 255.255.255.0`

    C. `Router(config)#interface loopback`
       `Router(config-if)#ip address 192.168.1.2/24`

    D. `Router(config)#interface loopback`
       `Router(config-if)#ip address 192.168.1.2 255.255.255.0`

62. Which command will configure logging stored in RAM to include only logs with a severity level of emergencies and alerts?

    A. `Switch(config)#logging buffered 1`

    B. `Switch(config)#logging 1`

    C. `Switch(config)#logging buffered 2`

    D. `Switch(config)#logging 2`

63. Which command will allow you to see the commands you previously entered?

    A. `Switch#show commands`

    B. `Switch#show log`

    C. `Switch#show history`

    D. `Switch#show buffer`

64. Which command will extend the history buffer to 30 for all users?

    A. `Switch#terminal history size 30`

    B. `Switch(config)#history size 30`

    C. `Switch#history size 30`

    D. `Switch(config-line)#history size 30`

65. Which command will extend the history buffer to 30 for only the current session?

    A. `Switch#terminal history size 30`

    B. `Switch(config)#history size 30`

    C. `Switch#history size 30`

    D. `Switch(config-line)#history size 30`

66. Which command will set the name of a router to PGH-4-209?

    A. `Router#name PGH-4-209`

    B. `Router(config)#name PGH-4-209`

    C. `Router(config)#hostname PGH-4-209`

    D. `Router(config)#system-name PGH-4-209`

67. You need to jump to the beginning of a long command string you just entered. Which key combination will achieve this?

A. Ctrl+B

B. Ctrl+A

C. Ctrl+E

D. Ctrl+1

68. You need to jump to the end of a long command string you just edited but has not been committed yet. Which key combination will achieve this?

A. Ctrl+B

B. Ctrl+A

C. Ctrl+E

D. Ctrl+1

69. Which command will allow you to enter privileged exec mode from user exec mode?

A. `Router>enable`

B. `Router>login`

C. `Router>priv`

D. `Router>enter`

70. You start up a brand-new router out of the box with no configuration on it. What will be displayed when it boots?

A. Setup mode

B. User exec mode

C. Privileged exec mode

D. Global configuration mode

71. Which key combination will escape you out of configuration mode and bring you back to privileged exec mode?

A. Ctrl+D

B. Ctrl+Z

C. Ctrl+F

D. Ctrl+C

72. Which command will show the current time and date on the switch?

A. `Switch#show date`

B. `Switch#show time`

C. `Switch#show clock`

D. `Switch#show ntp`

73. Which command will allow you to create short notes about an interface that will remain with the configuration?

A. Router(config-if)#remark Connection to Switch1

B. Router(config-if)#note Connection to Switch1

C. Router(config-if)#description Connection to Switch1

D. Router(config-if)#!Connection to Switch1

74. You are in configuration mode and need to remain in configuration mode but want to see the running-config. Which command combination will allow you to do this?

A. Router(config-if)#show running-config

B. Router(config-if)#do show running-config

C. Router(config-if)#!show running-config

D. Router(config-if)#[CTRL-Z]

75. You want to filter the results of show running-config to see only SNMP configuration commands. Which command will allow you to do this?

A. Switch#show running-config filter snmp

B. Switch#show filter running-config snmp

C. Switch#show running-config snmp

D. Switch#show running-config | include snmp

76. You have a switch with several hundred interfaces. You only want to see the running-config for one interface, Gi3/45. Which command will allow you to see the running-config for only Gi3/45?

A. Switch#show interface gi 3/45

B. Switch#show running-config | include 3/45

C. Switch#show running-config interface gi 3/45

D. Switch#show running gi 3/45

77. Which command will set the router's internal clock to 2:24 December 1, 2016?

A. Router(config)#clock set 2:24:00 1 august 2016

B. Router#clock set 2:24:00 1 august 2016

C. Router(config)#clock set 2:24:00 august 1 2016

D. Router#clock 2:24:00 1 august 2016

78. You are mapping a network with the use of CDP. On the entry of cs-main.ntw, what is the connection of Gig 0/1 used for in the following exhibit?

```
es-switch2#show cdp neighbors
[Output Cut]
Device ID       Local Intrfce   Holdtme   Capability   Platform   Port ID
cs-main.ntw     Gig 0/1         138          R S C     WS-C3560X  Gig 0/40
es-layer2.ntw   Gig 0/2         178            S I     WS-C3560X  Gig 1/1
es-switch3.ntw  Gig 0/3         178            S I     WS-C3560X  Gig 1/2
es-switch2#
```

    A. The Gig 0/1 interface on es-switch2

    B. The Gig 0/1 interface on cs-main.ntw

    C. The Gig 0/1 interface on es-layer2.ntw

    D. The Gig 0/1 interface on es-switch3.ntw

79. You are examining the output of the command `show cdp neighbors detail`. One of the devices has the capability of S and R. What does this mean?

    A. The device has source routing bridge capability.

    B. The device has switch capability.

    C. The device has router capability.

    D. The device has switch and router capability.

80. Your network is connected in a star topology. You are assessing a network upgrade. Which command will help you determine the version of IOS on the switches and routers in your network, with the least amount of effort?

    A. `Switch#show version`

    B. `Switch#show running-config`

    C. `Switch#show cdp neighbors detail`

    D. `Switch#show lldp neighbors`

81. Which command will allow you to enter global configuration mode for editing RAM?

    A. `Switch#configure network`

    B. `Switch#configure memory`

    C. `Switch#configure overwrite-network`

    D. `Switch#configure terminal`

82. Which command will allow you to verify the configured exec timeout?

    A. `Router#show version`

    B. `Router#show terminal`

    C. `Router#show exec-timeout`

    D. `Router#show timeout-exec`

83. Which key sequence will cause a break during a network command such as `ping` or `traceroute`?

    A. Ctrl+C

    B. Ctrl+4

    C. Ctrl+Shift+6

    D. Ctrl+Shift+1

84. Which command will display the serial number of the switch?

 A. `Switch#show version`

 B. `Switch#show serial`

 C. `Switch#show board`

 D. `Switch#show controller`

85. You have a rather large configuration on a switch. You want to see the running-config, but only after port gi4/45. Which command will achieve this?

 A. `Switch#show running-config begin 4/45`

 B. `Switch#show filter running-config 4/45`

 C. `Switch#show running-config interface gi 4/45`

 D. `Switch#show running-config | begin 4/45`

86. Which command will begin the upgrade of an IOS from a TFTP server?

 A. `Switch#copy tftp flash`

 B. `Switch#copy tftp ios`

 C. `Switch#copy tftp nvram`

 D. `Switch#upgrade tftp flash`

87. Which command will allow you to verify the size of flash memory and how much space is still free?

 A. `Switch#show version`

 B. `Switch#show free`

 C. `Switch#dir flash:`

 D. `Switch#show filesystem`

88. Which command will perform an MD5 hash against an image on flash memory so that you can verify its integrity?

 A. `Router#integrity md5 flash:/c2900-universalk9-mz.SPA.151-4.M4.bin`

 B. `Router#md5 flash:/c2900-universalk9-mz.SPA.151-4.M4.bin`

 C. `Router#verify /md5 flash:/c2900-universalk9-mz.SPA.151-4.M4.bin`
    `eef3f723c164f2af84ccfcbd642d121d`

 D. `Router#integrity /md5 flash:/c2900-universalk9-mz.SPA.151-4.M4.bin`
    `eef3f723c164f2af84ccfcbd642d121d`

89. What is the default configuration register for a Cisco switch or router?

 A. 0x2104

 B. 0x2102

 C. 0x2100

 D. 0x2012

90. Which command needs to be configured to enable the SSH Copy Protocol (SCP)?

A. `Switch(config)#ip ssh server enable`

B. `Switch(config)#ip scp server enable`

C. `Switch(config)#service scp enable`

D. `Switch(config)#service scp-server`

91. Which copy method will encrypt the IOS over the network during an upgrade?

A. HTTP

B. TFTP

C. FTP

D. SCP

92. You have enabled the SCP server on a switch, but when you try to log in it returns "access denied." Which command must you configure to allow access to the SCP server if your username was *scpadmin* and your password was *Sybex*?

A. `Switch(config)#ip scp user scpadmin password Sybex`

B. `Switch(config)#username scpadmin password Sybex`

C. `Switch(config)#username scpadmin privilege-level 15 password Sybex`

D. `Switch(config)#ip scp user scpadmin privilege-level 15 password Sybex`

93. Which command will allow you to view the contents of a file in the IOS File System (IFS)?

A. `Switch#type flash:/info`

B. `Switch#file flash:/info`

C. `Switch#cat flash:/info`

D. `Switch#more flash:/info`

94. After copying an IOS image named c2900-universalk9-mz.SPA.151-4.M4.bin, you reboot the router only to find that it has booted to the old IOS image. What needs to be configured to boot the new image?

A. `Router(config)#boot system flash:/c2900-universalk9-mz.SPA.151-4.M4.bin`

B. `Router(config)#boot image flash:/c2900-universalk9-mz.SPA.151-4.M4.bin`

C. `Router(config)#boot flash:/c2900-universalk9-mz.SPA.151-4.M4.bin`

D. `Router(config)#boot system-image flash:/c2900-universalk9-mz.SPA.151-4.M4.bin`

95. Which command will change the configuration register to 0x2100?

A. `Router(config)#confreg 0x2100`

B. `Router#confreg 0x2100`

C. `Router(config)#config-register 0x2100`

D. `Router#config-register 0x2100`

96. Which command will help you verify what the configuration register is currently set to?

   A. `Switch#show confreg`

   B. `Switch#show running-config`

   C. `Switch#show version`

   D. `Switch#show register`

97. What is the name of the system loaded on a router or switch when the primary IOS image fails to load?

   A. BIOS

   B. NVRAM

   C. OpenBIOS

   D. ROMMON

98. During a normal boot process, how does the bootstrap process decide which IOS version to load if multiple versions are present on flash?

   A. The bootstrap process checks the startup-config in NVRAM.

   B. The bootstrap process chooses the highest version.

   C. The bootstrap process checks the configuration register.

   D. The bootstrap process checks flash for a file named `version.txt`.

99. You have just updated the IOS on a router and you have configured the command `boot system flash:/c2900-universalk9-mz.SPA.151-4.M4.bin`. The command completes successfully, and you cycle the power. However, the original image boots. What is wrong?

   A. You have incorrectly typed the image name.

   B. You have not saved the configuration.

   C. You are not licensed for the Universal feature set.

   D. The IOS image needs to be verified before it can be used.

100. You need to make sure that the running-config is saved every night to the NVRAM. Which method will allow you to achieve this task?

   A. Training of network administrators to save configuration

   B. Configuring an archive process on the router

   C. Use of an external process such as Cisco Prime Infrastructure

   D. Configuration of a TCL script

101. Which command will allow you to boot a router from a TFTP server for the image of c2900-universalk9-mz.SPA.151-4.M4.bin on the TFTP server of 192.168.1.2?

   A. `Router#boot tftp://192.168.1.2`

   B. `Router(config)#boot tftp://192.168.1.2 c2900-universalk9-mz.SPA.151-4.M4.bin`

   C. `Router(config)#boot system tftp://192.168.1.2 c2900-universalk9-mz.SPA.151-4.M4.bin`

   D. `Router(config)#boot system c2900-universalk9-mz.SPA.151-4.M4.bin 192.168.1.2`

102. During the bootstrap process, where is the IOS image decompressed to?

   A. NVRAM

   B. RAM

   C. ROMMON

   D. Flash

103. When a password recovery is performed on a router, what should the configuration register be set to?

   A. 0x2100

   B. 0x2102

   C. 0x2142

   D. 0x2182

104. What command will allow you to verify the current running IOS version?

   A. `Router#show ios`

   B. `Router#show version`

   C. `Router#show running-config`

   D. `Router#show bootvar`

105. You're upgrading the flash memory on a 2900 router with a brand-new flash card. What needs to be done to restore the IOS?

   A. The new flash memory will have a mini-IOS installed. You will need to upgrade it from the mini-IOS.

   B. The router will boot into the ROMMON, and from there you will need to TFTP download the IOS.

   C. Nothing needs to be done because the IOS is not storage on the flash memory card.

   D. Format the flash card with the FAT operating system and copy the IOS image to the card.

106. Which command will allow you to back up the current IOS image to a TFTP server? Assume the image is named `c3560-advipservicesk9-mz.122-37.SE1.bin`.

   A. `Router#backup flash:/c3560-advipservicesk9-mz.122-37.SE1.bin tftp`

   B. `Router#copy flash:/c3560-advipservicesk9-mz.122-37.SE1.bin tftp`

   C. `Router#copy tftp flash:/c3560-advipservicesk9-mz.122-37.SE1.bin`

   D. `Router#archive flash:/c3560-advipservicesk9-mz.122-37.SE1.bin tftp`

107. Which command will allow you to view all of the archives of running-config stored in flash?

   A. `Switch#show archive`

   B. `Switch#show config`

C. `Switch#show flash`

D. `Switch#show running-config *`

108. Which command will roll back the third archive of the running-config?

A. `Switch#rollback flash:myconfig-3`

B. `Switch#configure replace flash:myconfig-3`

C. `Switch#configure restore flash:myconfig-3`

D. `Switch#restore flash:myconfig-3`

109. When configuring the archive process, which command will specify a time period of 24 hours?

A. `Switch(config-archive)#time-period 24`

B. `Switch(config-archive)#time 24`

C. `Switch(config-archive)#time 1440`

D. `Switch(config-archive)#time-period 1440`

110. Your router has a USB slot, and you need to back up the IOS to a flash drive. What format must the flash drive have in order to perform the backup?

A. FAT

B. NTFS

C. EXT3

D. Cisco IFS

111. You have connected to a switch via SSH and you want to see the logging messages. Which command should you use?

A. `Switch#terminal monitor`

B. `Switch#terminal logging`

C. `Switch(config-line)#terminal monitor`

D. `Switch(config-line)#terminal logging`

112. You have configured a switch so you can see all console logging in the current SSH session. You no longer wish to see the console logging. Which command will configure the SSH session back to the default?

A. `Switch#no terminal monitor`

B. `Switch#terminal no monitor`

C. `Switch#no terminal logging`

D. `Switch(config-line)#no terminal logging`

113. In the following exhibit, Host A suddenly cannot communicate with Host B. Using the `ping` command, which device will you ping first to diagnose the problem?

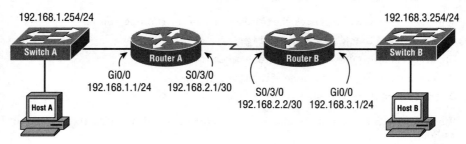

192.168.1.254/24   192.168.3.254/24

Switch A — Router A — Router B — Switch B

Gi0/0   S0/3/0
192.168.1.1/24   192.168.2.1/30   S0/3/0   Gi0/0
                                   192.168.2.2/30   192.168.3.1/24

Host A   Host B

- **A.** Switch A
- **B.** Router A
- **C.** Router B
- **D.** Switch B

114. Which command can you use to verify that a ping packet is exiting the interface you expect it to exit, which in this example is Gi0/1 with an IP address of 192.168.3.5?

- **A.** `Router#ping 192.168.3.5 Gi 0/1`
- **B.** `Router#ping Gi 0/1 192.168.3.5`
- **C.** `Router#debug ip packet`
- **D.** `Router#debug ip ping`

115. You are troubleshooting an application and need to capture the packets for an interface on a switch. Which method should you use to capture the packets?

- **A.** Netflow
- **B.** SPAN
- **C.** NIC teaming
- **D.** IP snooping

116. Which is a correct statement about the following exhibit?

```
Tracing the route to 192.168.3.1

  1   192.168.10.2    10 msec   1 msec    0 msec
  2   192.168.10.6     2 msec   2 msec    3 msec
  3        *               *         *
  4   192.168.20.3     2 msec   3 msec    3 msec
RouterA#
```

- **A.** The third hop is down.
- **B.** The third hop is not responding to ICMP.
- **C.** The traceroute never completed.
- **D.** The third hop is unavailable and packets have been rerouted.

117. Which tool can be used to analyze a packet capture?

   A. Netflow

   B. Wireshark

   C. SPAN

   D. RSPAN

118. Which feature is available when using an extended ping?

   A. Larger datagram size

   B. Larger repeat counts

   C. Changing the timeout

   D. Source interface or IP address

119. Which command will configure the source interface of Gi 1/1 for a SPAN session on a switch?

   A. `Switch(config)#span session 1 source interface gi 1/11 both`

   B. `Switch(config)#session span 1 source interface gi 1/11 both`

   C. `Switch(config)#monitor session 1 source interface gi 1/11 both`

   D. `Switch(config)#monitor session 1 gi 1/11 both`

120. Which command will allow you to see configured SPAN sessions on the switch?

   A. `Switch#show monitor span session`

   B. `Switch#show monitor session all`

   C. `Switch#show span`

   D. `Switch#show session`

121. Which command will configure a SPAN session for an entire VLAN as a source, assuming it's VLAN 23?

   A. `Switch(config)#monitor session 1 source vlan 23`

   B. `Switch(config)#session span 1 source vlan 23`

   C. `Switch(config)#monitor session 1 source interface vlan 23 both`

   D. `Switch(config)#monitor session 1 vlan 23 both`

122. You need to create a SPAN session for five Fast Ethernet ports. You want to watch both the tx (transmit) and rx (receive) on the ports. What is the sizing of the destination port you will require?

   A. 100 Mb/s

   B. 1 Gb/s

   C. 10 Gb/s

   D. 40 Gb/s

123. Which command will configure the removal of a SPAN session 1?

    A. `Switch(config)#no span session 1`

    B. `Switch(config)#no session span 1`

    C. `Switch(config)#no monitor session 1`

    D. `Switch(config)#clear monitor session 1`

124. Which command will configure the destination port for a SPAN session? Assume that you are working with session 1 and the destination port is Gi 1/14.

    A. `Switch(config)#monitor session 1 destination gi 1/14`

    B. `Switch(config)#monitor span 1 destination gi 1/14`

    C. `Switch(config)#monitor session 1 destination interface gi 1/14 both`

    D. `Switch(config)#monitor session 1 destination interface gi 1/14`

125. Which statement is correct about the following exhibit?

```
Switch#show monitor session 1 detail
Session 1
---------
Type                    : Local Session
Description             : -
Source Ports            :
    RX Only             : None
    TX Only             : None
    Both                : Fa0/1
Source VLANs            :
    RX Only             : None
    TX Only             : None
    Both                : 2
Source RSPAN VLAN       : None
Destination Ports       : Fa0/2
    Encapsulation       : Native
        Ingress         : Disabled
Filter VLANs            : None
Dest RSPAN VLAN         : None
```

    A. The source interface is Fa0/1 with a destination interface of Fa0/2.

    B. The source interface is Fa0/2 with a destination interface of Fa0/1.

    C. The source interface is Fa0/1 with a destination interface of Fa0/2 via VLAN 2.

    D. The source interface is Fa0/1 and VLAN 2 with a destination interface of Fa0/2.

126. What needs to be configured, when you want to create a SPAN session over multiple switches?

    A. RSPAN

    B. SPAN

    C. VPN-SPAN

    D. VSPAN

127. You want to perform a traceroute with more than three ICMP packets using an extended traceroute. Which attribute will you change to allow for multiple ICMP packets?

    A. Probe count

    B. Numeric display

    C. Maximum Time to Live

    D. Packet type

128. What severity is being logged to in the following exhibit?

```
RouterD#
%LINEPROTO-5-UPDOWN: Line protocol on Interface GigabitEthernet0/0, changed state to down
%LINEPROTO-5-UPDOWN: Line protocol on Interface GigabitEthernet0/0, changed state to up
```

  A. Informational

  B. Notifications

  C. Warnings

  D. Debug

129. You need to check the current CPU utilization on a router. Which command will achieve this?

  A. `Router#show cpu`

  B. `Router#show cpu-stats`

  C. `Router#show processes`

  D. `Router#show environment cpu`

130. Which command will direct logging to the internal log space?

  A. `Router(config)#logging buffered`

  B. `Router(config)#logging internal`

  C. `Router(config)#logging ram`

  D. `Router(config)#logging console`

131. Which network plane is used for Spanning Tree Protocol (STP)?

  A. Data plane

  B. Control plane

  C. Management plane

  D. Switch plane

132. Which network plane is used by syslog for delivering messages from the router or switch?

  A. Data plane

  B. Control plane

  C. Management plane

  D. Switch plane

133. Which statement is correct about the software-defined network (SDN) controller?

  A. The SDN controller configures the management plane of network devices.

  B. The SDN controller monitors data plane traffic.

  C. The SDN controller replaces the control plane of the SDN.

  D. The SDN controller complements the control plane of the SDN.

134. Which is used for communication directly to the SDN devices in the network?

    A. The northbound interface (NBI)

    B. The southbound interface (SBI)

    C. The core of the controller

    D. Applications hosted on the controller

135. What is an application program interface (API)?

    A. An API is a program that allows for data transfer.

    B. An API is a programming language for network programmability.

    C. An API is a programming interface or standard allowing one program to communicate with another program.

    D. An API allows for programs to be virtualized.

136. When a network packet is routed in a router, which network plane is facilitating the traffic?

    A. Data plane

    B. Control plane

    C. Management plane

    D. Switch plane

137. When an application communicates with a software-defined network (SDN) controller, which mechanism does it use to communicate?

    A. The southbound interface (SBI)

    B. The core of the controller

    C. The northbound interface (NBI)

    D. Simple Network Management Protocol (SNMP)

138. Which protocol is normally used with REST APIs?

    A. SNMP

    B. HTTP

    C. SNTP

    D. SOAP

139. Which platform is Cisco's software-defined network controller offering for enterprise connectivity?

    A. APIC-EM

    B. OpenSDN

    C. OpenStack

    D. OpenDaylight

140. On which network plane would a routing protocol perform?

    A. Data plane

    B. Control plane

    C. Management plane

    D. Routing plane

Chapter

8

Practice Test 1

THE CCNA EXAM TOPICS COVERED IN THIS PRACTICE TEST INCLUDE THE FOLLOWING:

- ✓ 1.0 Network Fundamentals (ICND1)
- ✓ 2.0 LAN Switching Technologies (ICND1) (ICND2)
- ✓ 3.0 Routing Technologies (ICND1) (ICND2)
- ✓ 4.0 WAN Technologies (ICND2)
- ✓ 5.0 Infrastructure Services (ICND1) (ICND2)
- ✓ 6.0 Infrastructure Security (ICND2)
- ✓ 7.0 Infrastructure Management (ICND1) (ICND2)

1. At which layer of the OSI model does Structured Query Language (SQL) operate?
    A. Application layer
    B. Session layer
    C. Presentation layer
    D. Transport layer

2. You are designing a wireless network for an office building. The building has a large number of tenants that utilize wireless already. Which protocol will least likely overlap with wireless channels the tenants are currently using?
    A. 802.11b
    B. 802.11g
    C. 802.11n
    D. 802.11ac

3. Which protocol is connectionless and is used for flow control?
    A. IP
    B. TCP
    C. UDP
    D. ICMP

4. Which cloud service is likely to be used for software development?
    A. SaaS
    B. IaaS
    C. PaaS
    D. DRaaS

5. Which statement is correct about straight-through cables and crossover cables?
    A. Crossover cables are wired with pins 1 through 8 on one side and 8 through 1 on the other side.
    B. Crossover cables are wired with the 568B specification on both sides.
    C. Straight-through cables are wired with the 568B specification on one side and the 568A specification on the other side.
    D. Crossover cables are wired with the 568B specification on one side and the 568A specification on the other side.

6. Which protocol is used by IPv6 to assist Stateless Address Autoconfiguration (SLAAC) in IPv6 addressing for hosts?
    A. ICMPv6
    B. DHCPv6
    C. UDP
    D. TCP

7. Which term best describes the IPv6 address of 2202:0ff8:0002:2344:3533:8eff:fe22:ae4c?

    A. Multicast address

    B. EUI-64 address

    C. Anycast address

    D. Link local address

8. Which network does the IP address 192.168.4.28/27 belong to?

    A. 192.168.4.8/27 network

    B. 192.168.4.16/27 network

    C. 192.168.4.32/27 network

    D. 192.168.4.64/27 network

9. The following exhibit is an Ethernet frame. What is field A in the exhibit?

7-byte preamble	SFD	Field A	Field B	Field C	Field D	Field E

    A. Source MAC address

    B. Destination MAC address

    C. Type Field

    D. Frame Checking Sequence (FCS)

10. Which switch function reads the frame and uses the MAC address table to decide the egress interface for the frame?

    A. Forward/filter

    B. Address learning

    C. Loop avoidance

    D. Frame flooding

11. Which type of switchport strips all VLAN information from the frame before it egresses the interface on the switch?

    A. Trunk port

    B. Access port

    C. Voice port

    D. DTP port

12. You have VLAN 10 and VLAN 11 configured on a trunk switchport as allowed. What will happen if you enter the command `switchport trunk allowed vlan 12` on the trunk interface?

    A. VLAN 12 will be added to the existing allowed VLAN list.

    B. VLANs 1 through 12 will be added to the allowed VLAN list.

    C. The native VLAN will be switched to VLAN 12.

    D. Only VLAN 12 will be on the allowed VLAN list.

13.   Which statement is true about the following exhibit below?

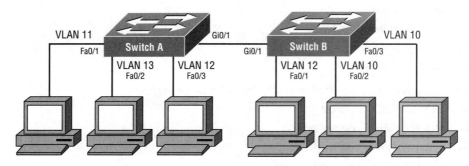

A.   Switch A interface Gi0/1 is configured as an access switchport to Switch B interface Gi0/1.

B.   Switch A interface Gi0/1 and Switch B interface Gi0/1 are both configured as trunk switchports.

C.   Switch B interface Fa0/1 is misconfigured with a duplicate VLAN ID.

D.   Switch A interface Fa0/3 is misconfigured with a duplicate VLAN ID.

14.   In the following exhibit, Rapid Spanning Tree Protocol (RSTP) is configured. Which interfaces will become the root ports?

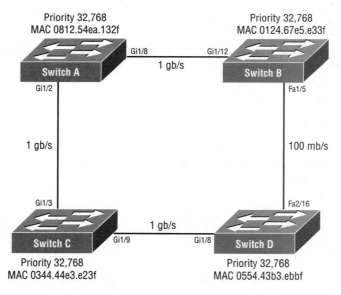

A.   Switch B interface Fa1/5 and Gi1/12

B.   Switch A interface Gi1/8 and Switch D interface Fa2/16

C.   Switch A interface Gi1/8, Switch D interface Fa2/16, and Switch C interface Gi1/3

D.   Switch A interface Gi1/2 and Switch D interface Gi1/8

15. On a switch you enter the commands `switchport mode access` and `switchport nonegotiate`. Which statement is true about the interface you've configured?

A. The interface will become a trunk switchport if a switch is plugged in and DTP is turned on for the other switch.

B. The interface will always remain an access switchport, regardless of whether another a switch is plugged in.

C. The interface will become a trunk switchport if a switch is plugged in and the other switch is set statically to a trunk switchport.

D. The interface will become a trunk switchport if a non-Cisco switch is plugged in and statically configured as a trunk switchport.

16. You are configuring a channel group for two interfaces. You configure the command `channel-group 1 mode passive`. What must be configured on the other switch to use Link Aggregation Control Protocol (LACP)?

A. The other switch must be configured with `channel-group 1 mode active`.

B. The other switch must be configured with `channel-group 1 mode desirable`.

C. The other switch must be configured with `channel-group 1 mode on`.

D. The other switch must be configured with `channel-group 1 mode auto`.

17. You have BPDU Guard configured on an interface. You receive a call that the interface is down. You perform a `show interface gi 0/1` only to find that the port is in an err-disable state. What caused the err-disable state?

A. A neighboring switch recalculated its Spanning Tree Protocol (STP).

B. The endpoint device connected to the interface sent a BPDU.

C. The endpoint device was disconnected for a long period of time.

D. The interface is transitioning between an up and down state rapidly, called interface flapping.

18. Which protocol assists in synchronizing a VLAN database across multiple Cisco switches?

A. NTP

B. IGMP

C. ISL

D. VTP

19. When you're using 802.1w, which switchport state will always forward traffic?

A. Disabled

B. Backup

C. Designated

D. Alternate

20. In the following exhibit, if Host A sends a packet to Host B, how many frames will be encapsulated during the process?

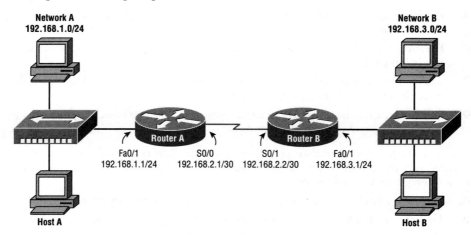

A. One

B. Three

C. Five

D. Six

21. What is the definition of route statement administrative distance (AD)?

A. The AD is a metric that routing protocols use to select the best route.

B. The AD is a value assigned by network administrators for route selection.

C. The AD is a rating of trust when multiple routes exist to the same destination.

D. The AD is a value associated with the cost to the destination.

22. Which must be configured so that EIGRP can calculate the best route?

A. Bandwidth

B. Delay

C. Reliability

D. Load

23. You perform a show ip route on the router and see several routes with an administrative distance (AD) of 90. Which routing protocol has generated these route statements?

A. IGRP

B. OSPF

C. EIGRP

D. RIP

24. You are configuring RIP for a network and you need to advertise the network. Which command will advertise the route for 203.244.234.0/24?

    A. `Router(config-router)#network 203.244.234.0`

    B. `Router(config-router)#network 203.244.234.0 255.255.255.0`

    C. `Router(config-router)#network 203.244.234.0 0.0.0.255`

    D. `Router(config-router)#network 203.244.234.0/24`

25. In the following exhibit, what type of routing is being used?

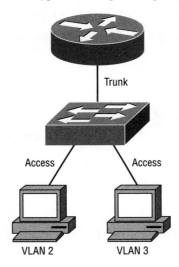

    A. Default routing

    B. SVI routing

    C. ROAS routing

    D. Stub routing

26. Which command must be enabled on a switch to enable routing between switched virtual interfaces for VLAN routing?

    A. `Switch(config)#ip route svi`

    B. `Switch(config)#feature svi routing`

    C. `Switch(config)#svi routing`

    D. `Switch(config)#ip routing`

27. Which network is part of the summary route of 172.16.32.0/21?

    A. 172.16.64.0/24

    B. 172.16.48.0/24

    C. 172.16.40.0/24

    D. 172.16.38.0/24

28. In the following exhibit, why does the first and third ARP entry have a dash for its age?

```
Switch#show ip arp
Protocol   Address       Age(min)  Hardware Addr   Type  Interface
Internet   172.16.10.1   -         00d0.565d.05ac  ARPA  Ethernet1
Internet   172.16.10.2   6         0030.9492.ee55  ARPA  Ethernet1
Internet   172.16.20.1   -         00d0.565d.05ab  ARPA  Ethernet0
```

    A. The entries are static ARP entries.

    B. The entries have just been added to the ARP table.

    C. The entries belong to the physical interfaces of the router.

    D. The entries have less than 1 minute before they expire.

29. Which OSPF packets contain link-state and routing information?

    A. Hello packets

    B. LSA packets

    C. LSU packets

    D. Dead packets

30. Which field in the IP header is used to prevent a packet from endlessly routing?

    A. Checksum

    B. Flags

    C. TTL

    D. Header length

31. Which layer 2 protocol has built-in security for WAN connections?

    A. HDLC

    B. PPP

    C. IPSec

    D. Metro Ethernet

32. Which QoS marking is used at layer 3 for routed packets?

    A. DSCP

    B. CEF

    C. CoS

    D. QoE

33. Which WAN protocol does not support multicast packets?

    A. GRE

    B. IPSec

    C. PPP

    D. MPLS

34. Which is a correct statement about support for OSPF on an MPLS network?

   A. The provider edge (PE) routers can only host area 0.

   B. The customer edge (CE) routers can only host area 0.

   C. The customer edge (CE) routers must use GRE for OSPF.

   D. Both the customer edge (CE) routers and the provider edge (PE) routers can participate in area 0.

35. What is the definition of a trust boundary in relation to QoS?

   A. A trust boundary is where the QoS markings are first configured.

   B. A trust boundary is where the QoS markings are stripped at the router.

   C. A trust boundary is where the network begins to trust the QoS markings from devices.

   D. A trust boundary is the separations of QoS queues based upon their priority.

36. Which WAN connectivity technology is always configured in a hub-and-spoke topology?

   A. IPSec

   B. MPLS

   C. DMVPN

   D. Metro Ethernet

37. Under which circumstance will a DHCP server issue a NACK message to the client?

   A. When the DHCP server IP address pool is depleted.

   B. When the DHCP client requests an IP address that has not been offered.

   C. When the DHCP client requests an IP address that the DHCP server cannot lease.

   D. When the DHCP client's lease time has ended.

38. You have four routers configured with Host Standby Routing Protocol (HSRP). Three routers—Router A, Router B, and Router C—are configured with the default priority. You change the priority of Router A to 80, Router B to 100, and Router C to 140. Which router will become the active router?

   A. Router A will become the active router.

   B. Router B will become the active router.

   C. Router C will become the active router.

   D. Router D will become the active router.

39. When a DHCP server is responding to a DHCP Discover message from a client, which address does the DHCP server use in its response?

   A. Broadcast MAC address

   B. Client's IP address

   C. Server's MAC address

   D. Client's MAC address

40. You have just configured NAT for the network in the following exhibit. What is wrong with the configuration?

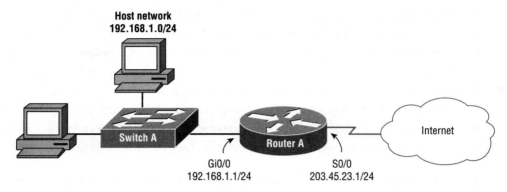

```
ip nat pool NATPOOL 203.45.23.1 203.45.23.7 netmask 255.255.255.0
ip nat inside source list 1 pool NATPOOL overload
!
interface GigabitEthernet 0/0
 ip address 192.168.1.1 255.255.255.0
 ip nat inside
!
interface Serial0/0
 ip address 203.45.23.1 255.255.255.0
 ip nat outside
!
access-list 1 permit 192.168.2.0 0.0.0.255
```

A. The inside source is on the wrong interface.

B. The access list is misconfigured.

C. The IP address in the NAT pool is overlapping with the physical interface IP address.

D. The source list pool is incorrect.

41. Refer to the following exhibit. What will happen when a computer with a different MAC address connects to the interface?

```
Switch(config)#int fa0/6
Switch(config-if)#switchport port-security
Switch(config-if)#switchport port-security mac-address sticky 00e4.6a51.8dd9
```

A. The computer will not be allowed to communicate, but the port will remain up.

B. The computer will be allowed to communicate.

C. The computer will not be allowed to communicate and the port will enter an err-disable state.

D. The computer will be allowed to communicate and the access will be logged.

42. Which authentication method will allow an authenticated user to be able to access only certain commands on a router or switch?

    A. TACACS+

    B. AAA

    C. RADIUS

    D. 802.1X

43. If a router has two interfaces and you only use IPv4, how many access control lists can be configured on the router's interfaces?

    A. One

    B. Two

    C. Four

    D. Eight

44. You have a router that you configured with a password, but you have forgotten the password. You have a copy of a recent configuration, and the password line reads as `password 7 06074352EFF6`. How can you access the router?

    A. You must call the Cisco Technical Assistance Center to reverse the password.

    B. You need to enter the password *06074352EFF6*.

    C. Log into another router and type `decrypt-password 06074352EFF6` in privilege exec mode.

    D. Perform a password recovery on the router.

45. Which command will achieve the same goal as the command `access-list 2 permit host 192.168.2.3`?

    A. `Router(config)#access-list 2 permit 192.168.2.3 255.255.255.255`

    B. `Router(config)#access-list 2 permit 192.168.2.3 0.0.0.0`

    C. `Router(config)#ip access-list 2 permit host 192.168.2.3`

    D. `Router(config)#access-list 2 permit 192.168.2.3`

46. You have a license on a USB drive. Which command would you use to install a license to a router that was obtained from Cisco?

    A. `Router#license install usbflash0:FTX3463434Z_2016030415234562345.lic`

    B. `Router(config)#license install usbflash0:FTX3463434Z_2016030415234562345.lic`

    C. `Router#license install file usbflash0:FTX3463434Z_2016030415234562345.lic`

    D. `Router#copy usbflash0:FTX3463434Z_2016030415234562345.lic flash:`

47.   What is the default destination of Cisco devices for sending syslog messages?

   A.   Broadcasts to a syslog server

   B.   Console

   C.   TTY

   D.   NVRAM

48.   You perform a show version and see the configuration register of 0x2142. What will the router do on the next reload?

   A.   The router will reboot with a console speed of 19200 baud.

   B.   The router will ignore breaks to the IOS.

   C.   The router will ignore the contents of NVRAM.

   D.   The router will boot into ROMMON mode.

49.   On which software-defined network (SDN) plane does CDP function?

   A.   Data plane

   B.   Control plane

   C.   Network plane

   D.   Management plane

50.   What must the network management station (NMS) be configured with before it can read the SNMP counters on a router or switch?

   A.   SNMP community

   B.   MIB

   C.   Version of SNMP

   D.   All of the above

Chapter

9

Practice Test 2

THE CCNA EXAM TOPICS COVERED IN THIS PRACTICE TEST INCLUDE THE FOLLOWING:

- ✓ 1.0   Network Fundamentals (ICND1)
- ✓ 2.0   LAN Switching Technologies (ICND1) (ICND2)
- ✓ 3.0   Routing Technologies (ICND1) (ICND2)
- ✓ 4.0   WAN Technologies (ICND2)
- ✓ 5.0   Infrastructure Services (ICND1) (ICND2)
- ✓ 6.0   Infrastructure Security (ICND2)
- ✓ 7.0   Infrastructure Management (ICND1) (ICND2)

1. On which OSI layer does the Address Resolution Protocol (ARP) function?
   A. Application layer
   B. Session layer
   C. Data Link layer
   D. Network layer

2. Which flags are used during the three-way-handshake process for TCP?
   A. FIN and ACK
   B. SYN and ACK
   C. SYN and FIN
   D. SYN and RDY

3. You are running several web servers in a cloud with a server load balancer. As demand increases, you add web servers. According to the NIST standard of cloud computing, which feature can you use to increase your compute capability for demand?
   A. Resource pooling
   B. Measured services
   C. Broad network access
   D. Rapid elasticity

4. In Cisco's three-tier architecture, the links between the distribution layer indicate what kind of topology?
   A. Full mesh topology
   B. Partial mesh topology
   C. Star topology
   D. Ring topology

5. Which type of cabling is used for high-speed long-distance transmission of data?
   A. T1 serial lines
   B. Single-mode fiber
   C. Twinax
   D. Multi-mode fiber

6. What is the last step in the diagnosis and resolution of a problem?
   A. Isolating the problem
   B. Escalating the problem
   C. Documenting the problem
   D. Analyzing the problem

7. Which classification of IP address does 225.34.5.4 belong to?

   A. Class A

   B. Class B

   C. Class C

   D. Class D

8. In IPv6, the solicited-node multicast message is used for what?

   A. Discovery of the gateway

   B. Discovery of the network ID

   C. Resolution of the MAC address for an IPv6 address

   D. Capability discovery of neighboring devices

9. In the following exhibit, what is Field C used for?

7-byte preamble	SFD	Field A	Field B	Field C	Field D	Field E

   A. The destination MAC address

   B. The next upper-layer protocol to send the information to

   C. The beginning of data, also called the start frame delimiter

   D. The cyclical redundancy checksum value

10. Under what circumstance will a switch flood a frame to all ports on the switch?

   A. When the source MAC address is unknown by the switch

   B. When the destination MAC address is a multicast address

   C. When the destination MAC address is unknown by the switch

   D. When the destination MAC address is 0000.0000.0000

11. Which is a correct statement about the output in the following exhibit?

```
Switch#show interface trunk
Port    Mode        Encapsulation   Status      Native vlan
Gi0/1   auto        n-802.1q        trunking    1
[output Cut]
```

   A. The default native VLAN has been changed.

   B. The encapsulation has been negotiated.

   C. The switch is sending DTP frames.

   D. The adjacent switch is also set to auto for DTP.

12. In the following exhibit, interface Gi 1/1 on both switches is configured as a trunk, between the switches. Which statement is correct about the following exhibit?

```
SwitchA#show interfaces status

Port       Name         Status    Vlan      Duplex   Speed Type
Gi1/1      Switch B     trunk     full      auto     10/100/1000-TX
Gi1/2      Computer A   23        auto      auto     10/100/1000-TX
Gi1/3      Computer B   23        auto      auto     10/100/1000-TX
Gi1/4      Computer C   23        a-full    a-10     10/100/1000-TX
[Output Cut]


SwitchB#show interfaces status

Port       Name         Status    Vlan      Duplex   Speed Type
Gi1/1      Switch A     trunk     a-half    auto     10/100/1000-TX
Gi1/2      Computer D   41        auto      auto     10/100/1000-TX
Gi1/3      Computer E   41        auto      auto     10/100/1000-TX
Gi1/4      Computer F   41        a-full    a-10     10/100/1000-TX
[Output Cut]
```

A. The interface Gi1/1, which is connecting the switches, has a wiring fault.

B. The interface Gi1/1 is operating nominally.

C. The interface Gi1/1, which is connecting the switches, has the wrong duplex configured.

D. The two switches have a VLAN mismatch.

13. You have several VLANs and need to route between them. You configure a trunk between your router and switch. What will you need to configure on the router to support each VLAN for routing?

A. Virtual interface

B. Switched virtual interface

C. Subinterface

D. VLAN database

14. How many bytes are used in an 802.1Q frame for tagging of VLANs?

A. 2 bytes

B. 4 bytes

C. 8 bytes

D. 16 bytes

15. What can be concluded about the output in the following exhibit?

```
SwitchA#show  mac address-table
Unicast Entries
 vlan    mac address    type      protocols                port
-------+---------------+--------+---------------------+---------------------
   2    000f.e504.6ad3  dynamic  ip,ipx,assigned,other GigabitEthernet1/1
   2    0017.e060.a640  dynamic  ip,ipx,assigned,other GigabitEthernet1/1
   2    0051.c4c3.560c  dynamic  ip,ipx,assigned,other GigabitEthernet1/1
   2    0051.c4c3.56b4  dynamic  ip,ipx,assigned,other GigabitEthernet1/1
   2    0051.c4c8.ba18  dynamic  ip,ipx,assigned,other GigabitEthernet1/2
   4    0051.c4c8.c344  dynamic  ip,ipx,assigned,other GigabitEthernet1/3
   5    0051.c4c8.c358  dynamic  ip,ipx,assigned,other GigabitEthernet1/4
[Output Cut]
```

A. Interface Gi1/1 is a trunk link.

B. Interface Gi1/1 is an access link.

C. Interface Gi1/1 has several static MAC addresses.

D. Interface Gi1/1 has a switch or hub connected to it.

16. When VLANs are configured in global configuration mode, where are the VLANs stored by default?

   A. In the running configuration or RAM

   B. In the startup configuration or NVRAM

   C. In the `vlan.dat` on the flash

   D. In the `vlan.dat` on the NVRAM

17. Which statement is correct about VLAN Trunking Protocol (VTP) transparent mode?

   A. Switches participating in transparent mode will receive VTP updates and merge them with their VLAN database.

   B. Switches participating in transparent mode will not forward VTP updates when received.

   C. Switches participating in transparent mode contain their own `vlan.dat` file for the VLAN database.

   D. Switches participating in transparent mode will not process VTP updates but will forward them to other switches.

18. When you connect a device to a switch, the device takes a minute before it is reachable via its IP address. What should be configured to fix this issue so that you can get immediate access to the device?

   A. Turn off auto-negotiation on the interface.

   B. Configure PortFast mode for spanning tree.

   C. Configure BPDU Guard mode for spanning tree.

   D. Turn off port security.

19. Under which circumstance will two switches not form a trunk link with Dynamic Trunking Protocol (DTP)?

   A. Switch A is configured as auto and Switch B is configured as auto.

   B. Switch A is configured as auto and Switch B is configured as desirable.

   C. Switch A is configured as desirable and Switch B is configured as desirable.

   D. Switch A is configured as auto and Switch B is configured as a trunk.

20. You perform the `show spanning-tree vlan 100` command on a switch. The output shows that all ports on the switch are in designated mode. What can be determined from this?

   A. This switch is connected to a root bridge.

   B. This switch is the root bridge.

   C. This switch is not participating in STP.

   D. This switch is a backup root bridge.

21. Which routing protocol will not contain a topology of the network?

   A. EIGRP

   B. RIP

   C. OSPF

   D. BGP

22. Which routing loop avoidance method is used by routers to prevent routing updates to exit an interface in which they have been learned?

   A. Routing to infinity

   B. Route poisoning

   C. Holddowns

   D. Split horizons

23. What is the default priority for Open Shortest Path First (OSPF) routers?

   A. 1

   B. 100

   C. 255

   D. 32,768

24. You have changed the router's priority for Open Shortest Path First (OSPF) to make the router the designated router (DR), but the router has not become a DR. What must be done to force the election?

   A. You must use the `shutdown` and `no shutdown` commands on the interface with the highest IP address.

   B. In global configuration mode, you must enter the command `ospf election force`.

   C. In privileged exec mode, you must enter the command `clear ip ospf process x`.

   D. In privileged exec mode on the DR, you must enter the command `clear ip ospf process x`.

25. Which command will allow you to change the default number of unequal-cost load-balancing paths for Enhanced Interior Gateway Routing Protocol (EIGRP)?

   A. `Router(config)#unequal-paths 6`

   B. `Router(config-router)#paths 6`

   C. `Router(config-router)#maximum-paths 6`

   D. `Router(config)#maximum-paths 6`

26. Which packet forwarding method is the fastest and does not directly use the central processing unit (CPU)?

   A. Cisco Express Forwarding (CEF)

   B. Process switching

   C. Fast switching

   D. Expedited forwarding

27. You see a number of IPv6 packets on your network with a destination address of ff02::a. What can be concluded about what is running on your network?

   A. Routing Information Protocol Next Generation (RIPng) is running on the network.

   B. Open Shortest Path First version 3 (OSPFv3) is running on the network.

   C. Enhanced Interior Gateway Routing Protocol (EIGRP) for IPv6 is running on the network.

   D. Stateless Address Autoconfiguration (SLAAC) is running on the network.

28. You need to configure an IP address on a switchport interface. However, when you enter the command `ip address 192.168.1.1 255.255.255.0`, it returns an error. Which command will fix the issue?

A. `Switch(config)#ip routing`

B. `Switch(config-if)#switchport routed`

C. `Switch(config-if)#no switchport`

D. `Switch(config-if)#switchport mode routed`

29. How can you suppress all hello messages out of a router by default for Enhanced Interior Gateway Routing Protocol (EIGRP)?

A. `Router(config)#passive-interface default`

B. `Router(config-router)#passive-interface all`

C. `Router(config-router)#passive-interface default`

D. `Router(config)#passive-interface all`

30. Which command would allow you to see the next hop information for Cisco Express Forwarding (CEF)?

A. `Router#show cef`

B. `Router#show ip cef`

C. `Router#show cef nop`

D. `Router#show cef route`

31. Which WAN connectivity method supports error detection and correction?

A. MPLS

B. HDLC

C. PPP

D. Metro Ethernet

32. In the following exhibit, Point -to -Point Protocol (PPP) is negotiating the username and password for the adjacent router. You are debugging PPP on the local router. What needs to be done to fix the problem?

```
*Feb  3 12:23:57.559: Se0:3 PAP: I AUTH-REQ id 25 Len 18 from "PAPUSER"
*Feb  3 12:23:57.559: Se0:3 PPP: Phase is FORWARDING
*Feb  3 12:23:57.559: Se0:3 PPP: Phase is AUTHENTICATING
*Feb  3 12:23:57.559: Se0:3 PAP: Authenticating peer PAPUSER
*Feb  3 12:23:57.559: Se0:3 PAP: O AUTH-NAK id 25 Len 32 msg is
```

A. Configure PAP on this router.

B. Configure PPP encapsulation on this router.

C. Verify that the local username matches the adjacent router's hostname and the passwords match.

D. Verify that the remote username matches the adjacent router's hostname and the passwords match.

33. Which device is responsible for adding the label to a Multiprotocol Label Switching (MPLS) packet?

   A. Customer edge (CE) router

   B. Provider edge (PE) router

   C. Customer premise switch

   D. Label switch routers (LSR)

34. Which WAN connectivity method is quickly scalable?

   A. MPLS

   B. VPN

   C. PPP

   D. Metro Ethernet

35. Which command will configure a policy map on an interface?

   A. `Router(config-if)#policy-map USER-MAP out`

   B. `Router(config-if)#service-map USER-MAP out`

   C. `Router(config-if)#service-policy USER-MAP out`

   D. `Router(config-if)#policy-class USER-MAP out`

36. When a packet it sent through Network Address Translation (NAT) to a remote web server on the Internet, what term is used to refer to the web server's IP address?

   A. Inside local

   B. Outside local

   C. Inside global

   D. Outside global

37. When configuring the Network Time Protocol (NTP), what is the stratum used for?

   A. The stratum designates the location of the time clock.

   B. The stratum designates the type of time clock.

   C. The stratum designates the level of precision associated with the time clock.

   D. The stratum designates a level of trust associated with the time clock.

38. A client has an IP address of 192.168.1.5/24 and a default gateway of 192.168.1.1. Hot Standby Router Protocol (HSRP) is in use in the network. Which type of router is the default gateway?

   A. Active router

   B. Standby router

   C. Virtual router

   D. Support router

39. What option should be configured along with interface tracking that will allow the original router to regain its active status once a failed link is repaired?

A. Interface tracking resets

B. Failback option

C. Preempt option

D. Priority tracking

40. Which record sets the time to live (TTL) for a Domain Name System (DNS) resource record when the resource record does not have one explicitly configured?

A. A record

B. SOA record

C. TTL record

D. PTR record

41. In a basic VLAN hopping attack, which switch feature do attackers take advantage of?

A. An open Telnet connection

B. Automatic encapsulation negotiation

C. Forwarding of broadcasts

D. The default automatic trunking configuration

42. When you are protecting an interface with port security, to which mode should you set the switchport?

A. Access mode

B. Dynamic mode

C. Trunk mode

D. Voice mode

43. Which security mitigation technique can be used to stop a MAC address flooding attack?

A. Access control lists (ACLs)

B. Network Address Translation (NAT)

C. Port security

D. VLAN access control lists (VACLs)

44. Which command will configure an access list that will deny Telnet access from the 192.168.2.0/24 network and allow all other traffic?

A. `Router(config)#access-list 101 deny tcp 192.168.2.0 0.0.0.255 any eq 23`
`Router(config)#access-list 101 permit ip any any`

B. `Router(config)#access-list 101 deny 192.168.2.0 0.0.0.255 eq 23`
`Router(config)#access-list 101 permit ip any any`

C. `Router(config)#access-list 101 block tcp 192.168.2.0 0.0.0.255 any eq 23`
`Router(config)#access-list 101 permit ip any any`

D. `Router(config)#access-list 101 deny 192.168.2.0 0.0.0.255 any eq 23`
`Router(config)#access-list 101 permit any any`

45. You need to make a modification to a rule in a standard conventional access list. How can you achieve this?

   A. Enter the ACL editor and change the entry.

   B. Remove the entire ACL and add it back with the modification.

   C. Remove the line number and add the new line number back with the modification.

   D. Remove the entry with the no command and add it back.

46. What type of message is generated from an SNMP agent to the network management station (NMS)?

   A. Trap

   B. Set

   C. Get

   D. Alert

47. What can you use to secure SNMP version 2c?

   A. Complex passwords

   B. Complex community names

   C. MD5 hashing

   D. SHA hashing

48. Which command will allow you to configure interfaces Gi1/1 to Gi1/12?

   A. `Switch(config)#interface gigabitethernet range 1/1 - 12`

   B. `Switch(config)#interface range gigabitethernet 1/1 - 12`

   C. `Switch(config)#interface range gigabitethernet 1/1 1/12`

   D. `Switch(config)#interface range gigabitethernet range 1/1,12`

49. What is the default level for syslog facility logging?

   A. Notice

   B. Informational

   C. Warning

   D. Debug

50. Which command(s) are required before you can use an FTP server for backing up configuration? Assume that the username is USER and the password is USERPASS.

   A. `Router(config)#ip ftp username USER password USERPASS`

   B. `Router(config)#ftp USER password USERPASS`

   C. `Router(config)#ip ftp username USER`
   `Router(config)#ip ftp password USERPASS`

   D. `Router(config)#username USER password USERPASS`

Appendix

Answers to Review Questions

Chapter 1: Network Fundamentals (Domain 1)

1. **D.** The OSI reference model was created to divide the network communication process into smaller components for standardization, design, and troubleshooting purposes. It also allows for a nonproprietary standardization of components and prevents a change at one layer from affecting other layers.

2. **A.** The Presentation layer is responsible for encryption and decryption. Web servers use SSL to encrypt data and the client uses SSL to decrypt the data. SSL processing for both server and client is done at the Presentation layer.

3. **D.** Switches primarily function at the Data Link layer. They inspect frames to direct traffic to the appropriate port by employing source MAC address learning and forward/filter decisions.

4. **C.** A simple way of remembering the order of the OSI layers is with a mnemonic such as All People Seem To Need Drinking Parties or All People Seem To Need Data Processing.

5. **B.** The Network layer is responsible for logical addressing. Routers use logical addressing for path determination to remote networks the same way the post office uses zip codes and street addresses to route mail.

6. **A.** Connection-oriented communication happens at the Transport layer with TCP. TCP uses a three-way handshake to establish a connection. Once it is established, sequences and acknowledgments make sure that data is delivered. Both server and client have a virtual circuit during the establishment.

7. **D.** The Presentation layer is responsible for compression and decompression. Compression methods can be MP3, JPG, and ZIP, which reduce the number of bits that need to be transmitted over the network. Often web servers use gzip to speed up page delivery. One end compresses and the other end decompresses the data.

8. **C.** Applications are found in the upper three layers and dialog control is found in the session layer. An example of dialog control is how an application such as instant messaging sends messages with half-duplex conversations like a walkie-talkie.

9. **B.** DTE and DCE interfaces are defined at the Physical layer. The original interfaces referred to computers and modems, respectively. However, today the DTE and DCE interfaces define the equipment such as hosts and switches, respectively.

10. **B.** Telnet, TFTP, SNMP, and SMTP all function at the Process/Application layer according to the DoD model. The Process/Application layer is a macro layer combining the Application, Presentation, and Session layers of the OSI model.

11. **A.** Since SNMP is an application, if it returns back successfully, then we can conclude that the Application layer on the client successfully made a connection to the Application layer on the server.

12. B. The Data Link layer is responsible for checking the FCS, or Frame Checking Sequence, which is a checksum of the frame. This occurs on the MAC sublayer of the Data Link layer.

13. C. The Internet layer of the DoD model maps to the Network layer of the OSI model. The Network layer is where routing occurs.

14. D. Switches create collision domains by isolating the possibility of a collision to the segment it is transmitting to or receiving frames from. This in turn raises effective bandwidth for the rest of the segments.

15. B. A hub is a multiport repeater. When a hub receives a frame, it will repeat the frame on all other ports, regardless of whether or not the port is the destination host.

16. D. The segment PDU is found at the Transport layer of the OSI. TCP/IP comprises two protocols at this layer: TCP and UDP, which create segments.

17. C. A router will stop broadcasts by default. If you add a router to a flat network, which is a single broadcast domain, you effectively raise bandwidth by reducing the number of broadcasts.

18. D. When the Individual/Group (I/G) high order bit is set to 1, the frame is a broadcast or a multicast transmission. The OUI assigned by the IEEE is only partially responsible for MAC uniqueness. The vendor is responsible for the last 24 bits of a MAC address.

19. B. Carrier Sense Multiple Access/Collision Detection (CSMA/CD) is a contention method that allows multiple devices to share the access media and detect collisions of frames.

20. C. The correct order of encapsulation starting with the Application layer is user datagrams, segments, packets, frames, and bits.

21. B. Telnet is used for terminal emulation over a network to a device expecting terminal emulation, such as a router or switch.

22. A. Logical Link Control (LLC) is responsible for identifying network protocols at the Data Link layer. This allows the Data Link layer to forward the packet to the appropriate upper-layer protocol.

23. C. The Presentation layer is responsible for translation such as ASCII to EBCDIC. All translation, encryption/decryption, and compression/decompression happens at the Presentation layer.

24. C. Broadcasts, multicasts, and multiple hubs for connectivity are all common causes of LAN congestion. Adding switches for connectivity has no direct relationship to LAN congestion, since switches create collision domains and raise effective bandwidth.

25. A. The Transport layer is responsible for flow control via the TCP/IP protocols of TCP and UDP.

26. C. User Datagram Protocol (UDP) does not guarantee segments are delivered. Therefore, the programmer must account for segments that are never received or out of order.

27. D. TCP is a connection-based protocol via the three-way handshake. It is not faster than UDP. However, it allows for the retransmission of lost segments because of sequences and acknowledgments.

28. A. The sender allocates a port dynamically above 1024 and associates it with the request through a process called a handle. This way if a web browser creates three requests for three different web pages, the pages are loaded to their respective windows.

29. D. The Simple Mail Transfer Protocol (SMTP) uses TCP port 25 to send mail.

30. D. TCP guarantees delivery of segments with sequence and acknowledgment numbers. At the Transport layer, each segment is given a sequence number that is acknowledged by the receiver.

31. A. When a programmer decides to use UDP, it is normally because the programmer is sequencing and acknowledging datagrams already. The redundancy of acknowledgments at the Transport layer is not needed.

32. B. When a daemon or server process starts, it binds to a port number on which to listen for a request. An example is when a web server binds to the port number of TCP/80.

33. A. The window size, which is a buffer, is established and agreed upon by the sender and receiver during the three-way handshake.

34. C. DNS requests are usually small and do not require the overhead of sequence and acknowledgment of TCP. If a segment is dropped, the DNS protocol will ask again.

35. A. A three-way handshake is required between sender and receiver before TCP can begin sending traffic. During this three-way handshake, the sender's window buffer size is synchronized with the receiver's window buffer size.

36. C. When more than one WAP covers the same SSID, it is called an extended service set (ESS). A wireless LAN (WLAN) controller coordinates the cell or coverage area so the same SSID is on two different channels.

37. D. Control and Provisioning of Wireless Access Points is a protocol that's responsible for provisioning of LWAPs and forwarding of data to the wireless LAN controller.

38. C. The wireless LAN controller (WLC) is responsible for centralized authentication of users and/or computers on a wireless network. When a wireless device is roaming, the WLC is responsible for maintaining the authentication between access points.

39. A. Centralized authentication of clients is a valid reason to implement a WLC. Although a WLC makes it easier to implement multiple SSIDs and VLANs, this task can be performed with autonomous WAPs, each performing its own authentication.

40. B. To achieve density and/or bandwidth in a relatively small area, you will need to deploy lightweight WAPs with a WLC. Although autonomous WAPs without a WLC would work, it would be problematic due to frequency coordination and roaming.

41. C. The 5 GHz band for 802.11 a/n/ac has 24 non-overlapping channels. The 2.4 GHz band for 802.11 b/g/n has only 3 non-overlapping channels. If the clients are compatible with 802.11 a/n/ac, it is desirable to use 5 GHz.

42. D. A wireless LAN controller keeps track of which LWAP a client has associated to and centrally forwards the packets to the appropriate LWAP.

43. C. In the 2.4 GHz spectrum for 802.11, there are three non-overlapping channels—1, 6, and 11, each of which is 22 MHz wide. Although channel 14 technically is non-overlapping, it is only allowed in Japan.

44. B. When WAPs are introduced to the wireless LAN controller, the WLC is responsible for synchronizing the WAPs to a standardized IOS. This allows for uniform support and features of the wireless system and is dependent on the model of WAP.

45. A. 802.11 uses a contention method of Carrier Sense Multiple Access/Collision Avoidance. 802.11 implements a Request to Send/Clear to Send mechanism that avoids collisions.

46. C. The demilitarized zone (DMZ) is where Internet-facing servers/services are placed.

47. B. Firewalls should always be placed at key security boundaries, which can be the Internet and your internal network. However, proper placement is not exclusive to the boundaries of the Internet and internal networks. For example, it could be placed between two internal networks, such as R&D and guest networks.

48. B. Firewalls cannot provide protection from internal attacks on internal resources. They are designed to protect networks from external attacks or attacks emanating from the outside or directed toward the Internet.

49. A. All physical access to a firewall should be controlled tightly so that it is not tampered with, which could allow external threats to enter the network. This control should include vendors and approved administrators. Physical access to the firewall is a security principal and therefore not a consideration for the management of a firewall.

50. C. Firewalls keep track of the TCP conversation via the SYN-SYN/ACK-ACK three-way handshake. This is done so that a DoS attack such as a SYN flood can be mitigated.

51. A. ASA allow for zones to be created and the connections applied to the zones. This methodology allows for security rules to be applied uniformly to the outside zone.

52. B. Servers should be placed in the DMZ so they can access both the inside zone and outside zone. This will allow a server such as a web server to allow client access from the Web (outside). Rules could also be applied so that the server (for example, a database server) could allow access to data from within the internal network (inside).

53. C. An IDS, or intrusion detection system, will detect unauthorized access. However, it will not prevent unauthorized access. It is a form of audit control in a network.

54. A. When a firewall matches a Uniform Resource Identifier (URI), such as a URL, it is operating at layer 7. This is known as a web application firewall, or WAF.

55. D. Since the email server needs access to the Internet to send and receive mail, it should be placed in the demilitarized zone (DMZ). This will also allow access to internal clients in the inside zone.

56. A. AWS and Microsoft Azure are examples of public cloud providers. Private clouds are internally created, and hybrid clouds are a combination of services between your private cloud and the public cloud.

57. B. If you were looking to create a fault tolerant colocation site as a cloud provider, you would be searching for an Infrastructure as a Service provider. This would allow you to install your own operation system and applications.

58. B. The hypervisor allows for multiple operating systems to share CPUs, RAM, network, and storage of a physical server.

59. D. A virtual machine, or VM, is an operating system that is running on hardware but is not directly attached to the hardware. It is decoupled from the hardware through the use of a hypervisor. The hypervisor creates an abstraction layer between the hardware and the operating system.

60. A. The physical hardware (such as a server) used in virtualization is the host.

61. C. A virtual switch connects the virtual machine NIC to the physical network.

62. B. The End of Row (EoR) switch acts as a distribution switch for the Top of Rack (ToR) switches.

63. C. Automated billing is not a NIST criteria for cloud computing. It is essential for the cloud computing vendor, but is not relevant if you are hosting it yourself. The five NIST criteria for cloud computing are on-demand self-service, broad network access, resource pooling, rapid elasticity, and measured service.

64. C. When an internal IT department hosts the virtualization for a company, it is called a private cloud.

65. B. A cloud services catalog satisfies the self-service aspect of cloud computing. It does this by listing all of the available VMs that can be created in the cloud environment, such as web servers, application server, databases, and so on.

66. C. A hosted medical records service is an example of a SaaS, or Software as a Service, model. The customer cannot choose variables such as vCPU or RAM. The cloud provider is responsible for the delivery of the software, maintenance of the OS, and maintenance of the hardware.

67. A. A hosted service that allows you to develop upon it is an example of the Platform as a Service (PaaS) model. The cloud provider is responsible for the delivery of APIs that developers can use to create programs.

68. C. An intercloud exchange is a service that connects multiple public clouds through a common private WAN connection. This allows a network engineer to configure the private WAN once and be able to transition between the public clouds on the service side without reconfiguration of the private WAN.

69. A. Internal bandwidth usage is not a consideration after conversion to a SaaS application. External bandwidth should be considered since internal users will access the application through the Internet. Location of the users should also be a deciding factor in moving to a SaaS model. Branch office connectivity to the Internet should be considered also when converting.

70. B. A virtual firewall or virtual router is an example of a VNF. These devices are typically network functions that are found in internal networks such as firewalls and routers. These devices perform basic network functionality and run as a virtual machine or virtual instance.

71. C. You will need a virtual router running static NAT to translate the two different IP networks. This type of service is called a virtual network function, or VNF.

72. C. Network Time Protocol (NTP) is a standardized protocol for network time synchronization.

73. D. If you wanted to scale a web server out to several other web servers, you would use Server Load Balancing as a Server (SLBaaS) from your cloud provider.

74. C. Lowering bandwidth between the premises and your VMs on the public cloud is a direct benefit if locating NTP on the public cloud for VM time synchronization.

75. A. Bandwidth is the primary decision factor for moving DNS closer to the application in the public cloud. However, if the majority of DNS users are on premises, then it should remain on premises for bandwidth reasons.

76. B. Access layer switches connect to users and are edge network devices.

77. A. Distribution layer switches connect to access layer switches and core switches to provide redundancy.

78. C. Core layer switches connect campuses together via the distribution layer switches.

79. C. The two-tier, or collapsed-core, model contains only the distribution and access layer switches.

80. A. Based on the layout of your network, the collapsed-core model is the most appropriate model to design. If at a later time other campuses are joined to the network, the core layer can be added.

81. B. Based on the layout of your network the three-tier model is the most appropriate model to design. Since there are four campuses, the core layer is recommended for connectivity.

82. D. Only switching between campus (distribution) switches should be performed at the core layer. Nothing should be done to slow down forwarding of traffic, such as using ACLs, supporting clients, or routing between VLANs.

83. B. The distribution layer is where redistribution of routing protocols should be performed. It should never be performed at the core or access layer.

84. C. The access layer is where collision domains should be created. This is called network segmentation.

85. C. The collapsed-core design model is best suited for small enterprises. It can later be expanded out to a three-tier model as an enterprise grows in size. It has no effect on bandwidth if designed right.

86. A. A star topology has a centralized switch connecting all of the devices outward like a star.

87. B. Increased redundancy of connections is a direct benefit of a full mesh topology. Although bandwidth will increase because of multiple paths, additional dynamic routing protocols will need to be implemented to achieve this.

88. C. The hybrid topology is most often seen at the access layer. The devices are connected in a star topology and the access layer switches are partially meshed to the distribution layer switches.

89. B. Distribution layer switches are fully meshed for redundancy. The number of links can be calculated with the formula of $N(N-1)$. So if you had four distribution switches, the ports required for a full mesh would be $4(4-1) = 4 \times 3 = 12$ ports among the four switches. The formula of $N(N-1)/2$ would give you the number of links (connected ports): $4(4-1)/2 = 4 \times 3/2 = 6$ links.

90. A. Core layer switches are commonly set up in a star topology. This is because core layer switches connect multiple campuses via distribution layer switches.

91. A. The collapsed core layer switch uses a star topology connecting outward to the access layer switches. This design is often found in small enterprise and single campus design.

92. B. All links between switches are connected redundantly. This allows for both the forwarding plane and control plane to have multiple paths and redundancy. The forwarding plane forwards traffic, and the control plane controls routing between VLANs.

93. A. In a star topology, the central switch is connected outward to all edge switches. This is commonly seen at the core layer switch.

94. A. An autonomous WAP acts similarly to an access layer switch. However, WAPs normally do not have redundant links back to the distribution switches. So it acts more like a star topology, connecting the Ethernet and wireless clients together.

95. C. Generally, office buildings do not have direct runs to each switch closet from the other closets. Although a full mesh is desirable, sometimes only a partial mesh is achievable.

96. A. 1000Base-T is short for 1000 Baseband – Twisted pair. 1000Base-T utilizes all four pairs over standard Cat5e, whereas 100Base-T utilizes only two pairs of Cat5.

97. C. Single-mode fiber is 9 microns at its core. With proper transceivers, the signal can span 10 km to 70 km without needing to be retransmitted.

98. A. A straight-through cable would be used since routers are DTE, or data terminal equipment, and switches are DCE, or data communications equipment. DTE to DCE requires a straight-through cable.

99. A. 1000Base-T can be run up to 100 meters, or 328 feet, per its specification.

100. B. You connect to Cisco switches and routers via 900 baud, 8 data bits, no parity, and 1 stop bit.

101. B. You would use a crossover cable because a switch is a DCE device. When connecting DCE to DCE, you would need to cross the connection with a crossover cable. Newer switches have MDI-X capabilities to detect the need for a crossover cable and will automatically switch the cable over if a straight-through cable is used.

102. B. Multi-mode fiber can be either 50 microns or 62.5 microns at its core. The maximum distance for 50 micron fiber is 550 meters utilizing the 1000Base-LX specification.

103. C. Although operation of computers connected to a switch uses a straight-through cable, management via the console port requires a rolled cable and an EIA/TIA 232 adapter.

104. C. 10GBase-CX is commonly used in data centers. It is referred to by its nickname of Twinax. It is a fixed, balanced coaxial pair that can be run up to 25 meters.

105. C. Cat5e can support up to 1 Gb/s via the 1000Base-T specification. Since 10Base-T, 100Base-T, and 1000Base-T can be run up to 100 meters in length, it allows for interchangeability with speeds. It was very common when Cat5e came out 16 years ago for installers to future-proof wiring installations with it.

106. B. It is most likely, since the interface was working before, that someone "shut down" the interface with the shutdown command. This can be seen in the show interface serial 0/0 command; the interface is reporting it is administratively shut down.

107. C. Traceroute should be used from the originating IP when the problem is to the destination IP. When the traceroute times out is most likely where the problem is located.

108. C. When you're checking for speed and/or duplex issues, the show interface status command will detail all of the ports with their negotiated speed and duplex.

109. B. When you're diagnosing frame forwarding on a switch, the MAC address table needs to be inspected to see if the switch has learned the destination MAC address.

110. A. When you're trying to diagnose port security, the first command should be show port-security. This will detail all of the ports with port security and their expected behavior when port security is violated.

111. D. After isolating the problem, performing root cause analysis, and ultimately solving the problem, the implemented solution should be monitored or verified.

112. A. The first step to troubleshooting a problem is isolating the problem. This can be done various ways and can sometime include documenting the problem to understand the root cause.

113. B. The first command used to diagnose a VLAN forwarding issue is the show vlan command. This command will show all of the VLANs that are defined on the switch either manually or dynamically through the VLAN Trunking Protocol (VTP).

114. C. Since you only have access to the local switches at your facility and you have checked the local user's connection status, your only option is to escalate the problem.

115. A. The command that you should begin with is show interfaces fast 0/0 switchport. This command will show the trunk status of the port as well as the operational status.

116. B. The IP address of 172.23.23.2 is a Class B address.

117. A. The default subnet mask of a Class A address is 255.0.0.0.

118. C. The multicast range begins with 224 to 239 in the first octet. Therefore, only the IP address 238.20.80.4 is correct.

119. B. The IP address 135.20.255.255 is a Class B broadcast address.

120. B. The CIDR notation for 255.255.240.0 is /20. The first two subnets are 8 bits (8 × 2 = 16), and the 240 is 4 more bits (16 + 4 = 20).

121. A. The mask you will need to use is 255.255.255.252. This will allow for two hosts per network for a total of 64 networks. The formula for solving for hosts is: $2^X - 2$ is equal to or greater than 2(hosts), which in this case is $(2^2 - 2) = (4 - 2) = 2$. So 2 bits are used for the host side, leaving 6 bits for the subnet side. 6 bits + 24 bits (original subnet mask) = /30, or 255.255.255.252.

122. D. The mask you will need to use is 255.255.255.224. This will allow for 30 hosts per network for a total of eight networks. The formula for solving for hosts is: $2^X - 2$ is equal to or greater than 22 hosts, which in this case is $(2^5 - 2) = (32 - 2) = 30$. So 5 bits are used for the host side, leaving 3 bits for the subnet side. 3 bits + 24 bits (original subnet mask) = /27, or 255.255.255.224.

123. A. The valid IP address range for the 192.168.32.0/26 network is 192.168.32.1 to 192.168.32.62, 192.168.32.65 to 192.168.32.126, etc. Therefore, 192.168.32.59 is within the valid IP range of 192.168.32.61/26.

124. B. The subnet mask will be 255.255.240.0. Since you need to solve for the number of networks, the equation is: 2^x is equal to or greater than 15 networks. $2^4 = 16$ completed the equation; the 4 bits represent the subnet side; you add the 4 bits to the 16 bits of the class B subnet mandated by the IETF. 16 + 4 = /20 = 255.255.240.0.

125. C. The valid IP address range for 209.183.160.45/30 is 209.183.160.45–209.183.160.46. Both IP addresses are part of the 209.183.160.44/30 network. 209.183.160.47/30 is the broadcast address for the network.

126. C. Computer A's default gateway address is 192.168.1.63. This address is the broadcast address for the 192.168.1.0/26 network and cannot be used as that network's gateway.

127. A. Computer A needs to have its IP address changed to align with the network that its gateway is in. Computer A is in the 192.168.1.32/27 network, while its gateway address is in the 192.168.1.0/27 network. Although changing the gateway address would work, the least amount of effort needs to be done. Changing the gateway address, which is a valid IP address, would create more work for other clients.

128. B. The /21 subnet mask has subnets in multiples of 8. So the networks would be 131.50.8.0/21, 131.50.16.0/21, 131.50.32.0/21, and 131.50.40.0/21. The IP address of 131.50.39.23/21 would belong to the 131.50.32.0/21 network with a valid range of 131.50.32.1 to 131.50.39.254.

129. D. The network for the computer with an IP address of 145.50.23.1/22 is 145.50.20.0/22. Its valid range is 145.50.20.1 to 145.50.23.254; the broadcast address for the range is 145.50.23.255.

130. B. The valid IP address range for the network of 132.59.34.0/23 is 132.59.34.1 to 132.59.35.254. The first address of 132.59.34.0/23 is the network ID and the last address of 132.59.35.255 is the broadcast ID.

131. B. The /20 CIDR notation written out is 255.255.240.0. The first two 8 bits are 255.255, and the last 4 bits make up the subnet mask of 250 to make a complete mask of 255.255.240.0.

132. C. The network mask of 255.255.255.248 borrows 5 bits for the network mask. Using the formula of 2^x = subnets, 2^5 = 32 subnets.

133. D. The valid number of hosts for a network with a subnet mask of 255.255.255.224 is 30. If 224 uses 3 bits of the 8 bits available for the network ID, then 5 bits remain for the host portion of the IP address. Using the formula of $2^x - 2$ = valid hosts, $2^5 - 2 = 32 - 2 = 30$ valid hosts.

134. D. The valid IP range for the network of 141.23.64.0/19 is 141.23.64.1 to 141.23.95.254. The IP address of 141.23.90.255/19 is a valid IP address within this range.

135. C. Summarization is similar to subnetting, with the exception that you are grouping IP addresses together. Think of it as reverse subnetting. Since /22 is multiples of 4, the statement of 141.24.4.0/22 would give the following range of IP addresses to be blocked: 141.24.4.1 to 141.24.7.254.

136. B. Summarization is similar to subnetting, with the exception that you are grouping IP addresses together. Think of it as reverse subnetting. Since /21 is multiples of 8, the statement of 132.22.24.0/21 would give the following range of IP addresses to be blocked: 132.22.24.1 to 132.22.31.254.

137. A. Using the subnet of 198.33.20.0/25 will give you 126 nodes. Since you are using 1 bit of the 8 bits in the 4th octet for the network ID, you have 7 bits left for the hosts. Using the formula of $2^x - 2$ = valid hosts, $2^7 - 2 = 128 - 2 = 126$ valid hosts.

138. C. Using the subnet of 198.33.20.0/26 will give you 62 nodes. Since you are using 2 bits of the 8 bits in the 4th octet for the network ID, you have 6 bits left for the hosts. Using the formula of $2^x - 2$ = valid hosts, $2^6 - 2 = 64 - 2 = 62$ valid hosts.

139. D. Using the subnet of 198.33.20.0/28 will give you 16 nodes. Since you are using 4 bits of the 8 bits in the 4th octet for the network ID, you have 4 bits left for the hosts. Using the formula of $2^x - 2$ = valid hosts, $2^4 - 2 = 16 - 2 = 14$ valid hosts.

140. D. The computer had an IP address of 172.18.40.5/12 and it belongs to the 172.16.0.0/12 network, which has a range of 172.16.0.1 to 172.31.255.254. Therefore, the internal server is within the same network as the computer, and the default gateway has no effect on the problem. The conclusion is that the network is not the problem.

141. C. The computer and the gateway address are correct; the IP address of the remote server is wrong. It is a loopback address and can only be internally used by the local computer. The valid range for loopback is 127.0.0.1 to 127.255.255.254.

142. B. A layer 3 broadcast is always all ones in the host portion of the IP address. When the IP stack see this, it puts all *F*s in the destination Ethernet MAC address.

143. A. A unicast address is a single valid IP address for direct communications purposes between two hosts.

144. D. Anycast is a way of allowing the same IP address on multiple machines in different geographical areas. The routing protocol is used to advertise in routing tables the closest IP by the use of metrics. Currently this is how DNS root servers work.

145. C. Multicast is used to allow computers to opt into a transmission. Examples of uses for multicast are imaging of computers, video, and routing protocols, to name a few.

146. D. The multicast address range is 224.0.0.0 to 239.255.255.255. The /4 depicts a subnet of 16.

147. B. IGMP, or Internet Group Messaging Protocol, allows switches to join computers to the multicast group table. This allows the selective process of snooping to occur when a transmission is sent.

148. B. DHCP uses a packet called a Discover packet. This packet is addressed to 255.255.255.255. Although ARP uses a broadcast, it is a layer 2 broadcast, not a layer 3 broadcast.

149. B. A broadcast will forward a message to all computers in the same subnet.

150. C. The multicast address range is 224.0.0.0 to 239.255.255.255.

151. C. RFC 1918 defines three private address ranges, which are not routable on the Internet.

152. A. The private IP address space was created to preserve the number of public IP addresses.

153. D. Network Address Translation (NAT) is required to communicate over the Internet with private IP addresses.

154. A. The Class A private IP address range is defined as 10.0.0.0/8. The address range is 10.0.0.0 to 10.255.255.255.

155. C. The Class B private IP address range is defined as 172.16.0.0/12. The address range is 172.16.0.0 to 172.31.255.255.

156. C. Although a Class C address has a classful subnet mask of 255.255.255.0, the private IP address range put aside for Class C addresses is 192.168.0.0 to 192.168.255.255, written in CIDR notation as 192.168.0.0/16.

157. D. Any address in the range of 169.254.0.0/16 is a link-local address. It means that the computer has sensed that a network connection is present, but no DHCP is present. The network only allows local communications and no routing. Microsoft refers to this as an APIPA address.

158. C. The network seems to be configured properly. You have received a valid address in the Class A space of the RFC 1918 private address range.

159. D. 198.168.55.45 is a valid IPv4 public address. All of the other addresses are RFC 1918 compliant and thus non-routable on the Internet.

160. A. IANA, or the Internet Assigned Numbers Authority, is the governing body, which distributes public IP addresses and registers them to ISPs.

161. B. IPv4 allows for 2^{32} = 4.3 billion addresses. However, only 3.7 billion are usable, because of reservations and classful addressing. The current IPv4 address space is exhausted and IPv6 allows for 2^{128} = 3.4 × 10^{38}.

162. C. An IPv6 address is 128 bits: 64 bits is the network ID, and 64 bits is the host ID.

163. D. A 6to4 tunnel can be achieved between the routers. This encapsulates the IPv6 header in an IPv4 header so that it can be routed across the Internet.

164. D. In order to enable IPv6 on a router, you must globally configure the router with the command `ipv6 unicast-routing`. Although `ipv6 enable` will work, it will allow only link-local addressing.

165. D. When you configure routers, always use the rule of major/minor. The major protocol is `ipv6`, and the minor command is `address`. So the correct command is `ipv6 address 2001:0db8:85aa:0000:0000:8a2e:1343:1337/64`. The additional rule is to specify the network portion with a `/64`.

166. A. The first 4 bits of an IPv6 header contain the version number. In an IPv4 packet, this is set to 0100, but in an IPv6 packet, this number is set to 0110. This allows for the host to decide which stack to process the packet in.

167. D. When you configure routers, always use the rule of major/minor. The major protocol is `ipv6` and the minor command is `route`. So the correct command is `ipv6 route ::0/0 s0/0`, specifying the `::0/0 s0/0` to mean everything out of the existing interface of s0/0.

168. A. When you use a `show` command, always follow it with the major protocol and then the parameters. The `show ipv6 interfaces brief` command would show all of the interfaces configured with an IPv6 address.

169. D. RIPng, OSPFv3, and EIGRPv6 are all dynamic routing protocols that work with IPv6.

170. C. The command `show ipv6 route` will display only the IPv6 routes in the routing table.

171. D. You can remove leading 0s in the quartet, and you can condense four zeros to one zero. However, you can use the :: to remove zeros only once.

172. C. Expanding out the IP of 2001::0456:0:ada4, you first expand the :0: to four zeros. Then expand the remainder of the quartets to 0s to make a 32-digit number again.

173. B. The first 48 bits of an IPv6 address is the global prefix; the next 16 bits is the subnet portion of the IPv6 address. 48 bits + 16 bits = 64 bits for the network ID.

174. A. The network prefix is 2001:db8::/64. Expanded it is written as 2001:0db8:0000:0000/64. However, the condensed version written in the answer is valid.

175. C. The command to ping an IPv6 address is ping6. The valid condensed address for fc00:0000:0000:0000:0000:0000:0000:0004 is fc00::4. You cannot condense trailing zeros such as fc00. You can only condense leading zeros.

176. B. The address 2001:db8::2435 is a valid IP address. It is shortened by removing leading zeros and condensed. You cannot clip off the trailing zeros in an address like fe80::1. Also, ff02::1 is a multicast address and cannot be used for host addressing.

177. C. A single interface can be configured with multiple addresses. Most host interfaces will have a link-local address for duplicate address detection.

178. B. The answer is 4,096 subnets. You have been given the first 52 bits from your ISP. However, the complete network ID is 64 bits. You subtract 52 bits from 64 bits = 12 bits, then 2^{12} = 4,096.

179. B. The answer is 16,384 networks. You subtract 34 bits from 48 bits = 14 bits, then 2^{14} = 16384.

180. D. In between each set of colons or field there are four hex numbers, and each hex number represents 4 bits. Four numbers × 4 bits = 16 bits. In an IPv6 address, there are eight fields of 16 bits. Eight fields x 16 bits = 128 bit address.

181. D. The correct command to configure Stateless Address Autoconfiguration is ipv6 address autoconfig. Although ipv6 address dhcp is a valid command, it requires a stateful DHCP server.

182. B. Router solicitations are sent on a multicast address of ff02:2. This address is a local scope multicast to all IPv6 routers.

183. D. Router advertisements are sent on a multicast address of ff02:1. This address is a local scope multicast to all IPv6 hosts.

184. A. The Neighbor Discovery Protocol uses Neighbor Solicitation and Neighbor Advertisements messages to look up an IP address from a MAC address through the use of multicast.

185. C. The layer 3 protocol that Neighbor Discovery Protocol uses to process Stateless Address Autoconfiguration are ICMPv6 messages.

186. D. Stateless DHCPv6 servers are used to configure DHCP options only. The one option that all clients need is the DNS server.

187. D. You can set the IPv6 DHCP relay agent on the interface for a stateful DHCPv6 server using the command ipv6 dhcp relay destination 2001:db8:1234::1.

188. B. Duplicate Address Detection, or DAD, uses Neighbor Solicitation and Neighbor Advertisement messages to avoid duplicate addresses when SLAAC is being used.

189. B. Stateful DHCPv6 uses a process similar to DORA for IPv4. However, IPv6 uses multicast in lieu of broadcasts via the DHCPv6 Solicit multicast address.

190. C. Before a host can communicate via an RS packet, it first needs a valid IP address. The first address is a link-local address so that it can send an RS packet and receive an RA packet. The client performs DAD on both the link-local address and the proposed address.

191. B. The global unicast address is defined as 2000::/3. This provides a valid range of 2000:: to 3fff::.

192. A. The link-local address is defined as fe80::/10. Any address starting with fe80 is non-routable.

193. A. The first 23 bits are allotted to the ISP by the RIR for the region of the world for which the ISP is requesting the prefix.

194. C. The unique-local address is defined as fc00::/7. Unique-local addresses have replaced site-local addresses as of 2004 and are non-routable. The valid IPv6 range is fc00:: to fd00:: despite IANA reserving fc00::/7 as the fc00:: range. The range should not be used since the 8th bit is considered the "local bit" and is required to be a 1, as in, for example, 1111 1101 = fd.

195. D. The multicast address is defined as ff00::/8. Multicast addresses always start with *ff*.

196. A. IPv4 RFC 1918 addresses are defined as private non-routable IP addresses. In IPv6, link-local addresses are the equivalent to RFC 1918 addresses and are non-routable.

197. D. The command to configure an anycast address on an interface would be `ipv6 address 2001:db8:1:1:1::12/128 anycast`. The /128 defines a single IP to advertise in routing tables.

198. A. When converting a MAC address to an EUI-64 host address, the first step is to split the MAC address into 6-byte sections of f42356 and 345623 and place *fffe* in between them, f423:56ff:fe34:5623. This gives you a 64-bit value comprised of a 48-bit MAC address and a 16-bit filler. You must then invert "flip" the 7th bit. Example: f4 = 1111 01<u>0</u>0 = flipped = 1111 01<u>1</u>0 = f6.

199. C. The EUI-64 address can always be found by looking at the last 64 bits. In between the last 64 bits of the address, you will always find *fffe*.

200. C. The command to set an EUI-64 address for the host portion of the IPv6 address on an interface is `ipv6 address 2001:db8:1234::/64 eui-64`.

201. C. When converting a MAC address to an EUI-64 host address, the first step is to split the MAC address into 6-byte sections of e5eef5 and 562434 and place *fffe* in between them: e5ee:f5ff:fe56:2434. This gives you a 64-bit value comprised of a 48-bit MAC address and a 16-bit filler. You must then invert "flip" the 7th bit. Example: e5 = 1110 01<u>0</u>1 = flipped = 1110 01<u>1</u>1 = e7.

202. B. The output of show ipv6 interface gi 0/1 shows the multicast groups the interface has joined.

203. A. A one-to-many IPv6 address is a multicast address. One multicast address will allow many IPv6 clients to receive the transmission.

204. D. The ::1 address is a special address called a loopback address, similar to 127.0.0.1 in IPv4.

205. B. A one-to-closest IPv6 address is an anycast address. Many routers or services can have the same address. However, routing protocols allow for the client to be directed to the closest resource.

206. C. Stateful DHCPv6 addressing will not allow EUI-64 addressing. This is because the DHCPv6 server is responsible for allocating an IPv6 address from a predefined pool.

207. A. Link-local addresses starting with fe80::/10 always configure the host portion of the address with an EUI-64 address. Note that Microsoft products default to a random host ID and can be configured to generate the host ID with EUI-64.

208. C. The IPv6 address has been given to you by the ISP with your company's unique identifier. The first 32 bits are allocated to the ISPs, and they in turn add a unique 16-bit address for your company. This makes 32 bits + 16 bits = 48 bits. You have 16 bits for subnetting after the first 48 bits to make a full 64-bit network ID.

209. B. When converting a MAC address to an EUI-64 host address, the first step is to split the MAC address into 6-byte sections of 401e32 and e4ff03 and place *fffe* in between them: 401e:32ff:fee4:ff03. This gives you a 64-bit value comprised of a 48 bit MAC address and a 16 bit filler. You must then invert "flip" the 7th bit. Example: 40 = 0100 00<u>0</u>0 = flipped = 0100 00<u>1</u>0 = 42.

210. C. Although the unique-local address scope is defined as fc00::/7, RFC 4193 states that the 8th bit must equal a one for the local (L) bit. This requires the address to always start with fd which in binary is 1111 = f and 1101 = d or 1111 1101 = fd.

Chapter 2: LAN Switching Technologies (Domain 2)

1. B. Switches break up collision domains by allowing full-duplex. Switches are set to auto-negotiate duplex and speed by default, and they do not force full-duplex.

2. C. MAC address tables, also called CAM tables, are always built and stored temporarily in RAM. When the switch is turned off or the clear command is issued, the table no longer exists.

3. A. Switches allow for low latency because frames are forwarded. They utilize ASIC hardware-based switching and have low cost.

4. A. Switches make forward/filter decisions based upon the MAC address to port association in the MAC address table.

5. B. The mechanism that switches use for loop avoidance is STP, or Spanning Tree Protocol.

6. B. Switches learn MAC addresses by inspecting the frame's source MAC address on the incoming port. They then associate the source MAC address with the port it came in on.

7. A. In the exhibit, only one broadcast domain exists because a PC on the left hub can send an ARP request, and the PC on the right hub can hear it. If you wanted to create multiple broadcast domains, you would need to create VLANs and route them.

8. C. In the exhibit, there are three collision domains present.

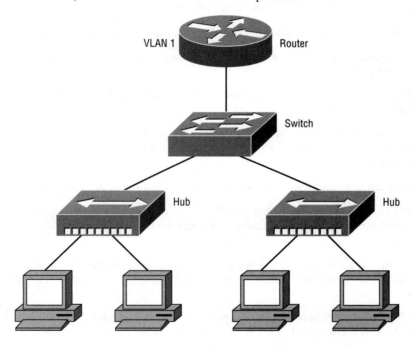

9. C. Computer A will create an ARP (broadcast) request. When that request is received on port Fa0/0, the switch will record Computer A's MAC address on Fa0/0. Then it will forward the message to all ports.

10. B. Since the MAC address table has the MAC address for Computer B, the switch will direct the frame to port Fa0/1 only.

11. B. The command to see the MAC address table is show mac address-table. However, on some 4000 and 6500 series switches, show cam dynamic will perform the same function.

12. A. Computer A will no longer forward traffic because the static entry will override a dynamic entry.

13. C. Computer A's frames will be forwarded to its new port of Fa0/3, since the entries will be cleared out when the cables are disconnected and relearned.

14. B. The destination MAC address for broadcasts are always all *F*s, such as ffff.ffff.ffff.

15. D. The show interfaces status command will display the port number, connected status, VLAN, duplex, speed, and type of interface.

16. D. When loop avoidance such as STP is not employed and loops exist, you will get duplicate unicast frames and broadcast storms. This will inevitably thrash the MAC address table and degrade bandwidth to nothing.

17. C. The default MAC address aging time for dynamic entries is 300 seconds, or 5 minutes.

18. A. The replacement of hubs with switches increases collision domains and effectively increases bandwidth.

19. C. The computer is connected to either another switch or hub on Gi0/1, since there are multiple MAC address entries on Gi0/1.

20. B. The command to show the current MAC address entry count in the MAC address table is show mac address-table count. This command will also show the maximum number of entries the table can hold.

21. A. Forward filter decisions are made upon the destination MAC address in the frame.

22. C. Store-and-forward mode is the default mode for mode edge switching equipment. Store-and-forward receives the frame, calculates the CRC, and then makes a forwarding decision.

23. A. A collision domain is defined as a group of computers that can potentially have a frame collision. Adding switches that can negotiate full-duplex and forward/filter fixes these issues.

24. B. When a MAC address is unknown by the switch, the switch will forward the frame to all ports; this is also called flooding the frame. When the destination system acts upon it, the switch learns its MAC address through source MAC address learning.

25. B. Fragment-free mode reads the first 64 bytes and deems the frame intact and forwardable. This is because most collisions that would create frame fragments happen within the first 64 bytes of a frame. This method of switching is often found on SOHO switching equipment.

26. B. Address Resolution Protocol (ARP) is used to map remote IPs on the current LAN to MAC addresses. It does this by broadcasting at layer 2 to all nodes for a response for the MAC address. Thus, it is a mapping of IP address to MAC address.

27. D. The collisions vs. packets shows a high number of collisions. In a full-duplex network connection, there should be no collisions. This would suggest that the port on the switch or the NIC card in the computer is set to half-duplex. Half-duplex causes collisions, which can degrade bandwidth by 40% to 60%.

28. A. Currently all of the computers are within one giant collision domain. Replacing the hub with a switch will create four separate potential collision domains. Switches create micro-segmentation, which increases the number of collision domains and increases bandwidth.

29. C. In the exhibit there are two broadcast domains, VLAN 1 and VLAN 2. In each of the broadcast domains there exists a single collision domain, along with the collision domain between the switch and router.

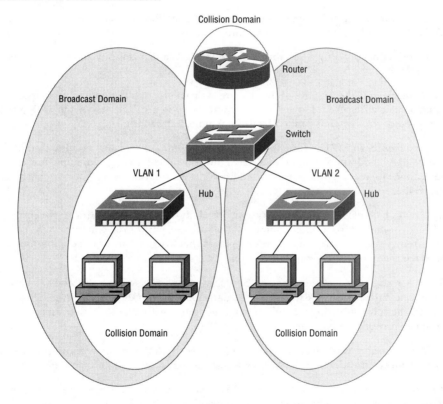

30. C. Reverse Address Resolution Protocol (RARP) is used to map MAC addresses on the current LAN to IPs. BOOTP also uses this method to allocate an IP address via the MAC address. Thus, it is a mapping of MAC address to IP address.

31. B. The command used to reset the MAC address table is `clear mac-address-table dynamic`.

32. A. In the exhibit, duplicate frames are being delivered to a router on segment 1. This is because Spanning Tree Protocol is not configured for loop avoidance.

33. A. The command to see all of the MAC addresses on a single interface is show mac address-table interfaces fast 0/1. This command can be entered in either privileged exec mode or user exec mode.

34. A. Cut-through mode copies the first 6 bytes after the preamble into memory and makes a switching decision on the destination MAC address. Many data center switches use this method of switching to provide low latency while assuming no collisions will exist.

35. B. Latency in switching is the total time it takes to forward an incoming frame to its destination interface. Latency of frame forwarding adversely affects total bandwidth.

36. C. Hardware-based bridging uses specialized application-specific integrated circuits (ASICs) to provide low latency in switching frames.

37. B. Flooding occurs only when the destination MAC address is not in the current MAC address table.

38. C. Wire speed is the switch's ability to process packets both incoming and outgoing on the same port at wire speed. However, this is not the switch's ability to switch at that speed; the speed of the switch is limited by its backplane bandwidth.

39. D. Switches learn MAC addresses based upon incoming ports and examination of the source MAC address. It will build a MAC address table for future lookups. It then determines forwarding interfaces based upon the destination MAC address contained in the frame.

40. D. A switch creates micro-segmentation, which in turns isolates traffic between two talking computers from other computers that are not part of the communications. This in turn increases bandwidth for the computers that are not part of the communications between the two talking computers.

41. B. The store and forward method of switching allows the switch to receive the entire frame and calculate the CRC against the data contained in the frame. If the CRC does not match, the frame is dropped, and the sending node must retransmit after an expiry timer or upper-protocol timer times out.

42. B. When a frame is received on an incoming port, both the incoming port and the source MAC address are added to the MAC address table and set with an aging timer.

43. A. Since there is nothing in the current MAC address tables or either switch, the incoming frame on Switch A will be flooded to all ports. This will include the port connecting Switch B. Switch B in turn will flood the frame to all ports. However, nothing will respond on Switch B since the host is on Switch A. Although this is wasted traffic, it is minimal since it is only the initial communications.

44. A. Wire speed of a single port on a 48-port gigabit switch would be 1 Gb/s, or 1,000 Mb/s.

45. C. MAC address aging time can be configured via the command `mac-address-table aging-time 400`. You can additionally specify a VLAN ID.

46. A. Since there is nothing in the current MAC address tables or either switch, the incoming frame on Switch A will be flooded to all ports. This will include the port connecting Switch B. Switch B in turn will flood the frame to all ports.

47. C. Each port on a switch creates its own collision domain. An increase in collision domains raises bandwidth since each port creates its own segment (micro-segmentation) and isolates possible collisions on other ports.

48. B. Since the MAC address table is empty on Switch A, Switch A will flood the frame to all ports on the switch. This will include the router attached to interface Fa0/3. However, a router does not perform forward/filter decisions, so the frame will not be flooded any further on Router A.

49. C. The only time a frame is dropped is when the cyclic redundancy check (CRC) calculated against the frame's payload deems the frame corrupt. If the destination MAC address is not known, it will be flooded to all active ports on the switch, but it will not be dropped.

50. A. In the exhibit, a broadcast storm is occurring due to improper configuration of STP for loop avoidance.

51. A. The 6-byte destination MAC address is after the preamble/SFD so that it can be read by the switch for forwarding.

52. C. The preamble allows for the source computer to sync its timing of the physical media independent interface with the destination computer. It achieves this via an alternating 1 and 0 pattern at a specific frequency, depending on data transfer speed. The Start Frame Delimiter (SFD) has an extra bit to let the destination computer know anything that follows is data.

53. C. The organizationally unique identifier, or OUI, is 24 bits, or the first 3 bytes of the MAC address.

54. B. The Frame Check Sequence is a 4-byte cyclical redundancy check (CRC) calculation. Its only function is to detect erroneous frames; it will not correct data and contains no parity to do so.

55. C. When the I/G bit is set, it means that the MAC address is intended to be a broadcast or multicast for a group of recipients.

56. B. When the G/L bit (sometimes referred to as the U/L bit) is set, it means that the MAC address is locally governed. This means that the user has manually set the MAC address.

57. C. MAC addresses are physical addresses that are burned into every NIC card and network device. They are unique at the Data Link layer for direct communication purposes.

58. A. The nominal MTU size is 1,500 bytes of data. It may also be advertised as 1,518 bytes, which is calculated from 1,500-bytes (payload) + 6 bytes (source MAC address) + 6 bytes (destination MAC address) + 2 bytes (type field) + 4 bytes (FCS) = 1,518 bytes. If 802.1Q VLAN tagging is being used, it can be advertised as 1,522 bytes to allow for 4 bytes for tagging. If ISL VLAN tagging is being used, ISL requires 30 bytes + 1,518 bytes = 1,548 bytes.

59. B. The Ethernet type field is 2 bytes and it identifies at layer 2 which upper-layer protocol to send the data to. When IPv4 is used, the type field is 08-00. When IPv6 is used, the type field is 86-dd.

60. C. The preamble is 7 bytes of alternating 1s and 0s at a frequency that matches the bandwidth of the link. It is important to note that the 1s and 0s pattern starts with a 1 and ends with a 0 for 7 bytes (10101010). The SFD has an extra lower bit signaling the end of timing and the start of data (10101011).

61. C. Although cabling could create an issue similar to this, it would not disable the interface. The most probable cause is that there is a duplex mismatch since there are a good number of late collisions. The most probable scenario is that the far end is set to half-duplex and the interface is set to full-duplex.

62. A. The interface has been administratively down, which means that the interface has been "shutdown". To resolve the problem a no shutdown command must be configured on the interface.

63. C. In order to clear the counters for a single interface, you would use the command clear counters interface fast 0/1. After it's entered, you will need to confirm clearing of the counters. Then you can monitor the solution provided on the interface.

64. D. The counters on this interface are all nominal, but the interface and line protocol are down/down. This most likely suggests that the cable is disconnected.

65. A. It is recommended to set all servers and networking hardware statically for speed and duplex. If a network interface flaps (transitions between up and down), auto-negotiation of speed and duplex will be performed again, which could create a service outage.

66. D. The txload and rxload counters are extremely high. This depicts that the interface is not fast enough for the data being transferred. The speed and duplex currently is 10 Mb/s and full-duplex. However, the interface on the switch is capable of 100 Mb/s. It is recommended to upgrade the node's NIC.

67. A. The commands to set the port back to auto-negotiation are speed auto and duplex auto. You can also negate the command with no speed and no duplex commands. Both methods will set auto-negotiation back on the port.

68. B. Cisco switches can auto-detect speed, so the speed sensed will be 100 Mb/s. However, if the switch cannot detect the speed, then it will fall back to 10 Mb/s. Duplex is decided upon bandwidth when IEEE auto-negotiation is turned off. If the speed is 10 Mb/s or 100 Mb/s, then the duplex will be half-duplex; otherwise it will be full-duplex on 1000 Mb/s links.

69. B. Hubs do not participate in IEEE negotiation, and therefore the speed will be detected. However, since duplex cannot be negotiated, 10 Mb/s and 100 Mb/s connections will be half-duplex and 1000 Mb/s connections will be full-duplex.

70. C. The show interfaces status command will display the port number, description, connected status, VLAN, duplex, speed, and type of interface.

71. D. The vlan.dat is the database for VLANs configured on a switch either manually or through VTP. It is persistent even if config.text (startup-config) is deleted. You must manually delete the vlan.dat.

72. D. All switches are configured by default with all interfaces in VLAN 1. This simplifies configuration if the switch is to be used as a direct replacement for a hub since nothing needs to be configured.

73. A. The normal VLAN range is 1 through 1001 before you must use the extended VLAN range.

74. C. The flexibility of design for workgroups of people and the ongoing management of moving and adding people is a benefit of a routed VLAN-enabled network.

75. C. When you're configuring an interface for a VLAN, only the VLAN number can be used. The correct command is switchport access vlan 9.

76. A. The switchport voice vlan 4 command will configure the interface to switch traffic with a COS value of 5 set by the phone to the voice VLAN of 4.

77. C. The switchport is configured as a trunk, but since the computer was originally in VLAN 1 and the native VLAN of the interface is VLAN 1 by default, all traffic untagged was directed to the native VLAN.

78. A. All VLAN tagging is removed from the frame before it egresses an access port to the end device.

79. C. VLANs 1 and 1002 through 1005 are protected by the IOS and cannot be changed, renamed, or deleted.

80. B. By default, the VTP mode is server. VTP v1 and v2 do not support storage and propagation of extended VLANs. However, when the switch is put into transparent mode, it does not participate in VTP, so the VLANs can be configured.

81. C. The extended VLAN range is VLAN 1006 to 4094.

82. C. The port needs to be changed from trunk mode to access mode, via the command switchport mode access. Although switchport native vlan 12 would remedy the problem, it would be an improper configuration since you are expecting tagged traffic and directing untagged traffic to VLAN 12.

83. D. For security concerns, it should not be used in production. It is the default VLAN configured on all switches. Potentially, a computer can be plugged into an interface defaulted to VLAN 1 and expose resources such as the switch management network.

84. B. Configuration of jumbo frames requires creation of the VLAN from a global configuration prompt and then setting the maximum transmission unit (MTU). The value of the MTU will differ from switch to switch but is usually 9,000 bytes or higher.

85. B. The command to verify that a VLAN is created and the port(s) it is associated with is show vlan.

86. C. The command to delete VLAN 9 is no vlan 9 performed from a global configuration prompt.

87. D. Frames with MAC addresses that are not in the MAC address table are flooded only to the ports in the respective VLAN.

88. B. When the command is invoked inside of the interface, it will create the VLAN automatically.

89. D. The normal range of VLANs on a default Cisco switch is VLAN 1 to 1001. However, VLAN 1 cannot be modified.

90. C. Static VLANs are VLANs that have been manually configured vs. dynamic VLANs that are configured via a VLAN Membership Policy Server (VMPS). A node will not know which VLAN it is assigned to when it is statically set via the command switchport access vlan 3.

91. D. The addition of another VLAN will increase the effective bandwidth by adding additional broadcast domains. A router is required to route between VLANs. However, it will not be required if you are logically partitioning the switch via VLANs.

92. B. When adding VLANs, you immediately increase the number of broadcast domains. At the same time you increase collision domains. If a switch had 12 ports and they all negotiated at 100 Mb/s half-duplex (one collision domain), when a VLAN is added you will automatically create two collision domains while adding an additional broadcast domain.

93. C. Dynamic VLANs are deprecated, but you may still see them in operations. A switch configured with dynamic VLANs checks a VLAN Management Policy Server (VMPS) when clients plug in. The VMPS has a list of MAC addresses to their respective VLANs. It is now recommended that dynamic VLAN installations are converted to 802.1x.

94. D. To verify a VLAN name change, you would use the command show vlan id 3. This would only show you the one VLAN configured in the database. show vlans is incorrect because the command is not plural; it is singular, show vlan. It will give you a complete listing of all VLANs.

95. A. Creating the new VLAN will logically segment this work group. Creating a Switched Virtual Interface (SVI) will allow routing on the layer 3 switch. The ACLs should only be applied to VLAN interfaces. Although the other solutions achieve a similar goal, they do not provide flexibility.

96. A. The Cisco Discovery Protocol (CDP) is required for Cisco VoIP phones. It allows the switch to learn capabilities and power requirements.

97. D. The command `show interfaces switchport` will display a detail of all ports in respect to VLAN operational status. The command will show the operational mode of the interface, such as trunk or access mode.

98. D. The proper way to enable a VLAN to forward traffic is to first enter the VLAN database for ID 3 and then issue the `no shutdown` command. On some IOS versions, this can also be done via the command `no shutdown vlan 3` from global config mode.

99. C. The command `show interfaces FastEthernet 0/3 switchport` will show the switchport details for only Fa0/3, to include its operational mode. This command is similar to `show interfaces switchport`, which will show all ports.

100. B. The VLAN is disabled from forwarding traffic in the VLAN database. The `no shutdown vlan 5` must be performed in global config. The VLAN interface being shut down would have no effect on traffic being forwarded on the VLAN, only routed.

101. C. The client computer connected to an access port cannot see any VLAN tagging information. It is removed before egress of the interface.

102. D. When the MTU is changed on the VLAN, it has little consequence to normal MTU communications. However, if you are going to utilize the new MTU for something like iSCSI, it must be supported end to end or it can actually decrease performance. All switching equipment between the two end devices must support jumbo frames.

103. B. Since the remote office has no onsite IT personnel, there is a risk of workers plugging in unauthorized equipment such as a WAP. If port security is implemented, the interface can be secured to allow only the MAC address of the computer to pass; all other traffic can be dropped.

104. C. When layer 3 or routed VLANs are implemented, it allows for a more secure network with the use of ACLs applied to the VLAN interface.

105. B. Wireless LAN controllers allow trunks to be used so that multiple VLANs can be used. Once the VLANs are accessible to the WLC, you need to create one SSID tied to the VLAN configured for production and another SSID tied to the VLAN configured for guests.

106. A. The default VLAN for all switches is VLAN 1. It is the default configuration for all access ports from the factory.

107. D. The extended VLAN database will be stored in the startup-config. Only normal VLANs are stored in the VLAN database (`vlan.dat`). When configuring extended VLANs, you must have the switch in VTP transparent mode.

108. A. You should first create the VLAN in the VLAN database and add its name. Then you need to enter the interface and configure the port for the VLAN.

109. B. VLAN 4 is an active VLAN. However, it has not been given a name, so the default name is VLAN0004.

110. B. You must manually configure the VLAN on the Cisco switch(s). VTP is a protocol that allows for VLAN autoconfiguration in the VLAN database. However, only Cisco switches support it.

111. D. A router will not function as a switch and a router. You cannot configure two router interfaces for the same network. The recommended change is that Switch A and Switch B are trunked together. Then a single connection from either Router A or Router B is connected to Router A.

112. B. When a VLAN is created, so is a broadcast domain. The broadcast domain/VLAN requires its own unique IP network addressing and a router to route between the networks.

113. D. Only one switch in the network needs to provide routing functionality. Since Computers A and C can ping each other, the SVI is configured properly for routing. The most probable cause is that a trunk does not exist between the switches.

114. B. In global configuration, you first need to enter the entry of the VLAN in the VLAN database. Then you can issue a `name` command to overwrite the existing entry. Negating the VLAN 4 and re-creating it would also work but would create interruption when it was destroyed.

115. C. The command used to configure an access port for VLAN 8 is `switchport access vlan 8`, and the command to configure the VOIP phone is `switchport voice vlan 6`.

116. D. The port is set up as a trunk. Since the phone is normally configured for 801.Q tagging of COS values, it will work in this diagram. However, since the computer is not tagging traffic for data, the communications will be directed to the native VLAN on the configured trunk.

117. C. One of the prerequisites for configuring extended VLANs is that the VTP mode must be transparent.

118. B. VLAN 1 is the default VLAN and it is not permitted by the IOS to change the VLAN in any way. This includes name changes.

119. C. The computer is on another switch connected via a trunk link, since there are multiple VLANs on the interface of Gi0/1.

120. A. Although the MTU is configured on the VLAN, all switches and devices connected end to end must be configured to support jumbo frames. If you fail to do this, you can expect to see a performance decrease. An MTU of 9128 is defined as a jumbo frame.

121. B. Since the Dell switch cannot support the proprietary protocol of ISL, both switches need to be set up to use 802.1Q.

122. B. The command to specify 802.1Q encapsulation on a trunk interface is `switchport trunk encapsulation 802.1q`.

123. D. This error is very common when configuring Cisco switches, since many switches only support 802.1Q and configuration is not necessary. The ISL trunking protocol is not supported on certain platforms, such as the 2900 series switches.

124. B. The command `show interfaces trunk` will display all of the configured trunks on the switch.

125. C. When a frame traverses a trunk and does not have VLAN tagging information in the 802.1Q encapsulation format (untagged), it is sent to the native VLAN configured on the trunk.

126. A. All switches are configured by default as a VTP server.

127. B. The command to display the mode settings for VTP is `show vtp status`.

128. B. When setting up VTP on a new switch connected to your existing VTP infrastructure, you need to change the mode of the switch. Then you must configure the VTP domain that is serving the VTP information.

129. C. The 802.1Q protocol is supported by all switches' vendors for trunking. It is an open standard that was developed by the IEEE.

130. C. The command `show interface fastethernet 0/15 switchport` will show the operational mode, and if configured as a trunk, it will show the native VLAN.

131. A. The command to change the native VLAN of a trunk to VLAN 999 is `switchport trunk native vlan 999`.

132. B. This error is normal if it is the first interface to be changed over to the new native VLAN since the other interface has not been changed yet. However, if the other interface was changed already and you received this error, then CDP is letting you know that the other side is mismatched.

133. B. The VLAN is not allowed over the trunk because of the `switchport trunk allowed vlan 4,6,12,15` command.

134. D. The Dynamic Trunking Protocol can be turned off with the command `switchport nonegotiate`, which when configured states not to negotiate trunks via DTP.

135. C. The command `switchport trunk allowed vlan remove 2-4` will remove VLANs 2 through 4 from the trunk.

136. D. The command `switchport trunk allowed vlan all` will restore the allowed VLAN list back to default.

137. A. Switch B will need to either have its interface set to `switchport mode trunk` or `switchport mode dynamic desirable` for Switch A to turn its interface into a trunk.

138. A. The command `switchport trunk allowed vlan add 4` will add VLAN 4 to the existing list of VLANs already allowed on the interface.

139. C. The command will not complete because the interface is set to `dynamic auto`, which implies the trunk protocol will be negotiated. You cannot set it to `switchport mode trunk` until you statically set the encapsulation via the command `switchport trunk encapsulation dot1q`.

140. D. On Switch A, DTP is turned on and the encapsulation is set to 802.1Q. However, on Switch B, DTP is turned off and ISL encapsulation is manually set. Switch B will need to have 802.1Q configured in order to have trunking complete.

141. B. VLAN Trunking Protocol, or VTP, propagates the VLAN database from an initial master copy on the "server" to all of the "clients."

142. A. Inter-Switch Link, or ISL, is a proprietary protocol used for trunking of switches. If you need to connect non-Cisco switches to a Cisco switch, you must use 802.1Q, the IEEE standard.

143. C. 802.1Q inserts a field containing the 16-bit Tag Protocol ID of 0x8100, a 3-bit COS field, a 1-bit drop-eligible indicator (used with COS), and the 12=bit VLAN ID, which equals 32 bits, or 4 bytes.

144. B. A switch in VTP transparent mode will not participate in VTP. However, if the VTP is v2, the switch will forward and receive VTP advertisements.

145. D. Both switches have a native VLAN mismatch. Since Switch B has an inactive VLAN, it would be recommended to change the native VLAN back to 1 on Switch B.

146. A. You must first set the encapsulation to 802.1Q, then you can statically set the mode to trunk. An alternative would be to set the port to dynamic desirable via the command `switchport mode dynamic desirable`. However, it is recommended to statically configure the link to trunk on one or both sides if possible.

147. B. VTP VLAN pruning removes forwarding traffic for VLANs that are not configured on remote switches. This saves bandwidth on trunks because if the remote switch does not have the VLAN configured on it, the frame destined for the VLAN will not traverse the trunk.

148. B. The command "vtp pruning in global configuration mode will enable VTP VLAN pruning.

149. D. The problems will not be apparent since the trunk will still function for tagged traffic. However, any traffic that is not tagged will be directed to the opposite side's native VLAN. So traffic expected for VLAN 1 will be directed to VLAN 10, and VLAN 10 traffic will be directed to VLAN 1 when not tagged.

150. A. VTP pruning needs to be configured only on the VTP server. The clients will receive the update and turn on VTP pruning automatically.

151. B. VLAN Trunking Protocol allows for conformity of VLANs across all Cisco switches. The protocol uses a master-slave database with a revision control of +1. If the server is 5 and the clients are 4, they will update the database to the latest revision.

152. C. Native VLANs are only used for traffic that is not tagged, which is placed on a trunk link. A common use for native VLANs is management traffic between switches, before both sides are configured as a trunk.

153. D. The VTP domains must match on both switches. Switch A has a VTP domain of Cisco, and Switch B has a VTP domain of cisco. The VTP domain, just like a password, is case sensitive.

154. B. The native VLAN on Switch A is set to VLAN 2, and the native VLAN on Switch B is VLAN 1. This will cause mismatch errors with CDP, although CDP will still function, it will continue to generate errors.

155. D. The switch is set up with a VTP mode of transparent. When a switch is set up with a mode of transparent, the VLAN information is stored in the running-config in lieu of the `vlan.dat` file.

156. B. If you issue the command `switchport nonegotiate`, the switch will not send Dynamic Trunking Protocol (DTP) frames for trunk negotiation. The default configuration for a port is the mode of access, so the port will remain in an access port.

157. A. You want Switch B to become a member of VLAN 5. So Switch A must change its interface to an access port, which will force Switch B to remain an access port. Then you configure the access VLAN of 5 on Switch A. If you tried to configure this with a native VLAN, you would result in a native VLAN mismatch and improper configuration.

158. D. The command `switchport mode dynamic desirable` is similar to `switchport mode dynamic auto` with the exception that it is desirable to become a trunk. So if the neighboring port is set to auto, desirable, or trunk, it becomes a trunk.

159. A. The command `switchport mode dynamic auto` will cause the port to remain an access port if the neighboring port is configured the same. However, if you configure the neighboring port as a trunk, it will become a trunk.

160. C. The command `show interfaces switchport` will show greater detail about the trunk than the command `show interfaces trunk`. Alternatively, you can specify a single port using the command `show interfaces Fa 0/5 switchport`, for example.

161. A. Configuring servers like VMware ESXi is no different than configuring other switches. The exception is that the VMware server will not participate in DTP. So we first configure the command to set the interface statically to a trunk. Then we turn off DTP with the command `switchport nonegotiate` since DTP is not needed.

162. B. Cisco Discovery Protocol (CDP) will alert you to a native VLAN mismatch. You will receive the error "%CDP-4-NATIVE_VLAN_MISMATCH: Native VLAN mismatch discovered…." When a trunk is configured, the native VLAN is always used for CDP exchanges.

163. C. The VTP clients track changes via a 32-bit number inside of the VTP frame called the revision number. By default, every 5 minutes a summary advertisement is sent from the server. However, when an update occurs, a new VTP frame called a subset advert message is sent.

164. B. The `show interfaces gi 0/1 switchport` on Switch B shows the interface in a static access mode. This means that you have an interface mismatch. Switch A is set to a mode of trunk, and Switch B is set to a mode of access.

165. A. Since the VTP clients in the network check the revision number in VTP, if a client is changed to a server, the database remains intact. So when a change is made, the revision number will increment and propagate to the rest of the network. Even if an existing server exists, its revision number will be lower.

166. D. The command show interfaces trunk will show the details of allowed VLANs. The show running-config command will also show you the allowed VLANs.

167. C. When trunking to a non-Cisco product, you cannot rely on DTP to form the trunk link. The port must explicitly be set to a trunk via the command switchport mode trunk. It is also advisable to turn off DTP via the command switchport nonegotiate.

168. A. The command show vtp status will tell you if VTP pruning is enabled or disabled.

169. C. VLAN 1002 is reserved for use with an FDDI VLAN and not allowed for Ethernet traffic. All Ethernet traffic must be a VLAN between 1 to 1001. You cannot use 1002 to 1005 because they are used for legacy applications.

170. D. Although switchport trunk allowed vlan all and switchport trunk allowed vlan 1-1001 would rectify the problem, it would cause network interruption if those VLANs were blocked for security concerns. The proper way to add a VLAN is switchport trunk allowed vlan add 9.

171. C. The original version of STP was created by Digital Equipment Corporation (DEC). The IEEE ratified the specification of STP as 802.1d in 1990.

172. B. Spanning Tree Protocol runs as a distributed process on each switch. Each switch creates and maintains its own topology database referencing the root bridge.

173. A. STP monitors all interfaces for BPDUs, which carry switches' identities. When it sees the same switch ID in BPDUs on multiple interfaces, a redundant link is detected.

174. C. The root bridge is elected by all of the switches and has the lowest MAC address and priority of them all.

175. B. The original STP specification was revamped in 2004 with RSTP 802.1w. This revamping of STP was to fix problems with the original specification.

176. A. The root bridge is a point of perspective for the rest of the STP network. It is important to have a point of perspective to calculate which ports are blocked and which remain in a forwarding mode.

177. C. The bridge ID is made up of a 2-byte bridge priority and a 6-byte MAC address for a total of 8 bytes.

178. D. The link cost is a numeric value that represents the cost in speed of a link. The higher the numbers, the lower the speed of the link, thus a higher cost.

179. B. The RSTP path cost is the calculation of all of the link costs that lead back to the root bridge. The link cost is a numeric value that signifies the speed. The lower the number "cost," the higher the speed of the link.

180. D. 802.1d STP convergence takes 50 seconds to complete before the port is put into a state of forwarding or blocking. This is dependent on the STA, or spanning-tree algorithm.

181. C. When a computer is connected to an STP-enabled interface, the port will transition between blocking, listening, learning, and forwarding. The time between the states of blocking and forwarding is called the convergence and is 50 seconds.

182. A. A designated port is a port that has the lowest cost compared to the higher cost of the redundant ports. It is placed into a forwarding state for a network segment.

183. A. Every switch in the network segment must have at least one root port. This is the port that leads back to the root bridge. The root bridge will have a designated port on the adjacent link.

184. C. The root port is the port that leads back to the root bridge on the adjacent switch. It has the lowest cost of the redundant ports.

185. C. An STP blocked port will block all frames from being forwarded. The blocking excludes BPDUs, which it will continue to listen for and calculate future topology decisions.

186. B. Per-VLAN Spanning Tree+ elects a root bridge for each VLAN and creates a topology table for each VLAN. It is a Cisco proprietary protocol due to the bridge ID calculation it must perform for each VLAN.

187. A. The designated port is the port with the lowest cost of the redundant links to the network segment. The adjacent port is normally the root port leading back to the root bridge.

188. D. RSTP has three transitions when a computer is plugged in (no loops). The transitions are discarding, learning, and forwarding, which allow for rapid convergence times.

189. C. The PVST+ bridge ID comprises a 4-bit bridge priority calculated in blocks of 4096, a 12-bit sys-ext-id that is the VLAN ID for the segment, and a 6-byte MAC address for the switch.

190. C. The default bridge priority for STP is 32,768.

191. A. Rapid Per-VLAN Spanning Tree+ elects a root bridge for each VLAN. It allows for fast convergence times and logical placement of the root bridge. However, it requires the most CPU and RAM of all implementations.

192. B. Common Spanning Tree elects a single root bridge for the entire network and all of the VLANs. This creates a problem when the center of your network may vary upon VLAN placement.

193. B. RSTP has three transition modes and converges faster than STP, which is 50 seconds. It is, however, backward compatible with STP 802.1d.

194. B. Each switch is responsible for sensing changes to the topology. Whenever the topology changes, a Topology Change Notification (TCN) is sent out all root ports and an acknowledgment is sent back. This happens until the root bridge sends back a notification.

195. B. 802.1s, which is called Multiple Spanning Tree (MST), is a standard based upon PVST+. It is an open standard created by the IEEE that will allow Per-VLAN Spanning Tree in multi-vendor switched networks. However, it is not fully supported on all Cisco platforms as of yet.

196. D. The root bridge always has all of its ports in a designated mode or forwarding mode. If there are redundant links, the adjacent switch to the designated port on the root bridge must be a non-designated or blocking state.

197. A. RSTP has three port states: discarding, learning, and forwarding. Blocking and listening are both mapped to discarding in RSTP. When a port is in a state of discarding, it means the interface is discarding all frames except for BPDUs.

198. B. The switch with the MAC address of 0011.03ae.d8aa will become the root bridge. Its MAC address is the lowest out of the four switches.

199. D. All Cisco switches are defaulted to the Cisco proprietary STP protocol of PVST+.

200. D. An alternate port is a port that is in a discarding state. If the root port fails on the switch with the alternate port, then the alternate port becomes the root port for that switch.

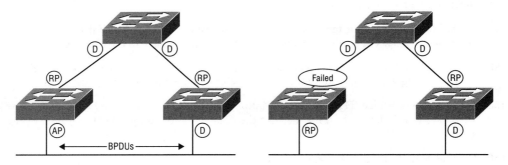

201. A. A backup port is a port in a discarding state. It receives BPDUs from another port on the same switch. If the forwarding port fails, then the backup port will become designated so that connectivity to the segment can be restored.

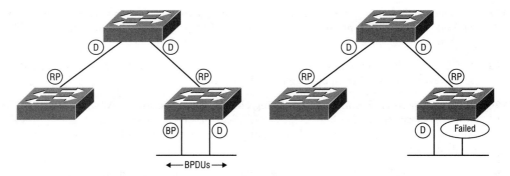

202. D. Although 00f8.034e.bede is the highest MAC address of the four switches, the priority is the lowest of the four. Since the priority and MAC address are added together, the priority allows the switch to win the election.

203. A. The command to set the STP priority for VLAN 5 is performed from a global config prompt. The full command is spanning-tree vlan 5 priority 16384.

204. D. The command show spanning-tree summary will show all of the VLANs for which the current switch is a root bridge.

```
SwitchA#sh spanning-tree summary
Switch is in pvst mode
Root bridge for: VLAN0005 VLAN0006
Extended System ID is enabled
PortFast Default is disabled
PortFast BPDU Guard Default is disabled
PortFast BPDU Filter Default is disabled
Loopguard Default is disabled
EtherChannel misconfig guard is disabled
UplinkFast is disabled
BackboneFast is disabled
Configured Pathcost method used is short
[output cut]
```

205. C. Enabling Rapid PVST is super simple. From a global config prompt you use the command spanning-tree mode rapid-pvst.

206. B. The command show spanning-tree vlan 6 would only show the spanning-tree configuration for VLAN 6.

207. D. The new port state that RTSP has is discarding, which replaces the blocking state of STP.

208. B. Switch B is the root bridge, therefore Switch A Fa0/0 is a root port and Switch C Fa0/4 is a root port.

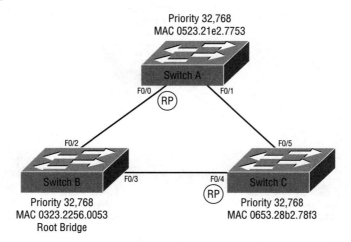

209. D. Switch B is the root port, therefore Switch A Fa0/0 and Switch C Fa0/4 are root ports. Between Switch A Fa0/1 and Switch C Fa0/5, one of the ports needs to be blocking. Since Switch C Fa0/5 has the highest MAC address, its port is put into a blocking state.

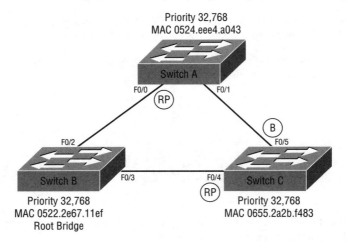

210. C. From the output of the show spanning-tree vlan 1 command, we see that the root bridge ID is a different MAC address from this bridge's ID. At the bottom of the output you can see the port role, which is root. This means that the port is connected to the root bridge.

211. D. Since Switch A is the root bridge because of the lower priority, the adjacent switch's interfaces become the root ports.

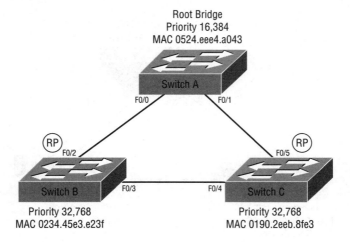

212. B. All of the switches have the same priority. However, Switch C has the lowest MAC address and has become the root bridge. The link between Switch A and Switch B is not a redundant connection. Since Switch A has a higher MAC address, its port of Fa0/0 will go into a blocking state and become non-designated.

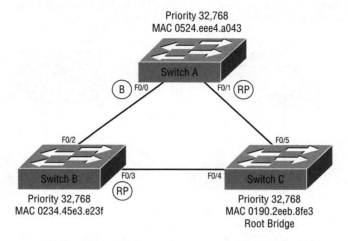

213. D. Nothing needs to be changed in this network because RSTP is backward compatible with STP. On some versions of IOS/models or switches, RSTP is not supported and therefore cannot be configured.

214. A. All switches have the default priority, so Switch A has the lowest MAC address of the four switches and becomes the root bridge.

215. C. All three switches will have a root port leading back to the root bridge since Switch A is the root bridge. The total path cost is lower for Switch D Gi0/8 than it is for Switch D Fa0/10.

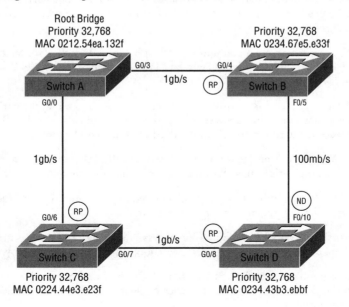

216. B. All switches have the default priority. The lowest MAC address is Switch C, so the adjacent interfaces of Switch A Gi0/0 and Switch D Gi0/10 become root ports. Next we need to calculate the total path cost, and since the total path cost is higher between Switch B and Switch D, we turn the furthest port into a blocking state.

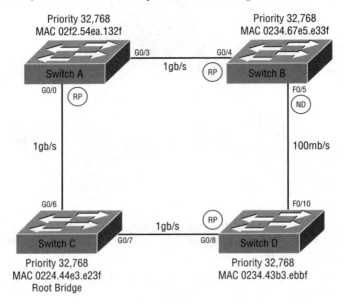

Priority 32,768
MAC 02f2.54ea.132f

Priority 32,768
MAC 0234.67e5.e33f

217. A. The network is running Rapid PVST+ since this is the default when you configure RSTP via the command spanning-tree mode rapid-pvst. The correct command is spanning-tree vlan 1 priority 16384. Priorities must always be configured in increments of 4,096.

218. B. The first switch you must configure as a root bridge is Switch A for VLAN 2 with a priority of 16,384. Then configure Switch C as a root bridge for VLAN 7 with a priority of 16,384.

219. B. With RSTP, path cost is the total calculated value of costs along the path to the root bridge. If another switch has a lower path cost to the root bridge for the VLAN, then its port will become the root port and any redundant links will become alternate ports.

220. C. Switch A is the root bridge for VLAN 1 because all of the interfaces are in a designated state. Only the root bridge has all of the interfaces in a designated state for a VLAN.

221. D. The command spanning-tree portfast" entered into the interface will turn on PortFast mode. This will allow the interface to forward first.

222. B. PortFast should only be configured on access links where end devices are plugged in because these devices will not typically create loops in the switch topology.

223. B. This command turns on PortFast globally for only access ports on the switch. This command should be used on access switches because end devices are connected at this level in the hierarchy.

224. A. You will create a temporary switching loop until the BPDUs are heard from each interface over the hub. However, during this period you will have a switching loop and degrade traffic over the entire switching topology until convergence happens.

225. A. BPDU Guard will turn the interface to err-disable as soon as a BPDU is heard on the interface. This feature should be enabled on access switches when configuring PortFast.

226. A. PortFast mode allows an interface to bypass the blocking state and begin forwarding immediately. It then listens and learns of BPDUs on the interface and can make a decision to continue to forward frames or enter into a blocking state.

227. C. The correct command to configure BPDU Guard on a single interface is spanning-tree bpduguard entered into the interface you want to turn it on for.

228. C. BPDU Guard was turned on the trunk link. When the BPDU of the adjacent switch was seen, the switch turned the port into err-disabled mode.

229. B. Configuring BPDU Guard along with PortFast ensures that the end device will always be forwarding. BPDU Guard ensures that in the event a BPDU is heard on the interface, the interface will enter into an err-disable mode.

230. D. Using the command show spanning-tree interface fa 0/1 will show the spanning tree configuration for an interface. If PortFast has been configured, the last line will read, "The port is in the PortFast mode."

231. D. One way to disable BDPU Guard is to enter the command spanning-tree bpduguard disable. Another way is to negate the command with no spanning-tree bpduguard.

232. C. The switch's interface will become err-disabled immediately. Once it is in err-disable mode, an administrator is required to reset the interface.

233. B. The show spanning-tree summary command will show you which features are turned on globally or by default.

234. D. BPDU Guard will protect the edge switch from someone accidentally plugging in another switch to a port dedicated for end devices.

235. A. The command spanning-tree portfast default will configure all access ports on the switch as PortFast enabled.

236. B. Link Layer Discovery Protocol is an IEEE standard of 802.1ab. Most Cisco devices can perform LLDP.

237. D. The command to turn off CDP globally on a switch is no cdp run.

238. B. CDP frames are sent out all active interfaces every 60 seconds.

239. C. Cisco Discovery Protocol, or CDP, is a Cisco proprietary protocol used for gathering information from neighboring switches and routers.

240. D. The default holddown timer for CDP entries is three times the advertisement timer of 60 seconds. So entries have a holddowntimer value of 180 seconds.

241. B. To turn off or suppress CDP advertisements on a single interface, you would enter the interface and enter the command no cdp enable.

242. D. The sh cdp entry * command will give output that's identical to that of the show cdp neighbors detail command.

243. B. The command lldp run entered in global config mode will enable LLDP on all interfaces. When enabled, LLDP-MED, or LLDP for Media, will read capabilities on the phone such as name and power level.

244. C. The command show lldp neighbor detail will show output identical to the output of show cdp neighbor detail.

245. A. The default LLDP advertisement interval is 30 seconds. When turned on, it will advertise out all active interfaces every 30 seconds.

246. B. When you use the command no lldp transmit, it will suppress LLDP messages from exiting the interface it is configured on.

247. D. The default value of the LLDP holddown timer for entries is 120 seconds. This holddown timer is set every time the switch hears an advertisement for a device. The holddown is four times the advertisement interval.

248. C. Switch B is connected to Switch A via Gi0/2. Switch A Gi0/1 is the adjacent interface connecting the two switches.

249. D. The command no cdp enable will turn off CDP advertisements on the interface that you configure it on.

250. B. The command show cdp interface will display all of the interfaces CDP is enabled on along with their advertisement intervals.

251. B. EtherChannel can aggregate 2 interfaces to 8 interfaces together on a single switch when using PAgP.

252. D. When EtherChannel bonds interfaces together, they act as a single Ethernet link. Therefore, layer 2 and layer 3 sees it as a single link.

253. A. The highest configurable bandwidth is going to be 2 Gb/s. This is because you cannot mix speeds and duplex.

254. A. The Link Aggregation Control Protocol (LACP) is the IEEE standard 802.3ad.

255. B. LACP is an IEEE standard that is supported by non-Cisco devices to create aggregation links and negotiate the configuration.

256. C. EtherChannel can aggregate 2 interfaces to 16 interfaces together on a single switch when using LACP. Only eight ports can be used at any one time; the others are placed in standby mode.

257. C. If you configure the EtherChannel to on mode, it forces the aggregation of links together without the use of a control protocol.

258. A. The term *EtherChannel* is a Cisco-centric term. Most vendors will not recognize the term.

259. C. Port Aggregation Protocol (PAgP) is a Cisco proprietary control negotiation protocol.

260. A. PAgP sends control notifications every 30 seconds to the adjacent switch.

261. A. Using active mode on both sides assures us that the switches will start negotiation with only Link Aggregation Control Protocol (LACP).

262. C. When you use passive on one side and active on the other side of a port channel, the result is that Link Aggregation Control Protocol (LACP) will be used.

263. A. The command `show etherchannel` will display all EtherChannels on the switch along with their negotiated protocols.

264. B. Since both interfaces are set to passive mode, neither side will initiate the LACP control notifications. Although the port channel is configured on the switch, it is not communicated between the switches.

265. D. When both sides of the port channel are configured with the On mode, an unconditional port channel is created. This means there is no control protocol assisting the port channel.

266. C. When you configure the channel group command interfaces, it automatically creates a port channel interface. This pseudo interface should be used for all configurations of the collective ports.

267. A. When one side of the port channel is configured with the auto mode and the other is configured with desirable mode, the EtherChannel is formed with PAgP.

268. A. When the on mode is used, it means that no aggregation protocol will be used. On the adjacent switch, you must use the on mode.

269. D. By default, load balancing is performed on frames by the source MAC address.

270. B. When configuring PAgP, you will use either the auto and desirable mode or the desirable mode on both sides. When you use desirable mode on both sides, desirable mode will unconditionally configure the EtherChannel with PAgP.

271. B. When changing the EtherChannel load-balancing criteria, you must change it in global configuration mode via the `port-channel load-balance dst-ip` command.

272. A. Since the load-balancing method is globally configured, you use the `show etherchannel load-balance` command to verify the criteria load balancing is performed with.

273. C. When you want optimal load balancing, you would configure the source and destination IP address. On some versions of Cisco IOS, you can configure the source and destination IP address as well as the source and destination ports. Although this creates the most optimal load balancing, it creates a high amount of latency since layer 4 information must be calculated.

274. B. This option forces an interface, if configured with desirable or auto, to forcibly send notifications. When a port is configured in auto mode, it requires another adjacent switch to send PAgP notifications. This option forces the notifications with the desirable mode.

275. B. When configuring an access port for use with an EtherChannel, it is recommended to configure the `switchport access vlan #` command in each interface where the `channel-group` command has been configured.

276. C. The EtherChannel has been configured with no control protocol, which is a result of configuring each side of the EtherChannel with the command `channel-group 1 mode on`.

277. B. Since the auto mode was used on the first switch (Switch A), desirable should be used on the second switch to assure forming of an EtherChannel.

278. D. If the other switch is set to passive mode, an EtherChannel will not form. The recommended mode for the other side is active mode.

279. A. When one side is configured with on mode, it uses no control protocol. If a control protocol is sensed from the adjacent switch, the port will enter err-disable mode to protect it from a loop.

280. C. When you configure the `channel-group 1 mode active` command on the first interface, a pseudo interface is created called port-channel 1. All statistics and configuration should be referenced by this interface.

281. B. Switch stacking allows for all of the switches to be tied together so the uplink port can be shared at a nominal bandwidth of 32 Gb/s for the backplane loop.

282. C. Cross-stack EtherChannel allows you to configure EtherChannels between physical switches to act as one EtherChannel. If one switch or SPF transceiver goes bad, the rest of the switching will be supported by the other physical switches.

283. B. Cisco will support a maximum of 9 switches in a switch stack configuration.

284. D. When you create a switch stack, the subordinate switches will upgrade or downgrade the IOS software according to the master switch's IOS. Legally, you must purchase the highest IOS the master switch contains or downgrade the license the master contains.

285. C. The StackWise 3750 has a backend loop of two counter-rotating rings. Each ring supplies 16 Gb/s in each direction. This allows for up to 32 Gb/s total traffic flow and also allows for redundancy.

286. B. When you create a switch stack, you assign the IP address to the master switch. This IP address is used for the entire switch stack. If a master fails, a new master is elected and the original master IP is used.

287. C. Switches participating in stacking can be added, deleted, or replaced without powering the stack off. The provisioned switch that is being replaced must match the replacement's stack member number via the `switch {stack-member-number} provision` command.

288. D. The master switch is responsible for forwarding tables, ACL distribution, QOS, and multicast routing. The master switch is elected by the criteria of configured priority, hardware and software priority, configuration, uptime, and MAC address.

289. A. Configuration is downloaded to the replacement switch automatically when it is replaced. The switch responsible for hosting the configuration is the master switch.

290. A. Only the master switch needs to be upgraded. Once the master switch is upgraded, it will download the IOS to all other members of the switch stack.

291. B. The subordinate switch, often referred to as the slave switch, downloads all of its IOS, configuration, and forwarding tables from the master switch.

292. B. Switch stacking cables come in lengths of 50 centimeters, 1 meter, and 3 meters. The maximum length of the switch stack cable is 3 meters, or about 10 feet.

293. D. The command used to verify cabling of the switch stack is show switch stack-ports. This command will display a table of how the switches are connected.

294. B. The command show switch will display all switches in the stack along with their role. Within this information will be a switch labeled *master.*

295. D. Priority values can be configured from 1 to 15. The higher the priority, the better the chances of winning an election. If the switch is set to a priority of 15, it will always win the election and become the master.

Chapter 3: Routing Technologies (Domain 3)

1. B. All routing decisions are based upon destination IP address. The router examines the IP address and routes the packet to the next closest hop for the network it belongs to.

2. C. Static routing requires a network administrator to intervene and create a route in the routing table.

3. D. When an IP address is configured on a router's interface, the network is automatically put into the routing table. The IP address is also added to the routing table. When the routing table changes, this normally tells the routing protocol it should perform an update.

4. A. The subnet mask is used by the host to determine the immediate network and the destination network. It then decides to either route the packet or try to deliver itself without the router's help.

5. C. The Address Resolution Protocol (ARP) is employed by the host or router when a packet is determined to be local on one of its interfaces.

6. C. The destination MAC address is changed to the router's MAC address and the destination IP address is untouched.

7. B. The TTL, or time to live, is decremented usually by one. When the TTL reaches zero, a packet is considered un-routable. This prevents packets from eternally routing.

8. B. When an IP address is configured on an interface, the entry in the routing table is called the local route. The local routes always have a prefix of /32.

9. B. When a packet is determined to be local to the sending host, ARP is used to resolve the MAC address for the IP address of the destination host, and the frame is sent directly to the host.

10. B. The sending host ANDs its subnet mask against the destination IP address, then against its IP address, and this give a frame of reference for where it needs to go and where it is.

11. D. The current method of packet forwarding used by Cisco routers is Cisco Express Forwarding (CEF). CEF creates several cache tables used for determining the best route for the destination network.

12. B. The layer 2 process is called frame rewrite. When a packet hops from router to router, the destination frame is rewritten for the next destination MAC address.

13. C. When a MAC address is unknown for the destination IP address or the default gateway, the ARP request is sent in the form of a broadcast.

14. A. Every host contains an ARP cache. This cache allows for lookups of MAC addresses for destination IP addresses when the host frequently sends packets to the destination. Therefore, there are fewer ARP packets.

15. B. After the frame is verified to be addressed to the router and the FCS has been checked, the router decapsulates the packet and strips off the frame.

16. D. The command to display the router's ARP cache is show ip arp.

17. B. By default, all entries have a time to live, or TTL, of 240 seconds. They will be removed after that period if not used during the 240 seconds.

18. C. When traffic is remote to the immediate network, the host sends an ARP packet for the IP address of the default gateway. This determines the destination MAC address for the frame.

19. A. The command to view the routing table is show ip route.

20. D. Dynamic routing allows for the population of routing tables from advertisements of other routers. There are several dynamic routing protocols, such as, for example, EIGRP, RIP, OSPF.

21. B. When a route is found in the routing table, the router will find the gateway for the next hop and change the packet's destination MAC address for the next router.

22. D. The Internet Control Message Protocol (ICMP) is a layer 3 protocol that allows for end-to-end testing with a command such as traceroute.

23. C. The command `clear arp cache` will clear the ARP cache of a router. It is notable that the command `clear arp-cache` will clear the ARP cache of the local router as well as send a gratuitous ARP (GARP) for other devices to relinquish the ARP cache of the router's address.

24. B. The Routing Information Protocol (RIP) is a distance-vector protocol.

25. C. The `ping` command uses ICMP to check the status of a router. It also gives the round-trip time of the packet.

26. D. The last router will send an ICMP packet back to the originating host, which has the result code of destination unreachable.

27. C. When you're using the `ping` command, the exclamation marks signify that the ping was successful and the router is responding.

28. B. A routing loop occurs when packets are routed between two or more routers and never make it to their destination. Routing loops can occur with more than two routers; it is in effect making the packet travel in a loop till its TTL expires.

29. A. Open Shortest Path First (OSPF) is a link-state protocol. A link-state protocol tracks the state of a link between two routers and chooses the most efficient routes based upon the shortest path. EIGRP is an advanced distance-vector protocol.

30. A. Dynamic routes are stored in RAM. When the power is taken away from a router, all routes must be repopulated by neighboring routers.

31. A. Static routes are highly trusted routes since an administrator created them. Therefore, they have the lowest administrative distance with a number of 1.

32. B. Although this is a static route, it is a very special static route called a default route or gateway of last resort. The S signifies that it is static and the * signifies that it is the default route.

33. C. The 4 represents the metric for this route statement. Since this is a RIP entry, the metric is the number of hops for this particular route.

34. C. The destination address of 0.0.0.0/0 is a special route called the default route or gateway of last resort. The 0.0.0.0/0 addresses all hosts, and if a specific route is not matched in the routing table, then this route is the last resort.

35. B. The top line in the exhibit is the summarization of all three routes below. This is also called a supernet, since it is opposite of a subnet. It groups the networks that are independently routable into one statement, summarizing them.

36. C. The number represents the time the route had been in the routing table and signifies when the route had last been updated. This route is populated via a dynamic routing protocol, when the protocol updates the route, it will be reset to zero.

37. B. The correct command sequence is `ip route`, followed by the network ID, the subnet mask, and then the gateway. In this case, the gateway is a serial line.

38. B. The command ip default-gateway allows the management plane of the router to egress the network in which the router is configured upon through a different gateway.

39. C. Router A needs to be pointed to the adjacent router's far IP address. Imagine a hall with two doors; one door leads to Network A and the other leads to Network B. To get to Network B, you need to get to the router's IP interface (door).

40. A. In the routing table there is a static route for 192.168.4.0/24 via Serial 0/0/1.

41. D. Your packets are most likely making it to the destination host. However, there is no route back to your host on the other network's router.

42. D. When an IP address of 192.168.1.1/24 is configured, for example, the router will create a summary route for 192.168.1.0/24 as well as a route for 192.168.1.1/32. Both of these changes to the routing table will trigger an update depending on which dynamic routing protocol is being used.

43. B. The command show ip interfaces brief will display all of the interfaces and their configured IP addresses.

44. A. A route for the interface will not be populated in the routing table until the interface is in an up/up status. If the link was disconnected, this would create the same symptoms.

45. C. The route will exit the Serial 0/2/0 interface, since the gateway of last resort is set to Serial 0/2/0. This statement is identified by the S* 0.0.0.0/0 entry.

46. C. Static routing is suited for small networks, where the central admin has a good understanding of the network layout. It does reduce router-to-router communications because the overhead of routing dynamic protocols will not use up bandwidth.

47. C. When you configure a static route, it is stored in the startup-config, which is located on the NVRAM. When a router loads, the routes are held in RAM.

48. C. The easiest way to accomplish this is to super-net the addresses together. The network of 192.168.0.0/30 or 255.255.240.0 would capture traffic for the range of 192.168.0.1 to 192.168.3.254.

49. B. Secondary routes with higher administrative distance are used for failover. If the physical interface fails, the route statement will be taken out of the routing table. Then the second route will become active.

50. A. The IP address of 208.43.34.17/29 belongs to the network of 208.43.34.16/29. In addition to the statement for the network which owns the IP address, the individual IP address will be configured as a local route with a /32.

51. D. The 192.168.4.0/24 network is routable via the Serial 0/0/1 interface.

52. A. Serial interfaces are point-to-point connections. Any traffic directed down the interface will automatically appear on the adjacent router. Routers will not process traffic normally unless Proxy ARP is configured for the interface.

53. C. When routers select the next hop, the rule of most specific first is always used. Since there are three routes to 192.168.4.0/24 (including the gateway of last resort), the most specific of 192.168.4.0/24 via Serial 0/0/1 is selected.

54. D. The route you will need should address the 198.44.4.0/24 network with the network mask of 255.255.255.0. The exit interface is Serial 0/1, which is directly connected to the other router.

55. B. The IP address of 203.80.53.22/19 belongs to the network of 203.80.32.0/19.

56. D. Nothing needs to be done since the IP address of 198.44.4.5/24 is configured on Fa0/1. This shows that the network of 198.44.4.0/24 is connected to Fa0/1.

57. A. The IP address of 194.22.34.54/28 belongs to the network of 194.22.34.48/28.

58. B. The network of 205.34.54.85/29 is written out as 205.34.54.85 255.255.255.248. The next hop is 205.34.55.2, so the command would be `ip route 205.34.54.85 255.255.255.248 205.34.55.2`.

59. C. When entering IPv6 routes. you must use the command `ipv6 route`. It is then followed by the IPv6 prefix and mask and then the gateway. The default route would be `ipv6 route ::/0 serial 0/0`.

60. B. When configuring an IPv6 route, you use the `ipv6 route` command. You then must specify the network and mask using CIDR notation. Last, you specify the exit interface or next hop of `serial 0/0/0`. The complete command will be `ipv6 route fc00:0:0:1/64 serial 0/0/0`.

61. A. The packet will be routed to the IP address of 192.168.4.2. This will occur because the administrative distance is lower than the route for the gateway of 192.168.4.5.

62. D. The administrative distance of the Routing Information Protocol (RIP) is 120.

63. B. Administrative distance is an order of reliability between dynamic routing protocols and static routes.

64. A. A directly connected network has an administrative distance of 0 and is the most highly reliable.

65. A. Internal EIGRP has an administrative distance of 90.

66. B. The network of 192.168.1.0/24 is directly connected via Serial 0/0. The packet will be delivered out the exit interface of Serial 0/0. The administrative distance is the lowest on directly connected routes.

67. C. The administrative distance of Open Shortest Path First (OSPF) is 110.

68. C. The routing protocol with the lowest administrative distance is always chosen. Within that protocol, if there are multiple routes to the same network, then the lowest metric is chosen.

69. B. The administrative distance can be added to the end of the route statement. Since RIP has an administrative distance of 120, 130 will be chosen if the RIP route is not present.

70. A. Enhanced Interior Gateway Routing Protocol (EIGRP) has the lowest administrative distance of the three protocols. Therefore, regardless of the metric, the lowest AD will always be chosen.

71. A. Latency is lower with SVI inter-VLAN routing because of the use of ASICs. This is usually why IVR switches are more expensive.

72. C. The scalability of ROAS is a major disadvantage. It does not scale well when a large number of VLANs are configured.

73. D. The command `no switchport` does the opposite of configuring a port as a switch port. It turns the port into a routed interface in which an IP address can be configured.

74. A. The use of VLANs requires a unique IP network for each VLAN. This is how broadcast domains are increased, since all VLANs are behind a router interface (default gateway).

75. B. Router on a stick is created by configuring a trunk between the switch and the router. ROAS will receive tagged frames and route them, then send them back down the interface to the respective connected VLAN.

76. C. The `ip routing` command must be entered in global config. When this command is entered, a routing table will be created and populated.

77. B. When a router's interface is used to allow routing, the method is called router on a stick, or ROAS.

78. B. 802.1Q is the trunking protocol that should be used for tagging VLANs when you are routing between VLANs on a router.

79. B. Bandwidth is often a consideration because everything you send to the router must come back on the same port for routing to work. Routing between two VLANs on a 1 Gb/s interface will allow for the bandwidth of 1 Gb/s up and 1 Gb/s down. When a third VLAN is introduced they must all share the 1 Gb/s.

80. C. When you perform inter-VLAN routing on a layer 3 switch, it is called Switched Virtual Interface (SVI) VLAN routing.

81. D. The command `encapsulation dot1q 2` will associate the subinterface with VLAN 2. If you specify the `native` tag after the command, it will make this subinterface the native VLAN for the trunk.

82. A. When configuring an IP address on an SVI, you must enter the interface of the VLAN. Once in the pseudo interface, you enter the `ip address` command and then enter `no shutdown`.

83. A. When you are configuring a router on a stick, the switch port of the switch must be in trunk mode. This is so that traffic can be tagged as it gets sent to the router, which will see the tag and route it accordingly by the destination IP address.

84. B. A best practice is to always name the subinterface the same as the VLAN number you are going to route. An example is if you are connected to Fa0/1 on the router, and you want to create an IP address on the subinterface for VLAN 2. Then you would name the subinterface Fa0/1.2.

85. C. The command `encapsulation dot1q 5`, when configured inside of the subinterface, will program the subinterface to accept frames for VLAN 5.

86. B. On 2960-XR switches you must enable the Switching Database Manager (SDM) for LAN Base routing to enable routing. The switch then requires a reload before you can configure routable SVIs.

87. A. The same command used to verify physical interfaces on a router, is used to verify SVI interfaces on a switch. The command `show ip interface brief` will pull up the configured IP address on each VLAN interface.

88. C. The command `ip address 192.168.2.0 255.255.255.0` only defines the 192.168.2.0 network. It does not specify a valid host IP address for the SVI.

89. B. The LAN Base feature supports IP routing between SVIs. However, it must be enabled first via the Switching Database Manager (SDM) by using the `sdm prefer lanbase-routing` command.

90. C. The `no switchport` will configure a physical port of a switch to act as a routed interface. Once the physical port is configured as a non-switch port, you will be able to configure an IP address directly on the interface.

91. A. The command `show interface gi 0/2 switchport` will show the state of a port. It will display if the port is switched or routed among several other attributes.

92. C. You can build an EtherChannel between routers and switches to obtain more bandwidth when using ROAS. It is supported on certain models of routers, such as 7000, 7200, and 7500 routers.

93. D. The command `encapsulation isl 5` configured in the subinterface will achieve this. It specifies the encapsulation as ISL and a VLAN of 5 that it will be tagged with.

94. B. After configuring a VLAN and the respective SVI interface, a route will not show until at least one port is configured with the new VLAN.

95. B. Using Router On A Stick is a cheaper alternative to IVR if the current switch does not support layer 3 routing.

96. B. When configuring ROAS on a router's interface, you should always issue the `no ip address` command. No IPs can be configured on the main interface. All IPs are configured on the subinterfaces.

97. C. Verifying the proper operation of the switch would start with verifying that the port is correctly set as a trunk to the router. If it is not set as a trunk, it would not be able to tag frames for the router to direct to the proper interfaces.

98. C. When you're configuring a router interface to accept VLAN tagging, the subinterface numbering does not matter. It is recommended that the subinterface match the VLAN for readability. However, encapsulation dot1q 10 is the command that allows the subinterface to accept the frames for VLAN 10.

99. A. When ROAS is implemented, only the physical interface has a unique MAC address. All ARP requests for the IP addresses configured on the subinterfaces respond with the same MAC address. They are not unique MAC addresses, but on each VLAN they are unique in the sense that no other machines on the VLAN share the same MAC address.

100. A. Each IP address on a subinterface is the routed gateway for the VLAN on that subinterface. The main interface should be configured with the no ip address command when ROAS is configured. The default native VLAN of 1 is configured on the switch side only unless you explicitly configure a native VLAN on the router.

101. D. The scalability of routes between routers should always be considered when choosing a static routing design vs. a dynamic routing design. A few VLANs over many routers creates a lot of work when a new VLAN is created and static routing is being used. However, when one router is being used, the administrative overhead is low.

102. C. Default routing is a form of static routing. It is used on the edge of a network to direct all traffic to the inner core of the network.

103. B. Static routing is extremely secure, because it does not need to broadcast or multicast routing updates. These updates can be intercepted or injected into a network to create problems.

104. D. Static routing has the lowest bandwidth overhead because there is no bandwidth required to maintain static routes.

105. A. Dynamic routing does not require any administrator intervention when routes go down. This is because dynamic routes send route notifications and recalculate the routing tables of all participating routers.

106. C. Static routing requires increased time for configuration as networks grow in complexity. You will need to update routers that you add with all of the existing routes in the network. You will also need to update all of the existing routers with the new routes you add with the new router.

107. D. Default routing requires the least amount of RAM consumption because one routing statement is required for every route. This type of routing technique is best used on stub network routers.

108. C. Routing Information Protocol (RIP) has the lowest overhead of all of the routing protocols. However, it is not very scalable, the maximum number of hops is 15.

109. A. The benefits of a dynamic routing protocol is that it creates resiliency when routes become unavailable. It does this by recalculating the best route in the network around the outage.

110. A. Most dynamic routing protocols will summarize routes. They do this for efficiency, so the least number of route statements will need to exist in the routing table.

111. D. Static routing requires administrator intervention when a route goes down. Default routing is generally used for stub networks where the only route out of the network is the default route.

112. A. The Routing Information Protocol version 1 (RIPv1)broadcasts updates for routing tables.

113. B. Optimized route selection is a direct advantage of using dynamic routing protocols. A protocol such as OSPF uses the shortest path first algorithm for route selection.

114. C. The `show ip routes static` command will display all of the routes that are configured as static routes.

115. C. Static routing is best suited for small networks in which there is not a lot of change. It should be chosen when administrators want absolute control over the routing process.

116. A. The Routing Information Protocol (RIP) is a distance-vector routing protocol. This is because RIP only advertises the discovered distance of a route and the metric is the number of hops.

117. B. Open Shortest Path First (OSPF) is a true link-state protocol. Link-state protocols keep track of the state of the links as well as the bandwidth the link reports.

118. C. The Enhanced Interior Gateway Routing Protocol (EIGRP) is a hybrid protocol. It has features of a vector-based protocol and a link-state protocol, hence it is considered a hybrid protocol.

119. B. Protocols such as RIP re-advertise routes learned. This can be problematic since it is the equivalent of gossiping about what they have heard and nothing is checked.

120. B. RIP, which is a distance-vector protocol, is best suited for networks containing fewer than 15 routers. This is because RIP is limited to a 15 hop count. Any route that is more than 15 hops away is considered unreachable.

121. C. EIGRP metrics are bandwidth, delay, load, reliability, and MTU, while RIP is a distance-vector protocol and only takes hop count into consideration for the metric. BGP is not suited for optimal performance since a large amount of resources need to be dedicated for the protocol.

122. A. Routing loops are the most common problem when you're using a distance-vector routing protocol. Although they can occur with any dynamic routing protocol, distance-vector protocols are most susceptible due to how they converge routes.

123. C. The Dijkstra algorithm is used by OSPF to calculate the shortest path based on a cost calculation of the bandwidth of the link vs. distance vector, which is based on hop count.

124. A. Link-state protocols such as OSPF require all routers to maintain their own topology database of the network. This topology database is why routing loops are less likely to occur. Distance-vector protocols don't really have a topology of the network and thus suffer from routing loops.

125. B. The Diffusing Update Algorithm, or DUAL, is used by EIGRP to calculate the best route for the destination network.

126. B. Slow convergence of routing tables is a major disadvantage for distance-vector protocols like RIP. It could take several announcement cycles before the entire network registers a routing change.

127. D. OSPF employs Link-State-Announcement (LSA) flooding and triggered updates. When these occur, every participating router will recalculate its routing tables.

128. C. Link-state protocols, such as OSPF are best suited for large hierarchical networks such as global networks, since they can separate out the participating routers with areas and border area routers.

129. A. The Routing Information Protocol (RIP) use the Bellman-Ford routing algorithm to calculate the shortest path based on distance. The distance is computed from the shortest number of hops.

130. B. The use of holddown timers allows the convergence of the network routing tables. This is used to hold down changes to the routing table before convergence can happen and a routing decision is hastily made by RIP.

131. D. The Border Gateway Protocol (BGP) is an exterior gateway routing protocol, which is used on the exterior of your network.

132. C. Enhanced Interior Gateway Routing Protocol (EIGRP) is a Cisco proprietary interior gateway protocol.

133. C. Interior routing protocols are used internally inside of a network. The functional difference is that IGPs exchange information within an autonomous system, and EGPs exchange information between autonomous systems.

134. A. Routers are grouped into the same autonomous system (AS). When they are within the same AS, they can exchange information such as routes to destination networks and converge their routing tables.

135. B. Interior gateway protocols function within an administrative domain. This administrative domain is defined with a common autonomous system number or area ID.

136. D. The only time you need to use an exterior gateway protocol such as Border Gateway Protocol (BGP) is when you have a dual-homed connection between two ISPs. An example of this would be routing between the Internet and Internet 2. You would need to know the fastest path to the destination network via the Internet connection.

137. A. In order to use BGP to advertise a route, you must obtain an ASN, or autonomous system number, from IANA.

138. C. BGP uses the entire database of entries to calculate the entire autonomous system path to the destination. Then it routes the packet to the next router, which performs the same calculation using the shortest AS path or the least number of ASs the packet must traverse.

139. B. Open Shortest Path First (OSPF) is an interior gateway protocol and a nonproprietary standard.

140. B. Although you have different administrative units, all of the administrative units are in the same company. In this situation, it is recommended to use an interior gateway protocol that can segment each administrative unit. OSPF will perform this requirement with the use of area IDs.

141. C. The command `show ipv6 interfaces brief` will show all of the IPv6 addresses configured for each of the interfaces on the router.

142. C. The network ID of 2000:0db8:4400:2300::/64 will be calculated and assigned to the directly connected route of Serial 0/0.

143. B. The second address on an interface with the prefix of ff80::/64 is the link-local address for Duplicate Address Detection (DAD) and Stateless Address Autoconfiguration (SLAAC). Link-local addresses are non-routable, so they will not get added to the routing table.

144. A. The command `show ipv6 route` will display only the entries in the routing table for IPv6. The command `show ip route` will only display the entries in the routing table for IPv4.

145. C. You will need two route statements, one on each router. Each route should point to the far side network through the serial interface. Since the IP address is an IPv6 address, the easier way to configure the routes is to direct the packets to the exit interface of Serial 0/3/0.

146. B. The command `show ipv6 route connected` will display only the directly connected routes on the router.

147. C. The route statement `ipv6 route ::/0 serial 0/3/0` will route any network that is unknown by Router B to Router A via the exit interface of Serial 0/3/0.

148. D. You will need two route statements, one on each router. Each route points to the far side network through the gateway in the ff80::/64 network. Router A has a gateway of ff80::ff:f200:2/64 to the 2001:db8:4:/64 network, and Router B has a gateway of ff80::ff:f200:1/64 to the 2001:db8:400/64 network.

149. B. The backup route to network 192.168.3.0/24 is though the gateway of 192.168.2.6. However, the administrative distance of a normal static route is 1. So the AD must be higher than RIP, which is 120. An AD of 220 is higher than 90, so the RIP route will be the main route and the static route will become the backup floating route.

150. C. The command `ipv6 address autoconfig default` configures the interface of Serial 0/3/0 with an IP address via SLAAC. When the default subcommand is used, it allows the router to inherit the default route discovered via NDP RS/RA messages.

151. A. Area 0 must be present in an OSPF network. It is the backbone area and all other areas must connect to it.

152. C. Router A is on the boundary of the autonomous system, which OSPF manages, therefore it is an autonomous system boundary router, or ASBR.

153. B. OSPF uses 224.0.0.5 for neighbor discovery via Link-State Advertisements (LSAs).

154. A. Routers C, D, and E are called area border routers, or ABRs. They border both the backbone area and areas 1, 2, and 3, respectively.

155. D. OSPF updates are event triggered. These events could be a neighbor router not responding or a route going down.

156. B. The highest IP address configured on all of the loopback interfaces is chosen first. If a loopback is not configured, then the highest IP address on an active interface is chosen. However, if a RID is statically set via the OSPF process, it will override all of the above.

157. C. A link is a routed interface that is assigned to a network and participates in the OSPF process. This link will be tracked by the OSPF process for up/down information as well as the network it is associated with.

158. B. Adjacencies are formed between the designated router (DR) and its neighbors on the same LAN. This is done to ensure that all neighbor routers have the same Link State Database (LSDB).

159. D. The designated router is elected by the highest priority in the LAN. If the priorities are all the same, then the highest RID becomes the tiebreaker. OSPF will elect a DR for each broadcast network, such as a LAN. This is to minimize the number of adjacencies formed.

160. B. The neighborship database is where all of the routers can be found that have responded to hello packets. The neighborship database contains all of the routers by RID, and each router participating in OSPF manages its own neighborship database.

161. C. OSPF uses areas to create a hierarchal structure for routing. This structure begins with the backbone area of 0. All other areas connect to it to form a complete autonomous system. This enables scalability with OSPF, since each area works independently.

162. D. A LAN is an example of a broadcast multi-access network. All nodes in a network segment can hear a broadcast and have common access to the local area network. In OSPF, a broadcast (multi-access) network requires a DR and BDR.

163. C. The multicast address of 224.0.0.6 is used to communicate between the designated router and the adjacencies formed. This multicast address is used for LSA flooding on broadcast networks.

164. A. Cisco uses a metric for OSPF which is calculated as 10^8/bandwidth. This cost value is of 100 Mb/s (reference bandwidth) divided by the interface bandwidth.

165. A. The command `router ospf 20` configures a process ID of 20. This process identifies the databases for an OSPF process as well as its configuration. The process ID is only locally significant to the router on which it is configured. It can be an arbitrary number from 1 to 65535.

166. B. The command show interface will display the reported bandwidth or configured bandwidth of an interface. The command show ospf interface will only display the calculated cost.

167. D. When you're configuring Cisco routers to participate in OSPF with non-Cisco routers, each interface on the Cisco router needs to be configured. The ip ospf cost command can be tuned between 1 to 65,535 and will need to be matched with the other vendor.

168. D. The first command sets up the process ID of 1 via router ospf 1. The next command advertises the network of 192.168.1.0 with a wildcard-mask of 0.0.0.255 and specifies area 0 via network 192.168.1.0 0.0.0.255 area 0.

169. A. By default, Cisco routes will load-balance four equal-cost routes with OSPF.

170. C. The wildcard mask is 0.0.31.255 for a network advertisement of 131.40.32.0/27. A wildcard mask is a bitwise calculation that matches the bits that change. The /27 has subnets with multiples of 32. The easiest way to calculate wildcard masks for configuration is to subtract 1 from the subnet you are trying to match; for example, matching a subnet of 32 in the third octet minus 1 equals 31, and you want to match all bits in the fourth octet with 255.

171. D. The command maximum-paths 10 will configure a maximum of 10 routes of equal-cost for load balancing. This command must be entered under the OSPF router process.

172. D. The maximum number of equal-cost routes that can be configured for load balancing with OSPF on a Cisco router is 32.

173. A. The command show ip ospf will allow you to verify the currently configured router ID (RID) or the IP address acting as the router's RID.

174. C. The wildcard mask is 0.0.0.15 for a network advertisement of 192.168.1.16/28. A wildcard mask is a bitwise calculation that matches the bits that change. The /28 has subnets with multiples of 16. The easiest way to calculate wildcard masks for configuration is to subtract 1 from the subnet you are trying to match; for example, matching a subnet of 16 in the fourth octet minus 1 equals 15.

175. A. The command show ip ospf neighbor will show all of the adjacencies formed as well as the routers discovered.

176. B. The default hello interval is 10 seconds for a broadcast (multi-access) network such as a LAN.

177. B. The command passive-interface gigabitethernet 0/1 must be configured under the router process. This command will suppress hello packets from exiting the Gi0/1 interface.

178. C. The command show ip ospf interface will show all interfaces in which OSPF is configured and sending hello packets.

179. D. Although all of these are valid methods of possibly setting the router ID (RID) of the router for OSPF, the configuration of router-id 192.168.1.5 will override all others.

180. C. The command `passive-interface default` configured under the OSPF process will cease hello packets by default on all interfaces. The command `no passive-interface gigabitethernet 0/2` will allow hello packets to exit the interface and allow Gi0/2 to become a neighbor.

181. A. After the OSPF configuration is changed, OSPF needs to be restarted. This is achieved at the privileged exec prompt by typing `clear ip ospf`.

182. D. Type 3 Link-State Advertisements contain summary information about the networks on the other side of the ABR. These LSA announcements are called Summary Link Advertisements, or SLAs.

183. B. The network IDs of 128.24.1.0/24, 128.24.2.0/24, 128.24.3.0/24, and 128.24.4.0/24 can be summarized as 128.24.1.0/22. The wildcard-mask for /22 is 0.0.252.255.

184. A. The command `show ip ospf database` will show you a summary count of all the LSAs in the database.

185. D. Interface GigabitEthernet 0/0 is not participating because it is in a different network than what the wildcard mask is advertising. The wildcard mask of 0.0.0.63 is a /26 network mask with the range of 197.234.3.0 to 197.234.3.63. The interface Gi0/0 is in the 197.234.3.64/26 network and therefore will not participate.

186. C. The default hello interval on a LAN is 10 seconds. If a router is configured with a hello timer of 30, the hello/dead interval will not match. In order to form an adjacency, the hello/dead intervals must match.

187. A. Fast convergence of the Link State Database (LSDB) that feeds the routing tables, is a direct result of a hierarchical OSPF design. The use of areas allows for routers within an area to converge and send Summary Link Advertisements to other areas.

188. B. Designated routers are only elected on broadcast (multi-access) networks such as a LAN. The router with the highest IP address will become the designated router. Since Router B has an IP address of 192.168.10.2/30, 192.168.10.5/30, and 192.168.2.1/24, it will become the DR.

189. B. Router B is called the area border router since it sits between two areas of area 0 and area 1.

190. C. The wildcard mask is incorrect because it is a bitmask, which is the opposite of a subnet mask. The 1s in the host section, rather than 1s in the network section, define the wildcard. The correct wildcard mask is 0.0.0.255 for this configuration.

191. A. In order to form an adjacency, the area IDs must match as well as the hello and dead timers. If the hello timer is changed on one router, it must be changed on the other router to form an adjacency.

192. A. The FULL state is only achieved after the router has created an adjacency with a neighbor router and downloaded the LSAs to form its topological database.

193. D. Both routers have formed an adjacency. However, the LSDB on each router has not yet been fully synchronized. Once the LSDBs have been synchronized, the state will become FULL and OSPF will calculate costs.

194. C. The command `ip ospf cost 25` should be configured on the interface that will act as the backup route. This adjustment of cost will allow the router to prefer the other route first.

195. D. The router ID of 192.168.2.2 is neither a designated router nor a backup designated router. Since it is neither, it will only form an adjacency with the DR or BDR and will participate in future elections.

196. B. The command `ip ospf priority 10` will change the interface's default priority of 1 to 10. This router will always become the designated router on the LAN.

197. A. The command `show ip ospf interfaces` will display the interface details of each interface for OSPF. In this information, the DR and BDR router ID will be displayed.

198. D. In order to form an adjacency, the area IDs must match. In this exhibit, Router A has an area of 0 and Router B has an area of 1 configured.

199. C. The command `default-information originate` will propagate a default route originating from router 172.16.1.1. All OSPF routers will calculate their default routes back to this router.

200. A. Bandwidth is always specified in kilobits per second (Kb/s), so 2.048 Mb/s would be 2,048,000 bits per second, or 2,048 Kb/s.

201. C. Both routers have passive interfaces for OSPF. In order to fix this, the command `no passive-interface serial 0/0` would need to be entered. This command would need to be configured in the OSPF router process.

202. A. The command `show ip protocols` will list the router ID of the current router as well as the networks that are being advertised via OSPF on the current router.

203. C. An area defines a topology inside of the OSPF hierarchy. Since each router in an area calculates its own costs, they all contain the same topological database, or LSDB.

204. D. All routers by default have an OSPF priority of 1. If you set the priority to 0, the router will never become a designated router. This command must be set in the interface.

205. A. It identifies the administrative distance of 110 for OSPF. The cost calculation is the reference bandwidth of 100 Mb/s divided by the link bandwidth. This calculation would result in a cost of 1.

206. C. The command `ipv6 router ospf 4` will start an IPv6 process with an ID of 4. Most IPv6 commands will start with `ipv6`.

207. A. OSPFv3 used the multicast address ff02::6 to send communications to designated routers.

208. C. When an OSPFv3 process is configured, the process will handle IPv6. However, the router ID is still configured as an IPv4 address.

209. B. With OSPFv3 IPv6 configuration, the duplication of long IPv6 network addresses can cause erroneous entries. So OSPFv3 is configured directly on the IPv6 link with the command `ipv6 ospf 4 area 0`.

210. A. Configuring OSPFv3 for a passive interface it is similar to configuring OSPFv2. However, the configuration prompt for IPv6 is `Router(config-rtr)#`.

211. B. The easiest way to achieve this is to change the reference bandwidth from 100 Mb/s to 10 Gb/s. This is done as a command in the OSPFv3 router process with the command `auto-cost reference-bandwidth 10000`. This will adjust the reference-bandwidth for all links associated with this process ID.

212. B. OSPFv3 used the multicast address ff02::5 to send hello packets to neighbor routers.

213. D. The command `show ipv6 route ospf` will display only the OSPFv3 routes.

214. B. The command `show ipv6 ospf interface` will display numerous stats about the interfaces participating in OSPFv3. One of the stats is the hello/dead timers.

215. B. IPv4 allows for packet fragmentation. However, IPv6 does not fragment packets because at the layer 3 header there is no fragmentation functionality. So close attention needs to be made to link MTUs on adjacent neighbors.

216. D. The configuration of OSPFv3 for IPv6 is always done on the interface. Area 0 can be represented as 0.0.0.0, because the area as defined by the RFC is a 32-bit value. The Cisco IOS allows you to enter the last octet of the area or the whole 32-bit value.

217. C. You must enable IPv6 routing via the command `ipv6 unicast-routing` in order to use OSPFv3.

218. B. The command `show ipv6 ospf 5` will only show the OSPFv3 process ID of 5.

219. A. The hello interval timer is configured per the interface, since broadcast (multi-access) would apply to a LAN interface vs. a non-broadcast multiple access (NBMA) network interface. The command `no ipv6 ospf hello-interval` will set the hello timer back to the original default value.

220. A. The command to restart the OSPFv3 process is performed at the privileged exec command prompt. The command to be entered for OSPFv3 would be `clear ipv6 ospf process`. You will then be asked to confirm it.

221. C. When you're configuring an area border router, only one OSPF process is required. Both areas are added to the same process ID.

222. B. Router C is misconfigured. If it was configured properly, it would show as a neighbor when the `show ipv6 ospf neighbors` command is used.

223. C. When you configure the command `ipv6 ospf 1 area 0` on an IPv4 interface, the IP address on the interface is used as the router ID.

224. A. Unlike OSPFv2, OSPFv3 will advertise all of the networks that are configured on a link in which OSPFv3 is configured. This replaces the need to use the `network` command, which is used in OSPFv2.

225. B. Both routers have the same router-ID configured and therefore cannot become neighbors and form an adjacency.

226. D. Enhanced Interior Gateway Routing Protocol (EIGRP) is a Cisco proprietary dynamic routing protocol. Only Cisco routers can participate in EIGRP.

227. A. EIGRP can use bandwidth, delay, load, reliability, and MTU as the cost metrics. Default configuration of EIGRP only uses bandwidth and delay as the cost metrics, although others can be configured.

228. C. A requirement for routers to become neighbors is matching K metrics. The K metrics are values that can be adjusted for the EIGRP metrics of bandwidth, delay, load, reliability, and MTU.

229. C. The Reliable Transport Protocol (RTP), which is part of EIGRP, uses 224.0.0.10 to send hello messages.

230. A. The default metric calculation for EIGRP is metric = ((107 / least-bandwidth) + cumulative-delay) * 256.

231. B. A neighbor requirement is matching autonomous system numbers. The autonomous system number is EIGRP's scalability mechanism.

232. B. EIGRP has a default hop count of 100 hops before a packet is considered unroutable.

233. D. EIGRP uses AS numbers to segment routing updates to an autonomous system. This provides scalability of the EIGRP routing protocol.

234. A. The default hello timer for EIGRP is 5 seconds. This is performed by RTP.

235. C. Upon forming an adjacency with its neighbor, EIGRP neighboring routers will send their entire database. After the initial load of the database, each router will watch for updates.

236. C. The default hop count is 100 for EIGRP. However, the maximum stable hop count is 255 hops before a route is considered undeliverable.

237. A. Hello packets and the RTP table help to build the neighbor table. In return, the neighbor table sends this information to the topology table.

238. B. If an established neighbor does not respond to its multicast hello packet, the router will send unicast packets. After 16 missed unicast packets, the neighbor will be declared dead. This process is called reliable multicast.

239. C. When the hold interval has expired and a hello message has not been seen, the neighboring router is considered down or failed.

240. A. By default, EIGRP can load balance up to 4 equal-cost links.

241. D. EIGRP uses the Diffusing Update Algorithm to calculate route cost.

242. B. After the neighbor process has been established, the routers will exchange full topology tables with each other. These topology tables are sent in full, then maintained only by partial updates if a route changes.

243. B. The cost of the link between routing protocols is irrelevant. The administrative distance (AD) of EIGRP is 90, and the AD of OSPF is 110. Therefore, the lowest AD routing protocol is used. If the EIGRP route becomes invalid or is removed from the routing table, then OSPF will be used.

244. B. The EIGRP hold interval by default is three times the hello interval. Since the hello interval is 5 seconds, the hold interval is 15 seconds. Hold intervals are usually three times the initial discovery interval.

245. D. EIGRP metrics are not based on hops. EIGRP metrics are based on bandwidth and delay as a composite metric. The metric can be a very large number, but the limit to this metric in which the route is considered invalid is $2^{32} - 1$.

246. D. EIGRP only sends updates if a route has changed. Updates happen only after two routers have become neighbors and originally send their full route database and converge. If changes have not occurred, then the neighbor believes the route is still valid, under the condition that they are still neighbors.

247. A. When a router acknowledges a hello packet from a neighboring router, the router is added to the neighbor table of the router that sent the hello packet.

248. B. Although two routers can have different hello/hold intervals, they could still become neighbors. However, to do so they must be on the same subnet.

249. B. The reported distance is the remote router's calculated metric for the remote network. EIGRP uses this reported distance in its calculation for a feasible successor route.

250. C. After DUAL calculates the metrics of the topology table, a successor route is calculated using the feasible distance. This route is populated into the routing table. A feasible successor route is also calculated based upon the reported distance and feasible distance.

251. B. The topology table is used to calculate the feasible distance of a remote network. The DUAL routing algorithm interacts with the topology table to calculate this metric.

252. A. Serial interfaces will default to 1.544 Mb/s. They will not auto-correct the actual bandwidth. Therefore, changing the bandwidth between Router A and Router B will allow EIGRP to calculate the best route through Router C. This is done by using the bandwidth command and specifying bandwidth in Kb/s.

253. C. The command to configure EIGRP with an ASN of 20 is `router eigrp 20`.

254. B. The default variance is a value of 1 by default. This is because the variance is a multiplier that is applied to the feasible distance. All EIGRP routers multiply the feasible distance by 1 by default.

255. B. The command `eigrp router-id 2.2.2.2` configured in the sub-command of the router process will change the router ID to 2.2.2.2.

256. B. The command `no auto-summary` will stop the router process of EIGRP from auto-summarizing network addresses. In a discontiguous network, this is problematic and should be turned off.

257. A. The command `network 192.168.1.0 0.0.0.255` will advertise the network of 192.168.1.0/24 for EIGRP with an ASN of 20. The `0.0.0.255` is a wildcard mask and matches bits in the last octet of the IP address.

258. D. The autonomous system numbers do not match. Router A has an ASN of 10 and Router B has an ASN of 20.

259. D. The command `show ip eigrp neighbors` will allow you to inspect the routers that have created an adjacency with the current router you are working on.

260. A. The command `show ip protocols` will allow you to see specifics about the configured routing protocols. In the details of the output will be the K metrics for EIGRP.

261. C. The command `passive-interface serial 0/0` configured inside the router process for EIGRP will set the Serial 0/0 as a passive interface. This will suppress EIGRP hello packets exiting the interface.

262. B. The command `show ip eigrp topology` will allow you to see the calculated metrics for routes inside of the EIGRP topology table. For each network, the number of successors will be displayed. This information will help verify a feasible successor for a particular network.

263. B. The `variance` command is configured in the router instance of EIGRP. The command `variance 2` configures the router variance with a multiplier of 2.

264. C. The command `no passive-interface serial 0/0` is used when either `passive-interface serial 0/0` or `passive-interface default` has been used in the router instance.

265. B. The K metrics must match to allow Router A and Router B to form an adjacency. Router A has a K metric of K2=0 and Router B has a K metric of K2=1.

266. B. The routing table shows a path on Router A to 192.168.4.0/24 via 192.168.2.6. The IP address is configured on Router C, therefore the path will be Router A to Router C to Router B to the destination network.

267. D. Auto-summarization is configured by default with EIGRP. Since there are several networks in the 172.16.0.0/22 address range on Router A, they will be summarized. On Router B there is the network 172.16.4.0/24, which would be part of the summarization of the 172.16.0.0/22 network. Since the serial connection is a noncontiguous network, auto-summarization will prohibit proper routing operation.

268. B. The protocol-dependent module (PDM) allows for multiple protocols to be supported with EIGRP. This allows for the same algorithm and methodology to be applied and for PDM-compliant modules such as IPv6, IP, and IPX to be used.

269. C. The command to configure the K metrics back to their default setting is `no metric weights`. This command should be entered in the router instance. The default metrics are K1=1, K2=0, K3=1, K4=0, K5=0.

270. A. The command `show ip protocols` will display the networks that are being advertised on the current router.

271. C. The multicast address for neighbor discovery for EIGRPv6 is ff02::a.

272. C. The `ipv6 unicast-routing` command must be entered first to enable the IPv6 protocol stack for routing.

273. A. The command `no shutdown` must be entered in the router instance to start EIGRPv6. By default, it is shut down.

274. C. When configuring EIGRPv6 to avoid erroneous duplication of IPv6 addresses, the interface is added to the EIGRPv6 routing process. This advertises all networks that are configured on the interface.

275. C. The command `router-id 1.1.1.1` is required for EIGRPv6 operations. This command must be configured in the EIGRPv6 routing instance. The IPv4 address is the router's ID, since EIGRPv6 requires an IPv4 router ID.

276. B. The command to restrict hello packets from exiting the serial 0/0 interface is `passive-interface serial 0/0` entered in the EIGRPv6 router instance.

277. D. The command `show ipv6 protocols` will display the routing protocols running with IPv6. In the output of the EIGRPv6 instance, the K metrics will be displayed. Although `show running-configuration` will display the configured K-metrics, it will not show the default configuration.

278. D. The command `show ipv6 eigrp neighbors` will display the adjacencies the router has made with other EIGRPv6 routers.

279. B. The command `show ipv6 route eigrp` will display only the EIGRPv6 routes.

280. D. The command `show ipv6 protocols` will display the routing protocols for IPv6. Included in this output are the interfaces participating in EIGRPv6.

281. D. The command `ipv6 hello-interval eigrp 10 5` will change the hello timer. It must be entered in the interface on which you want to change the hello interval.

282. A. Interfaces for EIGRP must be on the same subnet for an adjacency to form. However, that is not a requirement for EIGRPv6.

283. B. The command `show ipv6 eigrp topology` will allow you to verify the metrics. From this, you can calculate the variance multiplier for unequal-cost load balancing.

284. A. The packets will take the path of Router A to Switch A to Switch B to Router B, since the feasible distance is lower, by taking the path of the switches. Although interface Gi0/0 on Router A and Gi0/0 on Router B are not in the same subnet, the link-local interfaces are used for routing the packets.

285. B. By configuring the command `passive-interface gi 0/0` in each router instance, you can prohibit the two routers from creating an adjacency across the Ethernet link. This will not hinder the advertisement of networks attached to the interface as long as the command `ipv6 eigrp 10"` is configured on the interfaces.

286. A. The maximum hop count for RIP is 15. A hop count over 15 hops is considered unroutable or unreachable.

287. C. By default, RIPv2 multicasts the full routing table on all active interfaces every 30 seconds.

288. C. RIPv2 uses hop count to calculate routes. When a router sends its routing table, the next router adds a +1 to the metric for the entries in the table.

289. B. RIPv2 uses the multicast address of 224.0.0.9 to advertise routes.

290. D. When you're configuring RIP on a router, the RIP process will default to RIPv1, which is classful. The command `version 2` must be configured in the router instance of RIP to allow for RIPv2.

291. A. The command `network 192.168.1.0` will configure the RIPv2 route process to advertise the network 192.168.1.0.

292. A. The command `show ip protocols` will display the next interval when RIPv2 advertisements are sent out.

293. B. The command `show ip rip database` will display all of the discovered routes and their calculated metrics.

294. D. The command `default-information originate` will advertise the default route to all other RIPv2 routers.

295. D. The command `debug ip rip` will allow you to see advertisements in real time.

296. B. The three Class C networks need to be advertised separately. RIPv2 uses the default class network mask when configuring networks.

297. C. The command `passive-interface serial 0/0` configured in the router instance will suppress updates from exiting interface Serial 0/0.

298. C. The default invalid timer for RIP is 180 seconds. This holddown timer is six times the advertisement interval of 30 seconds.

299. B. RIPv2 has extremely slow convergence time. This is because the advertisement of routes is every 30 seconds. So a router four hops away potentially could take 120 seconds before discovering the route.

300. A. Split horizons are used to stop routing loops with RIPv2. Split horizons prevent a router from advertising a route to a router in which the original route was discovered.

301. C. RIPv2 uses the Bellman-Ford algorithm to calculate its metrics.

302. D. The command no auto-summary will stop the router process of RIPv2 from auto-summarizing network addresses. In a discontiguous network, this is problematic and should be turned off.

303. B. Configuring RIPv2 begins with configuration of the router instance of RIP via the command router rip. RIPv2 is configured inside of the router instance with the command version 2. Then the network of 192.168.20.0/24 is advertised with the command network 192.168.20.0.

304. B. The holddown timer's job is to allow the network to stabilize after a route had become unreachable via an update. This limits the potential problems related to a flapping port and allows RIPv2 to converge route updates in the entire network.

305. B. To route packets over the higher-speed link, you would need to configure a static route for both Router A and Router B. If these links would go down, then the lower-speed link would become active. This is due to administrative distance.

306. B. The default number of routes that RIPv2 will load balance is a total of 4.

307. D. RIPng is the next generation of the RIP protocol for use with IPv6.

308. B. The command show ip rip database will display the routes being advertised by RIPv2. These routes will be identified with the directly connected statement.

309. B. The command ip spilt-horizon configured on the interface will configure split-horizon processing for RIPv2.

310. D. The route will be flushed from the routing table after 240 seconds. The flush timer should be 60 seconds higher than the invalid timer of 180 seconds.

311. B. The ping command will allow basic connectivity testing at layer 3.

312. D. The command traceroute will allow you to verify the path on which a packet gets routed.

313. C. The ARP request took time for the ARP reply, and during this time, the ICMP timeout threshold was exceeded. This is common on a router, and the following pings should not time out unless the ARP entry is cleared after its TTL expires.

314. C. The command ipconfig /all will help you verify the IP address, subnet mask, default gateway, and MAC address of your computer. The command of ipconfig doesn't show the MAC address.

315. A. The Windows command for tracing a route is tracert.

316. B. When you see an exclamation mark, it means that the packets were successfully acknowledged on the other side and an ICMP response was received.

317. C. The extended ping command allows you to specify a number of parameters such as repeat count, datagram size, and source address or exit interface. There are several other parameters that can be adjusted.

318. C. The three times are the minimum response time, average response time, and maximum response time of the ICMP Echo and Reply.

319. A. The IP address or hostname entered in privileged exec mode will create a direct Telnet request. Alternatively, you can specify the command `telnet 198.56.33.3`.

320. D. The command `show ip interface brief` will display only the necessary information of interface, IP, and status to aid in the diagnostic process.

321. A. The normal `ping` command will achieve this task. Originally in Windows XP, the command `ping6` was used in lieu of the command `ping`. The command `ping6` is also found in Linux. However, today, most operating systems have extended the `ping` command to both IPv4 and IPv6.

322. A. The command `show ipv6 neighbors` will display all of the neighboring routers that have sent a Router Advertisement message. This cache will normally contain the link-local addresses of the neighboring routers.

Chapter 4: WAN Technologies (Domain 4)

1. B. High-Level Data Link Control (HDLC) is the default encapsulation on a serial connection for Cisco.

2. B. The Point-to-Point Protocol (PPP) is an open standard. Cisco routers default to the HDLC protocol. However, HDLC is a proprietary standard for Cisco. So PPP should be used for compatibility.

3. B. The Network Control Protocol (NCP) works at layer 3 tagging the network protocols from end to end when PPP is used. This gives PPP the ability to offer multi-protocol transport.

4. A. The command `encapsulation ppp` configures the serial interface with the Point to Point Protocol (PPP). PPP is an encapsulation protocol.

5. C. The Link Control Protocol (LCP) provides the authentication phase of a PPP connection.

6. B. The High-Level Data Link Control protocol is used as the encapsulation method for serial links. This protocol is the open standard HDLC compared to the native Cisco-proprietary version.

7. C. The Challenge Handshake Authentication Protocol (CHAP) works by sending a random number called the challenge. This challenge is received by the authenticating router and used to hash the password. The password is transferred to the challenging router and authenticates the authenticating router.

8. C. The Link Control Protocol provides the facility for multilink connections.

9. A. MultiLink PPP simplifies layer 3 configuration. It does this by bundling the connections together at layer 2. It provides a pseudo interface representing the individual interface where all layer 3 configuration is applied.

10. A. The pseudo interface must be created first with the command `interface multilink 1`. Then the encapsulation must be set to PPP with `encapsulation ppp`. The `ppp multilink` command configures the ability to use multilink for the encapsulation of PPP. Then the IP address is configured. Last, the `ppp multilink group 1` command associates the interface multilink 1 with the multilink group to be used for bundling.

11. B. The command `show ppp multilink` will display the active links of a multilink connection.

12. B. The first step is to set the username of RouterB to use for authentication via `username RouterB password cisco`. Then enter the interface and configure authentication with the command `ppp authentication chap pap`.

13. A. The command `debug ppp authentication` will allow you to watch the authentication exchange between two routers in real time. This will help you diagnose an authentication problem between two routers.

14. B. The command `show ppp all` will show the current authentication protocol used between two routers. The output will look similar to this:

Se0/3/0 LCP+ CHAP+ IPCP+ CDPC> LocalT 192.168.1.1 RouterB

15. D. The LCP closed line states that the LCP process has not completed. This could be due to numerous reasons, such as conflicting options or authentication failure.

16. B. The command `ppp authentication chap pap` will configure PPP authentication. The first authentication protocol is preferred, and if that protocol is not supported, then authentication will fall back to PAP.

17. C. Serial interface 0/3/1 has a mismatched multilink group. All multilink group numbers should match the multilink group specified in the multilink interface.

18. D. This configuration has an encapsulation mismatch. Router A is configured to use the PPP encapsulation protocol. Router B is defaulted to the HDLC protocol because no encapsulation is configured.

19. C. Layer 2 functionality such as authentication is configured on the interfaces in the bundle. Layer 3 configuration is on the multilink interface, such as the IP address of the bundle.

20. D. The passwords do not match on both routers. Passwords configured on routers are case sensitive. Router A's password begins with a lowercase *c* and Router B's begins with an uppercase *C*. The IP addresses on Router A and Router B do not match, but this will not hinder the PPP link to be formed.

21. A. Point-to-Point Protocol over Ethernet (PPPoE) is used for DSL connections. PPPoE allows CHAP to be used to authenticate users over an Ethernet network that is configured on the customer side.

22. B. The MTU for PPPoE should be set to 1,492 bytes. Normal MTU size is 1,500, but when PPPoE is used, there is an overhead of 2 bytes for PPP and 6 bytes for the PPPoE headers. 1500 bytes – 8 overhead bytes = 1,492 bytes MTU for data.

23. A. Internal connections between the customer router and the ISP router do not get configured with IP addresses. The customer-side interface can be configured with an IP address or it can be configured via DHCP from the ISP side.

24. D. When PPPoE is configured, the dialer interface serves as the exit interface. The command ip route 0.0.0.0 0.0.0.0 dialer 1 will configure the gateway of last resort to the ISP.

25. C. The command show pppoe session will display all of the interfaces involved with the PPPoE establishment and shows the status of each interface.

26. C. The Internet Protocol Control Protocol (IPCP) is an NCP protocol that is responsible for configuring the IP address on the PPPoE client.

27. A. The PPP authentication is configured on the interface Dialer1 for PPPoE. The interface Dialer1 passes the LCP authentication information to the ISP router during the authentication phase of PPPoE.

28. A. Router A does not have the correct hostname configured. The hostname that the aggregation router (Router B) is expecting is *client* with a password of *ccna*. The hostname of the aggregation router is only locally significant to the aggregation router.

29. C. The command show pppoe summary entered on the aggregation router (ISP router) will show you how many PPPoE sessions are terminated (active) on the router.

30. D. The state of PTA stands for PPP Termination Aggregation. This means that the client has successfully created and terminated a PPPoE session with this router.

31. C. The dialer pool value configured on the interface Dialer1 must match the pppoe-client dial-pool-number value configured on interface GigabitEthernet 0/2. The interface of Dialer1 does not need to match the dialer pool and dial-pool-number.

32. B. The command ip local pool poolname 192.168.1.2 192.168.1.254 configures a local IP pool with a name of *poolname*. The address range is configured first with the starting address of 192.168.1.2 (leaving 192.168.1.1 for the router) to 192.168.1.254, the end of the range.

33. D. The passwords on Router A and Router B do not match. Router A has a password of *ccna* and Router B (aggregation router) expects *CCNA*. Passwords are case sensitive and therefore the two routers will not create a session.

34. B. When using PPPoE, the MTU is smaller than the standard 1,500 MTU on Ethernet. If attention is not taken to the MTU, it can be problematic.

35. C. The authentication protocol on Router A and Router B does not match. Router A has an authentication protocol of PAP, and Router B (aggregation router) has an authentication protocol of CHAP configured. The authentication protocols must match or the two routers will not create a session.

36. D. GRE tunnels provide packet-in-packet encapsulation. It takes the original IP packet and encapsulates it, adding another IP packet for the GRE tunnel. GRE tunnels alone do not provide any encryption.

37. A. Generic Routing Encapsulation is a Cisco proprietary standard for encapsulating layer 3 protocols over an IP network, such as the Internet.

38. C. GRE uses the layer 3 protocol 47, which is the protocol that is stated in the layer 3 header.

39. C. The network is un-routable, since interface G0/1 on Router A is configured with a 192.168.1.0/24 network, and interface G0/1 on Router B is configured with a 192.168.1.0/24. The route statement that needs to be configured will not pass any traffic since 192.168.1.0/24 is directly configured on both routers.

40. D. The correct route statement is `ip route 192.168.3.0 255.255.255.0 192.168.2.2`, because the network of 192.168.2.0/24 is built between these two routers. The tunnel acts as a routed interface between the routers.

41. A. The maximum transmission unit of a GRE tunnel is 1,476, because there are 24 bytes of overhead for the GRE header—20 bytes are used by the public IP header and 4 bytes are used for GRE.

42. B. The command `show interface tunnel 0` will show in the output the source and destination of the tunnel.

43. A. If a traceroute is performed to 192.168.3.50 on Router A, it will show one hop. This is because the 192.168.3.0 network is on the other side of the tunnel interface, which is one hop away.

44. C. The routes are wrong. They should be set to the destination of the opposite tunnel IP address.

45. B. The Next Hop Router Protocol (NHRP) is responsible for resolving and directing traffic for Dynamic Multipoint VPN (DMVPN) traffic.

46. C. The default keepalive time is 10 seconds. The keepalive allows both adjoining routers to know when the connection should be turned to a down state so routing protocols can choose a new route.

47. B. A T1 is a leased line from the phone company that is a dedicated point-to-point connection between two facilities. T1 lines are serial communications lines, which guarantees a bandwidth of 1.544 Mb/s between two locations.

48. C. The problem is a layer 2 problem because both routers are in an UP/DOWN state for the connecting serial interfaces. Router A has a protocol of HDLC configured and Router B has a protocol of PPP configured.

49. B. A fault-tolerant connection to a single ISP would be a dual-homed connection. With a dual-homed connection, two dedicated lines will terminate from the ISP to your facility. If one line were to fail, the other would be the fault-tolerant line.

50. A. A single-homed connection will provide no fault tolerance in the event of an outage of the line itself at the ISP.

51. C. The keepalive function on a serial interface helps the router notice when a connection no longer functions. The router can then bring the interface to a DOWN status and recalculate routes.

52. D. The problem is a layer 3 problem because both routers are in an UP/UP status for the connecting serial interfaces. Therefore, the problem must be a mismatch of IP addresses.

53. B. MultiLink Point-to-Point Protocol is used as a point-to-point connectivity method. Although there are multiple connections, they are dual-homed to the same locations.

54. A. The E-Tree services of Metro Ethernet allows for a root to be established to serve the remote sites or leaf endpoints. The root can communicate to the leaf endpoints and the leaf endpoints can communicate to the root. However, the leaf endpoints cannot communicate to each other.

55. C. Ethernet Line services, or E-Line services, provided with Metro Ethernet, is a dedicated point-to-point topology. This is commonly done with the use of an Ethernet Virtual Circuit defined at the service provider.

56. D. E-LAN is a service of Metro Ethernet. It provides a full mesh capability between endpoints. E-LAN services perform this by allowing all endpoints participating in E-LAN to communicate with each other. This type of communication is normally found on a common network LAN. This allows all sites to communicate with each other while only requiring a single line to the point of presence (PoP).

57. B. The most common hub-and-spoke WAN design is the way an Internet service provider is connected to their customers. The Internet connection is centrally located in a common physical location of the Internet provider called the point-of-presence or meet-me-room. All lines connect out from this point in a hub-and-spoke design.

58. B. The line status and the protocol status are both in a DOWN state. Since the interface does not explicitly state it is administratively shut down, it is either a wiring problem or a physical problem.

59. A. The command `show controllers serial 0/0` will show the controller configuration and status. If clocking is detected, you will see `DTE V.35 TX and RX clocks detected`.

60. C. A T1 or DS1 comprises 24 DS0 channels at 64 kb/s. $24 \times 64 = 1.536$ Mb/s (advertised as 1.544 Mb/s).

61. A. Point-to-Point over Ethernet (PPPoE) is a point-to-point technology. It creates a connection between two facilities.

62. C. The command `clock-rate 64000` will set the interface as a DCE interface and provide a clock rate of 64000 bits per second.

63. D. The Telco provider network is responsible for providing clocking for data alignment. If clocking is not detected, then the status of the interface will show as DOWN/DOWN since this is considered a layer 1 requirement.

64. B. MultiLink Point to Point Protocol (MLPPP) is an example of a dual-homed topology. This is because there are two links to the same location for aggregation of bandwidth and failover.

65. B. Dynamic Multipoint VPN (DMVPN) is an example of a hub-and-spoke or point-to-multipoint topology. All of the satellite connections terminate back to the central location.

66. B. The requirement for multiple protocols is a compelling reason to use MPLS. The protocols moving across MPLS nodes are irrelevant to the technology. This is because layer 3 information is not examined to route packets.

67. C. The term *customer edge* defines the edge of the customer's network. The router at the customer's edge is usually only responsible for routing packets to the provider edge.

68. B. The field in the layer 3 header is called Differentiated Services, or DiffServ. The value is an 8-bit Differentiated Services Code Point. This DSCP value helps classify QoS for MPLS.

69. A. The term *provider edge* router is the router closest to the customer edge router. This router is responsible for labeling traffic and redistribution of routing protocols for the customer edge router.

70. D. Metro Ethernet provides a layer 2 connection between sites defined by the MEF services. Distances are overcome by the use of fiber optics.

71. B. MPLS is referred to as a layer 2.5 protocol. This is because it shims a header between the layer 2 and layer 3 protocols; the header contains the label for the traffic.

72. B. Date integrity is one of the benefits of using a secure VPN protocol. To ensure its integrity, a packet is sealed with a hash which must equate to the same hash on the other side when it is received and decrypted.

73. C. Cisco Adaptive Security Appliance (ASA) devices are used to create VPN tunnels between sites. ASA devices run the Cisco ASA software, which allows for firewall, intrusion prevention, and VPNs among other security-related functions.

74. C. Since you have several remote workers who telecommute, the best connectivity option would be client SSL/VPN connectivity. A product called Cisco AnyConnect Secure Mobility Client allows for SSL encryption for VPN tunnels back to the main site.

75. B. Asymmetrical Digital Subscriber Line (ADSL) connectivity typically uses PPPoE to authenticate subscribers. The subscriber's credentials are often relayed to a RADIUS server for subscription checks.

76. C. The central office, sometimes referred to as the CO, is the local switching office. The CO is where your data lines meet the public network for data and voice.

77. B. Private WANs secure transmissions of their clients by providing isolation between them. It is up to the customer to use encryption for an added level of security, depending on the nature of the business.

78. A. An EVC defines the endpoints inside of a Metro Ethernet network. These endpoints are the customers' sites in which traffic will flow.

79. B. *Point of presence (PoP)* is the term that defines the access point of the provider's services. These services might be Internet, private WAN, or cloud resources.

80. A. A Metro Ethernet E-LAN service allows for a full-mesh topology between all of the sites. Since all of the sites are connected in a method similar to a layer 2 (LAN) network, all of the routers will become neighbors. This is similar to having multiple routers on a LAN.

81. A. MPLS providers typically use Multiprotocol-Border Gateway Protocol (MP-BGP) internally. This is because MP-BGP can advertise multiple routes while allowing logical separation between customers' routes.

82. A. DSL access multipliers, or DSLAMs, share the local loop with analog phone traffic to intercept communications from the DSL modem. DASLAMs provide the switching of data to the Internet.

83. B. IPSec uses the Encapsulating Security Payload protocol to encrypt data.

84. C. Site-to-site IPSec VPNs offer scalability as a benefit. This is because each remote office only needs an Internet connection to create a VPN tunnel back to the main office.

85. A. Multiprotocol Label Switching allows for varied access links such as serial leased lines, Frame Relay, Metro Ethernet, and so on. You can leverage the existing connectivity methods to form a private WAN.

86. D. E-Tree services allow the root to talk to the leafs in the tree. The leafs cannot forward traffic to each other without going through the root. Routing protocols are no different in traffic patterns.

87. C. CE routers do not form adjacencies or neighbors (depending on protocol) with other CE routers. They depend on PE routers and route redistribution of routing protocols to receive their routing updates and tables.

88. B. Every area must connect back to the backbone area, or area 0. However, CE routers cannot create neighborships with other sites. So the MPLS PE routers can either extend area 0 or create the area 0 network, which is called a super backbone.

89. B. Service providers use policing on Ethernet virtual circuits to allow the customer to burst up to the line's potential bandwidth yet only allow sustained data rates according to the contracted committed information rate (CIR).

90. B. Although all of these can be considerations for the customer, the largest impact can be the access link technology used between the PE and CE routers. If the customer uses Frame Relay, the QOS can be unusable because of discarded frames due to congestion.

91. A. IPSec uses the Authentication Header protocol to check data integrity. This is done by creating a numerical hash of the data via SHA1, SHA2, or MD5 algorithms.

92. B. ACLs are a major consideration since they are neither TCP nor UDP; they are a layer 3 protocol of their own. The ACL required for the tunnel creation is permit gre {source} {destination}, which would be for a named access list.

93. C. The CIR, or committed information rate, is the sustainable speed that the customer can communicate on the Ethernet virtual circuit. This CIR is directly tied to the price of the Monthly Recurring Charge (MRC), since the service provider must dedicate this bandwidth for the customer agreement.

94. D. Metro Ethernet service providers employ policing of traffic on Ethernet virtual circuits according to the committed information rate (CIR). The policing of traffic discards any traffic over the CIR without prejudice to the type of traffic. Therefore, the customer should shape traffic according to their preference of QoS on important traffic so that important packets are not discarded by the provider during high utilization.

95. B. The customer has the option to configure each site with a different Autonomous System Number (ASN) for EIGRP, or they can configure all sites with the same ASN. Regardless, the routes would be route redistributed from the internal Multiprotocol-Border Gateway Protocol (MP-BGP) process on the Provider Edge (PE) routers.

96. C. eBGP stands for external Border Gateway Protocol. It is the only protocol used on the Internet to route traffic from one edge of the Internet to the other.

97. B. A major difference between iBGP and eBGP is that iBGP routers peer with other iBGP routers in the same Autonomous System (AS), whereas eBGP routers peer with other eBGP routers in different Autonomous Systems (ASs). iBGP routers will not advertise routes learned within their common AS number.

98. C. BGP neighbors are formed via static neighbor assignment. BGP neighboring routers will not form a neighborship without manual intervention.

99. A. EBGP is not very fast in terms of convergence, due to the volume of routes it must handle and calculate. However, it is extremely scalable and that is why it is used specifically for the routing functionality of the Internet.

100. B. EBGP uses path attributes to calculate best path selection. Rather than relying on one metric, a number of calculations are derived from the path attributes, which are updated with the network prefixes.

101. A. Best path algorithm is used with EBGP for path selection. The algorithm is a path-vector-based algorithm. Path-vector algorithms closely resemble distance-vector algorithms. However, with EBGP, there are about 14 pieces of criteria examined rather than just hop count, although AS path count is weighted heavily in the decision process.

102. C. Single-homed EBGP connections are found on the Internet edge. It is the link connecting the enterprise structure with a single ISP.

103. C. EBGP tables are initially loaded and updated via TCP port 179 by peer routers in a neighborship as well as by messages for peer setup. This is different than other routing protocols that use layer 3 protocols. EBGP uses the layer 4 protocol TCP to move data.

104. D. Only public address blocks such as 180.45.65.0/24 should be advertised with EBGP. Subnets can be advertised, but often policies with your ISP will prohibit it. Private IPs should not be advertised with EBGP and are usually filtered at the ISP.

105. B. In a single-homed Internet edge design, the default gateway will always be the ISP's router. Therefore, to reduce the load on the enterprise router, the default gateway can be advertised as the ISP router.

106. A. The command `router bgp 2001` will start a router process of BGP for the AS number of 2001.

107. A. The administrative distance of external BGP is a value of 20. The AD of internal BGP is a value of 200.

108. D. The network address 120.187.230.0 is a Class B address. Therefore, the mask of 255.255.255.0 must be specified, via the command `network 120.187.230.0 mask 255.255.255.0`.

109. C. The command `show ip bgp neighbors` will display all of the BGP neighbors that the router is peered with. The command will also show statistics about the peer(s).

110. B. The command `clear ip bgp 198.23.45.2 soft in` will soft-reset the BGP neighbor of 198.23.45.2 for inbound connections. This will soft-refresh the BGP table for the peer of 198.23.45.2 and cause a new set of inbound updates.

111. D. The command `neighbor 207.178.17.1 remote-as 2002` configured in the BGP router process will configure the neighbor as a peer. You first specify the remote IP of the peer and then the remote-as (autonomous system) of the peer.

112. C. The command `show tcp brief` will allow you to see TCP terminated connections on the router. Since BGP uses TCP 179 for BGP messages, there should be an "established" connection on the router from the remote peer.

113. C. The command `neighbor 198.45.32.2 shutdown` will put the neighbor into an Administratively Shutdown status. When you are ready to reestablish the peer, the `no neighbor 198.45.32.2 shutdown` command will return BGP back to normal. This is done to retain neighbor configuration while being able to disable the neighbor.

114. B. Using a route statement of `ip route 194.56.32.0 255.255.255.0 null0` will create a discard route. This route will allow BGP to advertise the network prefix as a /24. The routing to the /29 networks will be overridden in Router A's route table since the connected route is more specific than the /24 route.

115. A. The command `show ip route 160.45.23.0 255.255.255.0 longer-prefixes` will detail all of the specific routes contained in the route for 16.45.23.0/24.

116. A. Bandwidth describes the speed of a link in terms of bits per second.

117. A. QoS marking should always be performed closest to the source of the traffic. All switches and routers in the network should be configured to properly prioritize markings of traffic in queues.

118. B. Delay is the time it takes for a packet to travel from source to destination, which is a description of one-way delay. Round-trip delay is the time it takes for the packet to travel from source to destination (one-way delay) plus the time it takes for the destination computer to send the packet back to the originating node to form a round-trip.

119. A. QoS classifies traffic with access control lists and applies markings to the packets.

120. C. Jitter is the measurement of variation between consecutive packet times from source to destination (one-way delay). For example, if the first packet takes 10 ms, and the second, third, and fourth take 10 ms, the jitter or variance is 0 ms. The simple calculation is an average of packet times. However, data size has an influence on jitter, so the more accurate calculation is $J = J + (D (I - 1 , I) - J) / 16$.

121. B. The Class of Service field is only found in layer 2 transmissions, specifically only across trunks due to the dependency of 802.1Q. The CoS field is a 3-bit field in the 802.1Q frame type.

122. D. Loss is the measurement of discarded packets. The measurement is a percentage of transmitted packets. For example, if 100 packets are transmitted and 3 packets are dropped, then the loss is 3%. Loss can be attributed to congestions, faulty wiring, EMI, or device queue congestion.

123. C. Network Based Application Recognition version 2 is used to classify applications based on a Protocol Description Language Module (PDLM).

124. A. The Differentiated Services Code Point (DSCP) is a 6-bit value in the Type of Service (ToS) field of the IP header. The DSCP value defines the importance of packets at layer 3.

125. A. A malicious user can mark all of his or her traffic as high priority. Therefore, a trust boundary must be established by the network administrator. A common trust boundary device is the IP phone, but it is any device that is in control of the network administrator.

126. B. The standardized marking of DSCP EF, or Expedite Forwarding, is a decimal equivalent of 46. This marking has the highest priority and should be used for VoIP traffic and video.

127. C. The maximum delay that VOIP traffic should not exceed is 150 ms. At 150 ms, you will have call disruption.

128. B. Low Latency Queue (LLQ) overrides Class Based Weighted Fair Queuing (CBWFQ). CBWFQ uses a weighted round-robin scheduling of packets. LLQ has priority override when packets come in matching the classification for LLQ.

129. B. QoS queue starvation occurs when the Low Latency Queuing (LLQ) is given priority over the Class-Based Weighted Fair Queuing. Therefore, policing of the LLQ will help limit queue starvation and allow those queues an equal share of the total output bandwidth.

130. A. Shaping monitors the bit rate of packets. If the bit rate is exceeded for a configured queue, then shaping holds packets over the configured bit rate, causing a delay.

131. C. Class-Based Weighted Fair Queuing, or CBWFQ, is driven by a round-robin scheduler. The queues are weighted for priority in the scheduler and the packets are put into the queues upon classification.

132. B. Policing monitors the bit rate of packets. If the bit rate is exceeded for a configured queue, then policing drops packets over the configured bit rate, causing loss. In some cases it can be configured to re-mark the packets.

133. B. QoS policing should be implemented to adhere network traffic to a contracted CIR. As an example, if your enterprise contracted a Metro Ethernet connection with an access link of 1 Gb/s and a CIR of 400 Mb/s, you would need to make sure that traffic does not exceed the CIR except for occasional bursts.

134. C. Tail drop happens when the QoS queues are full and cannot send packets fast enough. There is no more room in the queue, and any packets being added to the tail of the queue are dropped.

135. D. QoS shaping should be used when the service provider is policing traffic. If the traffic is policed and exceeds the CIR, the ISP will drop packets. Therefore, traffic shaping can delay the packets to slow the protocols vs. being dropped by the ISP.

136. A. The command `auto qos trust cos` will configure the interface to be trusted for the CoS value. This type of QoS will happen at layer 2 with the CoS field. Based upon the CoS value, the interface will be trusted for QoS. Normally, devices should not be trusted for QoS since the CoS value could be forged so that the user can gain preferential treatment of their packets.

137. B. QoS packet shapers work by measuring traffic over a time interval. If the time interval is too large, the packets will be sent in the initial start of the interval. Then the router will wait until the interval is over to transmit again. Configuring a small time interval is desired so that the router is not waiting for the next interval to send packets. It is recommended to use a time interval of 10 milliseconds (ms) for voice and video traffic.

138. D. When the queue depth is above the minimum threshold, a percentage of TCP packets are dropped. This allows the TCP window to shrink and allows a normal slowdown of TCP transmissions. This is done in hopes that the queue will fall under the minimum threshold and return to normal.

139. B. The command `show mls qos interface` will display information related to the current QoS trust level on the interface along with the default CoS value.

140. B. AF41 marked traffic has a better position in the queue than traffic marked AF31. During high congestion times, traffic with lower positions in the queues (AF3x, AF2x, AF1x) would have more chances of being dropped than AF41.

Chapter 5: Infrastructure Services (Domain 5)

1. C. Domain Name Services (DNS) is a distributed database of fully qualified domain names (FQDNs) to IP addresses.

2. B. Forward lookups resolve fully qualified domain names (FQDNs) to an IP address.

3. A. Domain Name Services direct queries are performed over the UDP protocol to port 53. The queries do not require the TCP setup and teardown because the queries are simple request and reply messages, so UDP is used for direct queries.

4. D. Fully qualified domain names are significant from right to left, starting with a period to signify the root. The period is normally not visible on the FQDN, but it is processed as the root lookup.

5. B. A reverse lookup is when the fully qualified domain name (FQDN) is resolved from an IP address. This is useful when you want to identify an IP address. From the IP address, you can derive the FQDN.

6. C. The PTR, or pointer record, is used to look up IP addresses and return FQDNs that are mapped to them. This is helpful to identify an IP address, and in the case of SSH, it is used to positively identify the host you are connecting to.

7. A. The configured DNS domain name is appended to the hostname query. As an example, if you query a hostname of routera and the configured domain name is network.local, the DNS server will see a query for rotuera.network.local.

8. C. Static hostname entries are the most secure name resolution method for routers and switches. This is because the switch or router does not need to forward-query a server. However, static hostname entries are not scalable.

9. A. The A record is the DNS record that is queried when you want to resolve a hostname to an IP address.

10. B. The time to live, or TTL, limits the amount of time in which a DNS entry will be available in the DNS cache. The TTL can be defined by the DNS administrator on the entry, or it can be defined in the SOA record as the default TTL.

11. D. The alternative to DNS lookup on routers is configuring static hostname entries. This method unfortunately is not scalable.

12. D. The Quad-A (AAAA) record type is used for IPv6 hostname lookup on DNS servers.

13. B. The protocol TCP and port number 53 are used for DNS domain zone transfers. UDP port 53 is used for iterative queries, since the message is short. However, zone transfers require the help of TCP because there is more information than there is in a query.

14. C. Configuring DNS on a router or switch allows for ease of administration from the router or switch. It enables DNS resolution from the console. It does not enable DNS resolution from external sources unless you have configured the hostnames on the DNS server.

15. D. By default, all routers and switches are set for `ip domain-lookup`. Because no IP address is set, the router or switch will try to broadcast the DNS query. If you configure `no ip domain-lookup`, the query will just fail, and you will not need to break out of it.

16. D. The command `ip host routerb 10.1.2.3` will configure the local resolution of the host routerb to an IP address of 10.1.2.3.

17. C. The command `ip name-server 172.16.1.5` will configure the router or switch to query the DNS server of 172.16.1.5 for hostname lookups. You can specify multiple DNS servers by using a space as a delimiter between each name for fault tolerance.

18. D. The command `ip domain-name sybex.com` will set the appended domain name of sybex.com for DNS queries. This command will allow the proper FQDN to be resolved by DNS.

19. A. A period is always appended to all FQDNs. This is significant because it represents the root, where all DNS resolution begins. The root or period is not often visible, but it is part of the DNS recursion process.

20. C. A best practice for security is to always use a trusted DNS server. This is normally a server under the control of the enterprise, so it is a private DNS server.

21. B. The command `show hosts` will allow you to verify the statically configured hosts.

22. B. If the cache is cleared after the change has been made to DNS and you still get the same IP address, the reason is most likely that there is a host entry configured. The command `show running-configuration` will show you if there is an entry.

23. C. The command `nslookup routerb.sybex.com` will allow you to positively verify name resolution. Ping should not be used because the failure of ICMP echo will make the command fail, giving you a false result.

24. B. The command to verify DNS server(s) configured for name lookup is `show running-configuration`. The line to look for in the output is `ip name-server` *x.x.x.x*.

25. D. Options A, B, and C will return the error ""% Unrecognized host or address or protocol not running."

26. C. DNS changes can be made on-the-fly. However, the results will not be seen immediately unless all cache is cleared and routers request the new address. The problem would be that this router had resolved routerb.sybex.com already and the entry still exists in the cache, which needs to be cleared.

27. A. RouterB has not accessed the cache in 9 hours. The age represents when the IOS has last referred to the entry in cache. The age is represented in hours.

28. D. The command to clear only the host routerb.sybex.com from the DNS cache is `clear host routerb.sybex.com`. This will remove only that particular host from the cache.

29. C. The router is pointed to a public DNS server. The domain name of the router is sybex.local, and .local is not a valid top level domain (TLD). Therefore, the DNS server should be private, that is hosting the sybex.local DNS zone.

30. B. There is most likely an ACL on Router B that is blocking UDP port 53. The ACL on Router A would not affect traffic generating from Router A.

31. C. The DHCP Discover packet is a broadcast to discover a DHCP server. The layer 3 packet and layer 2 frame are broadcasts. Since the client does not have an IP address yet, the layer 3 source address is all zeros. However, the layer 2 source MAC address is filled out in the frame.

32. C. The command ip address dhcp will configure the router to use DHCP for IP address assignment. This command needs to be issued on the interface in which you want the IP address to be configured, similar to static IP address assignment.

33. B. The command show ip interface will display the IP addresses configured on the router's interfaces. It will detail which are static and which have been allocated through DHCP.

34. A. The DHCP client uses the source port UDP/68 to await connections back from the server. It keeps this protocol and port open in an active state until DHCP is complete.

35. A. The command show dhcp lease will help you verify the IP address configured on the router, the DHCP server that served the lease, and the lease time in seconds.

36. C. The DHCP Offer packet is a broadcast packet from the DHCP server to the DHCP client. The layer 3 packet and layer 2 frame are both broadcasts.

37. D. The command ip helper-address 10.10.1.101 will configure the interface to become a DHCP relay agent. This command must be configured on the interface in which you want the DHCP relay agent to listen and respond.

38. B. The Gateway Address (GIADDR) field is filled out by the DHCP relay agent before the DHCP packet is sent to the DHCP server. This field helps the DHCP server decide which scope to send an Offer message back for.

39. D. The DHCP server bind port of UDP/67 is used for awaiting connections from DHCP clients.

40. D. A DHCP relay agent installed on Router A interface Gi0/0 will allow clients on Host A's network to obtain IP addressing from DHCP.

41. B. The command ipconfig /all will display the generic information of IP, subnet mask, and gateway. It will also display the DHCP server that configured the client with an IP address.

42. A. The DHCP acknowledgment message is sent from the DHCP client to the DHCP server to acknowledge that the IP address offered will be used by the client.

43. A. DHCP uses layer 3 broadcasts by sending packets to 255.255.255.255 for initial DHCP discovery.

44. B. DHCP clients request a renewal of the lease halfway through the lease time of the IP address.

45. C. After the initial Discover, Offer, Request, and Acknowledge, it is the client's responsibility to maintain the lease of the IP address. This includes release and renewal.

46. A. DHCP uses UDP as a connectionless protocol for the Discover, Offer, Request, and Acknowledge packets.

47. C. The command debug ip dhcp server packet will show the details of a DHCP relay agent conversation. It will detail conversation between the client and router and the router and the DHCP server.

48. C. Stateless Address Autoconfiguration (SLAAC) allows for the client to learn the network ID and calculate a host ID that is unique. However, SLAAC is lacking the ability to configure options such as DNS time servers, etc. DHCPv6 allows for the configuration of these options when used in conjunction with SLAAC.

49. D. They will lose their IP after their entire lease has expired. Until the lease expires, they will have functioning IP addresses.

50. B. The command ipv6 dhcp relay destination 2001:db8:1:2::2 will configure the router interface to relay DHCP requests to 2001:db8:1:2::2. This command must be configured on the interface that is to listen for DHCPv6 requests.

51. A. The command lease 0 4 0 will configure the DHCP pool for a duration of 0 days, 4 hours, and 0 minutes.

52. D. The command ip dhcp exclusion-address 192.168.1.16 192.168.1.31 will configure an exclusion address range by specifying the low IP address and the high IP address. This command is configured from the global configuration prompt.

53. D. The command option 66 ip 10.1.1.5 sets the TFTP server to boot from. The command bootfile boot\x86\wdsnbp.com sets the bootfile on the TFTP server to boot\x86\wdsnbp.com. Some clients may need other options, such as option 60, which is the vendor class identifier.

54. B. The default gateway option is configured under the DHCP pool with the command default-router 10.1.1.1. This will set the default gateway to 10.1.1.1 for the DHCP clients.

55. A. The DNS server is configured with the command dns-server 10.1.1.5. This command is used in lieu of the option command so that multiple DNS servers can be configured on the same line.

56. C. The command network 192.168.1.0 255.255.255.0 will configure the network ID and subnet mask required for DHCP.

57. A. Stateful DHCPv6 supplies the network ID and host ID. The default router is discovered through the Neighbor Discovery Protocol.

58. C. The command `ipv6 address dhcp` will configure the interface to obtain its IP address via stateful DHCPv6.

59. B. The command `show ipv6 dhcp interface` will display which mode the client is in, the address, and the DHCP Unique Identifier (DUID) as well as the stateful DHCPv6 server address.

60. C. When the lease for a node is deleted on the DHCP server, the DHCP server is free to hand out the lease to another node. This happens independently from the client, as there is no communication from server to client about the lease. The client will retain the IP address until the renewal period, which will cause a duplication of IP addressing.

61. A. At seven-eighths of the lease cycle, the DHCP client will perform a rebinding. The rebinding process means that the original DHCP server was down at the one-half mark of the lease, so now the client will try to rebind with any responding DHCP server.

62. A. The command `renew dhcp gi 0/0` will force the DHCP client to renew the current lease.

63. C. When the DHCP server issues an IP address to a client, it records the MAC address in the DHCP bindings table. This is recorded along with the lease expiration.

64. B. During the DHCP rebinding process, a DHCP Request is sent. However, it is not sent to the originating server since rebinding occurs after the renewal period was missed. So the DHCP Request is broadcast to any listening DHCP server.

65. C. The DHCP pool is configured for the network of 192.168.1.0/24. However, there is an exclusion range of 192.168.1.0 to 192.168.1.25. Therefore, the first IP address handed out via DHCP is 192.168.1.26.

66. C. The DHCP server is not configured properly. When a Windows client configures itself with an IP address of 169.254.x.x, it is using APIPA, or Automatic Private IP Addressing (link-local addressing).

67. C. DHCP clients use a protocol called Gratuitous Address Resolution Protocol (GARP). The GARP packet is a broadcast to the other clients in the network. If no response is heard, there are no conflicts.

68. B. When DHCP detects a duplicate IP address in the pool, it will remove the duplicate IP address from the DHCP pool and place it into the conflict table. It will require manual intervention to reserve the IP address.

69. C. It is recommended that you create an exclusion for the router interface and any statically configured hosts in the network for the DHCP pool. This will prevent duplicate IP address conflicts.

70. B. The command `show ip dhcp conflict` will display the IP address conflicts on the router or switch. The table will display how the conflict was discovered with GARP or Ping as well as the detection time.

71. D. The DHCP pool network is incorrectly set to the wrong scope. The DHCP pool network should be set to 192.168.1.0 255.255.255.0.

72. D. The command show ip dhcp pool will allow you to see the current utilization of the scopes configured on the router.

73. D. The command to remove an IP address from the conflict table is clear ip dhcp conflict 192.168.1.6. This command will remove a single IP address of 192.168.1.6 from the table and place it back in the DHCP pool. Alternatively, all of the conflicts can be cleared with an * in lieu of the IP address.

74. B. The exclusions are configured for the entire 254 block of IP addresses in the network of 192.168.1.0/24. No IP addresses will be served until the exclusions are corrected.

75. A. The command show ip dhcp bindings will allow you to verify all of the current DHCP leases served by the router or switch.

76. B. Virtual Router Redundancy Protocol (VRRP) is an IEEE open standard that is supported freely on many router products.

77. D. The well-known HSRP ID is 07.ac. Anytime you see the 07.ac in the second part of the MAC address along with the Cisco OUI, you can identify that HSRP is being employed.

78. C. Gateway Load Balancing Protocol (GLBP) is a Cisco Proprietary protocol that supports redundancy and per-subnet load balancing.

79. C. The HSRP group number in the MAC address 0000.0c07.ac01 is 01. After the Cisco OUI and well-known HSPR ID, the last two digits are the HSRP group identifier.

80. A. The default priority of HSRP is 100.

81. D. You can create up to 256 HSRP groups on a router. This would include group 0 to 255 for a total of 256 groups.

82. B. HSRP routers communicate with each other on port 1985 using UDP.

83. B. Only one router can be active at a time in an HSRP group. All other routers are standby routers, until the active router fails.

84. C. HSRP uses multicasting to communicate among HSRP group members. For HSRPv1, the address is 224.0.0.2, and for HSRPv2, the address is 224.0.0.102.

85. A. The virtual router is responsible for host communications such as an ARP request for the host's default gateway. Technically, this is served by the active router since it is hosting the virtual router. However, it is the virtual router's IP address and MAC address that are used for outgoing packets.

86. C. The hold timer must expire for the standby router to become an active router. The hold timer is three times the hello timer, so three hello packets must be missed before the standby becomes active.

87. D. Gateway Load Balancing Protocol (GLBP) use the port number 3222 and the protocol UDP for router communications.

88. D. HSRP version 2 allows for timers to be configured in milliseconds in lieu of seconds. This allows for quicker failover between active and standby routers.

89. C. The active virtual gateway (AVG) is responsible for responding to ARP requests from hosts. The AVG will reply with the MAC address of any one of the active virtual forwarders (AVFs).

90. D. The router with the highest priority will become the AVG. However, if all routers have the same priority, then the router with the highest IP address configured becomes the tiebreaker.

91. B. Gateway Load Balancing Protocol (GLBP) supports up to four active virtual forwarders per GLBP group.

92. A. The command standby 1 priority 150 will set the HSRP group of 1 on this router to a priority of 150. As long as all other routers are set to the default of 100, this router will become the default router on the next election.

93. D. You can create up to 4,096 HSRP groups on a router. This would include group 0 to 4096 for a total of 4,096 groups.

94. C. Hot Standby Router Protocol version 2 (HSRPv2) is being employed. It uses an OUI of 0000.0c and a well-known identifier of 9f.f, and the last three digits identify the HSRP group, which has been expanded from two digits in version 1.

95. D. Preemption allows for the election process to happen for a newly added HSRP router. If preemption is not enabled, then the newly added HSRP router will become a standby router.

96. B. Hot Standby Router Protocol (HSRP) allows for only one active router per HSRP group. However, you can configure multiple VLANs with HSRP groups. You can then alternate a higher-than-default priority to force an active router per VLAN. This will give you a rudimentary way of balancing traffic.

97. C. The command show standby will allow you to verify the state of the current router for HSRP.

98. C. The HSRP group is not set for preemption, which is the default behavior for HSRP. You need to enable preemption, which will allow a reelection when the priority is changed or if a new standby router comes online. If preemption is disabled, the active router will have affinity.

99. D. The command standby 1 preempt will configure HSRP group 1 for preemption. This command must be configured under the interface on which HSRP has been enabled. The command show standby will allow you to verify this.

100. B. The command vrrp 1 ip 10.1.2.3 will configure the interface with VRRP with a virtual IP address of 10.1.2.3.

101. C. Interface tracking is configured on the interface in which the HSRP group has been configured. The command `standby 1 track serial 0/0/1` tells the HSRP group of 1 to track the status of interface serial 0/0/1.

102. B. The command `tracert 10.1.2.33` will allow you to see the real IP address on the router that is responding for the ICMP packet. With HSRP, the virtual MAC address is returned for the virtual IP address of the default gateway. However, when ping is used the ping packet enters the real interface, and then the interface responds with the real IP address.

103. C. The command `debug standby` will allow you to see real-time information from HSRP on the router on which you have entered the command.

104. A. GLBP allows for per-host load balancing. It does this by allowing the active virtual router to respond for the virtual IP address. The AVG then hands out the MAC address in the ARP request for one of the active virtual forwarders. It does this in a round-robin fashion.

105. A. The command `standby 1 timers msec 200 msec 700` will set the HSRP group of 1 with a hello timer of 200 milliseconds and a hold timer of 700 milliseconds. This is configured inside of the interface in which the HSRP group was created.

106. C. Network Address Translation (NAT) was created to slow the depletion of Internet addresses. It does this by translating RFC 1918 privatized addresses to one or many public IP addresses. It allows the packets to masquerade as the public IP address on the Internet until is it translated back to the private IP address.

107. A. Network Address Translation creates packet switching path delay. This is because each address traveling through the NAT process requires lookup time for the translation.

108. B. Static Network Address Translation is a one-to-one mapping between a local (private) and global (public) IP address. This is used for servers, such as web servers and email servers, so that they are Internet reachable.

109. A. The inside local address is the address local to the enterprise (private), and the address is inside the enterprise. The inside local address will almost always be an RCF 1918 address, unless NAT is being used for purposes other than enterprise Internet access. If NAT is used for Internet access, then the inside local address is any host address destined for the Internet through NAT.

110. A. Dynamic Network Address Translation is a one-to-one mapping on the fly in which the IP address is allocated from a pool of addresses. This is often called many-to-many. When a host makes an attempt to go through the NAT process, an IP address is mapped to the host from the global pool. This type of NAT is useful in network address overlap situations because there is less latency than NAT Overloading.

111. C. Network Address Translation overloading, sometimes called Port Address Translation, allows for one public IP address to be used for NAT. The conversations between local and global IPs are sorted using the source and destination ports for the various applications. This is the most common NAT and can be found in any home, small office, or enterprise.

112. C. The inside global address is the address public to the enterprise. The address is inside of or controlled by the enterprise. The inside global address in this case is the public side of the NAT which is Router A's S0/0 IP address.

113. D. The outside global address is the address public to the enterprise. The address is outside of the enterprise or outside of its control. When using NAT for Internet access, the outside global address is the destination host on the Internet. The outside global address in this exhibit is the web server.

114. A. Static NAT translation entries are always present in the NAT table. Static NAT entries have the same amount of security and latency as dynamic NAT.

115. B. Network Address Translation overloading is also called Port Address Translation. This is because a single IP address can allow up to 65,535 simulations inside local connections, which are segregated in the NAT table by source and destination port number.

116. B. A decrease in public IP address utilization is a direct benefit of using NAT. Memory utilization will increase, latency of packets will increase, and some network applications could have problems with NAT.

117. C. Static NAT is mainly used for publishing internal resources on the Internet, Such services are email servers, web servers, collaboration servers, and so on.

118. A. The inside local address is "inside" the enterprise and under "local" control of the enterprise. This term is from the perspective of the NAT device.

119. C. The flexibility of Internet connections is usually a driving factor for PAT (NAT Overloading). Memory is significantly higher with PAT, since the source and destination port numbers must be recorded in the NAT table. There is no effect on packet loss, and jitter is marginally affected.

120. D. The command to configure the private side of the network interface for NAT is `ip nat inside`. This command is configured on the interface in which you want to define it as the "inside" of your network.

121. A. The command `show ip nat translations` will allow you to view the active NAT translations on the router.

122. D. The command `show ip nat statistics` will allow you to view the number of active NAT translations on the router. In addition, it will provide you with the current inside and outside interfaces.

123. A. After you define the inside and outside per each respective interface, the command `ip nat inside source static 192.168.1.3 179.43.44.1` will statically NAT (Network Address Translation) the inside local address of 192.168.1.3 to the inside global address of 179.43.44.1.

124. D. The command `ip nat pool EntPool 179.43.44.2 179.43.44.15 netmask 255.255.255.0` will configure the pool called EntPool with the range of IP addresses from 179.43.44.2 to 179.43.44.15 and the network mask of /24. The /24 is used in lieu of the /28 because the serial interface is a /24 and therefore all IP addresses in that network are /24.

125. B. The access list allows the inside local address to pass through the NAT process.

126. C. The command `clear ip nat translation *` will clear all IP NAT translations out of the NAT table. The asterisk is used as a wildcard for all addresses. You can alternatively specify a specific inside or outside NAT address.

127. C. When the NAT table clears, established TCP sessions will need to reestablish via the three-way handshake. This creates a problem for some secure protocols such as SSH, which will drop the established connection and not reestablish a new connection. UDP does not have a state to its connection, so little or no disturbance will be seen.

128. B. The command `debug ip nat` will allow you to see real-time NAT translations. When you issue this command, you should know that each NAT translation will log to the screen or logging server and will spike CPU usage.

129. C. The first command required is `access-list 1 permit 192.168.1.0 0.0.0.255`, which defines the allowed networks. The next command creates the NAT pool with `ip nat pool EntPool 179.43.44.1 179.43.44.1 netmask 255.255.255.0`. The last command, `ip nat inside source list 1 pool EntPool overload`, ties the access list together with the pool and defines PAT with the `overload` command.

130. D. The first command sets up the allowed network to be NATed with `access-list 1 permit 192.168.1.0 0.0.0.255`. The next command, `ip nat inside source list 1 interface serial 0/0 overload`, is where everything is tied together. The access list is applied and the interface of serial 0/0 is configured to overload.

131. B. The Network Time Protocol (NTP) is used to synchronize time for routers and switches.

132. C. Time synchronization is important for logging accuracy. Serial communication frame alignment is timed via DCE clocking and packet queues are timed by how fast they can respond.

133. A. The command `ntp server 129.6.15.28` will configure your router to connect to the server 129.6.15.28 as an NTP source. This command must be entered in global configuration mode.

134. B. The command `ntp master` configures the router or switch to trust its internal time clock.

135. A. The command `show clock detail` will result in either `no time source` or `time source is NTP` if the router or switch is configured to slave off a server for time.

136. C. The command `show ntp associations detail` will allow you to view the NTP clock details from the master NTP server.

137. D. The Network Time Protocol uses UDP port 123 for time synchronization.

138. C. The command `debug ntp packets` will allow you to verify packets received from an NTP server.

139. A. A best practice is to configure the main router in your network to a known good trusted time source by its DNS address. All devices in your network should then be configured to point to this trusted router. All time sources should pyramid out from the central source of time in your network.

140. C. The command show ntp status will allow you to see the current time source, the precision of the time source, and the drift from your internal time clock.

Chapter 6: Infrastructure Security (Domain 6)

1. B. Port security can restrict a port to a single device by MAC address. This will effectively make plugging in a wireless access point a non-event for a corporate network.

2. A. Port security blocks unauthorized access by examining the source address of a network device.

3. C. Port security is enabled by configuring the command switchport port-security. This command must be configured on the interface in which you want to enable port security.

4. A. By default, only a single MAC address is allowed on an interface when port security is enabled.

5. C. Port security operates at layer 2 by inspecting the source MAC addresses in frames. It allows the configured number of source MAC addresses to be switched into the port and onto the switch processor.

6. C. Configuring port security helps a network administrator prevent unauthorized access by MAC address.

7. C. Port security works best in static environments where there is minimal change to the environment. It does not require any more memory since the results are pulled from the MAC address table.

8. B. Both the computer and the VoIP phone have MAC addresses, and therefore you will need to allow the port to have two MAC addresses, one for the phone to communicate and the other for the computer to communicate on the port.

9. B. By default, when port security is configured on a port, the violation method is err-disabled shutdown.

10. C. When port security is configured, the port cannot be in dynamic mode for Dynamic Trunking Protocol (DTP) mode. You must configure the port as an access port first, then turn off DTP with the command switchport nonnegotiate. You can then configure switchport port security.

11. B. The command `switchport port-security maximum 2` will configure the port with a maximum of two MAC addresses that shall pass through the port.

12. D. The command `switchport port-security violation restrict` will set the violation mode to restrict. This will drop frames over the maximum number of learned MAC addresses and will log security violations to the counters.

13. B. The command `show port-security interface gi 2/13` will allow you to see a detailed view of an individual port configured for port security.

14. A. The command `switchport port-security violation shutdown` puts the interface into the err-disable state immediately and sends an SNMP trap notification to a syslog server.

15. C. The command `switchport port-security violation protect` will set the violation mode to protect. This will drop frames over the maximum number of learned MAC addresses but will not log security violations to the counters.

16. C. The command `show port-security` will show all ports that have logged port security violations.

17. C. When you configure sticky port security, the first MAC address seen by the switch will become bound to the port. Any other MAC addresses will trip the access violation set.

18. B. The default configuration for port security results in an access violation of shutdown. When a port-security violation occurs, the port will be shut down in an err-disable status.

19. A. The command `switchport port-security mac-address sticky` will configure the port to learn the first MAC address and allow only the first MAC address to pass traffic.

20. D. One way to clear an err-disable status is to issue the `shutdown` command and then the `no shutdown` command on the port. This will reset the port so that traffic can flow again. However, if the access violation still exists then it will enter an err-disable status again.

21. B. The command `switchport port-security mac-address 0334.56f3.e4e4` will configure the interface with a static MAC address of 0334.56f3.e4e4.

22. D. The command `show port-security` will show all of the ports that are actively participating in port security. In addition, you can see the maximum number of addresses configured, current addresses, security violations, and action.

23. D. The global config command `errdisable recovery cause psecure_violation` will reset all ports with an err-disable status.

24. A. The command `show running-configuration` will show you the learned MAC addresses from port security.

25. B. Sticky MAC addresses become part of the running-configuration. If the running-configuration is saved to the NVRAM, then the sticky MAC address will become part of the startup-configuration.

26. D. The command no switchport port-security mac-address sticky 0045.2342.e4c3 will remove the entry for the device. The command no switchport port-security mac-address sticky will remain, so the next device learned will create a new sticky entry.

27. C. The port is up and operational in a normal status. The port is configured for a maximum of two MAC addresses, both of which are sticky MAC addresses.

28. D. The command show port-security address will allow you to see all of the dynamically learned MAC addresses for port security. The command show running-configuration would allow you to see only dynamically learned MAC addresses that are sticky.

29. B. The port is currently in an access violation status. The current access violation mode is secure-shutdown, and therefore, the interface will require shutdown and no shutdown to reset the port.

30. C. The command show port-security address will allow you to see all of the MAC addresses and the ports they are assigned to for port security. In addition, it will show you the time left before the MAC addresses expire, if they have been obtained dynamically.

31. B. The interface switchport should be in an access mode before port security is applied to the interface. Trunks can participate in port security, but it is rare to use these two functions together.

32. C. The maximum number of MAC addresses is one, which is the default. The current port-security violation of restrict will restrict frames from any other MAC addresses by dropping the frames.

33. D. The command show port-security interface gi 2/3 will allow you to see detailed information about the interface in which port security is configured.

34. A. The default configuration for port security is dynamic port security and a violation of shutdown. If a new device is connected to the port, it will enter an err-disable status. Therefore, clearing the dynamic MAC addresses will be required via the command clear port-security dynamic interface gi 2/3. Alternatively, the command clear port-security dynamic would clear all dynamically learned MAC addresses on the entire switch.

35. B. The command switchport port-security aging time 1440 will configure the port to forget the dynamically learned MAC address after 1,440 minutes. This command is configured in minutes and saves an admin from entering a clear command. However, if a violation of shutdown is configured, the port will need to be manually reset if it enters violation mode within this time period.

36. B. The perimeter area, or perimeter network, is outside of the corporate firewall. The perimeter area generally holds equipment necessary for routing to the ISP.

37. B. The DHCP binding table tracks all interface, MAC address, VLAN, and IP information. This database is critical in snooping out other ports from using identical information.

38. A. The demilitarized zone (DMZ) is an area that is protected by the corporate firewall. However, it allows servers such as web servers, email servers, and application servers to be accessible via the Internet.

39. C. An intrusion prevention system, or IPS, can detect and prevent attacks based on their signature. They are commonly found in firewall systems such as Adaptive Security Appliance (ASA) devices.

40. A. The internal network is defined by the firewall. Anything protected by the firewall on the internal network is considered to be the trusted network.

41. B. Distributed denial of service, or DDoS, is a common attack technique used to deny others of service. It is performed by overwhelming the service with bogus traffic. When it is performed from multiple hosts on the Internet, it is very difficult to prevent and stop.

42. B. An intrusion detection system, or IDS, can detect an attack based upon its signature. They are commonly found in firewall systems such as Adaptive Security Appliance (ASA) devices.

43. A. By default, all ports are considered untrusted, which means they should never serve the request of a DHCP client. Only the port put into trusted mode is allowed to answer client requests.

44. C. Rate limiting is employed to thwart DHCP starvation attacks by limiting the number of DHCP packets a port can receive per second.

45. A. A spurious DHCP attack is when a rouge DHCP server is started on the network. It serves clients with incorrect DHCP information. DHCP snooping helps to mitigate this attack.

46. D. Ping sweep scans are used by attackers to discover hosts on a network. The scan sends a flood of ICMP echo requests to the perimeter network and awaits echo replies. When ICMP is blocked at the perimeter, an attacker would not be able to scan the network via ICMP.

47. C. An intrusion prevention system (IPS) will help mitigate denial of service attacks. Common features of IPS can be found in the Cisco Adaptive Security Appliance.

48. C. IP address spoofing is a common attack method used to attempt to gain access to a system by spoofing the originating IP address.

49. C. Secure Sockets Layer (SSL) communications offer both encryption and authentication of the data via certificate signing. This would prevent tampering of the data end to end.

50. D. This attack is called a man in the middle attack. The attacker sits in the middle of communications and relays it back while capturing it and possibly modifying it.

51. A. Access control lists are an effective way to mitigate spoofing of internal IPs from outside the trusted network.

52. A. A requirement of DHCP snooping is that the device is on the VLAN that DHCP snooping is monitoring.

53. D. Any service that allows the user to create a connection or access to information can be used as an attack vector. In the case of DHCP, the attacker will set the gateway to their IP address. In the case of DNS, the attacker could spoof a request to redirect the traffic.

54. D. The default mode of switchports on a switch configured with DHCP snooping is untrusted. An admin must trust ports manually.

55. A. The default native VLAN for Cisco switches is VLAN 1.

56. C. Ports that are connecting to trusted infrastructure devices such as routers and switches should be trusted. This is because legitimate DHCP traffic could originate from these ports.

57. C. The untrusted ports drop Offer and Acknowledgment DHCP messages. The only device that should offer and acknowledge IP addresses is the DHCP server on a trusted port.

58. A. Double tagging is an attack that can be used against the native VLAN. The attacker will tag the native VLAN on a frame and then tag another inside that frame for the VLAN that the attacker intends to compromise. When the switch receives the first frame, it removes the default VLAN tag and forwards it to other switches via a trunk port. When the other switch receives the frame with the second VLAN tag, it forwards it to the VLAN which the attacker is targeting the attack upon.

59. D. The command show ip dhcp snooping binding will display the DHCP snooping database. This database will have entries for the MAC address, IP address, lease time, VLAN, and interface.

60. A. The command ip dhcp snooping trust will configure the interface as a trusted port.

61. C. The native VLAN is the default configuration on all switches. It is very possible that a user could be configured by accident for the native VLAN of 1. This would allow management access to switching and routing.

62. C. 802.1x allows selective access to a network at layer 2. It allows this on the switch because the switch acts as an authenticator to an AAA server, only allowing access after the user or device has been authenticated.

63. B. The end device that sends credentials is called the supplicant. The supplicant is a piece of software in the operating system that supplies the credentials for AAA authentication.

64. A. The switch is responsible for communicating with the supplicant and sending information to the authenticating server. This device is called the authenticator.

65. A. The protocol used to communicate between the supplicants (OS) and the authenticator (switch) is 802.1x. 802.1x is a layer 2 protocol used specifically for authenticating devices to switch ports.

66. B. VLAN hopping is an attack in which DTP is exploited. The attacker negotiates a trunk with the switch via DTP and can hop from VLAN to VLAN.

67. C. EAP, or Extensible Authentication Protocol, is used for authentication between the supplicant and RADIUS server. The EAP frame is first transmitted over the layer 2 connection via EAP over LAN (EAPoL). The switch then sends it to the RADIUS server encapsulated in a UDP packet.

68. A. The device requesting access is the supplicant. The supplicant is built into the operating system in which it is authenticating.

69. B. EAP-TLS, or Extensible Authentication Protocol/Transport Layer Security, uses certificates to authenticate end devices. It also provides a layer of encryption via the certificate infrastructure.

70. C. The AAA server listens for requests on port 1812 UDP for authentication of credentials.

71. A. Standard access lists are within the range of 1 to 99.

72. C. Access control lists can be based upon only the source address of the packet.

73. C. Extended access lists are within the range of 100 to 199.

74. B. At the end of every access list there is a deny any any rule. If a permit is not configured in the access list, the ACL does not serve a purpose. All ACLs must contain at least one permit statement.

75. B. When packets are compared to an access control list, they are compared in a sequential order. When the first rule is found to match, the action is acted upon. There is no further rule processing after the first match.

76. B. An advantage to a standard access control list is that they require less processing overhead from the ASIC or CPU (depending on the platform). Since they only inspect layer 3 headers, no further decapsulation is required for layer 4.

77. C. The expanded range of a standard access list is 1300 to 1999.

78. C. A wildcard mask is the opposite of a network mask. The easy way to calculate a wildcard mask is to figure out what the subnet is and deduct 1 for the octet. For example, if the network address is 172.16.0.0/12 (Classless Inter-Domain Routing), or 255.240.0.0 (Dotted Decimal Notation), and each network number is a multiple of 16, the wildcard mask should be 0.15.255.255.

79. A. The command ip access-list 20 192.168.1.0 0.0.0.255 will configure an access list of 20, which is a standard access list. The source address of 192.168.1.0 is wildcard masked with 0.0.0.255.

80. D. A rule with an address or 0.0.0.0 and wildcard mask of 255.255.255.255 defines all addresses. Effectively, it is another way to specify the "any" source or destination.

81. D. Access lists can be applied per a port, per a protocol, and per a direction. For example, you could apply only one ACL per the interface of Fast 0/1, per the protocol of IP in the inbound direction.

82. B. An extended access list allows you to filter traffic by port, which defines an application being used, since web traffic is communicated on 80 or 443.

83. D. The expanded range of a standard access list is 2000 to 2699.

84. C. A wildcard mask is the opposite of a network mask. The easy way to calculate a wildcard mask is to figure out what the subnet is and deduct 1 for the octet. For example, if the network address is 192.168.1.0/25 (Classless Inter-Domain Routing), or 255.255.255.128 (Dotted Decimal Notation), and each network number is a multiple of 128, the wildcard mask should be 0.0.0.127.

85. D. A named access control list allows for removing and adding entries by their line number.

86. B. Once a successful login is performed at the router, the dynamic access control list is activated. This is also called lock and key security.

87. A. The statement access-list 20 deny 172.16.0.0 0.255.255.255 configures a standard access list for two reasons: the first is that the access list number is 20, which falls between the standard access list range of 1 to 99. The second reason is that you are depicting traffic by source address.

88. C. The command access-list 5 permit host 192.168.1.5 specifies the traffic coming from the host 192.168.1.5. The statement access-list 5 permit 192.168.1 .5 0.0.0.0 achieves the same thing.

89. B. The command access-list 101 deny tcp host 192.168.2.6 host 192.168.1.3 eq 80 denies access from the host 192.168.2.3 to the host 192.168.1.6 for port 80. The next command, access-list 101 permit ip any any, allows all IP traffic from any to any. With extended access lists, the protocol needs to be described.

90. D. Standard access lists only allow you to describe traffic by source address. This helps the processing of the access list because the router or switch does not need to de-capsulate packets further than layer 3.

91. D. The command access-list 199 deny tcp any host 192.168.1.5 eq 22 will create an extended access list of 199 and deny TCP communication from any computer to the host of 192.168.1.5 for port 22.

92. C. An extended access list is required because you want to block by the destination address of the HR web application server. If you blocked only by source, then all host network traffic would be blocked to all servers.

93. C. The command access-list 143 permit tcp host 192.168.8.3 eq 80 any is a valid statement. All extended access lists that describe a port must also describe the protocol.

94. D. The command ip access-group 198 in will apply access list 198 to the interface in which it is configured in the inbound direction.

95. D. The access list must be placed on the Gi0/2 interface outbound. Whenever you are evaluating access list placement, remember that packets are evaluated as they leave the interface, which is outbound. When packets enter the interface, they are evaluated inbound. It is always in the perspective of the router.

96. D. The command `show ip access-list` will show all access lists with the line numbers. If the command is specific, such as `show ip access-list named_list`, you will see the ACL lines but no line numbers.

97. A. Extended ACLs should always be placed closest to the source of traffic since they are extremely granular.

98. C. The command `ip access-list extended named_list` will create an extended named access list.

99. B. Standard ACLs should always be placed closest to the destination of traffic since they are broad in the traffic they control.

100. C. The command `no 10` when configured under the named access list will remove only line 10 on the access list.

101. D. The command `ip access-list resequence named_list 10 10` will resequence the line numbers for the named access list called named_list. The numbering will start with 10 and increment by 10.

102. D. The command `ip access-group named_list in` configured inside of the interface will apply an access list called named_list to the interface for the inbound direction.

103. B. The command `ip access-list 6 deny 192.168.1.0 0.0.0.255` will block the internal server network. Then the command `ip access-list 6 permit any` will allow everything else. We then apply this to the interface Serial 0/0 for the direction of outbound. The final result is that the servers will be able to talk internally and not allowed out to the Internet.

104. D. IPv6 access lists are created as named access lists. The command `ipv6 access-list named_list` will create an IPv6 named access list.

105. B. IPv6 access control lists implicitly allow Neighbor Discovery packets. This is to facilitate a number of features that IPv6 has built in, such as SLAAC and DAD.

106. C. The command `show ip interface fast 0/1` will show the IP address details of the interface Fast 0/1. Included with these details you will find any outbound and inbound ACLs set on the interface.

107. A. Using the command `remark` followed by the text is a way of adding notes in an ACL. This particular example is a named access list. However, remarks can also be used in traditional ACLs using a similar syntax in lieu of the permit and deny.

108. D. The command `show access-list` will show the number of matches for each statement. This command also works for IPv6 access lists.

109. B. The command `ip access-list 101 permit tcp host 192.168.1.6 any eq 80 log` will permit traffic from host 192.168.1.6 to any matching packets on port 80. When the `log` attribute is configured on the end of the command, the router or switch will send a syslog notification each time the packet is matched to the rule.

110. D. Since NDP (Neighbor Discovery Protocol) is used for finding the gateway, Duplicate Address Detection, and Stateless Address Autoconfiguration, all of these functions would be impacted.

111. D. The Path Trace tool was first debuted in version 1.0 of the APIC-EM (Application Policy Infrastructure Controller Enterprise Module). However, the ACL Analysis tool was not added as an option until version 1.2.

112. B. Before performing a path trace ACL analysis, you must perform an environment discovery on your network topology.

113. B. The Path Trace ACL Analysis tool is a basic application. Basic applications do not require licensing, similar to the APIC-EM itself. Solution applications are licensed apps from Cisco and third parties; both run on top of the base controller.

114. C. The APIC-EM is a Cisco Development Network (DevNet) tool. It requires a login to the Cisco DevNet site. This is because the APIC-EM is a tool you can use to create applications for network management.

115. C. The red square *X* means that router ISR4451X-A is blocking the destination traffic with an ACL.

116. A. The APIC-EM Path Trace ACL Analysis tool is used for end-to-end analysis of ACLs via the path an imaginary packet will take.

117. A. When performing path trace ACL analysis, you first start by selecting the Path Trace option. On the next screen, you select the ACL Analysis option, which will help you perform the ACL analysis.

118. C. When performing a path trace ACL analysis, you must select the starting device and end device as well at the egress port and ingress port. The path of analysis will be calculated by the tool.

119. A. The green square check means that router ISR4451X-A has a matching ACL, which is permitting the destination traffic.

120. C. If a packet is blocked, the analysis output will show you the access control entry (ACE) in the ACL that is blocking the packet.

121. C. The command `enable secret Password20!` will set the enable password and encrypt the *Password20!* password.

122. D. The command `line vty 0 5` will enter you into the line for the virtual teletype, which is where you configure your Telnet password.

123. B. If the enable password is set and the `enable secret` is set, the enable password will be ignored. Therefore the `enable secret` is being used to authenticate the user, and you are typing the wrong password. The command enable password exists for backward compatibility with pre 10.3 IOS and should no longer be used.

124. C. The command password Password20! will set the login password to *Password20!*. The sub-command login will require login for the line.

125. C. The line login password is not set when you receive the error Password required, but none set. If the enable secret was not set, you would just not be able to get to a privilege exec prompt, but still be able to get to a user exec prompt.

126. B. The hostname and domain name are required before you attempt to generate the encryption keys for SSH.

127. A. The command ip ssh version 2 will set your SSH version to 2. This command is to be entered at a global configuration prompt.

128. C. The command transport ssh telnet will configure the VTY line to accept SSH as a login protocol and fallback to Telnet.

129. D. SSH is encrypted and Telnet is in clear text. To keep passwords and configuration safe, SSH should always be used.

130. C. You must first create an access list to permit the host that will manage the router or switch with the command access-list 1 permit host 192.168.1.5. Then enter the VTY line in which it will be applied with the command line vty 0 5. Then apply it with the command ip access-class 1 in, which differs from the command ip access-group, which is used on interfaces.

131. B. When you're configuring a switch or router for SSH version 2, the key strength must be at least 768 bits for the modulus. The default is 512 bits, and it is standard practice to double the number to 1024 bits.

132. A. The command username user1 password Password20! will create a user account called user1 with a password of *Password20!*.

133. B. The command service password-encryption should be entered in global config. It should not be kept in the configuration as it will use CPU cycles. So after it is configured, you should perform a show running-configuration to double-check if the encryption worked and then perform a no service password-encryption to turn it off.

134. B. The command crypto key generate rsa will generate the encryption keys for SSH. You will be asked for the key strength, called the modulus, which should be over 768 bits to support SSH version 2.

135. A. The command exec-timeout 0 0 will disable auto-disconnect of idle privileged exec sessions.

136. B. The line on which you are connected is always preceded by an asterisk. In this example, you are connected to the router via line VTY 0.

137. D. After configuring the username and password combinations that will be used on the switch or router, you will need to configure the line(s) that will use local authentication. The command used inside of the line is `login local`. This will apply to all the transport methods configured on the line.

138. D. The command `enable algorithm-type scrypt secret Password20!` will change the enable password to *Password20!* and use the scrypt algorithm type.

139. D. The default for encryption method for passwords configured for lines is clear text. If you want to encrypt the password, you should use the `service password-encryption` command.

140. B. The command `exec-timeout 30 0` will change the idle time to 30 minutes and zero seconds. If a privileged exec session is idle for 30 minutes, the network admin will be disconnected.

141. D. The command `clear line vty 2` will disconnect a remote admin connected to the switch. Nothing stops the admin from reconnecting to the switch again.

142. C. The exec banner will display a message to authenticated users who have successfully logged in, regardless of whether they are connected via Telnet or SSH.

143. B. The login banner will be displayed during initial connection to a Cisco device via SSH.

144. C. The command `banner login ^CCNA Routing and Switching^` will configure the login banner to read "CCNA Routing and Switching." The marks at the beginning and end of the text are delimiters to mark the beginning and end of the banner.

145. A. When a user is connecting to a router via SSH, the MOTD banner is not displayed until after the user has authenticated to the router or switch. A login banner is always displayed pre-login.

146. B. The AAA server will centralize authentication for Cisco routers and switches. AAA stands for authentication, authorization, and accounting. It is pronounced "triple A."

147. B. RADIUS authentication uses the UDP protocol and port 1645 for communications between the switch or router and the AAA server.

148. B. TACACS+ (Terminal Access Controller Access Control System) is a protocol used for communications between a switch or router and the AAA server for authenticating users.

149. D. TACACS+ uses TCP and port 49 for communications between the switch or router and the AAA server.

150. C. TACACS+ is a Cisco defined protocol. One of the useful features it has is that it can authenticate a user and only allow that user to access certain commands on the router or switch.

151. A. The command `aaa authentication login default group tacacs+ local` will configure AAA authentication for login using the default list and a group of TACACS+ servers for TACACS+ login first and a backup of local for authentication.

152. C. The router will lock you out since you have not provided a local account to log in with. The password recovery procedure would need to be performed if the configuration was saved.

153. B. The local second method should always be configured. This will ensure that if the router's connection to the AAA server is down, you can still gain access to diagnose or repair.

154. B. The command `radius-server host 192.168.1.5 key aaaauth` will configure the radius server 192.168.1.5 with a secret key of aaaauth.

155. D. The TACACS+ protocol will encrypt the entire packet from the switch or router to the AAA server.

Chapter 7: Infrastructure Management (Domain 7)

1. C. The introduction of SNMP version 2c added the Inform and Get-bulk messages for SNMP.

2. A. SNMP uses UDP port 161 for communication from an SNMP network management station to a network device for information requests.

3. D. SNMP version 3 introduced message integrity, authentication, and encryption to the SNMP suite.

4. B. The management information base, or MIB, is a database of variables in which SNMP allows retrieval of information. The attributes in the MIB are the description, variable type, and read-write status.

5. B. The network management station (NMS) is a server to which SNMP is polled back or in which SNMP information is trapped. The NMS can escalate problems via email, text message, or even visual indicators. Examples of NMS systems are Tivoli Netcool and OpenNMS.

6. D. Trap messages are sent from the network device to the SNMP network management station when an event has triggered over a set threshold on the device. An example of an event to be trapped is an interface going down or a restriction by port security.

7. A. Object IDs are the variables that make up the management information base. Each object has a unique ID in a hierarchical format in the form of a tree. As an example, 1.3.6.1.4.9.2.1.58.0 is the object that holds the router CPU utilization variable.

8. D. Inform messages differ from trap messages with respect to acknowledgment. Trap messages employ a best effort delivery utilizing UDP. Inform messages employ acknowledgment; while they use the User Datagram Protocol (UDP), they rely on the Application layer for acknowledgment.

9. C. SNMP version 2c is identical to SNMP version 1 with respect to security. Both transmit information in clear text and use the security of community strings to authenticate users for access to information.

10. D. The command `snmp-server community snmpreadonly ro` will configure the SNMP agent with a community of "snmpreadonly" and set it to read only.

11. B. Standard access control lists can be used in conjunction with the SNMP agent configuration. First a standard ACL is created containing the NMS IP. Then, when the `snmp-server` command is used, it becomes the last argument. For example, a standard ACL of 2 would be added as follows: `snmp-server community snmpreadonly read-only 2`.

12. B. The command `snmp-server contact Sybex Publishing` will configure the contact information for the device. This information is polled into the network management station along with the `snmp-server location`. It is used in case of an outage so that the responsible person can be notified.

13. C. The command `snmp-server host 192.168.1.5 version 2c C0mmun1ty` will configure the SNMP agent to send traps to the host 192.168.1.5. The `version 2c C0mmun1ty` sets the SNMP version to 2c and the community to "C0mmun1ty".

14. B. The command `show snmp community` will display all of the configured SNMP community strings along with the applied access control list.

15. C. SNMP uses UDP port 162 for communication from an SNMP agent to the network management station for trap and inform messages.

16. C. The command `show snmp host` will display the host that is configured to receive notifications of trap or inform messages from the router or switch.

17. B. When you begin to configure SNMPv3 for a restricted OID, the first step is configuring a view. The view allows or restricts what the user will have access to.

18. C. When you're configuring the SNMPv3 group, the `priv` parameter will configure privacy, which defines authentication and encryption. An example of the command is `snmp-server group1 v3 priv read view1 access read`.

19. A. The command `snmp-server view INT-VIEW ifIndex include` will configure an SNMPv3 view named INT-VIEW. The two parameters `ifIndex include` will include the ifIndex OID. This can also be expressed as the numerical OID four, but if it is expressed in word form, it is case sensitive.

20. C. The command `show snmp user` will display all SNMPv3 users. In the output you will find the group name, the authentication protocol, and the encryption protocol.

21. B. The command `show snmp group` will display all SNMPv3 groups. In the output, you will find the group name and the defined read view, write view, and notify view.

22. D. The router or switch sends syslog messages to the syslog server on port 514 with UDP.

23. C. The command `logging host 192.168.1.6` will configure all logs to be sent to the syslog server 192.168.1.6.

24. A. The command `show logging` will display the configured syslog server and the current severity level, for logs to be sent to the syslog server.

25. C. The command `logging trap debugging` will configure syslog events to be sent to the syslog server for the severity levels of debugging(7) through emergency(0).

26. D. A service-level agreement (SLA) is a contracted agreement between the Internet service provider (ISP) and the customer. This agreement defines the level of service. SLAs are based on uptime, quality of service, bandwidth, and any other stipulations the customer might deem necessary. Uptime is usually the most important when shopping for a provider.

27. A. The IP service-level agreement (IP SLA) feature in a Cisco router provides the network administrator with statistics on the performance, uptime, and monitoring of the provider's network connections.

28. C. Only Cisco routers contain the IP SLA feature; therefore, it can only be configured on Cisco routers for statistic collection. Switches with the LAN Base feature set can be used as responders, but they will lack the ability for the statistic collection.

29. C. The IP SLA responder in not required for ICMP echo testing. However, having an IP SLA responder allows for collection of more statistics.

30. D. The term used for the IP SLA router that sends packets and collects and compiles statistics on the packet is *IP SLA source*. The IP SLA source sends these packets to the IP SLA responder.

31. B. When you're configuring an IP SLA for ICMP echo, the first statement, `ip sla 1`, will configure the IP SLA operation. This command will present an IP SLA sub-configuration prompt, where you will enter `icmp-echo 192.168.1.2`. This command configures the ICMP echo probe to a destination of 192.168.1.2.

32. A. The default timer for an IP SLA ICMP echo probe is 60 seconds. This can be overridden with the `frequency {time in seconds}` command.

33. B. The command `ip sla 1 schedule life forever start-time now` will configure the IP SLA operation of 1 to run forever and start immediately. Using this command, you could create a schedule to start the probe during business hours and run it for a finite period of time. This command must be configured in global config mode.

34. C. The command `show ip sla history 1` will display the historical statistics collected from the ICMP echo probe for IP SLA operation 1. The command will allow you to see all of the buckets that were collected. The command `ip sla statistics 1` will only show the last collected bucket's statistical summary.

35. B. The Sense column of the statistics is the result code for the test. There are 10 different response codes, but only a few should be remembered. A result code of 1 means the test was OK, a result of 3 means the test was over the threshold, and a result code of 4 means the operation timed out and a response was not received.

36. C. The command `show file systems` will display all of the file storage types connected to the switch or router. In this output, the size in bits and the free space in bits will be displayed.

37. B. The start-configuration for the router or switch is stored in non-volatile random-access memory (NVRAM). This memory is similar to flash memory in that it retains data well after the power is removed from the device.

38. A. The command copy running-config startup-config will copy the running-config in RAM to the startup-config in NVRAM.

39. D. The command erase startup-config will erase the startup-config from NVRAM. The only copy left after that command is configured is in RAM. Once the power is removed, the RAM will be erased as well.

40. C. The command dir flash: will display all of the IOS images stored in the flash filesystem. The command show flash: will work also, but read-write attributes will be omitted.

41. C. The command copy startup-config tftp: will ask for the Trivial File Transfer Protocol (TFTP) server address, source filename, and destination filename. It will then proceed to copy the file over the network to the TFTP server.

42. C. The command copy tftp: running-config will ask for the TFTP server address, source filename, and destination filename. It will then proceed to copy the file over the network from the TFTP server.

43. A. All Cisco devices by default participate in the Cisco Discovery Protocol (CDP). By using CDP, you can begin mapping the network one node at a time, discovering all the nodes attached.

44. D. The command show cdp neighbors detail will display the IP addresses of the routers and switches connected to the current router. The show ip route command will only show the data plane IP addresses and not the management plane IP addresses.

45. B. By default, Cisco devices do not participate in Link Layer Discovery Protocol (LLDP). The first command that needs to be configured is lldp run, which starts the switch participating in LLDP. You then need to enter the command show lldp neighbors detail in the privileged exec mode prompt. This command will show all of the neighboring LLDP devices.

46. A. The term used to describe Cisco's current IOS image naming convention, which contains all the feature sets, is *universal image*. The universal image contains all of the features sets available, and a feature set can be "turned on" by providing a license key.

47. B. A current SMARTnet contract is required to download the latest IOS for your Cisco router or switch. SMARTnet contracts provide configuration support, parts replacement, and software maintenance on Cisco devices.

48. C. An activation key is required to activate the features, which are already installed in the universal image. SMARTnet agreements only cover you for upgrades to the IP Base IOS. They do not provide upgrades of features sets called Technology Package Licenses.

49. B. The Cisco License Manager (CLM) can be installed on Windows, Solaris, or Linux. It allows for discovery of Cisco devices and inventory of Cisco device licenses and connects to Cisco for access to current and new licenses purchased. The CLM allows for management of the software activation process through its user interface.

50. C. The command show license udi will display the product ID (PID) and the unique device identifier (UDI). Both the PID and UDI are required when activating a license from Cisco's license portal. The Cisco license portal will email or display the license key required to unlock the feature set purchased.

51. A. The command show license feature will display a matrix of all the features in the IOS, including the enforcement, evaluation, subscription, enabled, and right to use status.

52. B. A right-to-use license will allow a customer to evaluate a feature set for 60 days. After the 60-day period is expired, the feature set will remain active. However, after 60 days the customer is in violation of the license agreement if the feature set has not been purchased.

53. C. The command logging synchronous will configure console logging messages to synchronize with what is being typed so they will not disrupt the user's input.

54. B. The command clock timezone pst -8 will set the time zone to Pacific Standard Time with an offset of −8 from Coordinated Universal Time (UTC).

55. B. The command logging trap 4 will trap all messages with warnings to the syslog server.

56. D. The command service timestamps log datetime will configure syslog messages to be logged with the date and time rather than the arbitrary sequence number.

57. C. The command clock summer-time EDT recurring will configure the switch for Eastern Daylight Time (EDT).

58. A. The command logging console 0 will configure the logging to the console for the severity level of facility 0, which is alerts.

59. C. You should configure a loopback interface on the switch with the IP address of the NTP server the NTP clients will use. Although a Switched Virtual Interface (SVI) would work, it is not active until at least one port is configured with the VLAN. Therefore, the SVI is still tied to a physical interface state.

60. A. The command ntp source loopback 0 will configure the NTP service to respond to clients from the source address of the loopback 0 interface.

61. B. The command interface loopback 0 will configure and create a pseudo interface called loopback 0. The loopback number must be specified and the loopback should not overlap a loopback already configured. The command ip address 192.168.1.2 255.255.255.0 will configure the IP address on the loopback interface.

62. A. The command logging buffered 1 will configure the logs stored in RAM, which is buffered to a severity of 1. This command will include severity levels 1 and 0.

63. C. The command show history will show the last commands typed, which are kept in the buffer. The history normally includes the last 10 commands.

64. D. The command `history size 30` will extend the buffer to 30 commands for all users. This command must be configured on the line, such as the console or VTY.

65. A. The command `terminal history size 30` will extend the buffer to 30 commands for the current session. This command is configured in the privileged exec prompt and is only active until the user logs out.

66. C. The command `hostname PGH-4-209` will set the name of the router (before the prompt) to PGH-4-209. It is always advisable to create a name that is least specific to most specific from left to right. For example, PGH is the city, 4 is the building, and 209 is the room number where the equipment is located.

67. B. Pressing the key combination of Ctrl+A will take you to the beginning of a command string.

68. C. Pressing the key combination of Ctrl+E will take you to the end of a command string.

69. A. The command `enable`, sometimes shortened to `en` by seasoned Cisco admins, will allow you to enter into privileged exec mode. In privileged exec mode, you can change configuration.

70. A. When a router or switch boots and contains no startup-config, it will boot into setup mode. In setup mode, you can perform a basic setup of the management IP address and interface IP addresses. It is limited in its step-by-step configuration and can be useful in adding a quick IP address initially for management.

71. B. The key combination of Ctrl+Z will escape you back to privileged exec mode from configuration. If you are in a sub-configuration dialog, you would have to type `exit` several times to exit back to privileged exec mode. However, if you use Ctrl+Z, you will immediately exit back to privileged exec mode.

72. C. The command `show clock` will display the local time of the switch along with the date.

73. C. The command `description Connection to Switch1` will create a note that describes what the interface is for. The `description` command is useful in explaining what an interface connects to or providing service information in the case of an outage. Only one description can be used per interface.

74. B. The command `do show running-config` will allow you to "do" a command outside of the configuration prompt. This command was first introduced in IOS version 12.3.

75. D. The command `show running-config | include snmp` will show the running-config and only include lines that match `snmp`. Seasoned Cisco admins usually shorten this to `show running-config | i snmp`, since there are no other commands that start with the letter *i* after the pipe parameter.

76. C. The command `show running-config interface gi 3/45` will show the running-configuration for only interface Gi3/45.

77. B. The command `clock set 2:24:00 1 august 2016` will set the clock to 2:24 a.m. (24-hour format) and August 1, 2016.

78. A. The interface Gig 0/1 is used for the interface of es-switch2, which connects cs-main .ntw via its interface of Gig 0/40.

79. D. The device has the capability of both a switch and a router. It is most likely a switch that is performing SVI routing or has routing enabled.

80. C. The command show cdp neighbors detail will display all connected switches along with their IP addresses, hostnames, and IOS version. If this command is used from the central switch, you can quickly assess which switches need to be upgraded.

81. D. The command configure terminal allows you to enter global configuration mode. This command will enable editing of the RAM configuration, also known as the running-config. The command is usually shortened to conf t.

82. B. The command show terminal will allow you to verify the configured exec timeout. It will also display the current history size and the size of paging for output.

83. C. The Ctrl+Shift+6 key sequence will cause a break during a network command such as ping or traceroute.

84. A. The command show version will display the serial number of the switch or router. This is usually required when calling into support to open a support ticket.

85. D. The command show running-config | begin 4/45 will show the running-config and begin when the text *4/45* is found. It is important to note that after the | begin, everything is case sensitive.

86. A. The command copy tftp flash will begin an interactive upgrade dialog. The dialog will ask for the IP address of the TFTP server, the source filename on the TFTP server, and the destination filename. It will then begin transferring the image.

87. C. The command dir flash: will display the current images on the flash memory. It will also display how big the flash memory is and how much space is still free in bytes.

88. C. The command verify /md5 flash:/c2900-universalk9-mz.SPA.151-4.M4.bin eef3f723c164f2af84ccfcbd642d121d will verify the image specified for the MD5 hash included as the last parameter. The MD5 hash is always included with the image from Cisco's download center and is unique for each image.

89. B. The default configuration register for a Cisco switch or router is 0x2102. The configuration register tells the router to boot up normally and check the NVRAM for the IOS image to boot.

90. B. The command ip scp server enable needs to be configured to enable the SSH Copy Protocol (SCP). This command is entered in the global configuration.

91. D. The SSH Copy Protocol (SCP) will encrypt the IOS over the network during an upgrade from the client computer.

92. C. The command username scpadmin privilege-level 15 password sybex must be configured. This command will configure a user named scpadmin with a privilege level of 15 (enable access) and a password of *Sybex*.

93. D. The command `more flash:/info` will display the contents of the `flash:/info` file. This command is similar to the `type` command in the Windows OS.

94. A. The command `boot system flash:/c2900-universalk9-mz.SPA.151-4.M4.bin` will configure the system to boot from flash and load the image `c2900-universalk9-mz.SPA.151-4.M4.bin`.

95. C. The command `config-register 0x2100` will configure the configuration register to 0x2100. This command must be entered in global configuration mode.

96. C. The command `show version` will display the current configuration register. If you have just set the configuration register, it will state `on next reload` which will appear next to the configured configuration register.

97. D. When a router or switch fails to load its primary IOS image, it is reverted to a basic system called ROMMON, which stands for ROM Monitor. The ROMMON has very limited functionality, and it's mainly used for password recovery or diagnostics of the boot process.

98. A. The bootstrap process checks the startup-config in NVRAM for the `boot system` command. Although the startup-config is not loaded into the IOS at this point, the router or switch uses the startup-config to decide the IOS to load. The bootstrap process checks the configuration register, but the IOS version to load is not determined from the configuration register.

99. B. The command `boot system flash:/c2900-universalk9-mz.SPA.151-4.M4.bin` needs to be in the startup-config since it is used during the boot process. If you enter the command in global configuration mode, it is only resident in RAM (running-config) and needs to be saved before power cycling the router.

100. B. Cisco routers and switches have a built-in archive process, which is not configured by default. You can specify a time period to process the archive and specify to write the running-config to NVRAM. An added benefit is the second archive copy, which is saved with a time and date stamp to flash or a remote server.

101. D. The command `boot system c2900-universalk9-mz.SPA.151-4.M4 .bin 192.168.1.2` will configure the router for booting of the image named `c2900-universalk9-mz.SPA.151-4.M4.bin` from the 192.168.1.2 TFTP server. Under normal circumstances this should not be used in production environments since the router boot process is dependent upon the availability of the TFTP server.

102. B. During the bootstrap process, the IOS is decompressed to RAM. This can be seen during the boot process as `Loading "flash:/c3560-advipservicesk9-mz.122-37 .SE1.bin"...######`. Once the image is decompressed, it is executed by the CPU.

103. C. When you're performing a password recovery, the 6th bit of the configuration register should be set to a binary value of 1. The configuration register of 0x2142 will instruct the router to boot into the configured IOS and ignore loading the startup configuration.

104. B. The command `show version` will display the current running IOS version. Although the command `show running-config` or `show bootvar` will display the

IOS that should be loaded, only the command show version will display the current version that actually loaded.

105. B. The IOS is stored on the flash card. Since the flash card is brand-new, nothing is on it. When the router boots, it will not find the IOS and will boot into ROMMON mode. From ROMMON mode, you will configure an IP address, subnet mask, gateway, TFTP server, and image and initiate a TFTP download to flash. Once the IOS is downloaded to flash memory, you can boot the router and verify operations.

106. B. The command copy flash:/c3560-advipservicesk9-mz.122-37.SE1.bin tftp will copy the file in flash named c3560-advipservicesk9-mz.122-37.SE1.bin to a TFTP server. This command will enter an interactive copy procedure. You will have to enter the TFTP server address and confirm the source image filename and destination image filename.

107. A. The command show archive will display all of the archived versions of the running-config, which were archived by the archive timer.

108. B. The command configure replace flash:myconfig-3 will replace the running-config with the third archive of the running-config, which is stored in flash.

109. D. The command time-period 1440 will specify that the archive command runs every 1440 minutes, or 24 hours. This command must be configured in the archive process configuration.

110. A. Cisco routers and switches require any USB flash drive to be formatted in the FAT filesystem. Any other file system will not be recognized and mounted in the IOS on the router or switch.

111. A. The command terminal monitor will configure the current connected method with the ability to monitor console messages. This command is entered in privileged exec mode and is valid only for the current session.

112. B. The command terminal no monitor when entered in privileged exec mode will turn off the monitoring of console messages.

113. B. When you are diagnosing a network connectivity issue, you always start testing the closest IP address. In this case, the default gateway of Router A is the closest IP address. The switch is irrelevant because it is not a layer 3 device that can be tested at layer 3. The fact that it has an IP address and can return a ping means that you can communicate with its management plane, not the data plane.

114. C. The command debug ip packet will turn on debugging for IP packets. The output will display the exit interface that the traffic is taking, to include the source and destination IP addresses. This command should be used with caution because it could create high CPU utilization on the router. It is recommended to be used with an ACL.

115. B. Switch Port Analyzer (SPAN) should be used to mirror the port on the switch so that the network analyzer can capture the frames. When you use SPAN, you will see every frame on the switch port you are monitoring.

116. B. The third hop (router) is not responding to ICMP echo requests. The traceroute completes since the fourth hop responded and the user did not need to perform a break on the command.

117. B. Wireshark is a popular free packet capture utility. Once the packets are captured, they can be filtered and analyzed so that you can diagnose a networking problem.

118. D. An extended ping allows for the source interface or IP address to be specified. You can access the extended ping by entering the command ping without an IP address, then following the prompt till it asks if you want extended commands.

119. C. The command monitor session 1 source interface gi 1/11 both will create a monitor session 1 for SPAN, with the source interface in both directions. This session will capture and mirror frames for tx (transmit) and rx (receive) on the interface.

120. B. The command show monitor session all will display all of the SPAN session configured on the switch. The output will display the source port and destination port of the SPAN session.

121. A. The command monitor session 1 source vlan 23 will configure the SPAN session of 1 with a source of VLAN 23. When you're configuring a VLAN as the source of a SPAN session, the direction is irrelevant since the parameter of both is implied.

122. B. The sizing of the destination port should be equal to the amount of bandwidth that the source ports collectively can generate. When performing this calculation, you must take into account both the RX and TX. For example, five Fast Ethernet ports can transmit at 5×100 Mb/s = 500 Mb/s. They can also receive at 500 Mb/s since you are capturing both directions. The proper sizing of the destination port should be 1 Gb/s so that traffic is not lost out of the exit interface for the packet capture device.

123. C. The command no monitor session 1 will remove the currently configured monitor session of 1 from the configuration.

124. D. The command monitor session 1 destination interface gi 1/14 will configure the interface of Gi1/14 as the destination interface for the SPAN session. The direction can be omitted because it is specified on the source interface. The destination interface will receive a copy of the frames that are configured on the source interface.

125. D. The details of the output show that monitor session 1 is configured to capture interface Fa0/1 and VLAN 2 in both directions. The destination interface is Fa 0/2.

126. A. Remote Switch Port Analyzer (RSPAN) should be configured. This will allow a source port on a remote switch to be monitored for a SPAN session on another remote switch. An alternative to RSPAN is Encapsulated RSPAN (ERSPAN), which employs the GRE protocol to create a tunnel.

127. A. The probe count attribute must be changed to allow multiple packets to be sent to each hop. The default is three packets.

128. B. Line protocol up/down messages are logged to the Notifications severity level. This can be determined by looking up the 5 that appears after the affected component of line protocol in the syslog severity chart. For example %LINEPROTO-5-UPDOWN specifies the severity level of 5 for the line protocol.

129. C. The command show processes will display the utilization of the CPU. The first line of the output is broken down by 5 second utilization, 1 minute utilization, and 5 minute utilization.

130. A. The command logging buffered will direct buffering of log messages to RAM. This command can be undone by using the no directive in front of logging buffered. The command must be entered in global configuration mode.

131. B. The control plane refers to any mechanism that controls the data plane. Spanning Tree Protocol (STP) is used to control the data plane by removing redundant links.

132. C. The management plane is any mechanism that helps in the management of a router or switch. Some of the common mechanisms are SSH and Telnet. However, any mechanism that the router uses for management is considered part of the management plane.

133. C. The software-defined network (SDN) controller replaces the control plane on SDN devices. The SDN devices in the network do not contain a control plane locally and instead are controlled by the SDN controller.

134. B. The southbound interface (SBI) directly communicates with the SDN devices. This control is done via several different types of SBI protocols, such as OpenFlow, OpFlex, CLI (Telnet/SSH).

135. C. An application program interface (API) is a method the programmer has created to allow other programs to communicate with their program. The inter-programmability is required when another program wants to share data with the API.

136. A. The data plane is responsible for switching and routing data. Any data that is destined for endpoints is switched or routed on the data plane. For example, when one computer pings another, the ping is switched and routed on the data plane.

137. C. The northbound interface (NBI) is responsible for allowing communication between applications and the core of the controller. Applications therefore directly communicate with the core through the northbound interface.

138. B. Representational State Transfer (REST) APIs normally utilize HTTP for moving data. It performs this via a get URI and it receives a response in XML, JSON, or another date transfer language. Although you can encrypt the HTTP traffic with SSL (HTTPS), its core language is still HTTP.

139. A. The Application Policy Infrastructure Controller (APIC) is Cisco's SDN controller. This package is freely downloadable from the Cisco DevNet website as of the writing of this book. It comes with several built-in apps, such as a plug and play module and a path trace module. Many other apps can be built on top of the APIC to extend functionality of the controller.

140. B. Routing protocols such as OSPF and EIGRP would perform their function on the control plane, since they are controlling the routing of the data plane.

Chapter 8: Practice Test 1

1. B. Structured Query Language (SQL) operates at the Session layer of the OSI model. It uses half-duplex communications to request data and receive the reply. Other examples of Session layer protocols are Network File System (NFS), Server Message Block (SMB), and NetBIOS.

2. D. The 802.11ac protocol will be least likely to overlap the wireless channels the tenants are using. The 802.11ac protocol uses the 5 GHz wireless frequency spectrum. The 5 GHz spectrum defines 24 non-overlapping wireless channels. The 2.4 GHz spectrum defines 11 channels, but only 3 of them are non-overlapping. Although 802.11n operates on 2.4 GHz and 5 GHz, 802.11ac only operates on 5 GHz. Therefore, 802.11ac will have the least likely overlap of current channels.

3. C. Flow control is a function of the Transport layer of the Open Systems Interconnection (OSI) model. User Datagram Protocol (UDP) operates at the Transport layer. UDP provides a program with a connectionless method of transmitting segments. TCP is a connection-based protocol and maintains a state throughout the transfer of data.

4. C. Platform as a Service (PaaS) is commonly used by software developers. It provides a development platform that the software developer can use to create applications. An example of this is a web server with PHP and MySQL, which is hosted in the cloud.

5. D. Crossover cables are wired with the 568B specification on one side, and on the other side, the 568A specification is used. This change in wiring delivers the TX pair on pins 4 and 5 to the RX pair on pins 1 and 2. Straight-through cables are wired with the 568B specification on one side, and on the other side, the 568B specification is used.

6. A. Stateless Address Autoconfiguration (SLAAC) relies on the Neighbor Discovery Protocol (NDP). NDP works by using multicast and ICMPv6 message types. The host will multicast to ff02::1 an ICMPv6 Router Solicitation (RS) message, and the router will respond with a Router Advertisement (RA) message. This response will allow the host to obtain the network address and gateway of the network. The host will then create a host address portion of the IPv6 address and use the Duplicate Address Discovery (DAD) protocol to check for a duplicate address.

7. B. The IPv6 address 2202:0ff8:0002:2344:3533:8eff:fe22:ae4c is an EUI-64 generated address. The host portion of the address is 3533:8eff:fe22:ae4c, the fffe in the middle of it depicts that the address was generated from the MAC address. The MAC address of this host would be 37-33-8e-02-ae-4c. When EUI-64 is used, an ffee is placed in the middle of the MAC address, and then the 7th bit from the left is flipped. This changes the first two hex digits of the MAC address from 35 to 37.

8. C. The network 192.168.4.32/27 has a valid IP address range of 192.168.4.33 to 192.168.4.62. The /27 CIDR notation, or 255.255.255.224 dotted-decimal notation (DDN) defines networks in multiples of 32. Therefore, the address 192.168.4.28/27 is part of the 192.168.4.32/27 network.

9. B. The first field after the preamble and Start Frame Delimiter (SFD) is the destination MAC address. The destination MAC address is always first because switches need to make forwarding decisions upon reading the destination MAC address.

10. A. The forward/filter function of a switch is used to look up the destination MAC address in a MAC address table and decide the egress interface for the frame. If the MAC address is not in the table, the frame is forwarded out all of the interfaces. When the client responds, its source MAC address will be recorded in the MAC address table for future lookup.

11. B. Access ports strip all VLAN information before the frame egresses the destination interface. The endpoint on an access switchport will never see any of the VLAN information that was associated with the frame.

12. D. The command `switchport trunk allowed vlan 12` will remove all other VLANs and only VLAN 12 will be allowed on the trunk interface. The proper command to add an additional VLAN would be `switchport trunk allowed vlan add 12`. This command will add a VLAN to the already established list.

13. B. Switch A and Switch B are participating in VLAN tagging. Therefore, Switch A interface Gi0/1 and Switch B interface Gi0/1 are both configured as trunk switchports. This will allow VLAN tagging across the trunk link.

14. C. Switch B has the lowest MAC address of all of the switches. Therefore, Switch B will become the RSTP root bridge. All ports leading back to Switch B will become the root ports. Switch A interface Gi1/8, Switch D interface Fa2/16, and Switch C interface Gi1/3 will become root ports.

15. B. When you configure the switchport to a mode of access, you are statically configuring the interface to remain an access switchport. When you configure the switchport to nonegotiate, you are turning off Dynamic Trunking Protocol (DTP). The switch will never negotiate its switchport.

16. A. The command `channel-group 1 mode passive` configures the port to be placed in a passive negotiating state. The other switch must be placed into an active negotiating state for LACP to become the control protocol for the channel group.

17. B. When BPDU Guard is configured on a port, it guards the port from creating a loop. It also guards STP so that the STP calculation of redundant links is not affected by the device connect to the interface. If a BPDU is seen on the interface, the interface will immediately enter into an err-disable state. The most likely cause was that another switch was plugged into the interface.

18. D. The VLAN Trunking Protocol assists in synchronizing a VLAN database across all Cisco switches participating in VTP. You must initially configure the VTP domain on the switch that will hold the master database. Then all other switches must be configured as clients and the VTP domain must be configured as well.

19. C. The 802.1w Rapid Spanning Tree Protocol defines that designated switchports always forward traffic. The designated port is a port that is forwarding traffic and is opposite of the root port or blocking port if it is a redundant link.

20. B. There is a total of three frames that are encapsulated during the process of Host A sending a packet to Host B. In the exhibit, there are two hubs and two routers. The first frame is encapsulated from A to Router A. The second frame is encapsulated from Router A to Router B. The third frame is encapsulated from Router B to Host B.

21. C. The administrative distance (AD) is a rating of trust between different routing protocols and route methods. This trust scale is important when multiple routes exist to the same destination. Directly connected routes have ADs with the highest level of trust.

22. A. Enhanced Interior Gateway Routing Protocol (EIGRP) uses bandwidth and delay by default for calculating routes. The bandwidth should be set to the actual bandwidth of the link so that routing protocols such as EIGRP can calculate the best route. Delay cannot be set because it is a variable of the interface.

23. C. The administrative distance (AD) of EIGRP is 90. The most common ADs are 90 for EIGRP, 100 for IGRP, 110 for OSPF, and 120 for RIP. The mnemonic of 90 Exotic Indian Oval Rubies will help you remember the order; then starting with EIGRP with a value of 90, increment the following values by 10.

24. A. The command network 203.244.234.0 will advertise the 203.244.234.0 network. When you're configuring RIP, only the network address needs to be configured with the network command.

25. C. In the exhibit, packets are being sent to the router via a trunk link. A setup where the packets for VLANs are sent to a router for routing between VLANs is called Router on a Stick (ROAS) routing.

26. D. When you want to turn on the layer 3 functionality of a switch, you must configure the command ip routing in global configuration. This is required when you want to create switched virtual interfaces (SVIs) for VLANs and want to route on the switch between the VLANs. This method of routing is much more efficient since the traffic is routed in the ASICs on the switch.

27. D. The summary route of 172.16.32.0/21 contains 172.16.38.0/24 as a valid network route. The /21 CIDR mask defines networks in multiples of 8 in the third octet of the network address. Therefore, the next network address is 172.16.40.0/21.

28. C. The entries with the dash in the Age column represent the physical interfaces of the router. If the entries were configured statically, their type would reflect a status of static.

29. B. Link State Advertisement (LSA) packets communicate the topology of the local router with other routers in the OSPF area. The information contained in the LSA packet is a summary of links the local router's topology consists of.

30. C. Time to Live (TTL) is a field in the IP header that prevents packets from endlessly routing in networks. Each time a packet is routed, the router's responsibility is to decrement the TTL by one. When the TTL reaches zero, the packet is considered unrouteable and dropped.

31. B. Point-to-Point Protocol (PPP) is a layer 2 wide area network (WAN) protocol. PPP supports Challenge Handshake Authentication Protocol (CHAP), which secures connections. Although Metro Ethernet is built site to site by the service provider, there is no guarantee of security in the form of authentication.

32. A. The Differentiated Services Code Point (DSCP) is a layer 3 QoS marking for routers and layer 3 devices. The DSCP markings are located in the Type of Service (ToS) field in an IP header. Class of Service (CoS) is a layer 2 QoS service marking found in 802.1Q frames.

33. B. Internet Protocol Security (IPSec) does not support multicast packets. If you require both, you can set up a GRE tunnel for the multicast and broadcast traffic, then encrypt only the data over IPSec. However, by itself IPSec does not support multicast or broadcast traffic.

34. D. Both the customer edge (CE) routers and the provider edge (PE) routers can host area 0. However, the service provider must support area 0, called the super backbone, on its PE routers since all areas must be connected to area 0. The customer chooses whether the CE participates in area 0.

35. C. A trust boundary is the point in the network where the QoS markings are trusted from the devices connected to it. A network administrator will create a trust boundary where a VoIP phone will placed. Since the VoIP phone will be trusted, the markings will be accepted and used for priority throughout the network. The trust boundary should always be placed closest to the IT-controlled equipment.

36. C. The Cisco Dynamic Multipoint Virtual Private Network (DMVPN) is always configured in a hub-and-spoke topology. The central router creates a multiport GRE connection between all of the branch routers.

37. C. The DHCP Negative Acknowledgment (NACK) message is issued by the DHCP server to the client when a client requests an IP address the DHCP cannot lease. This often happens when two DHCP servers are misconfigured in the same LAN with two different scopes. One server will issue the NACK message when it hears the request destined for the other DHCP server.

38. C. Router C will become the active router since it has the highest priority. The default priority of HSRP is 100, and therefore, the router with the highest priority will become the active router. It is important to note that nothing will change if preemption is not configured on the routers.

39. D. When a DHCP server sends the DHCP Offer message in response to a DHCP Discover message, the client's MAC address is used in the response.

40. B. The access list is misconfigured. It must match the address that will be allowed through the NAT process. The access list is configured for 192.168.2.0/24. The private IP address network is 192.168.1.0/24. The NAT pool can overlap with a physical interface. It allows for the IP address configured on the physical interface to also be used for NAT.

41. C. The computer will not be allowed to communicate, and the port will enter an err-disable state. The defaults for port security allow for only one MAC address, and the default violation is shutdown. The violation of shutdown will shut the port down and place it into an err-disable state, which will require administrative intervention.

42. A. TACACS+ will allow for authentication of users, and it also provides a method of restricting users to specific commands. This allows for much granular control of lower-level administrators.

43. C. You can have only one access control list (ACL) per direction, per protocol, and per interface. Therefore, each of the two interfaces can have both an inbound and outbound ACL, per the protocol of IPv4. This allows for a total of four ACLs, which can be used to control access through the router.

44. D. Once the password has been forgotten, a password recovery must be performed on the router. Although you have the encrypted password, it cannot be reversed since it is a hash of the password. A hash is a one-way encryption of the password; only the same combination of letters and number will produce the same hash.

45. B. The command `access-list 2 permit 192.168.2.3 0.0.0.0` will perform the same function as `access-list 2 permit host 192.168.2.3`. The command configures the host 192.168.2.3 with a bit mask, which will only match the single IP address. Although it can be configured as a bit mask, it should be configured via the host parameter for readability.

46. A. The command `license install usbflash0:FTX3463434Z_2016030415234562345.lic` will install the license file to the router. This command must be entered in privileged exec mode.

47. B. By default, all syslog messages are sent to the console of the router or switch. It is recommended to configure a syslog server, because once the router or switch is powered off, the information is lost.

48. C. The configuration register of 0x2142 is used for the password recovery process. The configuration register will tell the boot process to ignore the contents of NVRAM, which is where the startup-configuration is located. It will only use NVRAM for the location of the boot system variable.

49. D. The Cisco Discovery Protocol functions on the management plane of the SDN model. It helps with management of the routers and switches and does not directly impact the data plane.

50. D. The network management station (NMS) must be configured with the version of SNMP, the community, and the management information base (MIB) before it can access the counters on a router or switch.

Chapter 9: Practice Test 2

1. C. The Address Resolution Protocol (ARP) functions on layer 2, the Data Link layer. It helps the Data Link layer resolve the destination MAC address for framing of data.

2. B. During the three-way-handshake, Computer A sends a SYN flag along with its receiving window size and initial sequence number. Then Computer B sends a SYN flag and ACK flag along with its receiving window and acknowledgment of the sequence number. Finally, Computer A sends an ACK flag, which acknowledges the synchronization of Computer B's receiving window. Communication begins and is considered to be in an established state.

3. D. Rapid elasticity is the ability to add and remove compute capability in the cloud. As demand is needed, compute power can be increased by adding more CPUs or servers. As demand for compute power decreases, CPUs or servers can be removed.

4. B. The distribution layer is a partial mesh topology. Links between the distribution switches and core switches are multi-homed to each device for redundancy. Also, the links between the distribution switches and access switches are multi-homed to each device for redundancy. Although, this might seems to be a full mesh topology, the distribution switches are not connected to each other.

5. B. Single-mode fiber is typically used in high-speed long-distance transmission of data. It can span up to 70 kilometers (km) with the proper transceivers. The speeds of single-mode fiber can be up the 100 Gb/s with the proper transceivers.

6. C. Documenting the problem is the last step in resolving a problem. After you monitor the problem for the implementation of the fix, the documentation should describe the problem, the root cause of the problem, and the resolution. The documentation can then be used for future problems that match the same criteria.

7. D. The IP address 225.34.5.4 is a multicast IP address. Multicast IP addresses are defined as Class D addresses in the range 224.0.0.1 to 239.255.255.254.

8. C. In IPv6, the solicited-node multicast message is used for resolution of the MAC address for an IPv6 address. The first 104 bits of the 128-bit IPv6 address is ff02::1:ff, and the last 24 bits comprise the last 24 bits of the IPv6 address that needs to be resolved. The solicited-node multicast message is also used for Duplicate Address Detection (DAD).

9. B. Field C in the exhibit is the type field. The type field is used to define the upper-layer protocol the data belongs to.

10. C. When the destination MAC address is not in the MAC address table, the switch will flood the frame to all ports on the switch. When the computer or device responds, the switch will memorize the source MAC address with the port on which it sees the traffic.

11. B. The switch has negotiated with the adjacent switch to become a trunk and set its trunking protocol to 802.1Q. The letter *n* in front of 802.1Q specifies it was negotiated. When a switch is set to auto for the Dynamic Trunking Protocol (DTP), it will respond to trunking requests but will not initiate DTP messages. The adjacent switch must be set to desirable, since the desirable mode will send DTP messages.

12. C. The two switches have a duplex mismatch. The duplex mismatch is a direct result of statically configuring only one side of the link to full-duplex. Switch A is not participating in port negotiation. Both sides must be configured statically the same or set to auto.

13. C. When implementing Router on a Stick (ROAS), you must first create a trunk to the router. Once the trunk is created, you must create subinterfaces for each VLAN to be routed and specify the IP address and 802.1Q encapsulation.

14. B. An 802.1Q frame is a modified Ethernet frame. The type field is relocated after the 4 bytes used for 802.1Q tagging. Two of the bytes are used for tagging the frame, and two of the bytes are used for controls such as Class of Service (CoS).

15. D. The exhibit shows several MAC addresses that have been dynamically assigned to the MAC address table. Since all of these MAC addresses have been seen on interface Gi1/1, it is safe to say that a switch or hub is connected to it. The output does not depict if the link is an access or trunk link.

16. C. Under normal circumstances, when VLANs are configured, they are stored in a file separate from the startup or running-configuration. The VLAN database is stored in a file called vlan.dat on the flash. When decommissioning a switch, if you were to erase the configuration of a switch, you would also need to delete the vlan.dat.

17. D. Switches that are configured in transparent mode will not process VTP updates. They will, however, forward the updates to switches that are connected to them. Transparent mode switches store their VLAN database in their running-configuration and startup-configuration.

18. B. The long delay for the device to become active on the interface is the wait time for convergence of Spanning Tree Protocol (STP). If the interface will only connect a device to the port, then the port should be configured with spanning-tree PortFast mode. This will skip the blocking mode during convergence of STP.

19. A. When both Switch A and Switch B are configured as auto for DTP, the link will not form a trunk since neither switch is sending negotiation messages. The ports will remain in access mode.

20. B. When all of the ports on a switch are in designated mode, it means that the switch is the root bridge for the Spanning Tree Protocol (STP).

21. B. Routing Information Protocol (RIP) does not contain a topology table. RIP compiles its table from multiple broadcasts or multicasts in the network from which it learns routes. However, it never has a full topological diagram of the network like OSPF, EIGRP, and BGP.

22. D. The split horizons method prevents routing updates from exiting an interface in which they have been learned. This stops false information from propagating in the network, which can cause a routing loop.

23. A. The Open Shortest Path First (OSPF) priority for a router is a value of 1. This priority is used when electing a designated router (DR) and backup designated router (BDR). The higher the value, the higher the chances of the router becoming a DR or BDR.

24. D. When configuring OSPF for the designated router (DR), if you configure another router with a higher priority, the original DR will remain the current DR. OSPF does not allow for preemption, and therefore you must force the election by clearing the OSPF process on the DR. This will force the DR to relinquish its status.

25. C. The command of maximum-paths 6 will configure the maximum number of unequal paths for load balancing with EIGRP to a value of 6. This command must be entered in the router EIGRP process.

26. A. Cisco Express Forwarding (CEF) allows the CPU to initially populate a sort of route cache called the forwarding information base (FIB). Any packets entering the router can be checked against the FIB and routed without the help of the CPU.

27. C. The multicast address of ff02::a is the multicast address for IPv6 EIGRP updates. Updates for routers participating in IPv6 EIGRP will be multicast to the IPv6 address of ff02::a.

28. C. The command `no switchport` will configure the interface as a layer 3 routed interface. The command `ip routing` needs to be configured for routing of the interface, but it will not hinder assigning an IP address.

29. C. The command `passive-interface default` when entered in the EIGRP router process will suppress hello messages for all interfaces. You can then include only the interfaces on which you want hello messages to be advertised with the command `no passive-interface gi 0/1`.

30. B. The command `show ip cef` will display all of the network prefixes and the next hop that Cisco Express Forwarding (CEF) has in the forwarding information base (FIB). The command will also display the exit interface for the next hop.

31. C. The Point-to-Point Protocol (PPP) supports compression, authentication, error detection, and correction. PPP can detect errors in the transmission and request retransmission of the packets.

32. C. This is a debug of outgoing packets, and therefore the configuration problem is on this router. This router's username must match the adjacent router's hostname and both passwords must match.

33. B. The provider edge (PE) router is responsible for adding the MPLS label to a packet.

34. B. Virtual Private Networks (VPNs) are extremely scalable because they only require an Internet connection at each site. We can reuse the existing Internet connection at each site to create a site-to-site VPN tunnel.

35. C. The command `service-policy USER-MAP out` will configure the policy map called USER-MAP on the interface in an outbound direction.

36. D. The web server's IP address is referred to as the outside global address in reference to Network Address Translation (NAT).

37. C. The Network Time Protocol (NTP) defines 16 levels of stratums. A stratum of zero has absolute precision, such as an atomic clock, which also has little or no delay. When an NTP clock is timed off a stratum zero clock, it becomes a stratum one, and when an NTP clock is timed off of a stratum one, it becomes a stratum two. The process continues onward, adding a one to each slave unit, as delay increases and you move further away from absolute precision.

38. C. When Hot Standby Router Protocol (HSRP) is used, the default gateway the client is issued is an IP address for the virtual router. The virtual router is not a physical router, but it is mapped to a physical router via HSRP. The active router processes requests for the virtual router IP address by responding to the virtual MAC address associated with the virtual router IP address.

39. C. When interface tracking is turned on and a link that is being tracked fails, the priority of the active router is lowered, and an election is forced. This will make the standby router become the active router. However, if the link is repaired, the priority will recover to its normal value, but the current active router will remain the active router. Preemption allows for the value to instantly reelect the original router as the active router.

40. B. The Start of Authority (SOA) record establishes several key pieces of information, such as the primary DNS server, the timers for refreshing DNS entries, and a default time to live (TTL). The default TTL is used when a resource record is not explicitly configured with a TTL.

41. D. An attacker will take advantage of the automatic trunking configuration of Dynamic Trunking Protocol (DTP). This will allow the attacker to create a trunk with the switch and tag packets so that they can hop onto different VLANs.

42. A. When you are configuring port security on an interface, the switchport should have a mode of access configured. This will also protect the switch from transitioning into a trunk if another switch is connected.

43. C. Port security can prevent MAC address flooding attacks by restricting the number of MAC addresses associated to an interface. This will prevent the Content Addressable Memory (CAM) from being overrun by bogus entries.

44. A. The command access-list 101 deny tcp 192.168.2.0 0.0.0.255 any eq 23 will deny TCP traffic from 192.168.2.0/24 to any address with a destination of 23 (Telnet). The command access-list 101 permit ip any any will permit all other traffic.

45. B. Conventional access lists lack the ability to edit a single entry. The entire ACL must be removed and re-added with the correct entry. An alternative to conventional access lists is named access lists. A named access list is referenced by line numbers, which allows for removal and additions of single entries.

46. A. Trap messages are sent from Simple Network Management Protocol (SNMP) agents to the network management station (NMS). This happens when an event that the router or switch is set to alert the NMS about is triggered. An example of this is overheating of the switch or an important link going down.

47. B. Simple Network Management Protocol version 2c lacks security. The only mechanism you can employ for security is complex community names. Security was introduced in version 3 of SNMP.

48. B. The command interface range gigabitethernet 1/1 - 12 will allow you to configure the interfaces Gigabit Ethernet 1/1 to 1/12.

49. D. The default syslog facility level is debug 7. All debug messages are logged to the internal buffer by default.

50. C. The command ip ftp username USER will configure the username *USER* for FTP connections. The command ip ftp password USERPASS will configure the password *USERPASS* for FTP connections.

Index

Comprehensive Online Learning Environment

Register on Sybex.com to gain access to the comprehensive online interactive learning environment and test bank to help you study for your CCNA Routing and Switching certification.

The online test bank includes:

- **Practice Test Questions** to reinforce what you learned
- **Bonus Practice Exams** to test your knowledge of the material

Go to `http://www.wiley.com/go/sybextestprep` to register and gain access to this comprehensive study tool package.

30% off On-Demand IT Video Training from ITProTV

ITProTV and Sybex have partnered to provide 30% off a Premium annual or monthly membership. ITProTV provides a unique, custom learning environment for IT professionals and students alike, looking to validate their skills through vendor certifications. On-demand courses provide over 1,000 hours of video training with new courses being added every month, while labs and practice exams provide additional hands-on experience. For more information on this offer and to start your membership today, visit `http://itpro.tv/sybex30/`.